SOUTHEAST ASIAN LIVES

SOUTHEAST ASIAN LIVES

Personal Narratives and Historical Experience

Edited by

Roxana Waterson

NUS PRESS
SINGAPORE

OHIO UNIVERSITY
RESEARCH IN INTERNATIONAL STUDIES
SOUTHEAST ASIA SERIES NO. 113

OHIO UNIVERSITY PRESS
ATHENS

First published by:

NUS Press
National University of Singapore
AS3-01-02, 3 Arts Link
Singapore 117569

Fax: (65) 6774-0652
E-mail: nusbooks@nus.edu.sg
Website: http://www.nus.edu.sg/npu

ISBN-10 9971-69-344-5 (Paper)
ISBN-13 978-9971-69-344-2

Published for distribution in the US by:

Ohio University Press
Athens, OH 45701, USA

Fax: (740) 593-4536
Website: http://www.ohio.edu/oupress

ISBN-10 0-89680-250-7
ISBN-13 978-0-89680-250-6

© 2007 NUS Press

National Library Board Singapore Cataloguing in Publication Data

Southeast Asian lives : personal narratives and historical experience /
    edited by Roxana Waterson.—Singapore : NUS Press, c2007.
        p. cm.
    Includes index.
    ISBN-13 : 978-9971-69-344-2 (pbk.)
    ISBN-10 : 9971-69-344-5 (pbk.)

    1. Oral biography. 2. Oral history. 3. Southeast Asia—Biography.
    4. Southeast Asia—History—20th century. 5. Southeast Asia—Social life and
    customs—20th century. I. Waterson, Roxana.

DS526.6
959.051—dc22   SLS2006044579

Typeset by: International Typesetters Pte. Ltd.
Printed by: Vetak Services

"The world is wide, but in us it is as deep as the sea."

– Reiner Maria Rilke

Contents

List of Contributors   ix

1. Introduction: Analysing Personal Narratives   1
   Roxana Waterson

PART I: SINGULAR LIVES

2. Madé Lebah: Reminiscences from "Jaman Setengah Bali"   41
   (Half-Bali Times)
   Carol Warren

3. Who Owns a Life History? Scholars and   88
   Family Members in Dialogue
   Janet Hoskins

4. A Toraja Pilgrimage: The Life of Fritz Basiang   125
   Roxana Waterson

PART II: VOICES AND FRAGMENTS

5. Arifin in the Iron Cap: Confessions of a Young Man,
   Drowning   181
   Robert Knox Dentan

6. Marking Time: Narratives of the Life-world in Thailand   221
   Annette Hamilton

7. Traversing Invisible Borders: Narratives of Women   253
   Between the Hills and the City
   Yoko Hayami

8. Gendered Lives, Gendered Narratives: Stories from a   278
   Muslim Fishing Village in Southern Thailand
   Saroja Dorairajoo

Index   315

List of Contributors

Robert Knox Dentan is Professor Emeritus, State University of New York at Buffalo. He was born in 1936. Since 1961 he has lived among Semai for a total of five years or so, and continues to keep in touch, visiting most recently in early 2006. This association with people who are experts on maintaining a peaceable way of life has given himself a reputation as an expert on the topic, an expertise for which he can take little credit. The experience has, however, kept him interested in the phenomena of (non)violence.

Saroja Dorairajoo is Assistant Professor of Sociology at the National University of Singapore. She has done fieldwork on a Muslim fishing community in Pattani, southern Thailand, researching on gender, food and Islam, environmental politics and fish trading.

Annette Hamilton is Professor of Anthropology and Dean of the Faculty of Arts and Social Sciences at the University of New South Wales in Sydney. She has carried out research in Thailand since 1985, with a focus on the impact of media and technological change, and social transformations at local and national level. She has worked in areas south of Bangkok, intensively in Prachuab Khiri Khan province and more recently in the southern border zones.

Yoko Hayami is Professor at the Center for Southeast Asian Studies, Kyoto University. She has done anthropological fieldwork among Sgaw Karen-speaking people in Northern Thailand since 1987, and more recently in Burma also, with interest in religious practices, ethnic relations and gender. She is the author of *Between Hills and Plains: Power and Practice in Socio-Religious Dynamics among Karen* (Japan: Kyoto University Press, 2004) and *Gender and Modernity: Perspectives* *from Asia and the Pacific*, co-edited with Akio Tanabe and Yumiko Tokita (Japan: Kyoto University Press, 2003).

Janet Hoskins is Professor of Anthropology at the University of Southern California, Los Angeles. She is the author of *The Play of Time: Kodi Perspectives on Calendars, History and Exchange* (Berkeley: University of California Press, 1994, awarded the 1996 Benda Prize in Southeast Asian Studies) and *Biographical Objects: How Things Tell the Stories of People's Lives* (New York: Routledge, 1998) and contributing editor of *Headhunting and the Social Imagination in Southeast Asia* (California: Stanford University Press, 1966), and *Fragments from Forests and Libraries* (Durham: Carolina Academic Press, 2001). She did research in Indonesia from 1979 to 2000 and has been working in California and Vietnam since 2002.

Carol Warren is Associate Professor in the School of Social Sciences and Humanities and a Research Fellow in the Asia Research Centre at Murdoch University, Australia. She is the author of *Adat and Dinas: Balinese Communities in the Indonesian State* (Kuala Lumpur, New York: Oxford University Press, 1993) and co-editor with Phil Hirsch of *The Politics of Environment in Southeast Asia* (London, New York: Routledge, 1998). She has carried out field research on community development, local governance, customary law and political ecology in Bali and Lombok in Indonesia, as well as Sabah, Malaysia.

Roxana Waterson is Associate Professor in the Department of Sociology, National University of Singapore, where she has been teaching since 1987. She has done field research with the Sa'dan Toraja people of Sulawesi, Indonesia, since 1978. She is the author of *The Living House: An Anthropology of Architecture in South-East Asia* (3rd edn., London: Thames & Hudson, 1997). As well as life history and personal narratives, her current interests include ethnohistory, indigenous religions, landscape, and social memory.

I

Introduction: Analysing Personal Narratives

Roxana Waterson

"Living in Interesting Times" — Looking at History through Life History

"May you live in interesting times": these are reputed to be the words of an ancient Chinese curse. It turns out that the author of this imprecation was actually Ernest Bramah, a British civil servant who, at the turn of the last century, composed a series of stories set in an imaginary China, which served him as the vehicle for an entertaining satire on the inscrutable workings of the bureaucratic hierarchy best known to him. It is one of a set of three curses, of escalating severity; the second is, "May you come to the attention of those in high places", and the third, "May the gods grant your prayers" (Bramah 1900). How many individuals in the century ahead were to experience both the ironies, and the mortal perils, of "living in interesting times"? There were many who, as the twentieth century opened, lived in the hope of witnessing radical social change. It was indeed to be an era of world-wide social transformations, so rapid and profound that Pierre Nora (1996: 1) has characterised it as a century marked by the "acceleration of history". But it has also been a period of unprecedented violence. At the start of the twenty-first century, we are in the position of being able to look back at the one recently concluded, and discern more clearly the shape it has taken. What was it like to live through it? Official histories can never capture all of the diversity of individual experiences; the study of personal narratives, on the other hand, multiplies the voices that reach us from the past. By turning the focus to that space where history intersects with personal experience, it offers new insights into wider social and political processes.

That such accounts promise a truer, fuller and more democratic picture of the past has for long been cogently and passionately argued by oral historians such as Thompson (1978) and Portelli (1997); increasingly since the 1980s, as anthropology has pursued a more and more historical turn, ethnographers have had much to learn from these practitioners. In our fieldwork, we sometimes have unique opportunities to record life history narratives, and thus have the potential, in our turn, to contribute to the development of oral history. This volume, although its contributors are all anthropologists, seeks to explore something of this overlap between history and anthropology. In the study of personal narratives generally, a further intersection with the field of literary studies must also be noted. From this field, the recent outpouring of new works on autobiography as a distinctive genre offers, as historian Timothy Ashplant (1998: 99) has observed, rich sources of fresh insight into the forms and structures of such narratives, from which both anthropologists and historians may benefit. We intend, then, that this collection provide a timely contribution not only to Southeast Asian studies, but also to the burgeoning field of research into life history and personal narratives. This project is motivated by a conviction that, in spite of all that has already been achieved in this field by oral historians, life history as a method has remained an under-utilised research tool within the social sciences. It is the aim of anthropology to make the diversity of human experiences intelligible across cultural boundaries; as Watson (1989: 4) has pointed out, personal narratives offer particularly rich seams of "shareable experience", and therefore ought to present special opportunities to the ethnographer. Yet, in spite of some outstanding examples of the use of life history within anthropology, attention to its possibilities has remained inconsistent. The relative rarity of its deployment by anthropologists suggests that there remain as yet unresolved theoretical questions and doubts about how best to present and analyse such materials. Since, however, there are currently signs of a renewed interest in its potentials in both anthropology and sociology, this volume sets out to interrogate and explore these potentials more fully.

In Southeast Asia, individuals whose lives have spanned a good part of the past century have frequently lived through several distinct regimes, sometimes including a pre-colonial past, through the period of European colonisation, followed by Japanese Occupation and struggles for Independence, to the emergence of independent nation-states. But for different people the encounters with modernity have taken many varying forms; while depending on their positions, what was at stake in these encounters was not necessarily the same either. While some people seized the new possibilities presented to them, others may have had good cause to distrust the intrusions of "progress" into their lives, while perhaps the majority have had no choice but to live out, in however dramatic a manner, the dilemmas of cultural collision. The lives lived by ordinary people have thus in fact been endlessly extraordinary. It is not that such lives merely reflect the history that was in the making, for their actions and experiences were also helping to shape it. In drawing together a selection of accounts from varied communities of both island and mainland Southeast Asia, another aim of this volume is therefore to present some fresh perspectives on the historical transformations which the region has undergone during the twentieth century.

Issues in the Analysis of Life Histories

We all tell stories about our lives, if only to ourselves; indeed, our mental health depends on our ability to do so, so that our lives may have coherence (Ross and Conway 1986; Rappaport 1990; Linde 1993). Without some coherent memory of the past, we should have no basis on which to act today. Accounts of lives may take many varied forms, however, some of them more formal than others: from published biography or autobiography, to what researchers in psychology have termed "life stories" — fragments of personal storytelling or oral discourse, which we all tell at various times and in different ways for different audiences, sometimes purely for entertainment (Linde 1993; Miller 1994; Ashplant 1998). Somewhere in the middle of this range of genres lie the life history accounts elicited by ethnographers or oral historians, which may be seen as one rather peculiar and specific kind of narrative, a collaborative product in which the dialogical relationship between teller and listener, and their probably mixed motives, shape the outcome. Autobiography, as a particular mode of telling about the self, is itself a distinctive genre with a relatively short history in European

cultures.[1] "Personal narratives" is a convenient term which covers all
of these genres, and may be extended to include other forms such as
letters and diaries (Caplan 1997).

In anthropology, life history has been described as "a venerable
but as yet little theorised genre of ethnographic writing" (Behar 1992:
122). This remark comes 20 years after Mandelbaum (1973: 178)
complained that "the study of lives for purposes of social science has
been more often advocated than practised".[2] In spite of some early
and remarkable works, as a research practice it has remained distinctly
marginal. One of the earliest examples was Paul Radin's *Crashing
Thunder: the Autobiography of an American Indian* (1926), an account
he elicited from a Winnebago man, which was written for him in the
Winnebago syllabary and directly translated by him into English. This
was presented as "a document absolutely unique of its kind — the only
account that has ever been obtained from a so-called 'primitive' man"
(Radin 1926: xvi), its presenter going so far as to propose that such
personal accounts provided the only possible way in to other cultures
and world views. From today's perspective, Radin may appear to have
been ahead of his time in drawing attention to the importance as well
as the elusiveness of "subjective values" in the effort to grasp another
culture. Few, however, seem to have taken him up on his challenge
to adopt the life history method as the only possible way to proceed.
Yet there are now signs of a renewed interest in exploring its still
unfulfilled potentials.[3]

What is it that has made life histories appear so problematic? How
does one sum up the meaning of a life? Analytical difficulties and
uncertainties present themselves; the very specificity of an individual life
seems to resist generalisations. We find ourselves faced simultaneously
with a feeling of incompleteness, and of excess. The incompleteness
stems from the fact that no-one is capable of telling everything about
themselves, and life itself is an "unfinished business"; the narrator must
make choices, and will certainly have withheld or passed over some topics
in favour of others.[4] The uniqueness of a life, at the same time, seems
to offer an embarrassing excess of meaning — how is one to derive
conclusions from all of its idiosyncrasies? This specificity might seem
less problematic in the case of famous persons, who attract us precisely
because of their uniqueness: such a person may be judged extraordinary,
or as in some way exemplary, and therefore worth reading about. We
may read their auto/biography for the light it sheds on their own role

in shaping historical events, or on their formation as a writer. In any case, an understanding of the individual might in such cases be taken as an end in itself, sustaining a "myth of genius" which has become an intrinsic dimension of the history of individualism in the western world. But what of the obscure and the non-famous? Why should we take an interest in their stories? Might there be things to be learned from them that cannot be found out in other ways? I want to suggest some arguments why personal narratives should be of interest in themselves, and how, in spite of their irreducible uniqueness, they can be made to generate more generalised insights about the historical and social contexts in which they are produced.

The extension of history into the area of social memory is part of a democratising urge to listen to the voices of the non-famous. The great radical historian E.P. Thompson spoke of "the enormous condescension of posterity" toward the defeated, and saw his own kind of historical enterprise as "a gigantic act of reparation" to them (cited in Samuel 1994: viii). Just as history is written by the victors, so auto/biographies have most often been written by or about the rich, the famous or the powerful. But within the disciplines of history, sociology and perhaps most especially anthropology, there has also been that other commitment to seeking out the voices of the marginalised and the disempowered, those who in Spivak's terms occupy a "position of the uninvestigated" (Spivak 1991: 71). Lucy Healey (1994: 113), an anthropologist who has written about the life histories of women from a fishing village on the east coast of Malaysia, discusses this idea, pointing out that investigating the uninvestigated has always been a *raison d'être* of anthropology, as well as an essential attitude of feminism. The project of developing a history capable of speaking from new perspectives (specifically, one that would displace the old Eurocentrism as well as an indigenous elitism) has been carried further by, among others, the historians of the Subaltern Studies group in India. Ranajit Guha (1982: 7) calls for a "rejection of the spurious and un-historical monism" characteristic of elite historiography, and instead, makes a passionate call for us to listen to the "small voice" of history (Guha 1996). He points out how even India's own nationalist historians, fed up with the "Cambridge History" approach to deciding what is significant about their past, have still too often replaced it with a focus on famous and powerful males of their own. They have thus continued to fail to tell the stories of the great mass of Indian people — peasants, workers, and most particularly women. In a similar way, historian John Smail (1993 [1961]) pointed out decades ago the need for what he called an "autonomous domestic history" of Indonesia, one that would break from the Eurocentric perspective which had left gaping lacunae in the understanding of the Indonesian past, and which would not be written only by the victors; a more recent Festschrift (Sears 1993) revives his argument. When an authoritarian regime collapses, history is characteristically one of the first things to come under re-examination; just a few years after the publication of that book, the watershed of 1998 in Indonesia brought the abrupt closure of the Suharto era, and suddenly opened up this possibility. The new outburst of historical activity, publicly encouraged by Abdurrahman Wahid during his brief and otherwise rather chaotic Presidency, has enabled Indonesian historians and the general public to re-examine for themselves many episodes of the recent past, as well as their often dubious presentation under the New Order. In this new atmosphere, previously taboo subjects are revisited, and it becomes possible for some people — former political prisoners, for example — to tell their stories for the first time.

The Self, the Social Context, and Historical Consciousness: Questions of Representativeness

The central problem about life narratives from the point of view of the anthropologist, sociologist or historian is the question of representativeness. What in the way of insights into generalities can be extracted from their uniqueness? Here we address, only in a more acute form, the issue of subjectivity that has been so endlessly debated in our disciplines. At one level, personal narratives are intrinsically about *the self*, however constructed, and how this is done is a matter that has to be addressed comparatively in terms of differing social contexts and available genres.

All life stories also present us with the intersection between a self and the social context in which that individual makes something of life with the resources available to them. In the current resurgence of interest in life histories, we find a number of works, by both psychologists and anthropologists, which use them principally as a means to comprehend the construction of the self (Neisser & Fivush 1994; Rosenwald and Ochberg 1992; Skinner, Pach and Holland 1998). In these analyses, the manner of telling the story is as significant as the content of the narrative itself. Rosenwald and Ochberg (1992: 8) talk of life stories as "an organisation of experience", and sometimes a process by which individuals "becom[e] aware of their social predicament" and perhaps even find a means to transcend it — a possibility which points to the potentially transformative power of narrative.[5] Skinner *et al.* (1998: 3) point to the links between identities, experience, and history, and call for "a new ethnography of personhood", one that will recognise the existence of "persons in history and history in persons". In their presentations of life stories from Nepal, they search for the interface between personal trajectories and the larger structures within which they "struggle to constitute themselves as particular kinds of actors and persons *vis-à-vis* others within and against powerful sociopolitical and cultural worlds". Women may typically experience different life trajectories from men, "improvising" multiple careers for themselves (Bateson 1989), or may choose a different style of telling about themselves, one that does not omit important relationships with others, or a sense of community solidarity, one that speaks of the "we" and not only the "I". Within oral traditions, the "I" itself may be revealed as a complex construction, "partaking of other Is", such that the teller may use "I" for events they could not have witnessed themselves, not in bad faith but through an intimate identification with ancestors or with group experiences (Tonkin 1992: 135). Temple (1995: 61) similarly notes with regard to the narratives of British Poles, looking back on their childhoods before the catastrophic events that displaced them during the Second World War, that "the self described is a social one which needs others to constitute itself". Even within the western world, then, we should recognise that the formal model of published autobiography represents one particular extreme of the imaging of an autonomous, bounded individual. Among her Polish interlocutors there is an intense ethnic identification of the "I" with the "we" of the Polish community, and a very active ongoing oral and written exchange of accounts of journeys made during the War, in which the irruption of historical events into personal life trajectories is painfully revealed. One of them summed up the importance of this narrative activity thus: "It is important to go on talking and writing so that we do not lose the lives of those we love in history. Otherwise history belongs to those who did such things [i.e. committed wartime atrocities]" (Temple 1995: 64).

The autobiographical self has its own particular history in the western world, and a whole literature already exists concerning the emergence of the idea of "the self" as part of the story of modernity: our taken-for-granted image of the self as atomised, bounded, authentic (the "true", or "inner" self), intrinsically psychological, unique and continuous in the story it tells itself, perfectible and therefore obsessively self-evaluating, the self in short as "project" (Rose 1998) is historically quite recent, and by no means universal. Portelli (1981: 177) has pointed out how much the emergence of a modern sense of the individual self has to do with writing, with the proliferation of texts brought about by printing, and with the development of the novel, a form which has powerfully influenced cultural expectations about the proper shape of an autobiography. Bruner and Weisser (1991) propose that this modern self is one which is apt to feel constrained by a particular set of thematic structures, dilemmas and constraints. Thus, when people in "western" societies are asked to give an account of themselves, they will do so in a way that is already heavily shaped by literacy in the culture they have grown up in.

That people in different cultures may choose different ways of telling (Cruikshank 1990), or may resist the task altogether (Röttger-Rössler 1993) is undeniable; but can we really assume that, once "modernised", their styles will converge? Whether we think of "modernity" as one story, one trajectory, or many, people's experiences of it, their resistances to or appropriations of it, certainly differ. Depending where you are, the social transformations involved may reach you at a different moment and in a different form (Gomes 1994). In Singapore, for instance, some Chinese families in the 1950s had members who were deeply politicised and followed with fascination the developments of the Chinese Revolution. A few made the decision to return to China in order to participate in the shaping of a different, revolutionary modernity. A prominent example is Tan Kah Kee, a hugely successful Singapore businessman, a noted philanthropist, and a legendary figure in the overseas Chinese story; but there were also others, more anonymous, who were not public figures. Needless to say, their decisions resulted in a sharp divergence in life trajectories between themselves and their siblings who chose to remain in Southeast Asia. Tan Kah Kee, upon his return to China in 1950, held various posts under the Communist government, and when he died in 1961 was given a state funeral; but this phase of his life receives a very muted attention in Singapore. He died before the country was engulfed in the turmoil of the Cultural Revolution, and it is impossible to say whether his high position would have protected him, or might have carried its own risks. Those who were longer-lived more likely paid the price of "living in interesting times". Historical vicissitudes, and the suppression of a communist "turn" in the life of a more obscure figure, emerged especially vividly in an essay once written for me by a student in my class on "Social Memory". His great-grandfather was a landowner, who had been tortured and killed by the Communists in China's Agrarian Land Reforms of 1950. His father had passed on the story to his children:

> My Grandfather owned land in China. When the land revolution happened, he was accused of being a landowner who had exploited his people. They then caught him and forced him to do hard labour in the fields. After he toiled in the fields, he was locked up in a cage — you know, those small, short little cages — and was not allowed any food. They taunted him by pulling his beard and ridiculed him. They then forced him to kneel on broken glass for three days and three nights before they executed him with a bullet. My grandmother was so upset after she saw what happened that she killed herself by jumping into the river.

The father had escaped to Singapore in the company of his other grandparents shortly before this tragedy occurred, and he still recalled his surviving grandfather recounting the story together with the injunction, "Never forget to hate the Communists!". But the gruesome tale awakened his own interest in history; beginning to delve into history books and to interview relatives, he became a keeper of family memories. He also transmitted them to his own children, who found them both thrilling and terrifying. In the process, though, he reached a deeper appreciation of how events had been shaped by bigger and inescapable social forces. Instead of passing on the message of hate, his advice to the next generation was to learn from past mistakes. One should strive to understand the past, he taught them, both in order to know where one comes from, and to be mentally prepared for the possible effects of an intrusion of history into one's own life. A further twist in family fortunes had been deliberately repressed from the archive of family stories: a cousin of the writer's father, enthused by the revolutionary events of the 1950s and '60s, had surrendered his Singapore citizenship in order to return to China to serve in the Red Army. In an effort to "forget" this betrayal, the family avoided mentioning his name at family gatherings, and the writer had learned of it only through his father, the keeper of family narratives. One can only speculate as to the fate of this cousin, and (assuming he survived to have any descendants) how differently his story may now be told by them. In this example, we see not only the violence with which history may shape individual lives, but also the constantly reinterpreted moral messages that families derive from the stories they choose to pass down across the generations — or to forget.

It is ironic that a particular sense of *historical consciousness* should appear to be so intricately linked with modernity, yet the connection has been pointed out by a variety of authors. Marshall Berman (1982: 17) has written that in Europe and America, "the nineteenth-century modern public can remember what it is like to live, materially and spiritually, in worlds that are not modern at all. From this inner dichotomy, this sense of living in two worlds simultaneously, the ideas of modernisation and modernism emerge and unfold." For many colonised people, the sense of living through a rupture comes somewhat later, in the twentieth century. Their experience has been one of living between two cultures, attempting to endure the clash between them and to make some sense of the contradictions involved. The life histories of some remarkable individuals provide great insight into that experience (Spradley 1969; Cruikshank 1990). Indeed, often it is precisely such exceptional individuals who have the sharpest insights to offer about their own society, its virtues and constraints, or its processes of change. Given the tumultuous events that many people have lived through in the twentieth century, whether in Southeast Asia or elsewhere, the question of historical consciousness is a crucial one in the construction of the self. So we can look at life histories both from the point of view of the light they shed on the experience of historical events themselves, and also in search of those critical moments in life when the protagonist tells us (explicitly or implicitly) how he or she first became aware of wider political issues and struggles that may have shaped the course of their life subsequently.

From another point of view, the mindset of modernity is often described as being partly the outcome of processes of industrialisation and capitalist penetration of an indigenous economy; but in this sense modernity is not necessarily an irrevocable process. The point is vividly made by Brenner (1998), who studied a quarter of the Central Javanese city of Solo which had in the 1920s been on the cutting edge of entrepreneurial development in the manufacture and trade of batik textiles, but which by the 1980s had become an oasis of nostalgia and backwardness as the tides of modernisation had swept on elsewhere. Once thriving neighbourhood businesses had failed to adapt to changing market conditions, and gone into a decline, which Brenner (1998: 126) interprets as a result of an "overidentification with the modernising moment, the moment of progress as the earlier generation had experienced it and as it was remembered in the community's individual and collective memories". Of individuals' identification, or otherwise, with the modern, Brenner (1998: 124–5) gives a striking and amusing example in the life story of one wealthy female entrepreneur, Bu Hamzuri, who was born in 1912:

> As a child, Bu Hamzuri's parents, who were also merchants, had sent her to an Islamic school. But one day while she was in her teens she heard a very attractive woman speaking Dutch, and she was impressed. She decided that she, too, would like to learn Dutch. With a note of modest pride in her voice, she told me, "I liked hearing people speak Dutch. I was rather modern." (*Aku seneng krungu wong omong cara Landa. Aku rada modhèren.*) But her father was old-fashioned (*kolot*), and forbade her to go to a modern school. She was determined, though, and with some savings of her own from her part-time trading she secretly went to a Dutch school (HIS) for a while. One night, she muttered some Dutch in her sleep, including the phrase, "I don't know" (*Ik weet 't niet*). Her father, convinced that she was possessed (*kesurupan*) by a Dutch-speaking spirit, shook her to wake her up and free her of its hold on her. As Bu Hamzuri recounted the story I was amused to think of the zeitgeist of modernity, the spirit of the age, almost literally being embodied in this woman as her old-fashioned father tried to exorcise it. The story is a nice metaphor for the sometimes unintended effects of encounters with the modern, which at times took the form of a casually borrowed Dutchness that could be put on or taken off at will like a hat or a pair of shoes.

The movement toward modernity may not always be one-way for individuals either. While some (like Fritz Basiang, in this volume, or Bu Hamzuri) may have embraced enthusiastically the new world proffered by colonial transformations in Southeast Asia, or chosen to appropriate those aspects of it that suited them, others may have tried and rejected it. For certain communities, especially those of indigenous minorities, their lives may have become a long-drawn-out struggle to negotiate and retain some measure of autonomy in a power structure which threatens entirely to displace and dispossess their own cultures. Such circumstances necessitate an evasion rather than an embrace of what

global capitalism, and an ever more intrusive state apparatus, may wish
to foist on them. It had been an original goal of this volume to include
contributions concerning the lives and experiences of indigenous peoples
in the region. Regrettably, contributions in this area have remained
elusive. Robert Dentan's chapter, however, provides one startling and
disturbing example of the agonies of cultural collision.

The self, then, is situated both in place and time, at a particular
historical moment. The individual, as narrator, may be engaged in
a struggle to make sense of that moment, so that as well as self-
consciousness, a historical consciousness simultaneously emerges from
the telling. A most remarkable example of this is the account of his life
given by an 84-year-old African-American sharecropper, "Nate Shaw"
(Ned Cobb) in Alabama to social historian Theodore Rosengarten
in the early 1970s (Rosengarten 1974). In this instance, one has
an uncanny sense of the researcher having arrived at just the right
historical moment, too: searching for the last surviving member of a
defunct sharecroppers' union formed in the 1920s, Rosengarten found
his way to Cobb's home and began what turned out to be an eight-
hour conversation, which was later followed by many more hours of
tape-recorded narrative. It is as if Cobb had been waiting years for an
audience to the story of his life's struggles — an encounter that might
very easily never have materialised. The resulting account, shaped as it
is by the narrator's own particular style, emotional tone, and turns of
phrase, conveys a vivid sense of his character and sense of self, while
simultaneously recreating in astonishing detail an incisive picture of
the social conditions endured by African-Americans in the deep south
in the early years of the twentieth century. It is this combination of
the deeply personal, and the social and political, embedded as it is in
the manner of telling, which can make the life history such a special
kind of document.

Watson (2000), examining a range of published autobiographies
from Indonesia, distinguishes between the several personae involved
in the production of an autobiographical account. These individuals
already have a *public persona*, either as politicians or literary figures,
but in the role of the *adult narrator* of their own past, they also look
back on another self, that of *childhood* and youth, now seen and judged
from a distance.[6] Watson is concerned to examine the range of play
that is possible between these three distinct personalities; does the adult
narrator, for example, wish to convey the way the world looked through

the eyes of the child he once was, or is he making judgements with the benefit of hindsight? He also demonstrates how the very specificities of these accounts can precisely be drawn upon for more general insights: each individual displays dimensions of identity which are locally and culturally specific (for instance, growing up as Batak, as Minangkabau or as Javanese); or which represent a specifically Indonesian style of historical consciousness, as the writer renders his own experience of the emergence of Indonesia as an independent nation-state; or which is gender-specific. The one woman writer in the collection has constructed her account in a way that deliberately resists the "normative" expectations of the masculine autobiographical narrative, such that its detailing of idiosyncrasies is ultimately just what makes it distinctively a woman's narrative.

Further examples in which the writer's position as a gendered subject is a vivid and dominant theme include Nawal el Saadawi's *A Daughter of Isis* (1999), or Graziella Parati's discussion of Italian women's autobiography, *Public Histories, Private Stories* (1996). Feminist analysts of autobiography have noted how male autobiographers tend to stress individual striving and success even to the virtual exclusion of discussion of their emotions or relationships with others; spouses often barely merit a mention. Women, by contrast, are much more likely to discuss these areas of life. To this extent, the typical western masculine narrative is strangely partial, for in reality individuals, and the choices they make in life, are much more socially embedded than such self-presentations suggest (Gluck and Patai 1991; Gergen 1992; Evans 1993). While that kind of account, notes Evans, offers the comforting fiction of people "who knew what they were doing", she sees a need to rescue biography from such individualism and use it to demonstrate that "without a social understanding individuals are unable to make personal choices" (1993: 12). Women, who typically must operate under very different cultural constraints than men, are much more likely to show an awareness of their social context, and may deliberately shape their lives, as well as their narratives, "against the grain" of conventional expectations. On the other hand, two still rare examples from Melanesian societies (Young 1983; Keesing 1985) show how, within markedly male-dominated societies, women may view their own careers and contributions to the maintenance of a social structure, and recount with pride their hard work and their efforts to excel in the expected female roles and occupations. The style of their narratives reveals a great deal about their own, gendered perspective on their society and its values. More recently, striking examples of feminist anthropologists' engagement with the personal narratives of women include Lila Abu-Lughod's account of Egyptian Bedouin society through women's stories, *Writing Women's Worlds: Bedouin Stories* (1993); Ruth Behar's presentation of the life stories of a Mexican woman street peddler, *Translated Woman: Crossing the Border with Esperanza's Story* (1993); and Gelya Frank's *Venus on Wheels* (2000), which records the life history of Diane, a woman born without limbs. Each of these works has enlarged the boundaries of what a study of personal narratives can achieve, while providing searching reflections on the author's own position within the dialogical relationship out of which their books have come into being.

What then is it that makes a life story representative? I argue that it is precisely this distinctive positioning of the subject that gives the narrative its authenticity, not the question of whether that individual is "average" or typical. However apparently unique, the individual's story will always be representative of the experience of living at that particular historical conjuncture, faced with those particular contradictions, opportunities or constraints. Nobody has written more penetratingly about the problems of representativeness than Portelli (1997). The authority of a personal narrative, he stresses, is closely tied to point of view. In telling of a historical event, an individual will generally tell it from their own, necessarily circumscribed, point of view, "a device," as Portelli points out, "that is widely shared both by oral sources and modern novels" (1997: 84). For instance, a worker from Terni, interviewed about the events of World War II, recalls his own memory of a day in 1942 when the factory hands were brought to the main square in order to hear Mussolini's radio broadcast announcing Italy's entry into the war. From his place in the crowd, he cannot see the whole scene; to do that, says Portelli, he would have had to be somewhere else:

> In order to take a stance as omnisicient narrator in that situation, one would have had to be located on top of the prefecture building — indeed, in the turret from which machine guns were aimed at the crowd in case of civil disturbances.

Once we accept the impossibility of a "neutral" position, the "problem" of a life's idiosyncracies no longer appears so disabling. Indeed, the particularity of an individual's story, according to Portelli (1997:

86), far from disqualifying it as a useful source, is always important insofar as it adds to our understanding of the range of possible human experience. As he puts it, "The representative quality of oral sources and life histories is related to the extent to which they open and define the *field of expressive possibilities*" [my italics]. And he adds:

> Texts do not become representative because of their statistically average quality. We do not dismiss Dante Alighieri's *Divine Comedy* from our reconstruction of the Middles Ages in Italy on the ground that he was not representative because the average Florentine citizen of that time would be unlikely to produce such a text. Rather, we include it precisely because of its exceptionality: on the one hand, *only* a Florentine citizen of that time could produce such a text; on the other, its uniqueness comprehends and defines the range of possibilities of its time and society.

In several of his writings, Portelli has examined instances of oral narratives he has collected in which specific details can be shown to be historically incorrect. Yet he is a master of analysing what such inconsistencies may reveal in terms of deeper emotional significances, both personal and collective, and he insists on acknowledging the importance of the imagination, or what he terms "the subjective projection of imaginable experience". Representativeness, he argues, rests not so much in "what materially happens to people" as in "what people imagine or know might happen". This applies as much to the possibility of being whipped in the narratives of African slaves in America, as to accidents and death on the job in the narratives of factory workers from Terni, or to Italian young people when they talk about the possible dangers of drugs. "Measurable or not, subjectivity is itself a fact, an essential ingredient of our humanity", is his inescapable conclusion (1997: 82). The study of life history narratives, then, falls within Portelli's description of oral history generally as a "science of the individual", offering "less a grid of standard experiences than a horizon of shared possibilities, real or imagined", one that is much closer to the texture of real life, in which "each person entertains, in each moment, multiple possible destinies, perceives different possibilities, and makes different choices from others in the same situation" (1997: 88).

Within the discipline of anthropology, Lila Abu-Lughod chooses to write about personal narratives as a means of "writing against culture" (Abu-Lughod 1991), resisting and destabilising anthropological generalisations about the structural features of certain types of society (in this case, "Arab" or "Middle Eastern" societies), which she fears have a tendency to congeal into too reified an idea of "cultures" as self-contained entities. In her book, *Writing Women's Worlds* (1993), Bedouin women's personal narratives about fragments of their lives are grouped under chapter headings that stand for classic anthropological categories of analysis of Arab societies: for instance, "Patrilineality", "Polygyny", "Patrilateral Parallel-Cousin Marriage", or "Honour and Shame". But the stories serve to unsettle our assumptions about those categories. The question that concerns her is, what is it like to *live* those institutions, those ideologies? In daily life, she notes:

> Individuals are confronted with choices; they struggle with others, make conflicting statements, argue about points of view on the same events, undergo ups and downs in various relationships and changes in their circumstances and desires, face new pressures, and fail to predict what will happen to them or those around them. Particular events always happen in time, becoming part of the history of the family, of the individuals involved, and of their relationships. In the events described in the women's stories I retell, one can even read the "larger forces" that made them possible (1993: 14).

The particularities of individual experiences and family disputes conveyed in the narratives serve to qualify, or even dissolve, the notion of "Bedouin culture"; they shed a more nuanced, and sometimes surprising, light on women's opinions, and their efforts to achieve their own goals and maintain their own honour within the constraints of the structures within which they must operate. Far from being passive victims of a patriarchal system, they drove home to her the point of some of their stories and poetic songs with such statements as these: "A woman can't be governed — anyone who tries to guard her will just get tired." "Whatever a woman wants to she can do. She's smart and she can think" (1993: 78). As the old nomadic life becomes more and more hemmed in, older women bemoan the reduced freedom of movement this can mean for women, and criticise today's young men for being too restrictive on their sisters, cousins and wives. When talking to an elderly grandmother, and her daughter-in-law from town, about the usual reactions to the birth of a boy or a girl, the daughter-in-law interrupts the grandmother's tale to insist that, where a boy is a cause of rejoicing, "the girl — well, her father will be sad and her relatives will be sad and they won't cook at all for her". The grandmother becomes agitated. "No, the girl...." The daughter-in-law heedlessly continues with her "normative" account: "The girl, poor thing, her mother is sad. That's how it is." But finally the grandmother firmly reasserts her own narrative: "No, the girl makes your heart happy. She's the one who should have a sheep slaughtered to celebrate her. It's just that people don't understand" (1993: 56).

Dialogical Relationships in the Interpretive Triangle: Narrator, Researcher, Audiences and the Choice of Genres

The context in which life stories are recorded is intrinsically a dialogical one, arising out of the interchange between narrator and researcher. A complete life history narrative would rarely, if ever, be told in a naturally arising social context; it is, instead, a product of that encounter. The story may well have been told in different ways before — most often in anecdotal fragments perhaps, to audiences of family and friends. Anecdote is likely to retain a central role within the larger structure of an elicited narrative, and rewards closer analysis as a "narrative resource" in its own right (Ashplant 1998). It must be remembered that oral genres invariably retain at least some of their vitality even within highly literate societies; Luisa Passerini (1987: 62), for instance, shows vividly how the oral testimonies she collected from members of the Turin working-class draw upon "genres older than writing"; their self-characterisations, often comic or rebellious, "could be put in that category that Bakhtin refers to as 'comic-serious', which includes genres such as mime, fable, dialogue and satire"; whereas, she notes, "one can observe a radical change in style when the same individual is writing rather than talking", when they adopt a more open kind of identity, whose conception has been markedly influenced by the novel. Similarly Ashplant, analysing the autobiographical account of a working-class man from Stratford and his experiences during and after the First World War, shows how closely many of the anecdotes embedded in his narrative echo the structure of music-hall comic sketches. This familiar, popular genre is skilfully deployed to parody those in positions of authority and to critique the cruelties of the class relations of the time, and ultimately to make a darker statement about the poverty and suffering endured by ordinary people. This individual was well known locally as a singer and story-teller, indeed was obliged to earn a living from these skills after being invalided in the Great War; his daughter-in-law, recording and piecing together his repertoire, constructs it in a new form as a complete life story, thus providing an intriguing example of the complex processes by which the oral may be preserved within the written (Ashplant 1998; Hewins 1981).

Even more, if we are dealing with societies whose traditions are predominantly oral, do we need to be alert to the indigenous contexts and styles of storytelling or performance which shape the way in which historical memory is preserved, or in which a narrator chooses to present her or his life. Tonkin (1992) argues cogently that the sum of "historical activity" in most societies extends far beyond the written work of professional historians. We therefore need to expand our definitions accordingly to include the strongly performative character of social memory in oral societies, as among the Jlao of Liberia with whom she herself has worked. Song, dance, ritual, painting, and a variety of mnemonic objects may all serve as vehicles of transmission within oral traditions, while performances may be constantly recreated and tailored to suit particular audiences or persons commissioning the performance. Yet ironically, any oral account that reaches us in the form of text on the printed page has clearly undergone a transformation, perhaps several if it has first been recorded on audio or video tape. There is also the question of translation. In all of this, the researcher is bound to play a shaping role. But where at one time the researcher as interlocutor might have attempted to efface themselves from the eventual presentation of what was originally a dialogue, we find it easier now to acknowledge that such an "objectivity" is necessarily false. Granted the essentially collaborative nature of the enterprise, it behoves the researcher to be more open about their own role in the production of the narrative.

The relationship between narrator and anthropologist can occasionally become so deeply personal as to become a journey of discovery for the investigator, who finds herself obliged to confront dimensions of her own identity and life struggle in a new way. Frank (1979, 1985, 1995), who has explored these issues in exceptional depth in her own work, suggests that the process of producing a life history may blend the consciousness of investigator and subject to such a degree that the resulting work must contain embedded within it a kind of hidden portrait of the investigator, a "shadow biography". Behar (1993) takes up and further explores the idea of "biography in the shadow", adding a chapter to her book about Esperanza's story in which she wrestles with her own complex background as the child of Cuban Jewish immigrants to the United States, and her own experiences of exclusion within the academy. Her personal experiences of border crossings preceded her bearing of Esperanza's story across the border from Mexico to the USA; her account becomes simultaneously a search for herself, "this woman who has been hiding behind the story of another woman's life", at the same time as she acknowledges shared authorship, seeking "to recognise Esperanza as a writer whose words are written in the sand of storytelling and conversation" (1993: 336).

Collaboration may well carry on through the writing process as further feedback and approval is sought from the original narrator (see for example Borland 1991; Echevarria-Howe 1995). Yet the possibilities for shared authorship have perhaps not yet been exhausted, since relatively few ethnographic works to date have actually named cultural consultants as co-authors.[7] In the work of editing, there are many choices to be made, and especially when working across cultures, the researcher must still be prepared to accept a certain responsibility for the work put in to the presentation of an account in a way that can ensure its accessibility to a wider audience. Caplan (1997: 22), reflecting on these issues, speaks of her decision to write "a seamed narrative in which the ethnographer sews the seams and is seen to do so, but in which the people who are its sources — their voices and the occasions on which they speak — are made explicit". And perhaps this is as fair a compromise as is possible.

In the study of lives, the resonances set up between narrator, researcher and reader are thus of particular interest and deserve our close attention. In the case of anthropologists, who often develop very long-term relationships with their cultural consultants in the field, they may find themselves drawn into the story being told (see Hoskins 1985 and this volume for a striking example). Who owns a life story? To whom, and with what purpose, is one to tell it? Family members and descendants may have their own concerns that a person's life should be remembered. One will have to consider how to frame the story in ways that are most culturally appropriate, for it is increasingly certain that the published account will be read not just in the academic community but also in the individual's own community of origin. Realistically, then, the readership is likely to comprise several very different audiences, who may have very different kinds of feedback to offer in this dynamic, triangular relationship. The relationship with audiences, and their possible variety, is an aspect of the life story that in this volume, we set out to explore more fully.

Individual Encounters with the Twentieth Century

My own interest in life history grew out of my fieldwork experiences in Tana Toraja, in the highlands of South Sulawesi, in the late 1970s and early '80s. During this period, I came to know a man named Fritz Basiang, whose story is told here in Chapter 4. He recounted his life to me in several long interviews in 1983, when he was 78 years old. His life was marked by the way he had eagerly reached for the new experiences ushered in with the colonial transformation of Toraja society. From the time he was a young boy, he had seized advantage of whatever opportunities presented themselves in order to pursue novel goals, and in the process, he created a new sort of life and identity for himself. Born in 1905, the same year that the Dutch entered the Toraja highlands, he was one of the first Toraja to attend school, and was also an early convert to Christianity. Though he never had the chance to complete a high school education, he seized the opportunity to train as a nurse, following his mentor, Dr Simon, to Germany, where he stayed during the years 1930–32. He was thus, so far as I am aware, the first Toraja to visit Europe. Escalating political tensions, and the rise of Hitler to power in 1932, eventually decided him to return home to Toraja. Although he was never able officially to qualify as a doctor, he ended up effectively working as one. For the remainder of his career, he worked in the mission-founded hospital at Rantepao; in fact he had to run it during the Japanese occupation when all Dutch personnel were interned. He married Marta Gora, Toraja's first trained midwife. After the Japanese surrender came the difficult years of struggle for Indonesian independence, and the troubled decade of the 1950s, when a long-drawn-out war was waged by Muslim guerrillas of the secessionist Darul Islam movement, who roamed the Toraja highlands terrorising the unconverted and co-opting villagers into their forces. In both these conflicts, Fritz was obliged to treat the wounded from both sides. He died in 1993, having lived almost the whole of the twentieth century.

The life of Fritz Basiang caused me to reflect how a single individual could in one lifetime experience so many social and political transformations, from the world he knew as a child in a remote highland village, to the emergence of Indonesia as an independent and modernising nation. Fritz was an unconventional person in his enthusiasm for new experience, and in the way he devised for himself a new kind of identity — modern, Indonesian, and Christian — while still to the end of his life retaining a strong respect for certain aspects of his own Toraja culture. His movement outward from his home village, first to school in a local town, thence to Java and finally to Europe, before returning full circle to his homeland, embodies precisely the kind of educational trajectory or "pilgrimage" through a political space which Anderson (1983: 111) has described as typifying the colonial experience. The newly "imagined reality" which grew out of these journeys, and the encounters with others along the way, contributed directly to the formation of nationalist identities and aspirations. Fritz's own life in a number of ways encapsulates the radical changes undergone in the whole region of the Sa'dan Toraja highlands during the twentieth century.

Although his story appears so remarkable, it is by no means entirely unique; if set within the framework of other published autobiographies of a similar period in Indonesia, we can at once see the emergence of some parallel themes. Indonesia's own, relatively short, tradition of published autobiographical and biographical writing has, as elsewhere, almost exclusively produced works by well-known public figures, whether politicians or literary figures. Fresh analytical attention has recently been paid to these works by a number of writers.[8] They provide many fascinating insights into the authors' encounters with modernity. A marked theme in many of them, particularly those published in the 1950s, is the simultaneous development both of the writer's own personality, and his (the writers are predominantly male) identification as "Indonesian" — the very idea of "Indonesia" itself being still emergent in the 1920s. In the process, a childhood world steeped in a more local ethnic identity is gradually left behind, assuming the qualities of a lost world, both romantically recalled and sharply criticised by the writer from his perspective as an adult and a nationalist. In Fritz's case, I am also able to situate his narrative within a distinctive subset of narratives — a handful of contemporary autobiographies published by individuals who, like him, received medical training under the Dutch (Anderson 1990; Soemarno 1981; Djelantik 1997). Like Fritz, they all experienced the Dutch colonial system and the passage toward a modern Indonesian identity. And for all of them this progression was also a political one, in which each came to share the vision of an independent Indonesia, and used their skills to contribute in the most practical way possible to improving life for ordinary people.

Although Fritz Basiang's reputation never spread beyond his own locality, his narrative has just as much to tell us about the experience of becoming Indonesian as those of more famous individuals. In reflecting on his life, however, I began to think how differently other Southeast Asians may have experienced the cultural collisions of the twentieth century, and responded to the threats or opportunities presented by the impacts of modernity. In Chapter 2, Carol Warren presents another fascinating life of a person who, like Fritz, lived almost the whole of the twentieth century. Madé Lebah (1905?–96) was born to a Balinese commoner family who were hereditary retainers to the Rajas of Peliatan. He describes his childhood in a world in which the Dutch presence was as yet barely felt, and his experience of the changes of the later colonial period, the Japanese Occupation and the emergence of an independent Indonesia. As Warren points out, the social transformations experienced in Bali during the Suharto era were in some ways still more radical than those of the first half of the century. A gifted musician in his own culture, his talents led Madé Lebah to have many encounters with Europeans. He formed a gamelan association which, besides playing for the court at Peliatan, was invited to perform at the Paris Colonial Exhibition of 1931; later he was employed by the musicologist Colin McPhee, performing a dual role as chauffeur and gamelan teacher. His account is full of detail and insightful commentary on many aspects of his changing social world: on Balinese ideas of illness, on magic, music, village co-operation, the declivities of the Rajas, and the changing costs of living. As an individual, Warren points out, his life is of interest for the way he represents Bali's "exceptional collective legacies", as much as for the details of his cross-cultural encounters; as a commoner, his down-to-earth view of life provides a valuable contrast to the upper-caste perspectives which, Warren suggests, have tended to dominate in many researchers' accounts of Balinese society. For all that he was clearly an exceptional individual, then, his account sheds light on a variety of broader social and historical issues.

Hoskins' account, in Chapter 3, of the life of Yoseph Malo of Sumba (1880?–1960), presents us with another highly unusual narrative of an extraordinary individual, who lived through the colonial encounter and its cultural collisions, yet whose life never the less exemplifies certain cultural ideals of Sumbanese society. Yoseph Malo was born into an aristocratic family, witnessed his father's beheading by enemy raiders at the age of nine, was sold into slavery, and ended up working for the first Catholic mission on Sumba in the early years of the twentieth century. He went on to take two heads himself, deliberately married into the family of his father's murderers in order to reclaim his head and recover his honour, and then became the Dutch-appointed Raja of the domain of Rara, and the husband of eight local wives.

Hoskins has worked in collaboration for 15 years with Yoseph Malo's son, Cornelius Djakababa, who has also been writing his own version of his father's story. Yoseph's grandson, who bears his name, is currently studying for a PhD in history at the University of Wisconsin, and may in turn produce his own account in future. Yoseph Malo was not himself literate enough to write his own autobiography, but he did tell his story to many people. During his lifetime he often performed it in an indigenous genre of storytelling that includes elements of ritual poetry, oratory and song. It is remarkable to note the parallel way in which the staging of ritual acts, with their accompanying orations, prayers, or laments, both act as critical turning-points in Malo's career as lived, as much as they provide high points in the dramatic narrative of his life as told. His own performances must have served to dramatise his persona and the reversals of fortune over which he had triumphed, in a form which clearly fits within an already familiar and socially salient narrative framework in Sumba.[9] Before he died, he also "bequeathed" the duty of telling his story to others, including an indigenous storyteller, Maru Daku, who has been a key consultant to Hoskins in her research on Sumba. The author's collaboration with Yoseph Malo's son has grown out of an initial difference of opinion over the appropriate way to present his story. In the written correspondence and repeated meetings that have followed, their accounts have borrowed from each other to the point where they have in Hoskins' words "served to construct one another". The circumstances therefore raise a number of demanding and thought-provoking questions: about the ownership of life histories, the possible ways of recording them, and not least the various prospective audiences who may read them. Hoskins' bibliography contains, as well as six papers of her own that refer in different ways to Malo's life, five versions locally produced by Sumbanese consultants. Two of these are tape recorded, two exist in manuscript form, while one is in press with a Jakarta publisher, and is due to appear in both Indonesian and English. One manuscript version has been lost, an ironic reminder — borne

out by similar experiences in my own fieldwork — of the potential
vulnerability of written materials, versus the tenacity of oral memory.
Hoskins has also videotaped Mr Djakababa telling his father's story,
thus producing still another kind of oral version, which differs in some
of its narrative dimensions from the written accounts.[10] A particularly
interesting dimension of Hoskins' analysis in this volume thus concerns
the manner in which these various versions of Malo's life have already
influenced each other and become interwoven. At the same time, the
number of possible audiences, and the different frameworks of ideas and
interests which each of these audiences is likely to bring to bear on their
interpretations of Malo's story, continues to multiply. With each new
account, our perspectives on Malo's life and its possible significances
multiply, yet none can be claimed as final. Even as the tale is enriched,
we are obliged to accept the inescapable sense of incompleteness that
is a feature of every life story.

Analysing Life Histories in Sets

Another major strategy by which to derive generalities from the unique
details of life stories is to analyse life histories in sets. Examples from
three different disciplines illustrate the fruitfulness of this method. The
sociologists Daniel Bertaux and Isabelle Bertaux-Wiame (1981) collected
a set of narratives from French bakers' apprentices; their systematic
correspondences proved highly revealing of long-established structures
of exploitation in the hierarchy of working relations in the bakers'
trade. Portelli (1991, 1997) and Luisa Passerini (1987) have both used
sets of life histories to analyse, respectively, the history of working-class
communists in Terni, and workers' oral memories of the Fascist period
in Turin. John Borneman (1991), an anthropologist, uses a set of life
histories to provide a vivid and compelling account of East Berliners'
lived experiences of socialism, and the variety and ambivalence of their
responses to the collapse of the Berlin Wall, based upon their very
different life trajectories and generational positions within the system
which the GDR had imposed upon its citizens. This variety he feared
would otherwise be lost to history in the "headlong rush to oblivion"
accompanying what he describes as effectively the corporate takeover of
the GDR by West Germany, and the media's simplified presentation of
reunification as one long moment of euphoria (1991: 17). Borneman's
book thus captures a more holistic picture of this fleeting yet most

dramatic of moments, so significant that, from a European perspective, it seemed to announce a premature close to the twentieth century. While he does not shy away from drawing certain generalisations about the distinctive features of the former East German society, we are enabled to see how differently these are played out in the lives of different individuals, not to mention their fantasies and desires. The narratives presented, far from adding up to a "typical" profile of the East Berliner, must remain a set of statements by individuals, illustrating how even within the most stifling and totalitarian of regimes, people's lived experiences and mental worlds can never be reduced to uniformity. Like Portelli, Borneman insists on the importance of documenting the diversity of human experience in any given time and place:

> In order to describe in the plural, in context, and in history, one must pay more attention to the exceptional than to typical lives, for only in the exceptional does one find the range of possibilities within the group. Thus I have chosen to portray individual lives of different generations, rare instances of crystallised meaning indicating how large scale political processes interact with personal histories and identities. Modern ethnographic fieldwork, which involves living over a substantial period of time with the people one studies and then focuses on the particular details of individual experience in historical context, is peculiarly suited to the task of linking the political and the personal (1991: 19).

In a subsequent paper (1998), Borneman discusses another set of life history interviews which he carried out with a set of Jewish individuals, all of whom had left Germany during the Nazi period but had later returned to either East or West Berlin. Some of these individuals, or their parents, had experienced multiple migrations across changing borders, as well as the forcible removal of their Germanness during the period of the Third Reich, followed by a renewed, if problematic, enculturation as either East or West German. The particular narrative he discusses in this paper comes from a person who has lived through so many ambiguities and redefinitions of identity that even this single story provides dramatic insights into the whole process of identity construction, as well as the complications possible in the modern experience of "resisting and resigning oneself to the boundaries imposed by states" (Borneman 1998: 131). This example illustrates sharply how the content and meaning of a narrative might be affected by the moment at which it is told; related in a moment of radical destabilisation, in 1989, just two months before the fall of the Berlin Wall, what was intended as primarily an account of kinship is constantly impinged upon by external happenings and the imminent disintegration of a former context or "form of belonging". Borneman thus uses the life history approach to show us that historical consciousness, or "the recognition and knowledge of one's own historicity", is "a condition to which one strives and not a state of being" (1998: 127). The individual struggles to make sense out of the tensions between personal, subjective experience and the shifting historical and social context within which that experience occurs.

Abu-Lughod's (1993) work on the Bedouin, already discussed above, shows how the use of sets of personal narratives can help to undermine taken-for-granted cultural stereotypes about Arab societies, as well as common feminist interpretations of gender relations in such settings. But more than this, Abu-Lughod has preserved in her book a focus on the way that stories are told for particular purposes in their original cultural setting, being deployed at particular moments to make a point for the benefit of specific audiences within the narrators' own community. She decided to resist the temptation to lift the narratives out of this setting and piece them together into coherent "life histories", fearing that this might give the reader a misleading impression of the narrators as isolated, separate individuals. They would hardly recognise themselves in such a portrait, but rather live their lives within a dense network of family relationships.

In her book, _Biographical Objects: How Things Tell the Stories of People's Lives_ (1998), Hoskins achieves a further innovation: she presents a set of Sumbanese men's and women's lives through the medium of the narratives they told her about deeply significant objects. Sumba is a society where certain possessions — textiles, jewellery, betel-bags, drums, horses, and other domestic animals — can acquire names, power and character of their own, or become so imbued with the personal characteristics of their possessors that their loss would cause soul loss to the owner. It is a society which Hoskins describes as being "saturated with gender" (1998: 15), where a principle of gendered pairing, as a metaphor of necessary completion or fertile sexual union, is a theme obsessively worked out in endless cultural contexts — whether in the naming of deities, house parts, or types of jewellery, for instance; and where in ritual contexts it is not uncommon for symbolically male or female objects to be made to substitute for real persons. In this setting, where people appeared to lack the "narcissistic preoccupation with telling and retelling about their own lives" more typical of Europe or America, Hoskins was often frustrated in her initial attempts to gather individual life histories (1998: 2). However, she found that people were often more comfortable talking allusively about themselves through the more distanced medium of tales about objects. These served as props and mnemonics in their efforts to define a personal and sexual identity, and to reflect, in a sometimes ironic way, upon the meaning of their lives. The use of a set of narratives in this instance is illuminating of the very different ways in which men and women tell their stories, using objects as mediating metaphors for the person, each having their own judgements to offer on the conflicts and tensions that may characterise gender relations in Sumba society.

The second half of this volume presents life stories analysed in sets — or, in the case of Dentan's paper, the tale of a single individual as it emerges from conflicting fragments told by multiple narrators. In all of them we hear partial stories, narrated by different voices. An older style of "realist" ethnography unproblematically assumed that the presentation of coherent accounts of whole societies was an achievable goal. But anthropology's "crisis of representation" since the 1980s has brought a break with that style, as a result of which the fragment has achieved a new ontological status. It has to be recognised that no ethnography can possibly say everything about a society, and if every account (whether life story narration, or written ethnography) is in fact incomplete and composed of fragments, so are identities themselves (Marcus 1998: 62). The papers in the second half of the book reflect this new respect for the potentialities of fragments and multiple voices.

Dentan's experimental contribution in Chapter 5, which claims as its literary touchstone Dostoyevsky's "Notes from Underground", concerns the disturbing story of a Semai/Malay child-murderer whom he met in the prison in Kuala Lumpur where the latter was awaiting trial for murder. It combines his own directly personal voice as author with fragments of narrative derived from several sources: Arifin himself, former workmates, police reports and newspaper articles. From the gaps within and between these fragments, like shards of shattered glass, a troubling picture can be more or less reassembled of this person's life story, referring back to the whole context in which Semai and other Orang Asli indigenous peoples have found themselves incorporated into the Malaysian state. Readers thus can form their own opinions of the investigation in which the author became tangentially involved, and of his own interpretation which concludes the chapter. Dentan postulates that Arifin may have suffered an attack of *Blnuul bhiip* or "blood intoxication", a trance-like episode of compulsive violence brought on by the sight of blood. This is a Semai cultural phenomenon which paradoxically runs directly counter to their established ethnographic image as "a nonviolent people" (Dentan 1979).

Bizarre though it may at first sight appear, the composition of this account raises much wider questions about the context of power structures out of which the life narratives of the powerless may emerge. It suggests compelling parallels with the work of British historian Carolyn Steedman (2000) on what she has called the "enforced narratives" extracted from men and women of the labouring poor in England, from the seventeenth century onward, in magistrates' courts when they applied for poor relief. Under legislation of 1661, to be entitled to relief, it was necessary that the applicant give an account of where they were born, when and where they were put to work, and crucially, how long they had worked in one place, for working consistently in one parish and receiving wages for a calendar year carried one of the most important entitlements to settlement. Thousands of these accounts, produced under magistrates' questioning and recorded by clerks of the court, have been preserved in county record offices across England. The chronological sequence of conventional autobiographies, with their opening sentence to the effect that: "I was born in X, on such-and-such a date", may owe more to the legal contexts in which the poor were coerced into telling their stories than to any creative impulse of the modern self. Like these narratives, Arifin's story is extracted under questioning, only in this case his life depends on the plausibility of the account he can give of himself. The anthropologist here takes the role of advocate, reluctantly drawn into a situation that is bound to prompt sharper reflections than usual on the circumstances of the ethnographic encounter. He is indeed in a position to offer a special kind of understanding and interpretation, yet is ultimately powerless to alter the outcome.

If Dentan's account presents us with the fate of one person related by many different voices, the remaining chapters of the book deal with sets of life stories told by different individuals who share a particular social context. In Chapter 6, Annette Hamilton, recording personal narratives from the southern Thai town of Hua Hin, shows how the lives of rural villagers or provincial townsfolk are revealing of their own particular interpretations of history, time and social circumstances. She found that the views of the past, of Thai politics, and of the intrusions of modern technology, which these narratives contained, were different from those of dwellers in the capital, and in many ways defied her own expectations. Ultimately, Hamilton is concerned to trace the outlines of a distinctive historical consciousness and experience of time in Thailand. Her project aims to displace persistently Eurocentric notions underpinning what she argues tend to be overly systematised and simplified interpretations of modernity, and of global social transformations under capitalism.

In Chapter 7, Yoko Hayami presents the narratives of young Karen women whom she befriended in the hills of northern Thailand and in the city of Chiang Mai. In this encounter the women relate to Hayami both as woman and as traveller. They recount with verve their travels and amorous encounters with men outside of their own communities. But for all of them, these adventures could have put their reputations at risk within their own communities. Hayami is an outsider, not bound by the same constraints which they face on their behaviour, and as such they may have found it easier to talk to her about their youthful experiences, rarely mentioned in conversation with other villagers. Hayami shows us how the women have tried to manage the social constraints they face, bound as they are by webs of power relations which give them far less room to manoeuvre than young Karen males enjoy. Nevertheless, they tell their stories in ways which emphasise their own enjoyment, agency and decision-making. Like the narratives of women recorded by Abu-Lughod (1993) or Skinner *et al.* (1998), their narratives shed an intimate light on women's lived experiences within the confines of a particular community and its cultural expectations.

In Chapter 8, Saroja Dorairajoo describes how the Pattani Malay villagers with whom she lived in South Thailand chose to situate her presence there in a particular way. This happened both as a result of pre-existing political tensions in that area, and of the large number of other researchers and NGO workers who had previously visited the village on brief fieldwork excursions. These latter had always focused on investigating the environmental problems created by new push-net trawling methods, which had destroyed both marine life and the local fishermen's livelihoods. As a result, the villagers already had a well-developed narrative of change ready to recount to any outside visitor, and they assumed that this was what she would want to hear, too. Over a much longer acquaintance, during which she tried to give up asking any questions at all, she gradually became the audience for narratives of a quite different nature. Like Abu-Lughod (1993), Dorairajoo retains a focus on the original contexts in which stories were related. The range of these narratives, the audiences to whom they were told, and the teller's purposes in telling them, provide the subject for analysis in her chapter. At one level, the stories told revealed a significant generational shift in how Pattani Malays are situating themselves in terms of ethnic and national identities, and in their relationship to Malays on the Malaysian side of the border. But the stories told by men and women also displayed notable gendered differences, revealing of their different responses to the changed opportunities for fishing. The stories told varied also according to whether they were being related to a mixed, or single-sex, audience, or whether, as Dorairajoo came to suspect, they were ostensibly addressed to her, but with a view to their effect on others present. Dorairajoo's work thus provides a close-grained account of the shifting content of life stories told at different moments of daily life, for different audiences and to different effects.

Conclusion: Selves, Lives and a Multivocal Anthropology

If in the early decades of modern anthropology, the over-riding concern tended to be with describing and modelling social structures, much ethnography since the 1980s has been distinguished by the turn toward a keener engagement with history. There is now a much stronger awareness of just how much history can be recovered, even of predominantly oral societies, and a greater concern with the ever more rapid processes of change engulfing societies everywhere. The current efforts to understand experience might be seen as a third turn in the evolution of the discipline, one in which the focus turns to what it is like to live in a given time and place, as an individual occupying a particular social location. The study of life histories offers us the opportunity to examine the intersections of history with personal experience, whether of single individuals, or of sets of people in similar circumstances. The apparent problem of representativeness is a matter of perspective and point of view, which far from disqualifying each unique narrative from any hope of generalisation, can be seen precisely as part of its value. Each narrative enlarges our sense of human possibilities, and enriches our understandings of what it has meant to live in the twentieth century. John Lukacs (1994: 357) avers that "the purpose of the historian should be the reduction of untruth"; the very diversity of the points of view that remain to be recorded can serve to reduce the dangers of oversimplifying the past, or of producing an overly "typified" picture of life in a particular community.

More than this, the study of personal narratives enables us to approach closer to the subjectivity of others, to record their own particular ways of telling, their skills in exploiting the variety of genres and social contexts available to them for the telling, and — even granted the dangers of "slippage" in translation — to capture something of the idiom and emotional tone of their speech. We see in these stories the self, however variably culturally construed, confronting a set of historical circumstances, and making a life out of the opportunities available. Such narratives shed light not only on particular historical events or conjunctures lived through, but in a more general sense, have things to tell us about the nature of the human experience. All the accounts presented here also bear the traces of the dialogical encounters between narrator, researcher, and other interested parties. We have seen how complex and prolonged these can be; for the anthropologist, this encounter exemplifies the enterprise in which we are engaged, and holds out the possibility of a knowledge that is itself more fully intersubjective.

Notes

I am grateful to Janet Hoskins for her comments on an earlier version of this paper.

1. See Gusdorf (1980), Graham *et al.* (1989), Mascuch (1997).
2. Comprehensive reviews of what have been achieved may be found in Langness and Frank (1981), and Watson and Watson-Franke (1985); important comments on method are made in Mandelbaum (1973), Agar (1980), Bruner (1987), Röttger-Rössler (1993) and Echevarria-Howe (1995).
3. Plummer (1990), while noting the same uneven pattern of attention to its possibilities, has gone so far as to declare a "renaissance" of interest in life history in the social sciences. Chamberlayne, Bornat and Wengraf (2000: 1) speak of a "burgeoning" of biographical methods. Some examples include Rosenwald and Ochberg (1992), and Cruikshank (1990). Rodgers (1995) draws attention to the potentials of published autobiography for the understanding of modern Indonesian history and society.
4. Evans (1999) proposes the "impossibility" of the project of auto/biography, and warns against the facile assumptions of modern biographers that more and more information about a subject's sex life will provide a complete

revelation. The very construction of the self involved in autobiography, as a genre with its own history in the western world, is based, she reminds us, upon certain cultural assumptions, not least, "the belief that we are an integrated 'individual' self, with a coherent persona" (1999: 23). On the inevitably self-serving nature of autobiography, see Peneff (1990).

5. On the therapeutic potentials of narrative, see White and Epston (1990).

6. On the autobiography of childhood as a distinctive genre in its own right, see Coe (1984).

7. A rare exception is *Piman Shamanism and Staying Sickness*, by Bahr, Gregorio, Lopez and Alvarez (1974). Here the authorship is shared between anthropologist, shaman, interpreter and editor.

8. See Watson (1989), Sweeney (1990), Anderson (1990), Rodgers (1995), and most recently, Watson (2000).

9. Some interesting parallels can be found in an example recorded by Keller (1994).

10. See Portelli (1998: 32–3) for some perceptive comments on the distinctive qualities and limitations of video as an interview medium.

References

Abu-Lughod, Lila. 1991. "Writing Against Culture", in *Recapturing Anthropology*, ed. R. Fox. Santa Fe: School of American Research Press, pp. 137–62.

———. 1993. *Writing Women's Worlds: Bedouin Stories*. Berkeley: University of California Press.

Agar, M. 1980. "Stories, Background Knowledge and Themes: Problems in the Analysis of Life History Narrative", *American Ethnologist* 7/2: 223–39.

Anderson, Benedict. 1983. *Imagined Communities: Reflections on the Origin and Spread of Nationalism*. London: Verso.

———. 1990 (1979). "A Time of Darkness and a Time of Light: Transposition in Early Indonesian Nationalist Thought", in *Language and Power: Exploring Political Cultures in Indonesia*, ed. B. Anderson. Ithaca: Cornell University Press, pp. 241–70.

Ashplant, Timothy. 1998. "Anecdote as Narrative Resource in Working-Class Life Stories: Parody, Dramatization and Sequence", in *Narrative and Genre*, ed. Mary Chamberlain and Paul Thompson. London: Routledge, pp. 99–113.

Bahr, Donald, Gregorio, Juan, Lopez, David and Alvarez, Albert. 1974. *Piman Shamanism and Staying Sickness*. Tucson: University of Arizona Press.

Bateson, Mary Catherine. 1989. *Composing a Life*. New York: Plume.

Behar, Ruth. 1992. "A Life Story to Take Across the Border: Notes on an

Exchange", in *Storied Lives: The Cultural Politics of Self-Understanding*, ed. George Rosenwald and Richard Ochberg. New Haven/London: Yale University Press, pp. 108–23.

———. 1993. *Translated Woman: Crossing the Border with Esperanza's Story*. Boston: Beacon Press.

Berman, Marshall. 1982. *All that is Solid Melts into Air*. London: Verso.

Bertaux, Daniel and Bertaux-Wiame, Isabelle. 1981. "Life Stories in the Bakers' Trade", in *Biography and Society: The Life History Approach in the Social Sciences*, ed. D. Bertaux. London: Sage, pp. 169–89.

Borland, Kathleen. 1991. "That's Not What I Said: Interpretive Conflict in Oral Narrative Research", in *Women's Words: The Feminist Practice of Oral History*, ed. S. Gluck and D. Patai. New York & London: Routledge, pp. 63–75.

Borneman, John. 1991. *After the Wall: East Meets West in the New Berlin*. New York: Basic Books.

———. 1998. "Narrative, Genealogy and Historical Consciousness: Selfhood in a Disintegrating State", in his *Subversions of International Order: Studies in the Political Anthropology of Culture*. New York: State University of New York Press, pp. 125–51.

Bramah, Ernest. 1938 (1900). *The Wallet of Kai Lung*. Harmondsworth: Penguin.

Brenner, Suzanne. 1998. *The Domestication of Desire: Women, Wealth and Modernity in Java*. Princeton: Princeton University Press.

Bruner, Jerome. 1987. "Life as Narrative", *Social Research* 54/1: 11–32.

Bruner, Jerome and Weisser, Susan. 1991. "The Invention of Self: Autobiography and its Forms", in *Literacy and Orality*, ed. D. Olson & N. Torrance. Cambridge: Cambridge University Press, pp. 129–48.

Caplan, Pat. 1997. *African Voices, African Lives: Personal Narratives from a Swahili Village*. London: Routledge.

Chamberlayne, Prue, Bornat, Joanna, and Wengraf, Tom. 2000. *The Turn to Biographical Methods in Social Science: Comparative Issues and Examples*. London: Routledge.

Coe, Richard. 1984. *When the Grass was Taller: Autobiography and the Experience of Childhood*. New Haven and London: Yale University Press.

Cruikshank, Julie. 1990. *Life Lived Like a Story: Life Stories of Three Yukon Native Elders*. Lincoln/London: University of Nebraska Press.

Dentan, Robert. 1979. *The Semai: A Nonviolent People of Malaysia*. New York: Harcourt Brace and World.

Djelantik, A.A.M. 1997. *The Birthmark: Memoirs of a Balinese Prince*. Hong Kong: Periplus.

Echevarria-Howe, Lynn. 1995. "Reflections from the Participants: The Process and Product of Life History Work", *Oral History* 23/2: 40–6.

El Saadawi, Nawal. 1999. *A Daughter of Isis.* London: Zed.

Evans, Mary. 1993. "Reading Lives: How the Personal Might be Social", *Sociology* 27/1: 5–13.

———. 1999. *Missing Persons: The Impossibility of Auto/biography.* London: Routledge.

Frank, Gelya. 1979. "Finding the Common Denominator: A Phenomenological Critique of Life History Method", *Ethos* 7/1: 68–94.

———. 1985. "'Becoming the Other': Empathy and Biographical Interpretation", *Biography* 8: 189–210.

———. 1995. "Anthropology and Individual Lives: The Story of the Life History and the History of the Life Story", *American Anthropologist* 97: 145–8.

———. 2000. *Venus on Wheels: Two Decades of Dialogue on Disability, Feminism and Cultural Biography.* Berkeley: University of California Press.

Gergen, Mary. 1992. "7 Life Stories: Pieces of a Dream", in *Storied Lives: The Cultural Politics of Self-Understanding*, ed. George Rosenwald and Richard Ochberg. New Haven/London: Yale University Press, pp. 127–44.

Gluck, Sherna and Patai, Daphne. 1991. *Women's Words: The Feminist Practice of Oral History.* New York: Routledge.

Gomes, Alberto (ed.). 1994. *Modernity and Identity: Asian Illustrations.* Bundoora, Victoria: La Trobe University Press.

Graham, E., *et al.* 1989. *Her own Life: Autobiographical Writings by Seventeenth-Century Englishwomen.* London: Routledge.

Guha, Ranajit. 1982. "On Some Aspects of the Historiography of Colonial India", in *Subaltern Studies: Writings on South Asian History and Society* I: 1–8, ed. R. Guha. Delhi: Oxford University Press.

———. 1996. "The Small Voice of History", in *Subaltern Studies: Writings on South Asian History and Society* IX: 1–12, ed. S. Amin and D. Chakrabaty. Delhi: Oxford University Press.

Gusdorf, Georges. 1980. "Conditions and Limits of Autobiography", in *Autobiography: Essays Theoretical and Critical*, ed. J. Olney. Princeton: Princeton University Press, pp. 28–48.

Healey, Lucy. 1994. "Modernity, Identity and Constructions of Malay Womanhood", in *Modernity and Identity: Asian Illustrations*, ed. A. Gomes. Bundoora, Victoria: La Trobe University Press, pp. 96–121.

Hewins, Angela. 1981. *The Dillen: Memories of a Man of Stratford-Upon-Avon.* Oxford: Oxford University Press.

Hoskins, Janet. 1985. "A Life History From Both Sides: The Changing Poetics of Personal Experience", *Journal of Anthropological Research* 41/2: 147–69.

———. 1998. *Biographical Objects: How Things Tell the Stories of People's Lives*. New York and London: Routledge.

Keesing, Roger. 1985. "Kwaio Women Speak: The Micropolitics of Auto-biography in a Solomon Island Society", *American Anthropologist* 87: 27–39.

Keller, Edgar. 1994. "Fashioned Words of Despair: An Autobiographical Speech of a Dispossessed in Laboya, West Sumba", in *Texts from the Islands*, ed. W. Marschall. Berne: University of Berne, Institute of Ethnology, pp. 265–309.

Langness, L. and Frank, G. 1981. *Lives: An Anthropological Approach to Biography*. Novato, CA.: Chandler & Sharp.

Linde, Charlotte. 1993. *Life Stories: The Creation of Coherence*. New York: Oxford University Press.

Lukacs, John. 1994 (1968). *Historical Consciousness: The Remembered Past*. New Brunswick/London: Transaction Publishers.

Mandelbaum, David. 1973. "The Study of Life History: Gandhi", *Current Anthropology* 14/3: 177–206.

Marcus, George. 1998. *Ethnography Through Thick and Thin*. Princeton: Princeton University Press.

Mascuch, Michael. 1997. *Origins of the Individualist Self: Autobiography and Self-Identity in England, 1591–1791*. Cambridge: Polity Press.

Miller, Peggy. 1994. "Narrative Practices: Their Role in Socialization and Self-Construction", in *The Remembering Self: Construction and Accuracy in the Self-Narrative*, ed. U. Neisser and R. Fivush. Cambridge: Cambridge University Press, pp. 158–79.

Neisser, Ulric and Fivush, Robyn (eds.). 1994. *The Remembering Self: Construction and Accuracy in the Self-Narrative*. Cambridge: Cambridge University Press.

Nora, Pierre. 1996. *Realms of Memory: Rethinking the French Past* (Volume I: Conflicts and Divisions). New York: Columbia University Press.

Parati, Graziella. 1996. *Public History, Private Stories: Italian Women's Auto-biography*. Minneapolis: University of Minnesota Press.

Passerini, Luisa. 1987. *Fascism in Popular Memory: The Cultural Experience of the Turin Working Class*. Cambridge/Paris: Cambridge University Press/ Editions de la Maison des Sciences de l'Homme.

Peneff, Jean. 1990. "Myths in Life Stories", in *The Myths We Live By*, ed. R. Samuel and P. Thompson. London: Routledge, pp. 36–48.

Plummer, Ken. 1990. "Herbert Blumer and the Life History Tradition", *Symbolic Interaction* 13/2: 125–44.

Portelli, Alessandro. 1981a. "The Time of My Life: Functions of Time in Oral History", *International Journal of Oral History* 2/3: 162–80.

———. 1990. "Uchronic Dreams: Working-Class Memory and Possible Worlds", in *The Myths We Live By*, ed. R. Samuel and P. Thompson. London: Routledge, pp. 143–60.

———. 1991. *The Death of Luigi Trastulli and Other Stories: Form and Meaning in Oral History*. Albany: State University of New York Press.

———. 1997. *The Battle of Valle Giulia: Oral History and the Art of Dialogue.* Madison: University of Wisconsin Press.

———. 1998. "Oral History as Genre", in *Narrative and Genre*, ed. Mary Chamberlain and Paul Thompson. London: Routledge, pp. 23–45.

Radin, Paul (ed.). 1926. *Crashing Thunder: The Autobiography of an American Indian*. New York/London: Appleton.

Rappaport, Herbert. 1990. *Marking Time*. New York: Simon and Schuster.

Rodgers, Susan. 1995. *Telling lives, Telling History: Autobiography and Historical Imagination in Modern Indonesia*. Berkeley: University of California Press.

Rose, Nikolas. 1998. *Inventing Our Selves: Psychology, Power and Personhood.* Cambridge: Cambridge University Press.

Rosengarten, Theodore. 1989 [1974]. *All God's Dangers: The Life of Nate Shaw (Ned Cobb, 1885–1973)*. New York: Vintage Books.

Rosenwald, George, and Ochberg, Richard (eds.). 1992. *Storied Lives: The Cultural Politics of Self-Understanding*. New Haven/London: Yale University Press.

Ross, M. and Conway, M. 1986. "Remembering One's Own Past: The Construction of Personal Histories", in *Handbook of Motivation and Cognition*, ed. R. Sorrentino and E. Higgins. New York: Guilford Press, pp. 122–44.

Röttger-Rössler, Birgitt. 1993. "Autobiography in Question: On Self-Presentation and Life Description in an Indonesian Society", *Anthropos* 88: 365–73.

Samuel, Raphael. 1994. *Theatres of Memory: Past and Present in Contemporary Culture*. London: Verso.

Sears, Laurie (ed.). 1993. *Autonomous Histories, Particular Truths: Essays in Honour of John W.R. Smail*. Madison: University of Wisconsin Center for Southeast Asian Studies.

Skinner, Debra, Pach, Alfred, and Holland, Dorothy (eds.). 1998. *Selves in Time and Place: Identities, Experience and History in Nepal*. Lanham: Rowman and Littlefield.

Smail, John. 1993 [1961]. "On the Possibility of an Autonomous History of Modern Southeast Asia", in *Autonomous Histories, Particular Truths: Essays in Honour of John W. R. Smail*, ed. Laurie Sears. Madison: University of Wisconsin Center for Southeast Asian Studies, pp. 39–70.

Soemarno Sosroatmodjo. 1981. *Dari Rimba Raya Ke Jakarta Raya: Subuah Otobiografi*. Jakarta: Gunung Agung.

Spivak, Gayatri Chakravorty with Nikos Papastergiadis. 1991. "Identity and Alterity: An Interview", *Arena* 97: 65–76.

Spradley, James. 1969. *Guests Never Leave Hungry: The Autobiography of James Sewid, a Kwakiutl Indian*. Montreal: McGill-Queen's University Press.

Steedman, Carolyn. 2000. "Enforced Narratives: Stories of Another Self", in *Feminism and Autobiography: Texts, Theories, Methods*, ed. T. Cosslett, C. Lury and P. Summerfield. London: Routledge, pp. 25–39.

Sweeney, Amin. 1990. "Some Observations on the Nature of Malay Autobiography", *Indonesia Circle* 51: 21–36.

Temple, Bogusia. 1995. "Telling Tales: Accounts and Selves in the Journeys of British Poles", *Oral History* 23/2: 60–4.

Thompson, Paul. 1978. *The Voice of the Past: Oral History*. Oxford, New York: Oxford University Press.

Tonkin, Elizabeth. 1992. *Narrating our Pasts*. Cambridge: Cambridge University Press.

Watson, C.W. 1989. "The Study of Indonesian and Malay Autobiography", *Indonesia Circle* 49 (June): 3–18.

———. 2000. *Of Self and Nation: Autobiography and the Representation of Modern Indonesia*. Honolulu: University of Hawaii Press.

Watson, Lawrence and Watson-Franke, Maria-Barbara. 1985. *Interpreting Life Histories: An Anthropological Inquiry*. New Brunswick: Rutgers University Press.

White, Michael and Epston, David. 1990. *Narrative Means to Therapeutic Ends*. New York: Norton.

Young, Michael. 1983. "'Our Name is Women; We are Bought with Limesticks and Limepots': An Analysis of the Autobiographical Narrative of a Kalauna Woman", *Man* (N.S.) 18: 478–501.

PART I

Singular Lives

2

Madé Lebah: Reminiscences from "Jaman Setengah Bali" (Half-Bali Times)

Carol Warren

This chapter focuses on perceptions of cultural place and social change in twentieth-century Bali through the eyes of one of its many extraordinary, "ordinary" people. Madé Lebah was born in the Gianyar village of Peliatan in the early years of the century and died just before its end. His reminiscences begin in the time he referred to as "jaman setengah Bali", when the regency of Gianyar was only nominally controlled by the Dutch, who had conquered the South Balinese kingdoms in 1906–8. This was the period of his childhood, his time as a servant in the royal court of Peliatan, and the beginnings of his life-long enchantment with Balinese music. He grew up under Dutch colonial rule, when he was given the first opportunity to travel the world as a performer in the Peliatan gamelan troupe, which he had helped to form. Thus began his first encounters with many of the Western musicians, scholars and students who flocked to Bali after the Peliatan performances at the Paris Colonial Exhibition in 1931 brought this stunning musical style to world attention. Subsequently Lebah worked for Colin McPhee, the Canadian composer who devoted himself to the study and exposition of Balinese music.[1] He had what might appear to be the unusual combination of jobs as music teacher and driver for McPhee. But in fact most performers in Bali of that era combined their artistic activities with more mundane pursuits as farmers or traders. And it remains the case today, that only a small number are able to support themselves as full-time professional performers.[2]

Madé Lebah's life (1905?³–96) spanned the Dutch conquest of Bali, the Indonesian Revolution, the Japanese occupation, and the massacres of 1965–66 that ended Indonesia's Old Order under Sukarno and ushered in Suharto's New Order. He died two years before the collapse of the regime that had brought changes to everyday life on this island of temples and art that were at least as profound as those accompanying colonisation. During the last two decades of his life, Bali was transformed from an agrarian economy to one primarily dependent upon tourism. The changes he witnessed in his society and culture over those decades would have been unimaginable in his youth. In economic terms, Bali had been one of the economically "poorest" provinces in one of the countries classified at independence as one of the least "developed" — at least according to the blunt instruments that international agencies use for measuring such things. Yet his story is strangely tempered with respect to the extremes the century brought. Perhaps it was his artistic perspective on these changes that filtered their impact, or perhaps it was the fact that his everyday life experience was not touched so directly or profoundly by these traumatic events.

For a number of reasons including his commoner "caste" status in the social system, the collectivist orientation of Balinese social organisation (there is a rather paradoxical Balinese version of the tall poppy syndrome in this celebrated "hierarchical" society), and his own rather shy and diffident disposition, Madé Lebah never achieved the prominence of individuals like the dancer Mario, or the painter Ida Bagus Madé, or even the co-founder of the Peliatan troupe, Anak Agung Mandera. Perhaps his talents were not to be regarded as exceptional on an island so well endowed,⁴ and in a culture which did not overly emphasise individual achievements.⁵ He may have been satisfied enough with the recognition and repute of fellow villagers and musicians. It was only very late in life that he received formal recognition from the state in the form of a provincial government citation for his contributions to the development of Balinese music.⁶

But it was not solely for his musician's perspective that I was interested in Madé Lebah's story. My research was on social change in Bali, and his extraordinary experiences as part of an ordinary life filled with everyday Balinese preoccupations, made his account of Bali in the twentieth century an interesting and down-to-earth counterpoint to the high-culture "babad" perspective which has tended to dominate the ethnography of Bali⁷ — a perspective which he also ambivalently shared. Over a period of six years between 1981 and 1987 I carried out a dozen lengthy interviews, most of them tape-recorded. There was no particular focus other than to get a sense of place and perceptions of changing times through the eyes of a person whose life was in some ways that of "everyman" while at the same time enmeshed in the cultural domains that give Bali its special interest to anthropology and its romantic appeal to the outside world. Madé Lebah's accounts did not dwell overly much on the more extravagant dimensions of what many regard as Bali's "uniqueness". For him music and magic were as much a part of everyday life as rice and village service obligations.

Although my research was primarily concerned with local-level social organisation and change, it was impossible to ignore the way in which musical traditions reflected cultural values and relationships in this village, the seat of a once wealthy and prominent principality and of a significant performing tradition. Music was also an important point of intersection between the vertical relationships associated with the court (puri, keraton), and the ideally horizontal ties of community (banjar, desa, subak, dadia and seka).[8] One of my early memories of Made Lebah, and one which influenced my thinking on the character of hierarchy in Balinese culture, involved a rehearsal session of the renowned Peliatan gamelan troupe, the Seka Gong Gunung Sari. Madé Lebah and Anak Agung Mandera were its founders, teachers and lead drummers. The latter was the elderly statesman from one of the prominent upper "caste"[9] families of Peliatan and inevitably became the public face representing the group. On this particular occasion, during rehearsals in preparation for an overseas trip, the two had a strong difference of opinion on how a particular piece should be played. The entire rehearsal came to revolve around the debate between them, each singing out his respective interpretation, other members entering the discussion, trying out the debated alternatives on their instruments, and it seemed collectively adjudicating between Lebah and Mandera. At moments the rivalry between the two took on the intensity of a cockfight and I was amazed at the forcefulness with which the usually quiet-spoken Lebah asserted his views. In the end it was his version that won the consensus of the seka on the day.[10]

Lebah's reminiscences provide an interesting commentary on both dimensions of the hierarchic-egalitarian grid that produced some of Bali's most interesting cultural obsessions. The desire for the respect of one's fellow villagers (banjar/desa), seka (association) members, or kin group (dadia/soroh) provokes powerful drives — both competitive and levelling. Balinese music is itself an interesting metaphor for these cultural and social tensions, as Keeler (1975) has speculatively suggested. The high pitch of the suling (bamboo flute), the clear tinkling of the upper-range of the kantilan metallophones, the deep driving beat of bronze gongs, the fast paced tempo of kendang drums, and the stunning sound of the bronze keys of the gangsa struck in perfect unison — now fused, then syncopated and interlocking, sometimes clashing — express Balinese cultural tastes for regulated rhythm and crowded busy-ness (ramai). They conjure the complementary oppositions of magic and ritual, social tension and ordered routine that colour the ebbs and flows of Balinese life. The structured aspects of life and ritual in this highly organised society are counterposed by a competitive and occasionally violent undercurrent. Bali's exuberant cultural expressiveness indicates a deep-seated desire for "order", while signalling at the same time the threat of explosive release.[11]

Madé Lebah's personality was somewhat more understated than the music he played; but he appreciated all its dimensions, as he did the complexity and paradoxes of other aspects of his society. It is very difficult to convey in written text the lilting narrative or the wry and sometimes impish sense of humour expressed through his speech.[12] His opinions were offered in a quietly quizzical manner. He had a voice that ranged from serious-deep to soft-meditative tones, and occasionally to a high-pitched and slightly raspy giggle that betrayed the effects of smoking and eventual emphysema. He spoke in a rather matter of fact and sometimes slightly amused or poignant tone about magic[13] and court life, European travels and family affairs. Of the many themes that his reminiscences revealed during these recorded interviews, the aspects of his life experience touching on hierarchy, reciprocity and social change receive most attention in the selection of excerpts included here. Most of his accounts focused on the early part of the twentieth century. His reflections on the latter decades are mainly asides drawn in comparison to the attitudes, passions, hardships and rhythms of earlier times.

Paul Radin, one of the contributors to the development of the cultural anthropological tradition, took the radical position that the only truly authentic ethnography could be through autobiography told in the original language. This piece could not pretend to such a claim. The interviews were prompted by my interest in the character of social relations in the pre-colonial and early colonial period; they were primarily in Indonesian rather than Balinese; and they have been edited and reordered to focus on themes selected for their salience to an early twenty-first century, largely non-Balinese audience.[14] Mediated as they are by these filters, by the slippages of the translation process, and the flatness of the printed word,[15] these translated narratives nevertheless attempt to convey to the reader the voice of one of the twentieth century's extraordinary "ordinary" people and his particular perspectives on Balinese culture and change over the last century.

* * *

Madé Lebah and *gangsa* (metalophone) (1980s).
Source: Photo courtesy of his family.

Madé Lebah with his son, Wayan Gandera, and granddaughter, Luh Mas Sriati (1980s).
Source: Photo courtesy of his family.

Madé Lebah with *kendang* (drum) in his youth (1930s) from the Colin McPhee collection.

Source: Photo courtesy of the UCLA Ethnomusicology Archive.

Madé Lebah's great-granddaughter, Luh Koming, as Legong dancer (2003).

Source: Photo courtesy of his family.

Childhood Memories of Family and Everyday Life

When I was small, my father was a *parekan* (servant) in the *Puri* (the royal court) of Peliatan. In our house compound there were two families. My father's older brother, my uncle, also lived in the household. He had wet rice (*sawah*) and dry farmland (*ladang*), but my father didn't have riceland. He was offered riceland by the Raja, but he didn't want it. Why didn't he want to accept it? Ya, my father like most people then was rather lazy about working in the fields. He didn't want to do farm work.[16] The Raja asked him, "Do you want to take riceland or eat food cooked in the Puri? If you wish to eat in the Puri every day, come and ask for food. If you have children at home, you can bring food from the Puri." So it was easier for him to ask for food already prepared — cooked rice, vegetables, everything he got from the Puri. Even after my mother died, and I was at home at the age of three, my father remained at court. Every afternoon, he brought food home from the Puri, then went straight to the Puri again. In the evening at about six, he brought food again. As soon as I ate, he went to the Puri again. Finally at ten at night he came home. He couldn't remarry because he was too busy in the Puri. If my father wasn't around, the Raja wasn't happy.

Our descent group, Batu Nginte, has a special relation to the court. A long time ago we were given the title "Batu Nginte" by the Raja. Batu Nginte means royal guardian. Whenever the Raja has a child, someone from our descent group becomes its care-giver. This role has been handed down from my ancestors. If others not close to the court commit a serious crime, they would be put to death by the Raja, but Batu Nginte are protected from capital punishment. Even for a serious crime, we may not be killed, but only expelled to another village. The *lontar* (palm leaf manuscript) granting our title is kept here in the main family temple. It tells the story of how our descent group received its title. The privileges have a history. It all has a history. If the Raja doesn't remember Nginte, he commits a wrong; if Nginte do not keep faith with the Raja, we commit a wrong. We must be together. But I think now it is nearly lost. When there is a ceremony in the palace, not everyone is called. Maybe they have forgotten, maybe they are a little embarrassed.

Back then there were only two of us at home. I had an older brother named Wayan Gedah. He looked after me while I was still small. Three years of age is too small to work, so I only stayed still at home. My brother looked after me, so that I didn't roam around. Because he was older, he understood more. So that I wouldn't go out, he stayed and took care of me. [By the time] I was six, I was old enough to know a little about how to look for food in the fields. After the villagers have finished harvesting the fields, the children would usually *munuh* (glean). *Munuh* means to collect the leftover grains in the fields that hadn't been taken [by the harvesters]. My brother and I could get a kilo of rice between us if we would glean from morning to late afternoon. We would come home and dry and pound the padi. If it was not sunny, we would lay the padi out on a shelf above the kitchen fire to dry. If no food came from the Puri we could cook for ourselves. The two of us would pound the padi to make rice, then make rice porridge. That was enough to eat with vegetables. Vegetables were easy to find. They could be picked from around the house, or along the road.

When my father went out, I would be given two *kepeng* (Chinese coins): two *kepeng* for me, and one for my brother, because he was big. One *kepeng* was enough to buy peanuts. Right in front of the house was a peanut hawker. One *kepeng*'s worth of nuts and a plate of porridge was plenty. In those days money had value. If you had five *kepeng* it was enough for a whole day from morning 'til night. That was strong money then. My father didn't get wages from the Raja. Whenever someone was sent on an errand from the Puri, the Raja gave money for, ya, who knows, on the road he might want to buy a drink, like *loloh*, squeezed from leaves. There weren't drinks like nowadays. In any case, because our family was like this with the Raja of Peliatan, my father could ask for money any time. He would come to the Raja and say, "I need money for this", and the Raja would give it. He wouldn't dare refuse.

We had family in Banjar Teges also. And whenever there was a harvest in Teges we would be called to join them. We went along with the harvest work group (*seka manyi*). They received a tenth share of the harvest, but my brother and I would take home whatever we could collect. We went to the fields together carrying a large basket for collecting the padi, but without any clothes. I didn't wear clothes until I was at least six. Before that we only used a cloth sheet to wrap around us. We only wore red *wanga* cloth. To have a covering of coloured cloth then, it meant you were already a bit well off.

Sometimes we would harvest cassava (*ketela*) for a quarter share of the harvest. The share of a day's harvest could be too heavy for one person to carry home. You could harvest padi in one place and cassava the next. For example, near Banjar Teges, they might be harvesting rice while in another part of Peliatan, near Banjar Kalah, they might harvest cassava. That's called *tulak sumur*, "ignoring the season" and rotating cassava or peanuts with padi. In this area it doesn't matter what season wet or dry crops are planted. Padi rotated with cassava or ground nuts or corn. Not long after that we were called to work in the Puri.

My father wanted to send me to school. There were no schools in Peliatan or in Ubud then, but there was one in Gianyar. My father wanted me to be schooled, but it wasn't permitted. No one could go except the children of the aristocracy. Basically, only the children of officials appointed by the Dutch could go. If you weren't the child of an official, you couldn't. There were other children who really wanted to go to school, but the Dutch were happier if Balinese didn't want schooling. After the revolution, adult literacy schools (PBH, *Pemberantasan Buta Huruf*) were set up in the *banjars*. I bought a book and I also studied at night in the *banjar* meeting house. I can read now, but I can't write. Some of my friends continued studying, but I couldn't because I had to leave home to seek a living (*merantau*). I travelled wherever I had to. Sometimes when I had the chance to come home for a month or so, then I could study. But if I had wanted to study straight through, then we wouldn't have had anything in the house.

I remember the earthquake in 1917. At the time, I was asked by Wayan Kerdep, who later became my father-in-law, to look after his cow because he couldn't do it himself. So I took it every day to the fields in Teges because there was good grass at the edge of the fields there. The *sawah* was flooded at the time. I had just climbed on the cow's back while it was eating grass, when the earthquake started. I fell in the *sawah*. The cow ran and almost fell too. It was a long time before you could walk. I wanted to go home, but the earth was still shaking. It lasted maybe two minutes. The water in the *sawah* fields completely disappeared and the cow was half a kilometre away by the time it ended! The houses in the village, the compound walls along the road, the gates, the temples, all were ruined. It was like photos I've seen of Germany after the World War — there were no houses left, absolutely nothing. When there is an earthquake, the *kulkul* (the village signal drum) is struck. The whole time people were striking drums and cans and plates, shouting "*hidup, hidup, hidup*" (live, live, live). It was a custom. I don't know why, but everyone did it.

People moved to the ricefields, because they thought it would be safer. Houses made of bamboo and thatch were not so dangerous. People had to build temporary shelters. But at night they slept in open houseyards or in the rice fields to be safe. Three days after the great earthquake, the earth started rumbling again, on and off all day until the next morning. Imagine that — Rrrrrr–Rrrr–Rrrrrr — like a violent storm. There have been earthquakes since, but the one in 1917 was the worst. I think the earthquakes have finished for now because Mount Batur and Mount Agung have erupted.

My mother may have died of malaria. At the time it wasn't called malaria, but she had fever. She was probably over 40 then, since in those days people were often 35 before they married. It was very different than these present times. Both men and women married late then.[17] If a boy went to visit at the girl's home, there was no certainty he would get to talk to her. If it were a holiday like Galungan or Saraswati and the unmarried women were pounding padi, along would come the young men to help. They could talk together. They would laugh. After a time, the young man would want to marry. But the young woman would still be reluctant. Ten times he would ask and she still wouldn't be ready. Until the young man becomes fed up and thinks, "What is it with her?" So, he would use any excuse to meet her. In the evenings before ritual ceremonial days he would come to plait coconut leaves to help his intended make flower offerings.

My father died when I was about twelve years old. He had been sick with a fever, but it was not like malaria, that fever. Then there were no doctors, only *dukun* Bali (traditional healers), who would give herbs and spices and peppers, chewing them to a fine paste and spraying the medicine from the mouth. But it wasn't strong enough. My father died. When my father died, the Raja sent white cloth, but of course he didn't come.

Many years later, after I returned from America in 1952, I was finally able to afford a cremation for my mother and father. No one could carry out cremations immediately in those days. We were permitted to have seven roofs [on the cremation tower] if we could afford it. We could use a *lembu* (bull sarcophagus), a *boma* (ritual tower); like the

Pandé (blacksmith descent group), we were permitted by the Raja to use the symbols they use.

It may have been six months after my father died that a servant was sent by the Raja to bring me to the Puri. Whether I wanted to or not, I went. Because I remembered my family had always lived from the court. Our family "belonged" to the Puri, since the time of my great grandfathers. Everything then belonged to the Raja. The Raja ruled my ancestors. Anything that was ours was by his permission. If he says to the right, ya, right. If he says left, left. So, I had nothing to say about it.

The Raja had a child. The name of the Raja's child was Tjok (Tjokorda) Putra. But he was already grown. So, I was taken into the Puri with my brother, leaving our house empty. My father had been a servant to Tjok Putra's father. So my brother and I became servants of Tjok Putra. Of course, in those days, we didn't say "Tjok". Then we were subjects and we called the members of the Puri family "Tjokorda" or "Dewa Agung".[18] Dewa Agung Anom, Dewa Agung Madé, Dewa Agung Alit. Only after independence did we start to use "Tjok". It's much easier to say Tjok Alit, Tjok Rai, if not quite proper. Nowadays people prefer to use easy informal speech.

Life as a Parekan at the Court of Peliatan

Actually, I had already been sent as a servant (*parekan*) to the court when I was still small. My father couldn't afford to keep me.[19] It was the hungry season. The rice had been eaten by tiny mice. They were not as long as my finger, but they ate it all. There weren't enough snakes I guess that year. In the end, the mice were washed away by the rain, but they had eaten it all. We were so hungry, we ate even the mice. That's when I was taken to the Puri for the first time — I swept in the morning, washed the clothes of the Raja and carried the betel (*sirih*) for him. At court I sat way behind and prepared *sirih* whenever he ordered it. In front of him sat all his court officials and retainers.

Puri Peliatan then was the part now called Puri Agung, but it isn't authentic (*asli*) any more; now that they have tourists, it's *moderen* (modern). All the buildings had beautiful carvings then. In the old days when you entered the Puri you had to wear a cloth sarong. Ordinary people's houses couldn't be built of brick — that was only for the Raja. We couldn't wear flowers over our ears; we couldn't have clean clothes like the Raja. We were frightened of the Raja, but the discipline was good.

The Raja had a person specifically for carrying out capital punishment. If the Raja said "kill so and so", nothing more had to be said. It didn't matter whether you were wrong or not. One time the Raja of Peliatan had a mirror as small as this biscuit. He liked to look at himself in it. It was stolen from him by a person from the *banjar*, and that person was put to death for it.

If you were sick you came to the Puri and asked for the leftover scraps from the Raja's meal. Then the sick person could become cured because he had a lot of rice, vegetables and meat. You weren't allowed to enter if you had malaria though — that disease was too strong. For that we used to take the root of the kind of cassava (*sela sawi*) over there in the garden. We boiled and ate it. It was very bitter. You wouldn't eat it for any other reason — but it made the malaria go away. The Rajas had a special healer (*balian*). He had to be an old person, because the Raja was jealous of young men.

I used to wash the Raja's clothes, but we didn't have soap in those days. We used something from a tree called *klerek*. In 1930 we first had soap that came from China. One *sen* (Dutch cent) or five *kepeng* would buy one piece cut from a bar. It smelled though. It was yellow and very different from the Dutch soap I saw at the hotel that was powdered and had a nice scent. We didn't have plates in those days either. We used smoothed out coconut shell. I made quite a large set for Colin McPhee. The Rajas had plates from China, both the fine (*halus*) and coarse (*kasar*) kinds. Chinese traders bought china to the royal courts; Arabs brought gold and gems; and Indian women came from Calcutta to sell precious stones to the Rajas. In the early '30s, metal plates that can't break began to be introduced — you could find all sorts in the shops in Denpasar.

They also began selling automobiles. The Rajas were "car crazy" (*gila mobil*). They pawned their riceland, their gongs, anything. They replaced the water caps on their cars with gold birds. A lot of the riceland changed hands then. Each Raja usually had 2,000 hectares of *sawah* and maybe 500 hectares of dry fields. The Rajas also owned many of the shops then. The shops on Gaja Mada Street [in Denpasar] were owned by the Raja of Ubud. The *sedahan* (tax collector and supervisor of the court's assets) looked after them for him. Since then the shops have been bought by Chinese. The *sedahan* knew what land was where, how many trees, animals, etc. It was he who went around ordering whatever was needed by the Raja. We always gave it — "as long as the Raja is happy...." They used to keep a lot of it for themselves. The Raja didn't know or care of course. If they collected a thousand coconuts — 600 went to the Raja, 200 to the *sedahan*, 200 to his subordinates.

The Raja in those days had wives like ducks — 40 or so. I followed wherever he went, carrying his *sirih* (betel chew). I was also sent to call whichever of his wives he chose for a particular night. He had a high pavilion (*balé tegeh*) at the edge of the Puri wall, where he sat and watched what was going on in the street. People were often afraid to pass by and waited until he left. We always bowed down passing in front of him — though not the children.

The Colonial Period — "Half-Bali Times"

At first, there was only a Dutch Controller in Gianyar. There was a Resident in Singaraja and an Assistant Resident in Denpasar and that was it. There were probably only eight Dutch in all of Bali then. One in each District [regencies now called *Kabupaten*] and one Resident [for what is now the Province of Bali]. He would come if something important were happening here. If there were an important case that had to be adjudicated, he would come. If he came, it was in an automobile and we had to show respect, just like a Raja. It had to be like that. There wasn't a real judicial court then. There was a *punggawa* (the former ruler of Peliatan), the Regent (the ruler of Gianyar) who was over him, and then the Controller. If they said "wrong", whether the person was wrong or not, that was it.

We had to work on the roads (*kerja rodi*) under the Dutch. Tjok Putra was the Raja in Peliatan by then. It was he who would order us to do *kerja rodi* [forced labour on the roads]. If you didn't want to work, you could pay one *ringgit* tax for a year. That was a lot of money in those days. *Rodi* was like this. Every year we would pay a head tax (*pajeg orang*). We paid 75 *sen*, which was called "*telung talen*", so you had to pay 3 *talen*.[20] If you weren't easily able to pay, you had to do *kerja rodi* wherever the government sent you. Even if the road being built was in Sukawati [15 kilometres away] we would have to walk from here. We would take turns — Peliatan one day, another *desa* the next. Once a year we would work three days. Pay tax with three days work and that was it. The next year then you did it again. In the morning when the *kulkul* (slit drum) was struck, the *banjar* would all come out carrying their hoes (*cangkul*), and we carried little stones to tap on the *cangkul*. Everyone would play little rhythms. T'-keng Tong-keng T'-keng Tong-tong. All the way it was full of sound and people — *ramai sekali!*

But if you could pay, you didn't have to work. A person who was a bit wealthy, someone who had a lot of riceland, would pay out his service. We could probably have afforded that amount, but we wouldn't have had money left for food. Those who organised the labour were *pemidjian* [exempted]. Brahmana and Anak Agung would usually pay and become *pemidjian*. One way or the other, everyone had to pay. The Dutch didn't care who you were.

In those days, at the time of the Dutch it was so different compared to now. Before, ya, it was completely Bali. I was already six years old or so, I didn't wear any clothes. Only when I grew up did I wear clothes. It's true! There wasn't much cloth around in those days. The Dutch thought it wasn't good [to be without clothes]. There were shops run by Arabs and Indians ("*orang Bombay*"), in Denpasar, but they sold only a few kinds of cloth — The Rajas all wore black cloth, called *bérem*. They also wore a white cloth coloured with the water from tumeric root to make it yellow. That was called *kuning sari*.

I was given black cloth when I went to the Puri. After black cloth had been used by the Raja, and had lost its colour from washing, it would be given to young servants such as me. There was black and white *kain poleng* in those days. There was woven Bali cloth, but it wasn't particularly good — there was no fine Balinese cloth. No one here could make really fine cloth then. Cotton like this came around the Japanese period. Only then could Balinese make fine cloth that was really *halus*. Before cotton was introduced, there were Chinese who sold imported thread, but it wasn't good. Only about 1937 could Balinese make *kain halus* with thread that came from China. There was gold thread, which we could use to make *songket* (cloth woven with gold threads). But only the aristocracy could wear them. Not the orang *sudra* (ordinary people).

Actually it was still *jaman kerajaan*, the time of the kingdoms, in those days. Even though the Dutch claimed to be in control, it was still *jaman kerajaan Bali* also. An ordinary person wouldn't dare wear a flower like this [over the ear]. The Raja would be outraged. The Rajas in those days wouldn't tolerate being copied in any way.

You couldn't use bricks in the walls. We had to use mud that didn't look so nice. Now it's no problem [he laughs] — if you want it, use it! I had a friend from Kutuh (near Ubud) who took a mirror in the Puri, which he had picked up along the road and taken home. It was a round mirror. They said that mirror belonged to the Raja, and because of that he was put to death. Ya, he was blamed and was killed. They said he stole it from the Puri, even though he didn't steal it. It was like this — half Belanda [Dutch], half Bali in those days. It wasn't yet really colonised. When it was all Dutch, the Raja wouldn't dare act that way any longer.

I was still small when that happened and still a servant in the Puri. The roads weren't that good. There was no car. Well, there was one car belonging to the Controller in Gianyar. The roads were gravel, not sealed at that time. Whenever the Controller came we all got ready. No one would dare to say anything. Ordinary people were afraid of the Raja in those days. The Raja had lots of spies who would tell him what was going on everywhere. That was the bad thing about those days. They would tell the Raja what was happening outside the palace. The spies were called *pecalang* — they were servants of the court who would see here were mangoes — ya, take them; there are durian that look good — take them. Every day they would circulate in the *desa* and take anything that looked good to the Puri. These were ordinary people. They were people from outside the Puri. From Banjar Tengah, Banjar Kalah, there were lots. They would go to the palace and be sent out to collect this and that. And they didn't ask for anything, they just took. Ya, if that person would be seen in the road, people would run away. I don't think the Dutch really ran things completely then. The Raja could still play around in those days.

My most important job was to follow the Raja's wives when they went home. If her brothers or sisters had a tooth-filing ceremony or a six-month birth anniversary (*oton*), the Raja's wife would want to go home. Four or five servants had to go with her. In the afternoon when she returned to the Puri from her house, the servants were called by the Raja. If five servants went, the five were called by the Raja. He would ask each of them one by one: "When she got to her home, what did she do? Who came to the house to visit? Did any man come?" [giggles] That was very tough work! If a man did come, you still said, "No, there were none. From the time she entered the house, no bachelors dared enter. She spoke with her brother, with her mother, with her father, but no one else." That satisfied the Raja. Actually on the road there were lots of men. But if you told the truth, watch out!

If the Raja became angry at a servant, he would strike him with a stick — *piak ... piak ...* until he bled. The Raja would do it himself. If the Raja happened to be smoking a cigarette, he might put it up the servant's nose. You didn't dare resist. You stood still, taking anything. If the Raja wanted to use the switch broom, you handed it to him yourself, as he willed. If he took a cigarette and put it in your nose until it burnt inside, you did nothing. In Bali you could say he was like a "dictator". He treated children however he wished. Even an old man, if he made a mistake, was not spared the Raja's anger. He might be sent home and could never return to the palace again. An old man would have a hard time then.

That was under the rule of Tjokorda Putra's father, the old Raja. Tjokorda Putra was a modern man. He wouldn't dare. When he called someone to go to Sukawati, he had to give money, buy rice, and coconuts. But his father, no! When he wanted something, he simply ordered. We always gave. We used to say, "as long as the Raja is happy, we are safe. If he's angry ... death!" So much has changed since then.

Musical Apprenticeship

When I was still attached to the Puri as a *parekan* (servant), at about the age of 12, I was sent to study the music of the Legong in Sukawati. The Raja of Peliatan loved Legong, so he sent me there with my brother to study. We were chosen to go because my forefathers were performers from long ago. If there were none in Banjar Kalah, then the court had no gamelan. It's true. To this day they come from my descent group, Batu Nginte. If there weren't musicians or dancers from our descent group, the Raja was not satisfied. The Raja's son, Tjok Putra, took us [to Sukawati] with three Legong dancers, five people all together. He gave rice, coconuts and 500 *kepeng* for our living costs.

Actually Tjok Putra fancied the daughter of the Raja from Sukawati. He pretended that forming the Legong was only to enliven the court of Peliatan. The truth was that he wanted to marry that princess — the beautiful one. So, I became a spy there. I would go back to the Puri after practising Legong to report to Tjok Putra because he wanted her for his wife. For nearly the whole six months I was there, she continued to refuse him. Only after she finished studying, when she was finally an accomplished Legong dancer, did she give in.

When I first went to study music with Anak Agung Rai Prit in Sukawati, it was about 1919. Before that time there was no Legong in Peliatan. It was only in Sukawati. Anak Agung Prit was truly gifted. Although he was already very old, well over 70 years then, he was still a strong teacher. As long as he could dance Legong he was happy. When he had children come to study Legong — he must have had 60 — he would dance like a madman. He loved to hear the sound of doves. He loved to hear them singing — *ngeneng ku'ung, ngeneng ku'ung*. Whenever he heard them he would dance and he would have the birds dance too! He loved to teach, though he was already extremely aged. Perhaps from his happiness, he lived so long. I think that came from his enthusiasm and his love of teaching. If the Legong dancers didn't come, he just slept, like someone in a stupor from smoking opium. But when the children came to practise Legong, he was up and active. The more children came to study, the stronger he became.

I studied hard there — myself, Nyoman Kaler from Denpasar and Lotring from Kuta, who came with his wife. We all stayed there. Rai Prit in fact had many students, but not for money. He didn't want money. He desired honour and respect. So that he would have many students, he didn't want to ask for money. If there was work to be done or there was a wedding or a tooth-filing ceremony for his child, he would ask for help from the people, or for rice, for palm leaves or coconuts, things of that sort. So the whole *seka* would bring these things. Whatever he needed he would ask from people and it would be brought there. It was easy. When I had students from Desa Mawang, Desa Pengosekan, Desa Bedulu, from Katih Lantang, Tatiapi, Sukawati — they weren't asked for money either. But if my sleeping place was broken down, I asked for help. All these *balé* [one room cottages] in the house compound were built with the help of my students. The *balé gedé* on the north side was built by the Seka Legong from Tatiapi. The stone entryway was built by my students from Mawang, and the building to the east was from Katih Lantang. To ask for a building even as large as this is easy, but to ask for money is difficult — in Bali it isn't done.

From that time I was only responsible for music at court. I taught the Legong. We had brilliant dancers and besides the classical music, there were new creations. To this day, the Legong Peliatan is famous. When we took the Legong to the palace in Gianyar, we walked. We arrived at four in the afteroon. When we finished dancing at seven we went home, also on foot. When we had become famous, the Raja of Klungkung requested performances, and the Raja of Bangli. We walked there too. We walked to Klungkung. We walked to Bangli. They didn't have Legong performers of their own. If we were asked to go there, in the morning we were brought two large packets of *ketipat* [packets of steamed rice], and 25 *kepeng* for each person's supplies on the way. Twenty-five *kepeng* in those days would last for five days. We would leave here at seven and arrive in Bangli at noon. There we could rest a bit and the Raja gave us food. In the afternoon we performed.

Of course it is the Legong for which the Peliatan gamelan became famous. The Legong originated in Sukawati. In the time of the Balinese Kingdoms, before the Dutch ruled, there was a prince in Ketewel named Tjokorda Karna. He was from the ruling house in Sukawati. Tjokorda Karna was brilliant and said to be s*akti* (to have magical powers).[21] When he was about 45, he died suddenly. They had already gone to the Priest to choose the correct day for the washing of the body and the cremation ceremony. But when they were preparing everything the day before the ceremony, the food and offerings, Tjokorda Karna suddenly revived! He was still sick but alive. In this sleep near death he had dreamed he was in heaven where he saw two heavenly sprites, the *legong*, and when he returned to life he remembered their dance and the sound of the music from his dream. That particular Legong in Sukawati became known as the Legong Dewa. The word *legong* means refined in every way, exquisite. The dancers must be striking with sweet eyes and mouth. So the Legong was created. But those Legong performers were still men who used masks with the face of a woman.

Eventually, Anak Agung Rai Prit from Sukawati, who was related to Tjokorda Karna, created a new version of the Legong. He wanted to dance the Nandir, the male form of Legong. So he looked for someone who would make a good pair with him. He chose Dewa Ketut Belatjing from Peliatan to make the Nandir. In the Gianyar court he was always called to perform whenever there was a ceremony. He became famous in Karangasem, Klungkung and Denpasar. But when he became an adult he stopped dancing and looked for female dancers for the Legong. Dewa Ketut Belatjing taught around the Peliatan area and from Bangli to Singaraja, while Rai Prit taught around Sukawati and as far as Denpasar.

Satria (gentry from the ruling "caste") were preferred to dance Legong, because the dancer must be very striking, you know, have bearing, presence, and Satria usually have presence. For that reason a Legong dancer should ideally be at least a Brahmana, Satria or Pradewa or Gusti. If there aren't any, ya, the Legong would have to be Sudra. In any case, it was the Raja who chose the dancers for their beauty and white skins. The Legong was especially performed for the Keraton [palace], the reason it is called "Legong Keraton" today.

It was Anak Agung Rai Prit who composed the particular version of Legong Keraton that was taken up here. When he first saw the Legong dance, he wanted to perform it himself and sought out Dewa Ketut Belatjing in Peliatan to make a pair. And it was Belatjing's protegé Gusti Biang Sengoh who taught Luh Man, Agung Sri and my granddaughter, Luh Mas. There were no dancers anywhere that compared because Gusti Biang was no ordinary teacher. Before their lessons, they had to be massaged with leaves and coconut oil so that their dance movements and skin would be fine and smooth. Teachers in those days were strict. A wrong movement was corrected with a slap. Now teachers wouldn't dare, but the dancers are much stiffer today. They say there is still a specialist Legong masseur (*tukang pijet legong*) named Anak Agung Raka Saba.

In the old days there was no *prada* (gold leaf) for dancer's costumes. A red cloth called *wanga* [?] was used, which I think came from France. This was still a Balinese kingdom, but somehow there was French cloth! I thought that was amazing. There was also cloth from China — cloth, shirts and incense. It was still the days of the Balinese kingdoms and there were goods from India. I don't know whether there were foreign traders as well. The headdresses were painted with a gold powder mixed with water. There wasn't anything like gold leaf until the Dutch came. Dutch *prada* was used for everything special. Whenever the Dutch brought a shipment of *prada*, the prince of Ubud would buy the whole lot for the Puri and for its shrines.

Ubud couldn't be rivalled in that period. In Peliatan, the court was still well off — not too rich, not too poor. But in Ubud how much rice land did they control! — at least 2,000 hectares, not including dry cropland. Ubud was so much wealthier by then because Ubud dared to fight wars anywhere and they always won. Whoever lost, lost everything. They got all that land in the Negara Wars.[22]

The Ubud Puri had ricelands and dryfields from as far as Desa Mawang, to Sumampang, up to Tegallalang and as far as Taro. That was from the time of kingdoms through the Dutch period. It wasn't divided up until the time of the PKI (Communist Party of Indonesia). What they did then was to divide their wealth among all their children, wives, etc. so they didn't have to redistribute too much. The aristocracy were a bit clever with that. Maybe the person responsible for redistribution was paid off — I don't know. The intent was to divide among the poor, among those who didn't have much land. They were the ones who were supposed to get it, but that wasn't what usually happened.[23] But lots of the Tjokordas had already sold their land too. They might have wanted to buy a motorbike and they liked to gamble at cockfights.

The Negara War was also when the Semar Pegulingan gamelan was brought [as booty][24] to the Peliatan court, the one that is still used in Teges today. The public prosecutor (*jaksa*) came from Puri Kaleran [Anak Agung Mandera's branch of the Peliatan aristocracy]. He had the authority to decide who was going to live or die, who would be punished in what way in the days of the Balinese kingdoms. Ya, that's the way it was. So as soon as the gamelan was brought from Negara, and Puri Kaleran asked for it, ya, that was the same as being in the hands of the Raja. *Majorog* we say in Balinese — an easy give-and-take relation — existed between the Puris. In those days with good relations, what belonged to one, could be used by the other.

Establishing a Musical Tradition

In 1926 I was living at home again, "free" from serving in the Puri. I had already learned to work as a driver. I would drive for a while, again I would study gamelan — like that. Then we formed the *seka* and looked for teachers from Batubulan. For maybe three months they worked with us — here for a week, returning home for a day, a week here, a day home. They stayed in the Puri. We gave them food and paid them each 25 cents a day from the *seka* treasury, if I'm not mistaken. For two teachers 50 cents was quite a lot. They were also given food, and if one of them went home, I would ride him on my bicycle. Five *ringgit* a bike cost in those days. We brought Mario (who created the Kebyar dance) here in 1928 or 1929. It only cost 25 cents to come from Tabanan by *opelet* (motorised transport service) in those days.

From the beginning, Anak Agung Mandera was the leader of the Peliatan *seka gong* and I was musical director. Mandera became the head since he was the oldest and he helped put the *seka* together. Only four of us are still alive now [in 1982] — myself, Anak Agung Mandera, and two others — only four of us. The group began performing at the Bali Hotel in Denpasar every week. The tourists then were very different — like Rajas — they made us feel very embarrassed. We had no shirts and were ashamed. They would ask, "Did you come here to bathe?" Before that we had only played in the temple for *odalan* (temple festivals), for weddings, tooth-filings, and didn't really have uniform costumes. Some wore headpieces (*dastar*), but all were different. In those days it was hard to buy things. The tourists at the Bali Hotel paid 12 *ringgit* each time we played. At that time it cost one silver *ringgit* for a day's car hire. One *sen* equalled 5 *kepeng*, which was enough for a serving of rice. The money was kept and divided evenly among all the members of the *seka*[25] every six months before the Galungan festival.

Each month, before the *seka* became a success, every member put in dues, sometimes as much as one *rupiah*, so we could find a teacher. There were 30 members then, so that was 30 *rupiah*. That was plenty in those days to pay for a teacher. If there were any money left, we would buy cotton singlets for the *seka*. We had begun wearing shirts, white singlets. They cost 12 cents.[26] We wanted them all to be the same.

Life was very hard then, but what was easy was that you could always borrow from someone for a few days. People would always give you rice if you asked. Now I don't usually give. You get people who are really wealthy asking for things. If I see the person is strong and healthy and has big muscles, I won't give him anything. Balinese were different [then], they didn't calculate.

In those days there was no other work. People "chased after" the best way to play, the best way to dance. Everyone practised faithfully. It was easy to set practice times because village people then had no other work besides farming ricefields and collecting fodder for their cows. It's different now. Now lots of people are carving, painting, making all sorts of things to sell. Now music like that can't be found. Ya, people play, but not so well. Where is there even one gamelan gong group like that today?

When we could play a little Tabuh Telu and Baris and Topeng, when we had enough of a musical repertoire, we went to Paris in 1931. We only began practising in 1926 and were already going to France in 1931, led by Tjokorda Raka Sukawati from Ubud. It was Tjokorda Raka who later became "President" of the NIT in Sulawesi.[27]

Our gamelan was still not complete. I heard that in Belaluan, Denpasar, there was a gamelan set that was perfect, so I went there to see if we could borrow or rent it. I couldn't believe the sound. That gamelan was extraordinarily sweet. I asked to borrow it and brought it to Peliatan. We took it to Holland. We took performers from other places too. We brought with us the Legong, Topeng Baris, Janger, and the Barong, because Europeans can't bear it unless the performances are short and varied.

We took a bus to Singaraja, then a ship to Batawi [Jakarta]. "Batanbara" was the boat we took from there to Holland. It burnt coal and we were black all over from it. It took 35 days from here. I couldn't sleep. But I was really happy. They gave us warm clothes and shoes. Even though it wasn't winter, it was cold to us. The food was Javanese or Chinese if we wanted it. We stayed near the palace in The Hague. Then we went on to Paris for the Colonial Exhibition. We had spent a week in Holland but about a month in France moving about and performing up to three times in each place. We went to France to earn money. All costs had been paid in Holland, but we hadn't received any money.

On that first trip, I was extremely happy. It was strange though. They took us to see a textile factory and things like that — I didn't really understand it much. It was exciting for the first week, but after that I couldn't sleep — too many cars, too much noise. I wanted to go home. When we went out to the city we used all of our money up. It was better to sleep — play — sleep — play. Then we could bring our money home.

What was interesting was the museum in Amsterdam. Tuan Goris[28] took us around. He was a very good speaker of Balinese and could read the *lontar* (palm-leaf) manuscripts in Kawi [Old Javanese]. At the museum they showed us the crown of gold that belonged to the Raja of Klungkung. There were *topeng* masks, legong costumes and keris that had been taken from different Rajas of Bali. I almost cried. I was almost angry, because they had taken it all.

We financed the making of our own gamelan from the Paris trip. The gamelan taken to Paris was borrowed. We had a new gamelan made in 1932 after we came back from Paris. We had each received 80 silver *ringgit*. Each member contributed to buy the new gamelan instruments, to bring Pandé (blacksmiths) from Tihingan for two months to make the gamelan set here. Every day each of us contributed one *rupiah* to pay the Pandé. Anak Agung Mandera also holds a share. Only I have two, because my wife had gone with the troupe to Paris and was also a member of the *seka*.

All the members joined in *gotong royong* (mutual assistance) to help make the instruments. They rotated five at a time — every hour the signal drum (*kulkul*) would beat for another team to come. They worked the bellows, carrying water, hammering the hot metal and dropping it in the *gerombong* [a large earthenware water vessel]. The *seka* members did all the carving work on the wooden instrument casings (*pelawah*). The big gong probably came from Siam. It has a much deeper tone than the ones that come from Java. We bought it from the pawn shop. Tjok Rai had pawned it because he was "*gila mobil*" (car crazy). There were two gongs, but that was the beautiful one.

Six craftsmen each with his own specialty came here from Desa Tihingin. Pandé Asem was the blacksmith. The *tukang datjin* determined the weight of the metal needed for each instrument. For the *trompong* we need this much, for the *riong*, this much, *gangsa* and so on. Each one is different. And gold has to be added so that the sound is sweeter. Only a little bit — maybe eight grams for the whole set. In other places this isn't heeded, but it really should be added. The bronze we used then was very good. Now they mix it with electric wire. They can buy broken cable from the PLN (electricity commission) and mix it with bronze. As a result the gamelans aren't good and the keys don't look yellow.

What a different feeling then. To play the gamelan was happiness. Why? Because its sound was so beautiful. Every day we practised. Even to go without food didn't matter. We had to play. In those days there was no other work. Now there is carving, painting, but not then, only padi farming. If you had no ricefields, you didn't have work. So people could study straight through. We practised in the morning until 12 and went home to eat. Practised from 2 to 4 o'clock. Home to bathe. Studied again at 7 and went home at 11 — three times a day. Because of that, the Peliatan Seka Gong became famous. Because of that, we could strike the gamelan without thinking, with perfect strokes.

From 1932 we played regularly in the kingdoms of Bangli, Klungkung, Gianyar — the others would send word to Gianyar, Gianyar would send word to us. Every five days or so we were called by Gianyar to play. Of course we had to walk. You wouldn't dare refuse. "*Inggih titiang ngiring*" [High Balinese, "Yes, I will follow"]. They didn't give anything but *sirih* (betel chew). Of course we had as much as we wanted to eat there — rice, saté, water. We didn't have coffee in those days. Yes, the Dutch and Chinese and maybe the Rajas drank it, but we drank cold water.

In the middle of 1937, Tjokorda Sukawati sponsored a Gong Festival competition in Gianyar. Gamelan groups from Negara, Denpasar, Buleleng, here, Bangli, Karangasem, Klungkung and Tabanan all competed. The Regents — the Rajas — were the judges. It was so crowded that no one could walk. Each group played in rotation. This went on for several days. The prize for the winning group was exemption from *kerja rodi* (corvée labour service). We won!!! Peliatan won and Denpasar came second. We didn't have to work *rodi* for 3 years! We also received 50 *rupiah* and a Dutch flag!

Livelihood and Family Responsibilities

As a servant in the Puri I only received food. Later if I wanted to marry a wife, I wanted to have something, and also I wanted to get experience working some place else. I went to work in Klungkung in 1933 for about a year. I drove a bus to the market and got a salary as well as 10 per cent of the income. Then after a year I changed jobs and worked in Denpasar. I became a driver for the father of Ida Bagus Mantra, [at the time of the interview] the Governor of Bali. His father looked after government money and had a 1929 Sprolet with wheels made from black wood. He had gotten it from the Dutch. He was wealthy and the car was used for the family, not as a taxi. I took Ida Bagus Mantra to school. After about a year of that I asked to be excused because my brother died and the house was empty.

The gamelan Gong group had gotten Mario from Tabanan as a teacher. They also had Lotring from Kuta. So I studied again. When I needed money, I'd take occasional jobs as a driver. There was a Chinese in Banjar Tengah who had a bus, and he often called me to drive for him. His grandson is still here, but he moved to Denpasar later. He liked me to drive because I was extremely careful with his vehicle and wouldn't go more than 40 kilometres an hour on these roads. I never had an accident in all those years. He initially joined the *banjar*, but eventually came into conflict in his relations with the locals. Because he was clever at making a living and became quickly wealthy, in the end people didn't have a good feeling about him. One of the local village leaders (*klian*) was jealous, so he made trouble. And because they didn't get along with him and made an issue of it, they had him expelled from the village. It was on the decision of the *banjar*, but at the instigation of its *klian* who didn't like him. The *banjar* just went along with it.[29]

I would work for a while as a chauffeur, then study again, then drive, then study. After a while I got bored of working as a driver, and came back to Peliatan to play in the gamelan. I was aged about 26. It wouldn't be right if there weren't any Nginte playing with the troupe. My wife then was a Legong dancer. I took her as my wife after we came back from Paris. She was from a family related to us. I was called by her father and asked to marry into the family. I married *sentana*[30] and became the inheritor there. I carried out the work of the *banjar* that was required from that house-compound. If there was work required for the *banjar*, I went; if there was work required for the *desa*, I went. The term is *maganti ayah* — to take over *ayahan* service obligations in the *banjar* from an elder member. After some years, again my father-in-law said to me: "Madé, you have to take my other daughter." He loved his two daughters and wanted them to remain in his household, so he didn't want to give them to anyone else. It's true what you heard that the Raja wanted to marry her, and my father-in-law wouldn't give her to him. Their parents only had the two daughters and didn't want them to marry out.[31]

After I had married the second time, I began to work in Denpasar as a driver for Bali Tour. If there weren't any tourists, I would come home to Peliatan for a while. Lots of Germans came by boat then, also tourists from Holland came on the Dutch boats. The boats arrived in Singaraja from May until about July. I would pick them up in the sedan in Singaraja and take them to the Bali Hotel in Denpasar. There was a guide to speak English and we would take them to the monkey forest in Sanggih, then to Ubud, Peliatan, Mas, Celuk, and Denpasar. In the afternoons they would watch the Kecak dance in Bona.

There is a 'Cak [Kecak] in the Sanghyang ritual which is still performed in Sasih Keenam (sixth month of the Balinese calendar) near Cemenggaung. That's the month when people often fall sick, so they carry out the Sanghyang, which is descended from the Deities. The 'Cak chorus is a kind of escape to forget about the sickness, and it would travel from one village to another for that month. The whole village would be there — men, women, the whole *desa* would pack in to see it. When the situation in the *desa* was calmed and there was no more sickness, the Sanghyang would disband. Even now in Cemenggaung it is performed in that month. But it depends upon the Sanghyang Dedari through whom the deities say whether they want to travel. They are young children who have never danced before, but they know how to dance as soon as they go into trance.[32]

When I was married I started selling cloth with my wife. When she went to Ubud, I would keep her company. I'd sell shirts and pants, just the two of us in the market. The next day we'd go to Tegallalang. The next day to Payangan on the three-day market cycle. My wife would go to Payangan and on that day I'd go to Tampaksiring. When I had gotten money from Colin McPhee, I would give the money to my wife. She would buy cloth at Toko Adil in Denpasar. At that time she began selling and sometimes I would go along. We would go by bicycle, she sitting on the back, carrying handcloths that sold for 3 cents, singlets for 12 cents; batik cloth like this would be 500 *kepeng* — 5 *kepeng* were worth 1 cent then. She would buy the singlets for 10 cents in Denpasar and sell them for 12 cents. Other than that there wasn't anything people could buy. I had lots of gamelan students at Tampaksiring. One was from Manukaya and two from Banjar Kawan. If I went to Tampaksiring at *odalan* temple festivals, they all came to buy *baju kaos* (cotton undershirts) for the *odalan*. They made me promise to come three days before the *odalan* and bring so many shirts of certain sizes. I brought dozens. They wanted to wear identical ones. They had begun to wear white cotton singlets. That was already considered really good.

Even through World War II, I had cloth. I had riceland too, given by my father-in-law; two pieces of *sawah*, altogether 42 *are* (0.42 ha). That was enough to support a family from one harvest to the next. I used to work it myself, but now I'm not strong. I just have to organise things occasionally helping to get the water. I attend the *subak* (irrigation association) meetings and go to the rituals every six months. If I can't attend, I send one of the tenants, and they usually watch the padi at night when it is nearly ready for harvest. You never know, otherwise it might disappear the night before harvest! There weren't usually any thieves in those days, only once in a while. It was no problem finding someone to watch the fields at night. When I went selling in the market, I'd bring back a shirt or something like that to give them.

In short, life with my wife was perfect. But then she became ill. She was coughing up blood every night. I took her to the hospital in Denpasar. The doctor said, "You must take your wife to Surabaya. There they have the equipment to treat her." Then I bought three tickets and went with my wife and Tjok Putri, from Puri Peliatan. She came along to keep us company. In Surabaya the doctor wrote down what to treat her with when she is bleeding, and they all said that she had cancer and had only two months to live. Aduuuh, I cried. As soon as we got home, I thought, where can I find a really good *dukun* (traditional healer) who can heal my wife? I heard that there was a good *dukun* far to the west from here in Tegal Canting, Jembrana. I took her there, using the sedan of Tjok Mayun. I borrowed it from him to take her. Sometimes he had let me use his sedan to take tourists places. After a month in Negara still she wasn't well. She stayed a second month, and I kept going back and forth with my granddaughter, Sriati. In the end she died there.

Then I was faced with the problem of how to bring her home. You couldn't carry her, as we would ritually, because she was so far away. I had a friend in the military, so I asked his help. He offered to borrow a car that belonged to a Dutchman. So I bought the petrol and food for the trip and he drove to pick her up. Then we had the cremation ritual (*ngaben*) in the *banjar*, shared with Madé Suta's family. There is a lot of work organising a cremation. Balinese are kept very busy, looking for this and that leaf [for required offerings], etc. More than a month before the ceremony you are already busy with preparations. The most important thing is that the *banjar* helps with all the work of the ceremony. Whatever has to be done, they do it — looking for cooking wood, slaughtering the pig, housework, whatever. All of it is *gotong royong* (mutual assistance). When they come you offer coffee, cigarettes, betelnut, that's all — everything else the *banjar* does. It's still like that. None of that has changed.

Ever since my wife died I didn't go to the market any more. After that I began to feel confused. I began to work in the ricefields myself again. Lots of people came to help. The *seka gong* in Pengosekan whom I had taught came to my ricefields bringing their hoes. All of them came, so that in an hour the fields were all cleared. They all came, the members of the *seka gong* from Pengosekan.

I had one child, Gandera, and could afford to send him to school. But he didn't want to continue. He sometimes wouldn't go to school for five days at a time. The teacher would come from Gianyar asking why he hadn't come. The teacher said he was very bright. He caught on to the Dutch language very quickly. He would go out every day, but he wasn't going to school. Sometimes I would accompany him to school by bicycle, to make sure he went. Every day he would ask for money. Sometimes he would go, sometimes he didn't. But in the end he didn't graduate — what a shame (*kasihan*)! He loved music and he came to play with the Seka Gong Gunung Sari. [Eventually he built a reputation as a composer and musician.] He was taken to California at UCLA and to Australia to teach gamelan. He became good at speaking English. But then he didn't want to work anymore — *Kasihan*! He didn't want to do anything when he came back from about a year in America. He didn't look after the family. He turned over responsibility for his family of eight children to me. To this day he doesn't pay any attention to them. He came back with a different character. He liked to marry. He would have one wife, then he'd take another. Then he had two and again he got involved with someone else. I don't know if it was the effect of being in America, I don't understand how he could be like that. I'm just tired. There is a story in Bali about a bird, named *bangau* ("egret"), ya. He climbs very high to fly. But when he becomes bored there, eventually he comes home. And so I just wait to see when he'll come home. My grandson Madé has now graduated from the Kolkar conservatory in Solo. He was supported by the government to study there for four years. He was asked to stay there to teach and would be given a salary. But he felt that he should come back to Bali.

Colin McPhee

McPhee used notes when he studied gamelan. He travelled all over Bali — two months in Kuta, then in Karangasem, in Desa Culik two months. He filled notebooks about Angklung, about Selonding, Gamelan Semar Pegulingan, about Legong, about Joged. Sampih, McPhee's adopted child, could perform the Gandrung, the male version of Joged.

Sampih was taken to Tabanan to study Kebyar Duduk. In those days the really famous Kebyar dancer from Tabanan was Mario. Sampih had two teachers, Mario and I Gusti Raka. After that McPhee said he would pay for his child, Sampih, to become a member of the Seka Gong [Peliatan]. He would pay the cost of the share in the gamelan, but it would be Sampih that would own it.

I was paid by Colin twice over. I got 17 ½ *rupiah* as a driver each month and 22 ½ *rupiah* for teaching gamelan to him. So I had 40 *rupiah* a month and I was extremely happy. And if a ship came in to Padang Bai, Colin would be called to play Balinese music — but with a piano on the ship! And I was his drummer. He used Balinese songs. He could make the piano sound like a Balinese gamelan. I could never do that.

Colin McPhee had three gong groups: the Semar Pegulingan from Teges, the Angklung in Sayan and the Joged. His child, Sampih, was a famous dancer from Bongkasa, but he isn't alive any longer. He used to bring tourists up and often asked one of the *gong* groups to play for them. Each tourist usually gave five *ringgit* or so, which was kept by the *seka*. Gambuh, which is extremely refined, was danced for ceremonies and the courts — but never for tourists. If McPhee had a Bali Night in his house, lots of visitors came. There was Bonnet, Spies. There were two English who lived in Desa Bayung in the mountains.[33] The visitors were very happy to hear Semar Pegulingan, Joged, Wayang. There was a *seka* of four people who performed Gender Wayang and would get five *ringgit*.

You could buy a big pig in those days with five *ringgit*. You could take a bus from Peliatan to Denpasar for ten cents then. Once every three days, McPhee would send me down with a note to Toko Betawi to buy vegetables and drinks. He would buy gas, meat, and vegetables on credit. I only had to collect them. He rented the car from the Raja of Ubud for 30 *rupiah*. The Raja had one '29 Sprolet and a '31. McPhee chose the '29. The roads were terrible — just pebbles. It took more than an hour and a half to go to Denpasar — very slowly. The roads were broad enough, but weren't looked after. If it poured rain, sometimes you couldn't walk on them.

He would drink and smoke and eat cheese or cake. I was a bit surprised. He ate only a little bit of rice. He liked *babi guling* (roasted piglet) though. Every day whenever they had a young pig they'd cook *babi guling* with *ketipat* (rice steamed in woven leaf packets). Other than that they didn't like meat. He would be here for six months at a time; then he'd go home and come back. I would watch his house for him. His wife's name was Jane Belo,[34] but she wasn't ever involved in McPhee's work. She went to the schools and collected pictures by the school children. She would buy them from the school children for five or ten cents, whatever they liked to draw. She would give them paper and pencils, and whatever they made she would buy. Strange, ya?

Whenever I'd go off, Colin would ask "Where is Madé?" He would get really angry. I was given a place to stay there, so I wouldn't go home. I ate there, he would tell me to drink, but I couldn't drink. He had a refrigerator. He'd tell me to go and take whatever from the fridge, but I didn't like it. I just ate rice.

Colin liked me. He gave me money to buy clothes. He said "I need Pak Madé to teach gamelan and to drive for me" [laughs], and sometimes I would organise the food for people who came with Bali Natour. His wife didn't like to go with him, except sometimes when we went shopping in Denpasar. We'd come home from Denpasar with a little pig in the back of the car for *babi guling*. Except if he was ill, Colin McPhee never stopped. There was a gamelan in Sukawati, an old *seka* with people on average 60 years old. Gambang, Joged, Gong, Luang, Angklung — he was always there asking for old songs.

Of Magic, Music and Changing Times

There was a dangerous season, *musim gering* we say in Bali, when there are fevers, cholera and other sicknesses. At that time the Barong[35] would go out at night followed by lots of people. They would carry small bamboo slit drums and hats made from *kukusan* (woven bamboo baskets in which rice is steamed) and they would be marked with lime and blood. So the sickness would disappear. The person would no longer feel sick, and would be given holy water by the *pemangku* (temple priest) asking for help from the deities. He would chant prayers asking help. "There's a person named Madé Lebah imploring Tuhan Yang Maha Esa (The Most Exalted God) so that his family will be safe.

He has someone in the family who is sick...." And the Barong would know the person causing it. Usually it was successful when the Barong tried to cure them. People can be entered by the deities (*kerauhan*). The Gods could enter the Barong being danced. As far as I know the Barong in Banjar Tengah is *keramat* (magically powerful) like that. The person who used to carry it was a Satriya, whose name was Gung Aji Ngungkus. He would know if someone was making trouble for the people. He suddenly came to the Barong, and the Barong would come out completely on its own. Everyone in the *desa* would come out and follow. Sometimes it would run to Tegallalang and everyone would follow. It was *ramai sekali* (enjoyably crowded and noisy). In short, in those days there was a season of sickness. But now there isn't. Ya, there is a season of sickness, but it isn't like before. There are those who come to ask for help from the Barong. But if they have money they go to the doctor. Before, there wasn't a doctor. Now there are lots of doctors, nurses, lots of people who give medicine.

I think that the Barong in Banjar Tengah belonged to Tjok Lingsir perhaps. That Raja was a *dukun* (healer). He knew Balinese letters and mantras. He was *sakti* (magically powerful). Now it is different, even if they can read letters. I don't understand now. Before if someone was sick, they would say a mantra and the person would become well. But nowadays they can't do it like that. If someone is sick, they won't necessarily be cured by mantras. Before they were. Maybe because [that power] has been extinguished — this age of change, everything is very different. Before if there was a priest saying prayers with the bells — deng-ninga-ninga, deng-ninga-ninga — people were so happy to hear that; now it's just ordinary (*biasa*).

In Bali, because there is a strong spirit of solidarity, if one person does his own thing, he has to watch out — he's likely to be struck down by magic. I couldn't believe that Cekek [an elderly man from the next *banjar* who was reputed to have magical powers and who had recently passed away] died in a magical night war. He couldn't read letters, so how could he know the mantra? I think he pretended to be a *pemangku* (priest) and have magic. He wasn't a *pemangku* in a temple (Pura). But I do believe Tjok Mangking from Puri Saren Kangin in Ubud was *sakti*. One night he came to me because he had been told that he could trust our descent group. He came in the middle of the night and asked me to come with him. I was married then and my child Gandera was still small. Tjok Mangking wanted to see Desak

Putu in Pengosekan with whom he had fallen in love. I could feel
my arm being held tight, but my feet didn't move. "What *is* this?" I
thought. We met a man from Pengosekan sitting on the road, bound
up and wearing two swords (*keris*). "What is *that*?", I asked "*Desti*",
said Tjok Mangking, "but he's afraid of me, and on his way to Pura
Batu Gaing", the temple where most Night Wars are held. Then we
entered the house of Desak Putu without any doors opening — "What
is this?" I was too scared to say no. She of course agreed to marry
him, since she was afraid to say no! He eventually died because he
lost during magical combat in a Night War.³⁶ Apparently it wasn't
actually during the duel, but while he was bathing, that is, while he
was becoming an ordinary person again. But the Tjokorda from Nyalian
hadn't bathed and struck him in his weak human form. He was given
petenga — a "stay of execution" until his next child was born, because
his wife had just become pregnant. In the end I was given a secret
three-word mantra from Tjok Mangking to protect me when out at
night. Sometimes I see *leyak* (witch) lights in the rice fields.³⁷ There
are no rays; that's how you know they aren't natural. Now *his* magic I
believe. I still can't imagine how it was possible to get to Pengosekan
without walking, and to enter a room without opening the door.

My opinion on the good and bad (*baik buruk*) of all these changes?
These days it is certain that people compete. All now have to have work
and they give priority to their own private enjoyment — to work, to get
money so that they can eat. If there is a performance, sometimes they
don't want to go. Each person will think about his work the next day.
If there is a performance after 10 o'clock, sometimes he won't want to
go out. "Better that I sleep because tomorrow I have to work." Before
it wasn't like that. If there was an Arja performance or a Prembon,
by 5 o'clock they would already be sitting there waiting. They would
bring *sirih*. If there were a performance until late the next morning,
they'd stay till it was over. It's different now. Like last night, I saw
some people watching the Prembon, but not that many.

In those days everywhere you heard *kotekan*.³⁸ They would pound
padi together in a *ketung* [a hollowed out log from a large tree about
five meters long.] All the padi would be put into the *ketung*. People
would bring wooden poles and were clever at making rhythms while they
pounded. Ting teng, ti-deng, te-ting teng ti-deng Everyone loved to hear
that sound of people working as padi became rice. "Ting teng, ti-deng,
te-ting-teng ti-deng." This is with a counterpoint: "kole dolé ken-tolé

dolé ken-tolé…." There were specialists at counterpoint, but not anymore. That was pure art (*paling seni sekali*). But now there are no more *ketung* to be found. Ya, the government of Indonesia has brought in mills. The rice isn't good to eat. Not that it isn't good — I don't mean to be accused of insulting — but it's not like real food. Some houses still have stone *lesung*, but the *ketung* from wood that was long enough for ten people, you don't see any more. The music they made was like "Cak". Women were extremely clever at making "Cak" rhythms with it. There were 3 Cak, 5 Cak and 7 Cak rhythms. Cak cak cak/ cak cak cak/ 'n-cak ke cak-cak 'n-cak ke cak…. If I used a *gumpang*, without any padi, it has an even finer sound: "tung tung tung te-di-tung di…" — very good! Now if I were to make a *seka* using that, maybe lots of tourists would come!

But now there are some good things too. In the old days, the Raja's Patih [minister] could go out and make trouble. For example, he might say to the Raja: "Oh, so-and-so's child is beautiful". So the Raja would call in the family of the girl, and they couldn't say no. They could make trouble (*pengacau*) for parents who had a daughter. The Patih would say to her mother and father, "this child, Wayan or Madé, is called to the Puri", so that she had to be presented to the Raja. The parents would cry, "*Aduh*, my child has been called by the Raja". The mother of the child would ask for help to the Raja's Patih, "Please, so that your Greatness would say to the Raja that she is sick." And she would give money to the Patih asking this favour — 400 or 500 *kepeng* — and would give him lots of food. He would make trouble like that. *Macam-macam*! (all kinds!) That was what was really bad, before. The Patih was very powerful under the kingdoms. He could do as he liked with the people. If there was a durian tree that was good and sweet, he would say, "I'll take that durian." Whatever was good would be taken. If he said it was for the Raja, it had to be accepted by the people.

A great deal changed when the Japanese came. You would see them in the street, but they didn't interact with people a lot. They took rice. At first they took half the rice; then they came back two weeks later and took the rest. Lots of Balinese were sent to Sulawesi. I heard some were thrown into the sea. If we answered back to them, they'd get angry, to the point of striking. Ya, they were really like that, the Japanese. Even people who hadn't done anything were taken and killed just like that, for no reason. We would sometimes hide the padi up in a coconut tree or a sugar palm in little sacks. People had to make pants/shorts from palm fibres.

In this place [Peliatan] today there are no thieves, no one gets angry. If someone has an argument, it is always broken up. People don't stay mad. That's because it is an area of artistic temperament (*seni*). It is peaceful (*tenang*). It's not like that in Singaraja or in Denpasar. In my lifetime, three people have been killed for stealing — the last time was in 1967.[39] If the *kentongan* rings like this — dung-dung-dung-dung-dung [rapid beat] — all the members of all the *banjar* come out — Teges, Teruna, Tebesaya etc. This area is very close knit and united. It is very safe (*aman*).[40]

* * *

Undoubtedly the most glaring gap in Madé Lebah's account is the understatement of the political violence that rocked Bali in the twentieth century — the Dutch invasion, the Japanese occupation,[41] the revolution, and the purge of communist party (PKI) sympathisers that swept the island in 1965–66.[42] He told stories he had heard from his father of the Negara war of the late nineteenth century in which Peliatan and Ubud participated, but doesn't mention the dramatic ritual suicides (puputan) which occurred around the time of his birth and which brought an end to the independence of the south Balinese kingdoms. He said little of the revolution or the anti-communist massacres. Although I did raise these subjects occasionally, they seemed to have been rather remote events which he observed with relative detachment from a distance, and about which he had not much to say. The Gianyar royal house had colluded with the Dutch, whose invasions resulted in the puputan massacre-suicides of the royal families in Badung and Klungkung.[43] Gianyar was also pro-Dutch in the revolutionary period. And although members of the Peliatan court — always at odds with its overlord in Gianyar — did mount a guerrilla style resistance to the return of the Dutch,[44] Madé Lebah and the majority of his village contemporaries were not involved. The same was the case with the violence surrounding the anti-communist purge in 1965–66. Unlike neighbouring Ubud, Peliatan was predominantly Nationalist Party (PNI) in its sympathies, and all but one banjar were unscathed by the brutal killings of that period.[45]

It might be assumed that Made Lebah's aesthetic sensibilities inclined him to an apolitical perspective, or that the Balinese cultural proclivity for muting climactic experience suggested by Bateson and Mead (1942) was at work.[46] But these silences highlight as well an intensely localised view of the world that is also characteristically Balinese (Couteau 2002). For someone who travelled as widely as he did as a trader, a driver, a music teacher and performer, Madé Lebah was decidedly local in his attachments, and his village-level view of the surrounding world is not unusual in contemporary Bali. He was curious about world events and avidly watched television and read the newspaper. But the relationships that mattered to him were those of his family and community. These relationships were not without ambivalence though. He spoke with great warmth of his wives, but there are also stories of extra-marital liaisons, of which he gave no hint in these interviews. He was proud of his grandchildren and great-grandchildren. But he was deeply disappointed by his son's irresponsibility, and what Lebah viewed as the squandering of undoubted musical talents.

Another feature that stands out in Lebah's narrative is his precise memory of the cost of living for the increasing number of items of everyday life that were commoditised over the century.[47] The cash economy was not an entirely new phenomenon. Traditional Balinese texts regulating village affairs (awig-awig) are litanies of fines, specifying how many kepeng were required to compensate for this or that infraction of local adat rules. At the same time, Lebah's account draws a sharp line between those kinds of goods and services which could be paid for in cash, and those which remained firmly outside commodity status because of their ritual or social importance. The Western students who came to learn from him paid for these services, but for Balinese the arts entered a different domain of aesthetic and social values.[48] Teaching was not typically reciprocated in cash — certainly not within one's own village, and only rarely beyond. The Peliatan seka did raise funds for the full-time services of the teachers that were brought to work with them in the early years of the gamelan orchestra's development. Although Lebah expressed considerable pride in the way his teaching was reciprocated through contributions for ceremonies and help in constructing the buildings around his house compound, he apparently did feel tension between the two kinds of valuation and reward. This was particularly acute in his later years, when the financial burdens of helping to support his son's large extended family with school fees and health costs became pressing. Tenzer (personal communication 1984) describes Lebah as expressing irritation that he was never offered honoraria by Anak Agung Mandera for teaching the new Semar Pegulingan orchestra that the aristocratic co-founder of the Peliatan Seka Gong started up in the late 1970s in Puri Kaleran, and disappointment that the Teges Seka which he also taught had never invited him on their trips to perform in Japan.

Today two of Madé Lebah's grandchildren and three of his great-grandchildren are accomplished performers in the Seka Gong Gunung Sari which he had helped to found and in several other performing troupes in Peliatan. His village had changed greatly over that period, many of its members achieving undreamed-of wealth through painting, carving and the production of handicrafts. Still his granddaughter, Ni Luh Mas Sriati, like so many of the inheritors of Bali's artistic traditions, continues to teach dance to children of the village by the old rules of reciprocal obligation, and with the same sense of service to the arts, the deities and the community as her grandfather.

Madé Lebah died in 1996. Bali had undergone a dramatic period of change in the last half of the twentieth century with impacts on everyday life arguably as great as the puputan, the revolution, and the massacres that shook the island's culture to its foundations in the course of this one life. In the new century, perhaps his quiet reflections, his sense of humour, his ambivalence about the contradictory and paradoxical processes of change, and his absorption with many of its continuities will find resonance and appreciation among new generations of Balinese who inherit the exceptional collective legacies, achieved as much by Bali's many extraordinary "ordinary" people, as by its celebrated heroic figures.

Notes

I would like to express my gratitude to Madé Lebah's family and other Peliatan villagers who provided insights into the life and times of Lebah and his community in the twentieth century. In particular, Ni Luh Mas Sriati, I Made Geriya, I Wayan Puja, Ni Ketut Ratna, Ni Wayan Puri, I Ketut Nesa and I Wayan Gandera. Interviews with Lebah's contemporaries, Dewa Putu Dani and Anak Agung Mandera, complemented his own reminiscences from the perspective of the titled gentry. Among Western researchers who worked with Lebah, Michael Tenzer shared recollections of his teacher from the point of view of a student and scholar of Balinese music. David Stuart-Fox made valuable comments on this manuscript. I particularly want to acknowledge Hildred Geertz for her advice on approaches to the use of biography as social history, and Jim Warren, who participated in several of the early interview sessions, contributing a historian's perspective to these explorations.

1. The painter Walter Spies arrived in Bali in 1927 and McPhee in 1931, but publications about Bali by Western scholars and artists who came to spend time on the island were not in wide circulation until some years later. It was the French theorist of drama, Antonin Artaud, whose writings after

witnessing the Balinese performances at the Paris exhibition recognised this among the great genres of world theatre (Vickers 1989: 108–9).

2. See, for example, the editorial in the *Bali Post* ("Sejahterakan 'Pragina' Bali", 16 Feb. 2005), decrying the lack of attention from the Provincial Department of Culture to the poor incomes of Balinese performers, who receive as little as Rp 20,000 (US$2) for performances at tourist venues.

3. This date is his own estimation. A regional government publication (Dinas Kebudayaan [Bali] 1990/91) profiling local artists gives his year of birth as 1915. However, Lebah's account of his experience of the devastating 1917 earthquake (see below) indicates that he would have to have been born much earlier.

4. McPhee's notes (*Bali Field Journal* VIII) describe Lebah as "an instinctive rather than a technical musician". His major contribution is generally regarded as that of teacher and transmitter of classical compositions to later generations. Tenzer (personal communication, 1984) remarked that Lebah's real forté was the complex and precise drumming demanded by Arja, a classical operatic genre by then in decline. He tells a lovely anecdote about his aging music teacher: "I think Lebah's ... true passion was for Arja drumming, which is a close relative of Legong drumming, but more complicated.... Lebah kept saying he was too old, he needed injections, he couldn't [perform any longer].... One night there was an Arja put on in Peliatan for the *odalan* (temple anniversary) at the Pura Dalem [Death Temple]. He stayed up all night performing.... That kind of Arja drumming is almost all lost. Next day I saw him at the *odalan* and he was in a great mood. Obviously performing the Arja again had made him feel wonderful and young.... He was one of the few really good performers of this genre." Harnish (2001: 37) says Lebah "spoke of how he would not feel pain, hunger, tiredness, and age when he played music". I too was taken by the ethereal expression that transformed his face when he played with the orchestra into his 80s. By then, he only performed the drumming for the Legong sequence, and was responsible for setting out the lanterns for stage lighting, which was his other duty for the Peliatan *seka* (club) at that stage in his life.

5. McPhee comments, "In the contributions of Lotring, Lebah and the Guru [apparently referring to Lunyuh from Payangan], the slow, plant-like growth of music revealed itself. There were none of the postures of genius. Not one considered himself an 'artist'. Each was a superb craftsman, professional, individual only as one leaf differs from another, changing things only to suit his fancy. Lotring created; Lebah rearranged. As for the Guru, he was simply a medium through which the past continued. At his age, withdrawn, he added nothing, gave nothing. His memory was unique and incredible, but that was all. He was too old, too set to

come out of his shell. Lebah was right, he was an old turtle" (McPhee Collection, *Field Journal* IV).

6. In 1991 Lebah was awarded the Piagam Dharma Kusuma for his contribution to the arts by the provincial government of Bali. He received other regional government awards in 1976 and 1985, but no national recognition (Dinas Kebudayaan [Bali] 1990/91: 9).

7. "*Babad*" here refers to the dynastic chronicles used to establish genealogy and descent group status, emblematic of the wider Indic traditions underwriting the royal courts and priestly authority (see Vickers 1990). The "high culture" focus of much of the popular and ethnographic writing on Bali, has in my view tended to under-rate or shift from focus the autochthonous sources of popular culture, and the complex interdependence of elite and popular value orientations and practices. The latter are expressed quintessentially in a range of forms of local social organisation and ancestral religious beliefs. For an elaborated presentation of this argument see Warren (1993a, 1993b). Clifford Geertz's work *Negara* (1981) is undoubtedly the most prominent of contemporary ethnographies focused on the "high culture" dimension, but many other of his own and Hildred Geertz's studies have contributed to our knowledge of popular culture as well. See in particular H. Geertz (1959), C. Geertz (1959), H. and C. Geertz (1975). More recently this issue has surfaced in debates concerning state as opposed to community control of the complex irrigation system in Bali. See Lansing (1991) and Hauser-Schäublin (2003).

8. For the classic account of the core institutions around which Balinese everyday life is structured — *banjar* (hamlet), *desa* (village), irrigation societies (*subak*), descent group (*dadia/soroh*), voluntary associations (*seka*), see C. Geertz (1959). For detailed studies of *banjar* and *desa* structures, see the early accounts by Dutch scholars Korn (1984 [1933]) and Goris (1984 [1935]) and more recent work by Warren (1993); on *subak*, see Lansing (1987); on *dadia*, see H. and C. Geertz (1975). *Seka* refers to a range of voluntary groups which are formed for special purposes such as harvesting (*seka manyi*), musical performance (*seka gong*), etc., but the term also refers to the general principle of equal participation in collective action. See discussion of the *seka* principle in H. and C. Geertz (1975: 30–1) and Warren (1993: 7–10).

9. The term "caste" is generally regarded as inappropriate for describing Balinese concepts of rank as opposed to the Indic system of social ordering from which the concept is derived, despite the contemporary use of the terms Brahmana, Satria, Wesia and Sudra for classifying descent groups in Bali. For one thing, reincarnation in Balinese religion is into one's own descent group rather than up or down a hierarchy of status achieved through deeds in past lives, and so a key concept legitimating the Indic

system is completely missing in Bali. Also, titles are not tied to occupations. Although some priestly and ruling title groups are described as Brahmana and Satria respectively, the power and authority claimed by these groups has never been exclusive and remains hotly contested in Bali. For discussions of the question of caste and hierarchy in general, see H. and C. Geertz (1975: 21–2), C. Geertz (1980: 26–33), Boon (1977), Schulte-Nordholt (1986), Warren (1993: 68–93).

10. For a similar description of collectivist approaches to musical development in Bali, see Covarrubbias 1977 [1937]: 211–2. McPhee remarks upon Lebah's brief foray into composition, inspired by the collectivist *seka* ethos: "As for Lebah, his compositions were slight, fresh, graceful, neatly put together and charming like himself. I was surprised when he began to compose these pieces, and, I think, so was he. He referred to them with extreme modesty. But he had now a club of his own to direct, and since it is a feather in the cap of any club if it can produce new music, Lebah was thus stimulated to produce compositions of his own. But he did it, not as the result of the desire for personal expression, but simply for the sake of the club [*seka*]. This, I think is important to note" (McPhee Collection, *Field Journal* IV).

11. Perhaps John Coast's account of the first time he heard the Peliatan Seka play Tabuh Teluh conveys something of the stunning complexity of Balinese music and the style which made this village troupe famous: "Madé Lebah gripped his hammer firmly; then he and the Anak Agung exchanged a lightning glance and drum and metallophone started on a terrific chord that I shall never forget, and straightaway we were drowned in the music — drowned, overwhelmed, carried away, submerged. For such music as this we had never heard in our lives, never heard hinted at by the dozens of gamelans which we had already listened to. This gamelan had a percussive attack, an electric virtuosity, a sort of appalling precision, which, as it echoed and rebounded off that long wall, almost pulsated us out of our seats, bringing tears of astonished emotion to our eyes.... My whole Balinese horizon had been violently broadened in these few minutes ... that such great music as this could have been devised had never entered my senses.... I told them, I think, that this was the most wonderful music I had heard in my life, anywhere, ever...." (1954: 58–9). Coast, an Englishman working in the Indonesian Ministry of Foreign Affairs, organised the first tour of the Peliatan troupe after Indonesian independence to Europe and America.

12. Recordings and transcripts of some of these interviews with Madé Lebah, along with those of other figures in Bali's recent artistic and political history, can be accessed through the Bali Oral History Archive at <http://wwwlib. murdoch.edu.au/boha>.

13. Lebah didn't express the almost paranoic concern with black magic that Unni Wikan (1990) describes for her primary informant in *Managing Turbulent Hearts: a Balinese Formula for Living.* He tells of his amazement at some unusual experiences that he attributed to magical powers, but rarely indicates strong fear or anxiety, and was occasionally sceptical. One of the Balinese language texts in Jane Belo's collection, written by her research assistant Gusti Madé, records Lebah's efforts to obtain a mantra from a spirit medium (*balian*) that would sicken a fellow *banjar* member, I Doewari, who was trying to seduce his wife. Another text recounts the story of his visit to a medium to find his lost or stolen bag (Pacific Ethnographic Archives N37 text #132 January 2, 1938 and #150 March 16, 1938). See also note 37 for a story told by Lebah indicating the exceptional interest of McPhee, Belo and their Western visitors in Balinese magic.

14. His stories were peppered with Balinese expressions that often lack adequate Indonesian — no less English — equivalents. I have reordered the content into roughly chronological-thematic sequence and interspersed background detail in notes to add information from other sources that helps set his personal narrative in a wider ethnographic context.

15. See Hildred Geertz's discussion of translation dilemmas involved in the shared project narrating the reminiscences of Batuan artist, I Madé Togog (Geertz and Togog 2005: 8–10).

16. This is a common complaint of families who explain their contemporary landlessness as a consequence of such decisions by their forebearers, a choice that reflected a very different set of values attached to land and relationships.

17. Since patrilineal marriage meant the loss of property rights, women were reluctant to leave home, and commoner families preferred marriages within the *banjar* and descent group to protect their daughters, who continued to participate in natal family rituals.

18. Tjokorda from Tjokor I Dewa "Foot of the Deity"; Dewa Agung means "Great Deity". These are generally regarded as the highest ranking titles among the ruling Satria "caste". Anak Agung and Gusti are also titles of ruling families in other parts of Bali, and there is considerable debate about the origin and significance of the classification and ranking system.

19. It was still common in the late twentieth century for poor people to send their children to work as servants at local courts in return for being fed and educated. Several in the family I lived with had been placed in the Puri in the 1960s and '70s because there were too many children to support. The last, Ketut, revolted and returned home after four days. To the present day, the family is informed of major ceremonies in the Puri

and is expected to assist with preparations in return for ritual food and gifts. Ketut, now a teacher, complained on one occasion that she felt taken advantage of and that the reciprocity for their labour was no longer what would have been expected from the court in the old days — gifts of cloth or jewellery.

20. Currency values in the early colonial period were as follows: 5 *kepeng* = 1 Dutch cent (*sen*); 500 *kepeng* = 100 *sen* or 1 *rupiah*; 2.5 *rupiah* = 1 *ringgit* (silver).

21. See H. Geertz (1994: 83–95) on the magical potency exercised in a variety of ways by kings, healers and sorcerers. Access to these powers may be through traditional *lontar* (palm leaf) texts or direct channelling through trance and magical formulae. The mystical power and inspiration expressed in extraordinary artistry is termed *taksu*.

22. Prior to the Negara conflict in the late nineteenth century, Ubud had been a client offshoot of the Peliatan court. The Raja of Peliatan was young and inexperienced at the time, and for this reason Peliatan did not profit to the extent that Ubud did from this military adventure. From that point Ubud became independent of Peliatan and the relative prominence of the Peliatan court began to wane, although it was the seat of District government in the early colonial period. See Agung (1989: 414–22) on the 1895 Negara War and the independence of the principalities of Peliatan, Ubud and Tegallalang from former overlords in Gianyar and Klungkung in the unsettled political situation in South Bali at the end of the nineteenth century.

23. One of the few first-person Balinese accounts available of the 1965–66 PKI massacres in Bali is provided in the autobiography of Anak Agung Made Jelantik from the royal house of Karangasem. His is decidedly written from the perspective of the landed gentry. Where Jelantik describes the "illegal occupation of farmland … instigated by the Communists" (1997: 304), Lebah's few remarks on the subject are critical instead of the subversion of land reform policy which he seems to take for granted as just in principle.

24. Many of the households in Peliatan including Lebah's family boasted *lesung*, stone rice pounding mortars which were said to have been booty (*mejara*) taken by their forefathers who fought in the Negara wars. The Semar Pegulingan instruments from Negara were in turn borrowed by the Teges *seka* on an agreement that is still binding. In its place they loaned a Ford Foundation granted gamelan to Puri Kaleran.

25. A basic *seka* (formal association) principle is equal division of proceeds and equal contribution to *seka* activities. Leaders (*klian*) will sometimes be given a double share for their extra responsibilities, and/or an additional

share of requisite food distributions on ritual occasions. In the past, income was usually saved until the Galungan festival every 210 days, and either divided among the members, or used to buy a pig for the ritual feast.

26. Covarrubias, writing in the mid-1930s, records a price of two guilders (US$1.36) for a complete outfit of clothes, and 20 cents for a meal in a *warung* stall. *Kepeng* were valued at 500–700 to the guilder. He comments, "It was always a mystery to us how the Balinese made the money they seemed to spend so lavishly in extravagant festivals and in [*sic*] beautiful clothes. They never appeared to work regularly for wages, and outside of the market, in which alone business was transacted, they never seemed interested in commerce" (1972 [1937]: 85–6).

27. Negara Indonesia Timor was the controversial federated State of Eastern Indonesia, a puppet government set up during the revolutionary war by the Dutch in an attempt to counter and contain the newly declared Indonesian Republic based on Java.

28. See Vickers (1989: 94–5) for background on this Dutch scholar of Balinese language and religion. He chose to remain in Bali after the Revolution, taking up Indonesian citizenship.

29. By other accounts, the expulsion was precipitated by an infraction of *adat* (customary) rules. It may well be that both interpretations are correct. The other long-standing residents of Chinese descent, remain today active members of this same *banjar*.

30. *Sentana* refers to the practice of a male marrying into another family line as the "jural female" in this patrilineal system. It is not the preferred marriage form, but nevertheless quite commonplace. Just as a female loses her right to inherit in her natal household upon out marriage, so the male marrying out as *sentana* would lose inheritance rights in his household of origin. Although theoretically the husband and wife have reversed legal relationship, normally they perform their everyday roles as in any other Balinese household.

31. Anak Agung Djelantik (1997: 20) tells a story I also heard in Peliatan, that villagers sometimes hid their daughters from the local ruler and "often the beautiful girls had their earlobes sliced through in order to become imperfect and thus escape the danger of being chosen". On the other hand, there were advantages to having a family member marry into wealthy and powerful ruling families, and such marriages could also be a source of pride.

32. For discussions of the Sanghyang and Kecak, and the relationship between the ritual and touristic versions of this trance and choral genre, see de Zoete and Spies (1973 [1938]) and Bandem and deBoer (1995).

33. This undoubtedly refers to Margaret Mead and Gregory Bateson, who carried out research in Bayung Gedé in 1936–37 and briefly in 1939.

34. There are several short Balinese language texts by Jane Belo's research assistant Gusti Madé in which Lebah features. These are held in the collection of her fieldnotes in the Pacific Ethnographic Archives of the Library of Congress (Nos. 30, 36, 132 and 150).

35. The Barong is a magically powerful dragon danced by two men. Barong masks are often regarded as *keramat* and kept in the village shrines. Several popular local legends surround the magical powers of the Barong of Banjar Tengah in particular (*Peliatan Legends* 1990: 8–11).

36. See the painting of "A War among Sorcerers" by the Batuan painter, Ida Bagus Ketut Rai, in H. Geertz (1994: 89).

37. Michael Tenzer (personal communication, 1984) recounts a cryptic anecdote told by Lebah of McPhee, Belo and guests asking him to find them someone who could conjure *leyak*, for which they would pay. Tenzer was left in the dark as to whether Lebah believed the lights they all saw that night were really the result of magic or not.

38. See Tenzer for a discussion of the instrumental expression of *kotekan*, which he vividly describes as "the crackling ornamental fireworks of Balinese music" (1991: 46).

39. I later found a newspaper article, dated 29 August 1965, describing the most frequently told of these incidents, in which I Lingkuh from the neighbouring village of Kutuh was eventually killed by a crowd drawn from 12 surrounding *banjar* in an *adat*-sanctioned form of village justice that still occurs in contemporary Bali. Lingkuh had been repeatedly jailed for theft and was reported to have interfered with the distribution of irrigation water. He was reputed to be a practitioner of magic and to be "*kebal*", magically invulnerable. ("I Lingkuh Pentjuri Ulung dan Kebal: Ahirnja mati melingkuh kena buah kates", *Suara Indonesia* 19 August 1965.) His demise according to both local lore and the press report was due, not to the stones and other weapons used to attack him, but to a mango thrown from the crowd, against which his magic was impotent. The men of the village of Peliatan were convicted by a court and received a sentence of collective labour, clearing what is still today the sports field adjacent to the Village Death Temple (Pura Dalem). McPhee recounts another incident in the 1930s told to him by Anak Agung Mandera, who was then a secretary in the District office. The story similarly involved a thief named I Kisid, who was captured with several hundred magical charms in his belt. "The men of Peliatan were summoned and tried for murder, but were released. In the old days thieves were always killed, and even today such a

collective murder was not rigorously punished" (McPhee Collection, *Field Journal* IV n.d.).

40. The connection between notions of aesthetic sensibility, order and harmony were common tropes in popular Balinese discourse under the New Order, a view seemingly at odds with the violent history upon which these concepts rested. Dewa Putu Dani drew on similar metaphors in his recounting of local legends revolving around the arts and cultural history of Peliatan (*Peliatan Legends* 1990).

41. Of these events, it was the Japanese occupation that most drastically affected everyday life in Lebah's experience.

42. See Geoffrey Robinson (1995) for the most complete study available of the violent events of the period from 1945 through 1966 in Bali.

43. See Margaret Wiener (1995) for a cultural historic analysis of the significance of the *puputan*. Her study particularly focuses on the paramount royal house in Klungkung.

44. See the account of tensions between Gianyar and Ubud/Peliatan after Dutch reoccupation of Gianyar in Sukawati (1979: 34–9). Two leaders of the resistance from Puri Peliatan, Tjokorda Gde Rai, the Punggawa of Peliatan, and Tjokorda Rai Pudak were killed in the confrontation.

45. Three PKI members from the northernmost *banjar* in Peliatan were killed during this time of terror, while other villages number those killed in the hundreds. In Banjar Tengah, a Kecak chorus was formed, daily bringing together all the adult males in the *banjar* meeting house, with the explicit intent of quelling the dangerous rumours and discouraging villagers from turning on one another. See Cribb (1990) and Robinson (1995) for two of the few extensive treatments of this traumatic period in Bali's history.

46. Hildred Geertz notes similar silences in the accounts of the Batuan painter, Ida Bagus Madé Togog, despite at least two of his own family and several friends having been imprisoned and killed during these violent times. She attributes these lacunae to Balinese conventions of civility (Geertz and Togog 2005: 7–8).

47. Sukawati (1979: 18) says, "At this time [1930s] life was still very simple. No one talked about money, it was not in general use. In the markets food and articles were exchanged in barter." He comments on the high price of 600 guilders offered by Walter Spies for ten years' rent on land in Ubud. "Well, I refused and he insisted and so on and on and eventually I just took 175 guilders from him. Had it been done today, three or ten times that would not have satisfied us. So things have changed."

48. Louise Koke (1987 [1953]: 140) remarks of the famed dancer Mario: "I marvelled at Balinese acceptance of great artistic gifts. Here was an outstanding artist accorded no more importance in his community than

any tiller of the soil. He had a humble job in the Controleur's office in Tabanan..., he received a pittance for his dancing, and he was paid nothing, or at most a few sheaves of rice, for his teaching. The only deference I ever saw him receive was from a high caste pupil who sat on the floor with him, as an equal, instead of on a chair."

References

Agung, Anak Agung Gde. 1989. *Bali pada Abad XIX: Perjuangan Rakyat dan Raja-Raja Menentang Kolonialisme Belanda 1808–1908*. Yogyakarta: Gadja Mada University Press.

Bandem, I Madé and deBoer, Fredrik. 1995. *Balinese Dance in Transition: Kaja and Kelod*. Kuala Lumpur: Oxford University Press.

Bateson, Gregory and Mead, Margaret. 1942. *Balinese Character: A Photographic Analysis*. New York: Academy of Sciences.

Boon, James. 1977. *The Anthropological Romance of Bali: 1597–1972: Dynamic Perspectives in Marriage and Caste, Politics and Religion*. Cambridge: Cambridge University Press.

Coast, John. 1954. *Dancing Out of Bali*. London: Faber and Faber.

Connor, Linda, Asch, Patsy and Asch, Timothy. 1996. *Jero Tapakan: A Balinese Healer*. Los Angeles: Ethnographies Press.

Couteau, J. 2002. "Bali: Crise en Paradis", *Archipel* 64: 231–54.

Covarrubias, Miguel. 1972 [1937]. *Island of Bali*. Kuala Lumpur: Oxford University Press.

Cribb, Robert. 1990. *The Indonesian Killings, 1965–66: Studies from Java and Bali*. Clayton: Centre of Southeast Asian Studies, Monash University.

De Zoete, Beryl and Spies, Walter. 1973 [1938]. *Dance and Drama in Bali*. Kuala Lumpur: Oxford University Press.

Dinas Kebudayaan [Bali]. 1990/91. Riwayat Hidup Para Weniman Penerima Penghargaan Seni Dharma Kusuma dan Dharma Kusuma Madya tahun 1990/1991. Denpasar: Dinas Kebudayaan Prinpinsi Daerah Tingkat I Bali.

Geertz, Clifford. 1980. *Negara: The Theatre State in Nineteenth-century Bali*. Princeton: Princeton University Press.

————. 1983. *Local Knowledge*. New York: Basic Books.

Geertz, Hildred. 1994. *Images of Power: Balinese Paintings Made for Gregory Bateson and Margaret Mead*. Honolulu: University of Hawai'i Press.

Geertz, Hildred and Geertz, Clifford. 1975. *Kinship in Bali*. Chicago: University of Chicago Press.

Geertz, Hildred and Togog, Ida Bagus Madé. 2005. *Tales from a Charmed Life: A Balinese Painter Reminisces*. Honolulu: University of Hawai'i Press.

Goris, R. 1984 [1935]. "The Religious Character of the Village Community", in *Bali: Studies in Life, Thought and Ritual*. Dordrecht: Foris Publications/ KITLV.

Harnish, David. 2001. "A Hermeneutical Arc in the Life of a Balinese Musician", *World of Music* 43/1: 21–41.

Hauser-Schäublin, Brigitte. 2003. "The Precolonial Balinese State Reconsidered", *Current Anthropology*, 44/2: 153–81.

Keeler, Ward. 1975. "Musical traditions in Java and Bali", *Indonesia* 19: 85–126.

Korn, V.E. 1984 [1933]. "The Village Republic of Tenganan Pegeringsingan", in *Bali: Studies in Life, Thought and Ritual*. Dordrecht: Foris Publications/ KITLV.

Lansing, J. Stephen. 1987. *Priests and Programmers: Technologies of Power in the Engineered Landscape of Bali*. Princeton: Princeton University Press.

McPhee, Colin. 1966. *Music in Bali: A Study in Form and Instrumental Organization*. New Haven: Yale University Press.

———. 1972 [1946]. *A House in Bali*. Kuala Lumpur: Oxford University Press.

Peliatan Legends. 1990. [accounts by Dewa Putu Dani and others] Desa Peliatan (photocopy booklet).

Radin, Paul. 1926. *Crashing Thunder: the Autobiography of an American Indian*. New York: D. Appleton. [In: Human Relations Area Files. Code no. NP12/7 [049107] 301 H918.]

Robinson, Geoffrey. 1995. *The Dark Side of Paradise: Political Violence in Bali*. Ithaca: Cornell University Press.

Schulte-Nordholt, Henk. 1986. *Bali: Colonial Conceptions and Political Change 1700–1940: From Shifting Hierarchies to Fixed Order*. Rotterdam: Comparative Asian Studies Program 15.

Sukawati, Tjokorda Gde Agung Sukawati. 1979. *Reminiscences of a Balinese Prince* (as dictated to Rosemary Hilbery), University of Hawaii, Southeast Asian Studies, Southeast Asia paper No. 14.

Tenzer, Michael. 1991. *Balinese Music*. Singapore: Periplus.

Vickers, Adrian. 1989. *Bali: A Paradise Created*. Ringwood, Vic.: Penguin.

———. 1990. "The Historiography of Balinese Texts", *History and Theory* 29/2: 158–78.

Warren, Carol. 1993a. *Adat and Dinas: Balinese Communities in the Indonesian State*. Kuala Lumpur: Oxford University Press.

———. 1993b. "Disrupted Death Ceremonies: Popular Culture and the Ethnography of Bali", *Oceania* 64/1: 36–56.

———. 1998. "Mediating Modernity in Bali", *International Journal of Cultural Studies*, 1/1: 83–108.

Wikan, Unni. 1990. *Managing Turbulent Hearts: A Balinese Formula for Living*. Chicago: Chicago University Press.

Archival Collections

McPhee Collection, Music Department, University of California at Los Angeles.

Pacific Ethnographic Archives, Jane Belo and Margaret Mead Collections, Library of Congress, Washington, D.C.

Suara Indonesia, microfilm, Centre for Research Libraries, Chicago.

3

Who Owns a Life History? Scholars and Family Members in Dialogue

Janet Hoskins

This article is dedicated to the memory of Cornelius Malo Djakababa
(1935–2004)

Anthropologists developed the life history method as a way of collecting ethnographic data that they hoped would be more sensitive to individual subjectivity and variation. While in its early years, the method was preoccupied with methodological questions about which lives were "typical" (Langness and Frank 1981; Dubois 1940) in more recent years it has been linked to a phenomenological turn in the discipline that has foregrounded positioned subjects and a diversity of different perspectives. Malinowski's adage that the anthropologist sought "the native's point of view" was re-interpreted to try to correct the universalising tenor of older ethnographic writings (Malinowski himself spoke glibly of "how the savage looks at the world") and restore a sense of the particularities of each person's perspective. Life histories were generally collected from people who were illiterate and unable to write their own accounts, and for this very reason they seemed to promise an escape from Eurocentric perspectives and a unique window onto the different texture of personal experience in other cultures.

The recent crisis of representation in ethnographic writing has problematised many of the ethical assumptions which surround the life history method: On what basis can western scholars accurately "give voice" to people from another culture? Life histories are no longer seen as simple documents which can be "collected", recorded and translated, but as complex, dialogically created narratives, in which the ethnographer's own questions, interests and expectations construct a series of topics which the subject is called upon to address. Recent critical life histories (Behar 1993; Frank 2000) have developed the notion of the "biography in the shadow", a term coined by Frank to designate the subtle, often unconfessed attractions that draw each ethnographer to his or her prime informants.

This paper examines a new level of these problems. It looks at different claims to "own" a life history — in this case, claims put forward about the life of a prominent man who played an important role in the period of contact and colonial conquest on the Eastern Indonesian island of Sumba. Although his father was beheaded when he was a young boy and he himself was sold as a slave, Yoseph Malo rose to take heads himself, and become both a traditional clan leader and the first Dutch-appointed Raja of Rara. He was the first convert to the Catholic Church on the island, and in 1960, after he retired and Indonesia achieved its independence, one of his last acts was to request a Catholic wedding to the last of his eight wives.

From 1984 to 2002, I have published several different versions of Yoseph Malo's life history (Hoskins 1984, 1989, 1996a, 1996b, 2002), and these versions have been criticised and challenged at times by Yoseph Malo's son, Cornelius Djakababa, an educated businessman fluent in English and deeply concerned with his family's heritage. In this article, I trace the history of our dialogue about this life history — a dialogue initiated through correspondence but then continued through personal encounters and, finally, a form of scholarly collaboration. I focus on the most sensitive issue in our dialogue: the representation of the period from about 1889–95 when Yoseph Malo was enslaved, transferred to the Jesuit fathers of the first Catholic Mission on the island, converted, and (depending on the interpretation offered) "freed" and/or "ransomed" to return to his natal family in Rara.

I choose this focus both because it was the subject of an early misunderstanding which meant that my relationship with Mr. Djakababa began as a hostile challenge, and only gradually shifted into a form of dialogue and eventually collaboration. Slavery is a sensitive topic, which can often be dealt with through "historical amnesia" or other devices (Larson 2000). It has, for this reason, often proved to be a "historiographic problem", and slave origins are sometimes concealed in archival records. In the case of Yoseph Malo, the fact that he was enslaved as a child of nine or ten after his father was beheaded was not disputed, but its interpretation was: Mr. Djakababa was very concerned that his father be represented as someone who had impressive, even aristocratic ancestry, so that his struggle to attain freedom and eventually an honorable burial for his father was a return to his rightful status, rather than a rise from "rags to riches". The initial misunderstanding between my account and the family tradition also sheds a fair amount of light on the related issues of whether "freedom" or manumission really was possible for former slaves, what the position of the first Jesuit missionaries was towards indigenous slavery, how a life story can be crafted to parallel a familiar genre in oral narrative (which I will call the "triumphant orphan" stories), and the relation of history to social memory.

Ethics and the Special Challenges of Non-Western Biography

Biographers of prominent persons in the Western world have written at length about the ethical and methodological problems of securing access to personal correspondence, getting interviews with friends and family members, and working as an "authorised" or non-authorised biographer. While there are now a number of biographies done under other conditions, I believe that not much has been written about these kinds of considerations in other settings.

The "anthropological life history" was born in an era that was still relatively "innocent" in relation to the politics of representation. Presenting a vivid portrait of a particular person was an effort to convey the subjective side of a culture, and to do a subtle form of propaganda which would make the subject of the study seem more human, although still culturally different. Lila Abu-Lughod has presented a more up-to-date version of this argument in her case for "tactical humanism", set forward in "Writing Against Culture" (1991) and *Writing Women's Worlds* (1993).

But this apparently easy task of "translating humanism" across cultures needs to be problematised in a number of ways. I will concentrate on four specific areas: (a) problems of genre; (b) problems of language and memory; (c) problems of interpretation; and (d) historiographic problems, opposing local views of history to scholarly ones. I will then discuss the "hybrid format" of Mr. Djakababa's own text — involving influences from both the traditional oral narration (which his father performed for him and for H.R. Horo, the Raja of Kodi, and which Maru Daku, a well-known storyteller and cultural expert of Kodi, performed for me in 1980), the scholarly article, and perhaps even the business report.

Problems of Genre

The life history can be considered a "genre" in a number of different cultural contexts, but in a somewhat different way from the way we usually understand it ourselves. When I wrote *Biographical Objects* (Hoskins 1998b), I argued that it was because there was not a widespread genre of biographical narratives that so many of my informants were most revealing about themselves when they spoke about objects. There were, however, a few exceptions to this rule, and Yoseph Malo was certainly the most well known of these: he was a famous storyteller, who performed the story of his own life as if it were a traditional epic, accompanying his narratives with strumming on the one-stringed fiddle (*dungga*) and even singing his own versions of a hero's laments for his misfortunes. I never saw him perform, but I spoke to many who had — and who said they would cry in listening to his account of all his troubles.

He also had a need to tell his story, since it was a narrative of triumph over the most humiliating of situations — the loss of his father's head, his own enslavement as a boy, and a fall from aristocratic rank to the lowest social level. When he became a Raja under the Dutch colonial government and successfully married eight different women, he still needed to ensure that his audiences understood all this. He made elaborate arrangements to marry into the family of his father's beheaders — the Kodi village of Ratenngaro, from which he took two wives — and to recover his father's skull and reunite it with his body in a splendid new tomb which became a symbol of the restoration of the family honour.

The traditional narratives that he modelled his tale on belong to particular lineage houses, which are said to "hold on to" them just as they hold on to heirloom weapons or gold valuables. In Kodi, these stories are usually called *ngara kedoko lodo*, "narratives with songs", since they combine interludes of realistic narrative and dialogue with sung sections in ritual verse. The stories may also, and typically do, contain orations — spoken passages in ritual verse which may be prayers to ancestors, laments, funeral dirges or various other reflections on the hero's trials and travails. Since the stories generally concern orphans who triumph over adversity, they are also called *ngara kedoko ana milya ana lalo*, "orphan stories", and usually bear the name of the orphan concerned as their title. (Since his father's death, Yoseph Malo could accurately be described as an *ana milya*, "a child who has lost one parent", although not fully an orphan — but his separation from his mother by slavery certainly made the connection almost complete.) The stories cannot be told just anywhere: the best place to tell them is in the lineage house in the ancestral village, at night, on an important ceremonial occasion. It is necessary to kill a chicken first and ask the permission of the ancestor who "gave the story" to share it with outsiders.

I was told this story by Maru Daku, a famous Kodi storyteller who also worked with Yoseph Malo on a number of occasions as a spokesperson, a go-between for marriage negotiations, and a confidant. Malo specifically told his story to Maru Daku because he "wanted him to remember it and tell it again", since he knew Maru Daku had an extremely impressive memory and the ability to narrate these kinds of stories in a mixture of ordinary language and ritual verse. Malo also told his story to Hermanus Rangga Horo, the Raja of Kodi, in the hopes that he "would make it into a book". Apparently, there was once a manuscript that Horo prepared — which was not quite a "book", but perhaps 12 to 15 pages long — but it "disappeared". (It was once consulted by Cornelius Djakababa, Malo's son, but apparently now it cannot be found.)

Thus, two of my interlocutors were in a sense "authorised" to tell this tale, and (since both had worked with earlier ethnographers F.A.E. Van Wouden and Rodney Needham in the 1950s), it was perhaps not inconceivable that they would pass it on to a foreign scholar — although neither of these ethnographers seems have met Malo before his death in 1960.

My first reference to Malo in print was in my 1984 dissertation, where I referred to his narrative as an "incredible rags to riches story", which demonstrated how important personal achievements (both military and oratorical) were in Sumba of the early twentieth century. I also noted that his account could almost be compared to the "Horatio Alger" story genre in American culture, where a young hero strives against adversity to achieve fame and fortune.

This remark, however, was what prompted Cornelius Djakababa to write to the Chair of the Harvard Anthropology Department that I had "attacked his family honour" and should not have received my degree. This letter, received by my advisor in 1986 and forwarded to me, seemed to have been a response to looking at a copy of the dissertation which I left in the home of H.R. Horo when I visited the island in 1985. Once I received it, I wrote directly to Mr. Djakababa, telling him I had the utmost respect for his father, and had collected about 60 pages of materials about him and his life. In 1987, I sent a full transcript of the material, in Kodi and in English, as well as copies of a number of articles about "Horatio Alger stories" as positive models for achievement.

Mr. Djakababa wrote back that he was happy to see that I had recorded so much about his father, and added that he himself wanted at some time to write a fuller account of his father's life. He invited me and my husband to visit him at his home in Jakarta the next time we were in Indonesia in 1988. At that visit, which was very pleasant, we also talked more about his father's life and his relations with both Maru Daku (who had died in 1982) and H.R. Horo (who died in 1986), and whom Djakababa called "mother's brother", since his mother's family was from Kodi Bangedo.

Six months after my return, Djakababa sent me an 80-page manuscript, in English, Kodi and the language of Rara, which dealt with his father's life. He incorporated much of my account verbatim, but took the speeches, which had originally been delivered in the languages of Rara or Weyewa, and translated them back into these languages from the Kodi in which the story had been narrated to me. He also added material concerning Yoseph Malo's different wives, explaining that he was raised primarily by a Weyewa wife; his own mother was from Kodi, but she was often absent, travelling with his father. He also added material on what happened after his grandfather's head was recovered, and the roles he had played in the Dutch administration, during the time of Japanese occupation, and in the newly-independent Indonesian state.

How should the story begin? Maru Daku's account began with a boy named Bili who was abducted from his village shortly after his father was beheaded. My 1989 article began with the same events, set into their historical context:

> At the end of the nineteenth century, the eastern Indonesian island of Sumba was torn by warfare, headhunting and slave raids. Hundreds or even thousands of Sumbanese were captured and sold overseas, and others were brought back as captives or killed in ritual vengeance (Needham 1983). Among those who perished in such raids was Rato Umbu Malo Rangga, an important nobleman from the traditional domain of Rara. He was travelling from his home in the highlands of the interior down to the coast where he hoped to sell ten of his slaves. His party was ambushed sometime around 1888 by a band of mounted warriors from the neighboring region of Kodi. His head was cut off, and his body left by the roadside, where local people who recognised him prepared a simple earthen burial. The head was carried, along with the captured slaves, in a triumphant procession back to the ancestral village of Ratenngaro, where it was greeted with a victorious celebration of singing, dancing, and sharp, ululating battle cries....
>
> For some 50 years, the head would remain as a trophy of war, displayed in the House of Silver Heads (*Uma Kataku Amaho*) and remembered by its proud owners as the head of an important man.[1] When Dutch colonial forces gained control of the island 30 years later, they prohibited warfare, headhunting and the slave trade, ushering in a new era of exchange, alliance, and trade between former enemies. One of the most prominent figures of this new age was Yoseph Malo, Rato Malo's son, who had been sold into slavery after his father's death but later rose to become a traditional ruler and official of the Dutch colonial administration. As his own career flourished, he remembered the early sorrow and humiliation of his father's death and his own sale into slavery, so he decided to recover his father's head and rebury it in a splendid stone tomb where all passers-by could gaze on a monument to the restoration of his family honor. To do so, he began an elaborate series of negotiations with the House of Silver Heads. The head had to be redefined from its former status as a trophy into a new one as an exchange valuable, and Yoseph Malo chose to do so by proposing a marriage alliance to his former enemies. Earlier exchange values of fierceness, warfare and vengeance

were transformed into modern ones of rivalrous diplomacy, feasting and alliance (Hoskins 1989: 419–20).

This passage also recurs in Djakababa's manuscript, referred to on p. iv of the Introduction and p. 12 of the main text, but it comes only after a Preface, a Foreword, and an Introduction to the subject and its value to family memory. The Preface begins with a mixture of the personal and the historical:

> The story of Yoseph Malo's life has impressed many people through the years.
>
> His extraordinary accomplishments and the anecdotes about his wisdom and diplomacy have made him a mythological figure of his time (1888–1961) throughout the western part of Sumba. Yoseph Malo did not put his biography in writing. He, instead, left the colorful characters of his life story in the monuments and villages that he built, in his verses and ritual speeches, and in the often retold stories of his life, that he handed down to the generations after him. This book is primarily a family record for Yoseph Malo's descendants to know, for example, that the magnificent megalithic tombstone by the road in Rara is not just like any others, and that Yoseph Malo is an extraordinary person with an extraordinary life story.... Some of my earliest memories were listening to my father ... repeatedly telling the stories of his earlier life. Even to this day some people are still telling the stories about Yoseph Malo, one of the last old time Rajas of Sumba (Djakababa 2002: iii).

The Foreword, later dropped from the published book, took a more distant view, contextualising the events of Yoseph's life in relation to the phenomenon of kidnappings:

> Kidnappings are nothing new in history. They have been big business for generations. It seems that each generation and each century had its most notorious kidnappings, starting with Richard the Lion-Heart in 1192–94 when he was offered to England for ransom by Emperor Leopold of Austria.... Of the past centuries, the nineteenth century seems to stand out as a century full of kidnappings, as it was in that century that the slavery business boomed in most parts of the world. The slave trade was a big business in Africa, America, Europe and also in Asia. This book is a biography of Yoseph Malo of Sumba island in Indonesia, who, although he was born into an important family, suffered and was sold as a slave, and forced to achieve prominence on his own, through a demonstration of the qualities of wisdom and diplomacy. "It presents an extraordinary documentation not only of

the life of an unusual and admirable man but also of a whole period in Sumbanese history" (Dr Janet A. Hoskins 1987).

The final line from me came from a letter I wrote him about my interest in his father. A few paragraphs later, he also quotes another line ("Yoseph Malo's life story, through the comparison with upward mobility, could be compared to that of Horatio Alger, who wrote stories of people who rose to riches and power".). He notes that his own book is a "testimony of the human struggle out of adversity ... and of God's love for Yoseph Malo ... who was called to the Catholic faith through a strange and extraordinary way ... slavery" (Djakababa 2000: iv, these lines occur in the published Preface, 2002: iii).

The early pages of Djakababa's book concern the history of Sumba, its population, and the founding of the ancestral villages of Rara, which establish Rato Malo's genealogy and his links to important ancestors. He then details how the boy Bili was kidnapped by Dairo Bobo and Dangga Kedu and sold to the domain of Laura, near the slave port. The details he provides reflect his hearing of the story directly from his father: "After tying his hands together with a rope, the kidnappers put a gag on Bili's mouth with piece of cloth to prevent him from crying out for help. Dragged away from his native village and from all his loved ones at the end of a rope, Bili's world was a very lonely and tearful world...." (Djakababa 2002: 14).

The 1889 Blessing: Language, Memory and Oral Tradition

The aspect of Yoseph Malo's life which is most similar to the night-long epics told in Sumbanese ancestral houses is his encounter with Sairo Luku, a prominent elder and ritual speaker in Elopada, the domain of Sumba known as Weyewa (and studied by Joel Kuipers 1990, 1999). In the "triumphant orphan stories", the hero (sometimes accompanied by his sister) survives the death of both parents, and is then left all alone to fend for himself. He is punished for a perceived misdeed (winning at tops, apparently stealing something, etc.) by being tied under the floorboards of the house, and sings a long lament to the spirits of his dead parents which is often overheard by an important person or a spiritual protector, who eventually comes to his aid.

In the story of Yoseph Malo, as narrated by Maru Daku and later endorsed by Djakababa, the events recounted closely parallel this sequence. The boy known then as Bili was brought to Sairo Luku's house with his hands bound in front of him and a gag on his mouth. He was then tied to the edge of the house, below the floorboards, shivering in the rain. Sario Luku is reported to have asked "Where did you get this boy? By his look, this boy is not a commoner" (Djakababa 2002: 16; Maru Daku 1980: 3). He then asked the boy the names of his father and mother, and — to check his story — the names of the father's father and mother's father. Sario Luku knew the boy's grandparents well, and he told the kidnappers "Aaa … you have committed a grave mistake in kidnapping this boy." He then took off his own headcloth, unwrapped it, and placed it on the boy's head to bless him. He then recited the following words, which begin as a blessing and end as a curse [recorded in Kodi by Maru Daku (1980), and translated into Rara by Djakababa (1986 and 2002: 17–21)]:

Lalu, ba anamu ba ana takka	Son, if your father is really the son of
Ndona Rato Umbu Kyaleka	The great Umbu Kyaleka
Manno ba innamy ba ana takka	And if your mother is really the daughter of
Ndona Kalenga Lelu Pyero la	The great Kalenga Lelu Pyero
Ka a konggola kunggu wango loko la	Let them bring you back from the flooding rivers
Ka a awleka kunggu mbonu nale la	Let them lift you out of the waves of the rainy season
Ka a pendende bali kunggu	Let them stand you again in the
Ne'e pandouna pakoda kere buku	Home of the elegant ram with snail shell horns
Ka a pamandi'i bali kunggu	Let them seat you once more in the
Ne'e pandouna tambola wua kapaka	Home of the round banyan seed
Nggai kaundende kuwu	So you will stand again at
Ne'e pandouna we ngiundu ngora tana	The home of the outreaching cape of the land
Kau mandi'i bali kuwu	So you will sit once again at
Ne'e pandouna papo ndara lewa	The home of the round cheeked horses of Lewa
Ka a pandende bali kunggu	Standing you once again at the
Ne'e pandouna wulu walio mandeta	Home of the high plumed rooster feathers

Monno ka a pandi'i bali kunggu	Standing once again at the
Ne'e pandouna padi mette katowa	Home of the black horse hair headdresses
Kau mandi'i bali kungguu	Standing once again back at the
Ne'e pandende konda la	Place where the nobles stand
kau pandi'i bali kuwu	Sitting once again back at the
Ne'e pamandi'i rato	Place where the great men sit
Nggailka ba nana inna monno ba ana ama takka duwala	So that if you are really a child of the mother and father you say
Kau deke walkona ngara mandeta	Then may you also achieve a name as noble as theirs!
Takka, ba inda umbu konanaggu	But if you are not really a grandson of
Rato Umbu Kyaleka	Rato Umbu Kyaleka
Manno ba inda umbu konanggu	And if you are not really the grandson
Kalengga Lelu Pyero la	of Kalengga Lelu Pyero la
Ka ettikunggu netti a tundu loko lera	Then you must walk along the river banks
Ka etikunggu netti a manena oro mara	Then you must follow the shifting tides
Ka etikunggu a lenda lara	You must fly from one owner to the other
Ka etitikunggu a samasa enggu	You must be sold continuously on and on
ka etikunggu a bekka watu batu	You must split pebbles from fallen stones
ka ettikunggu a dela domba tana	You must wander aimlessly in the dust
Ka ettikunggu a pangga nda ndoli	You must wander off with no resting
Manno ka ettikunggu a kako nda ndukka	And you must walk on with no stopping
Neti kamba la	Take this cloth here
Kana patondo kunggu urra	Let it shield you from the rain
kana panguimndi kunggu loddo	Let it protect you from the sun

Nggai ka inda patomdo	So you will not be struck by the ends
waikanaa uppu urra nale	of the rains of the wet season
Ka inda palodi waikana	So you will not be burned by the
lombo loddo poddu	edge of the last sun of the dry season
Saluri tipu urra walkona la	Let this be your shield from the rain
Kada ngindi loddo walkona la	Let this be your shelter from the sun

According to the beliefs of the *marapu* religion, speaking these words should place the power of the ancestral spirits (*marapu*) behind them. On hearing their names mentioned, the spirits of the boy's grandmother and grandfather would come to watch over him and assist him to regain his earlier position. If, however, he had invoked their names in vain and was not their descendant, they would come to punish him for this infraction by condemning him to perpetual slavery. Djakababa's manuscript speculates directly on the causality involved:

No one ever predicted, nor suspected then, that anything good would come out of this tragedy. But as the events of Bili's life would show, from the very beginning he was actually treading on an extraordinary life path that would eventually lead him to his destiny.... Was it his powerful ancestors answering Inna Koni's (his mother's) tearful prayers or was it Rato Malo's way of rescuing his son? Was it the power of Sario Luku's words or was it the lord's angel who led little Bili's every step all the way to Pakamandara (the location of a Catholic mission) and a new beginning? (Djakababa 2002: 21–2)

He here juxtaposes traditional and Christian interpretations of the same events — prayers to ancestors and the actions of angels — only to conclude, personally, that the Roman Catholic interpretation must prevail:

As one would proceed reading the episodes of Bili's life in this book, one may very well reach the conclusion that Bili's life must be guided by the combination of all those factors, as indeed they all sprang from the very same source.... The Divine Providence (Djakababa 2002: 22).

Here a story which took place in two worlds, one ruled by ancestral spirits and another by Catholic saints and angels, is brought into balance by his own weighting of the evidence in favour of Christian values.

How realistic is it to assume that these words were recalled perfectly by young Bili from the time he heard them in 1888, to the time he told the story again to Maru Daku and Raja Horo in the 1940s? It is interesting that this question was not seen as problematic by Sumbanese audiences who listened to this account. After all, these words had been preserved in *panggecango*, "paired speech" a special form of speaking in couplets used to preserve authoritative texts in what Western scholars like to call the "oral tradition". Using devices of repetition and recall that have been with us since the time of the Homeric epics [cf. A.B. Lord's *Singer of Tales* (1961)], these performers spoke with ease, fluency and traditional authority. [For a more formal account of Kodi ritual verse, see Hoskins (1988), and related regional studies by Kuipers (1990) and Keane (1997).] The formulaic character of many of the couplets would no doubt contribute to their exact recall (as it also contributes to the ethnographer's ability to recognise and transcribe them — and to Djakababa's ability to translate them from a text in one Sumbanese language into another).

In Sumbanese belief, verses of ritual language should be unchanging and authoritative, so I heard famous speeches quoted to me from periods as distant as 1913 (the first Dutch conquest of the island), while ancestral narratives allegedly quote speeches made in a period represented as "the dawn of time" (Kodi: *e nawu*, which is a bit like our "once upon a time", but is granted more historical veracity in local terms — even if it occasionally refers to a period when animals could speak as people do, before human mortality was definitive, and when cultural institutions were just taking shape).

The ritual verse passages of the story were an important part of the performance of the story by Yoseph Malo to his contemporaries, who reported that he would sometimes also sing and accompany himself with the one-stringed fiddle during these passages. While they are certainly standardised, it is significant that since these passages are seen as occurring in the "unchanging words of the ancestors", they were perceived by local interpreters as the most reliable sections of the narrative — the "proof" of its veracity. To a western readership, they may appear as rhetorical elaborations, but to a Sumbanese audience they are the evidence that these encounters really happened.

These exchanges originally took place in the late nineteenth century in remote parts of Sumba, and they were never recorded, although some were witnessed by many people. Sario Luku's blessing was heard only by Yoseph Malo, since it was whispered under the floorboards of his ancestral house in Elopada. Although there were no witnesses for that event, Malo remembered it so vividly that in the 1930s he returned to Elopada, with a ritual cortège of more than 50 people, to present Luku's descendants with two bulls, a riding horse and two colourful textile banners. He was greeted by men from all the surrounding villages singing and shouting, and women ululating as the drums and gongs were beaten. He then recited a prayer of thanks, witnessed by hundreds of people, to the listening spirit of the man who had blessed him and enabled him to return to his rightful place as an aristocrat (Djakababa 2000: 83). This is the text of that prayer which Djakababa included in his first (1986) version of his father's life, and also the published one (2002: 120–1), a text not included in Maru Daku's 1980 version:

Anguleba, hetti pa panau kimungga wainangge	Cousin, following your words spoken so many years ago
Ka ku dikki bana tana	I have reached my birthplace
Ku toma bana wanno	I have returned to my home village
A waleka bangga loko	Brought back by the flooding rivers
A konggola bangga bonnu nale	Lifted out by the great waves of the rainy seasons
A pandende bali bangga nee pandouna pakode kere bokku	They made me stand again at the home of the elegant ram with snail shell horns
A pamandi'i bali bangga nee pandouna tambola wua kapaka	They seated me again at the home of the round banyan seed
Ku ndende bali ba nee pandouna we ngyundu ngora tana	I stand again at the outreaching cape of the land
Ku mandi'i bali ba nee pandouna ndara lewa	I sit high again at the home of the round cheeked horses of Lewa
Ku ndende bali ba nee pandouna wullu wailo mandeta	I stand again among the high plumes of the tall rooster feathers
Ku mandi' bali ba nee pandouna padi mette katowa	I sit again at the home of the black horse-hair headdress
Ku ndende bali ba nee pandende konda	I stand again in a noble stance
Ku mandi'i bali a nee pamandi'i rato	And sit again in a lordly seat

Eia' kini Iama a magholo	It is Father, the Creator who
bana milla kingga ate	showed me a loving heart
Eia' kini Myori a marawi	It is the Lord, the provider who
darra kingga koko	showered me with a merciful
	throat

The effect of this prayer of thanks was to provide a sense of closure for Yoseph Malo, since he had finally fulfilled the prophecy of Sario Luku. The effect on his listeners was to use a commemorative celebration to both fix the memory of his enslavement and re-inscribe it in a triumphant narrative of accomplishment. As Djakababa's text describes it:

> Yoseph Malo's sentimental trip to Elopada, as reigning Raja and Chief, plus the return of his father's complete remains to Rara in fitting rituals and ceremonies, had finally completed the reverse cycle in the destiny of Yoseph Malo's family, from helplessness and humiliation, into triumphant return to honor and fame. In all of these, Yoseph Malo felt that God's guiding hand and divine providence played a major role (2002:122).

For a Western audience, it is somewhat astonishing that Yoseph Malo should have displayed such extraordinary gratitude for a gesture which — in a purely practical sense — did not actually free him from slavery or assist him in any perceptible way. The combined blessing and curse could only be called a form of psychological (or, in *marapu* terms, spiritual) assistance, from someone who recognised his noble origins. The prayer begins with a kin term that signals a genealogical connection that apparently neither Sario Luku nor Yoseph Malo were aware of in the nineteenth century. Djakababa provides this footnote:

> The extended family ... of Rato Malo Umbu Rangga was scattered after his tragic death. It was for this reason that Yoseph Malo, in his early years in power, traced his family lineage to reaffirm the position of his family in society. It was then discovered that Sario Luku was actually a distant cousin or *anguleba* of Yoseph Malo (Djakababa 2002: 120).

I should add my own historical footnote to this explanation, since it was a clearly defined policy of the Dutch colonial government to rule indirectly through the local nobility. In places like West Sumba, where there had been no centralised indigenous state, it was often hard to define exactly who the members of the nobility were. So all the

Dutch-appointed rulers were instructed to trace their own genealogies to verify their claims to power, and define their relations with other noble families. Maru Daku was, in effect, "hired" by both H.R. Horo and Yoseph Malo to help them to trace these genealogies, and this was one of the functions that he served during the colonial period (see Hoskins 1998: 25–58 for an account of Maru Daku's life, and 1998: 82–113 for the life of H.R. Horo and the colonial creation of kingship). It was Maru Daku who discovered that Horo and Malo were linked by alliance, and that Horo was the "mother's brother" or wife-giver of Yoseph Malo because his village was related to the one where Rato Malo's skull was once stored.[2]

Finding kinship and alliance ties to noble families in other domains was, of course, also an important part of the political strategy of colonial administrators, and from this perspective Yoseph Malo's commemoration of his blessing as a slave could be motivated also by other, more Machiavellian, expediencies, but he remembered it and recited it to his son as the culmination of a series of events which finally relieved him of the burden of humiliation and sorrow which he had suffered since his boyhood trauma.

In terms of the "politics of memory", it was this performance of thanks, staged in the 1930s, which was widely remembered by people throughout West Sumba, and which helped to fix these events in their minds. The date of this commemorative visit is not given, but it is said to have preceded the conception and birth of Cornelius Djakababa, whose birth certificate states that he came into the world in December 1935. In Sumbanese belief, a family is unable to produce descendants for as long as violent deaths have not been avenged and the ancestral spirits have not been placated. Although Yoseph Malo and a companion took a head in revenge in the last years of the nineteenth century (Djakababa 2002: 35–6), this was apparently not sufficient. He had to also recover his father's head from the village of Ratenggaro in Kodi by marrying two women from that village and requesting the head as part of the marriage counterpayment from the bride's family (see Djakababa 2002: 94–104; Hoskins 1989: 419–40).[3] Yoseph Malo married a total of eight women, from many of the surrounding domains; however, until he was past fifty he had many daughters, but all of his sons died in infancy. In local interpretations, he had to rebury his father in a splendid tomb and declare his thanks to Sario Luku as his spiritual benefactor before he was finally rewarded with a surviving male descendant and heir.

Problems of Interpretation: Controversies Over Events and Their Meanings

After receiving the package of materials which Djakababa sent me, I drafted what became Hoskins (1989) and sent it to him. There were several points where our accounts differed. In this article, I referred to Malo's being "bought" as a slave by the German Jesuit missionaries in Laura. Djakababa had noted that his father told him he became a Catholic "even before the Dutch came" — which is true — but for this reason Djakababa described the earliest Catholics as Portuguese, since the Portuguese did come to eastern Indonesia in the sixteenth and seventeenth centuries, and converted a certain number of people on the neighbouring islands of Flores and Timor. There was no Portuguese mission ever established on Sumba, however, and the official history of the Catholic Church on the island confirms that these particular people were German Jesuits. In this case, I corrected him, and he later confirmed this with Catholic Church records in Waitabula.

There was some controversy about how he was "bought" by the Jesuits. One local story that I heard in Kodi and in the town of Waitabula said he was exchanged for a corrugated iron roof (Ind.: *dibeli dengan harga seng*), while another says he was sold to a woman who was related to him, though she did not reveal this relationship to his kidnappers (specifically, she was said to be his father's sister or *kiyo*) , and she gave him to the Mission so that he could get an education (Maru Daku 1980: 3). In his written version of his father's life, Djakababa says that Maru Daku's version is closer to the truth. While he does not give the name of the nobleman (or woman) who bought Bili from his kidnappers, he says:

> The family who had bought Bili had come to like him and, likewise, Bili had become attached to them. It took numerous visits and much persuasion from Fr. Schweitz before Bili's owner finally agreed to free Bili and allowed him to go with the priest to the mission station in Pakamandara. There was, therefore, no truth in the story that Bili was sold to the mission with the price of corrugated iron strips for roofing (*seng*). Years later he related to this writer and to Martinus Maru Mahemba that he was simply freed through the intercession of a Catholic missionary, Fr. Bernardus Schweitz SJ (Djakababa 2002: 24).

It is interesting that Djakababa here reiterates the position of the German missionaries that they themselves did not participate in the slave trade by either buying or selling slaves, although it was the perception of the local people of Laura that they did so. People in Waitabula said that after Bili was transferred, the house of Rato Umbu Kondi (who owned the land where the Catholic Mission was built) was recovered with new metal roofing — which they believed to be payment for the boy slave. In any case, all parties agree that after he was "freed", Bili continued to tend sheep and goats for the Catholic priests, just as he had done for his previous masters.

Bili was given religious instruction by Fr. Schweitz along with several other boys. On 29 March 1891, at the estimated age of ten, Bili was baptised and become a Catholic: "Recognising a parallel to the Biblical story of Jacob's son the boy Joseph, who was sold as a slave to Egypt, the Jesuit priest baptised Bili with the Catholic name of Joseph" (Djakababa 2000: 24). Just a few days later, Yoseph Malo (using an Indonesian spelling of his name) became one of the first seven students in the first school on Sumba; five of the seven students were the sons of the Raja of Laura, while two others were described by the Mission historian as slaves from the mountain who were already freed. "They were not slaves from birth, but they were once kidnapped from their families and made slaves" (Haripranata 1984: 131). It is worth noting here that the German Jesuit fathers (and their Javanese SVD historian) thought it important to note the distinction that Sumbanese make between people who are born slaves (*ata pa helu*, "slaves by heritage") and those who were captured and sold (*ata pa kahi*, "bought slaves"). The implication of these added words of explanation is that they would not have considered people born to slavery as worthy of instruction, but they did not feel the same way about the young victims of tribal wars and feuds who happened to find themselves in that situation.

Yoseph Malo and his companions also received lessons in writing and mathematics from Renier Theedens, a Catholic teacher of mixed blood (he had a Dutch father and an Indonesian mother from the neighboring island of Roti). After two years, Yoseph Malo (who was reported by his son to have been "a very bright and intelligent student") was kicked out of the school because he was "naughty and mischievous". He became a full-time shepherd for the mission, but reportedly still listened to the lessons from the back porch. "When the teacher wrote on the blackboard and the students wrote on their papers or *batu tulis* (slates), Yoseph would write on the ground in front of him. That was how it went day after day, while at the same time he kept an eye on the grazing sheep nearby" (Djakababa 2002: 27). In this way, he supposedly completed all four grades with the other pupils, "although the teacher never suspected it". (This account is verbatim from Maru Daku's text, confirmed as corresponding to Djakababa's memory of his father's words.)

In my 1989 article, I wrote that when Yoseph's brothers heard he was at the Mission, "he asked permission of the priests to return home and was granted it" (1989: 421). I based my interpretation on the fact that the German Jesuits had written about the deplorable state of slavery on Sumba, and had condemned it in the strongest terms as inhuman and barbaric. Since they had already baptised Yoseph in 1891, it seemed they would no longer consider him a slave.

Other versions I heard on the island, however, were not that he was freed by his masters, since no real notion of manumission existed [see my discussion of Sumbanese slavery in Hoskins (2004)]. Instead, some family members said that he ransomed himself, buying his own freedom by putting his younger brother in his place. Djakababa offers a somewhat different explanation, writing that he received his freedom after exchanging his dog Fidel (this name must have been suggested by the Jesuit missionaries!) and a shirt for a slave boy named Kalowo ("banana") whom Yoseph called Gabriel ("bearer of good tidings"). The boy remained with the Mission, was baptised and later moved to Timor, where he remained a lifetime servant of the Catholic Church. One of Yoseph's younger brothers, Lede, also came to the mission and was baptised Adrianus. Adrianus later received a mission education and became a convert to the Catholic Church.

Traditional members of the Kodi family said Yoseph's freedom was exchanged for the slave and his younger brother. The more progressive interpretation (in Djakababa's 2002 manuscript) was that the two decided to stay there of their own free will, but leaving them in the care of the Jesuits was a way "to show his gratitude to the mission for all the kindness and good things he received, particularly his freedom from slavery, his education and his new faith...." (2002: 31). The Jesuits, however, did not stay long, since their homes were repeatedly burned and their horses stolen. Very few adults were baptised, and as soon as boys reached adolescence they were taken back by their families, leaving no mature converts to build the Catholic community. In 1898, the mission in Laura was disbanded and all the German Jesuit priests left the island. The Church was not to return for over 30 years (Haripranata

1984: 172–3). When it finally did so, it was because the Netherlands Indies government became sympathetic to the plea that many early converts (like Yoseph Malo) has "slipped back into paganism" without the guidance of local Catholic priests. Malo himself remained a lifelong friend of the Church, but had already married eight wives by the time new missionaries from the Societas Verbi Divini arrived.

The arguments about whether Malo was "freed" or ransomed by the Church (or was ever bought at all) remain, even though his son's account should now probably be taken as definitive. These discussions make clear, however, that there can be significant cultural differences in notions of "slavery" and "freedom". Notions of obligation and reciprocity also complicate this account, since if the Jesuit Mission was seen as assuming the role of a foster parent rather than a slave-master, then some compensatory gift at the time of departure would certainly have been appropriate in terms of local categories. The form that Djakababa's present text assumes has been "revised" in relation to my own earlier misunderstanding, and in some ways this interpretative difference remains a tension.

Local Historiography and Our Own

The problem of what language the events "happened" in and how accurately they can actually be recalled is related to the overall problem of "proof". Sumbanese are very interested in establishing the veracity of the narratives they recite, and they turn to material objects as their archive of the past, the "proof" (Ind.: *bukti*, rendered in Kodi as the "traces of the hands, traces of the feet" — *oro limya, oro witti* — which trace the trail back to the original source).

Djakababa, in trying to research his father's story, examined the Church records in Waitabula, the current seat of the Sumbanese Catholic Mission, and read the history of the mission on the island published in Indonesian by Haripranata, a Javanese priest. He also mobilised family networks to seek out and find Gabriel Kalowo, the slave boy his father bought and left behind to take his place at the Catholic Mission. He interviewed members of his own family in Kodi, Rara and Weyewa, including several older slave women who had helped raise him when he was a boy and who knew his father well. I also met several of these people in the summer of 2000 when I visited Puu Karudi, his ancestral village, and I conducted new interviews with his Kodi family members, especially Ngila Wora, the oldest member of the wife-giving group from Ratenggaro and the elder representative of Djakababa's mother's family.

I, in contrast, had access to libraries with some of the writings of the German Jesuits, and articles like Rodney Needham's "Sumba and the Slave Trade" (1983). This adopts a very pro-Dutch position that colonial conquest was a liberation from the "scourge of slavery" perpetrated by Makassarese-Endenese pirates. By contrast, Anthony Reid's comparative study, *Slavery, Bondage and Dependency in Southeast Asia* (1983) is written with a certain sympathy for the slave traders, and presents the view that slavery in the region was a somewhat softer, gentler form of debt bondage.

"Proof" in Kodi terms corresponds to having a direct line to the source, preferably a direct line of descent or, failing that, at least an "authorisation to retell". While Western scholars might argue that descendants may tend toward hagiography, that they may be biased because their own status is at stake in any biographical investigation, to local commentators it is not possible to be "too close" to the material. Comparative material may be interesting, but is basically beside the point, since the concern is not so much with a pattern or a system of relationships as it is with an original "point of truth". The greatest veracity is accorded to the storyteller who demonstrates both a blood tie and a number of significant objects — heirloom valuables, a stone tomb, cloth and personal possessions — which tie him to the biographical subject.

"Proof" for my profession involves convincing a community of scholars, who will expect a certain distance from the subject, objectivity (which does not preclude empathy and even transference, cf. Frank's idea of the "biography in the shadow" 1979), a search for archival evidence, and carefully recording the trail of evidence, inference and interpretation.

Cultural differences about how to preserve and commemorate the past may influence this process, but it would also probably be accurate to explain the distinctions between Djakababa's account and my own with the labels of "social memory" and "history". Larson's (2000: 39–40) effort to present a case for integrating studies of memory with history (rather than opposing them) is relevant here:

> An interest in social memory — defined as the way in which a community understands its history or, more precisely, conceptualizes

its experience through a variety of means including narrative, ritual, dance, customs, bodily practices, and other forms of socially meaningful action — requires scholars temporarily to set aside their own historical memories with all their professional techniques and hypotheses. In particular, understanding social memory requires modifying the idea that something verifiable and recoverable happened in the past that can be reconstructed if only factually accurate contemporary accounts can be located in the archives or extracted from "oral traditions" through proper historical procedure, processing, and analysis. Social memory emphasises "the conceptualisation of experience", human agency, and political (rather than technical) processes in the shaping of meaningful knowledge of the past.

Larson contrasts the goals of constructing a history of events (which he associates with *logos* and professional historians) with the goal of constructing a history of interpretations (which he associates with *mythos* and social memory). He criticises earlier generations of scholars for valuing the written words of European visitors more highly than the spoken words of local actors, noting that local narratives are "stories with their own histories whose evidence often lies subtly embedded in language, genre, emphasis, and historically developed silences" (2000: 280).

Working with the versions of Yoseph Malo's life which were performed for me by Maru Daku, then recreated on the page by H.R. Horo and Djakababa, I am dealing with several layers of memory — what Larson (2000: 40) refers to as a "laminate", a mixture of knowledge and understanding derived from experience and present interests. In this case, we are not dealing with myths about long passed times, but the life of an individual who had an important impact on Sumbanese history, who exemplified a heroic archetype and actively promoted himself as following in the footsteps of the heroes of traditional epics. Few if any of his contemporaries are alive today, but in the late 1970s and early 1980s there were still many people who remembered him vividly.

Social memory and family records are oriented not only toward preserving the past but also moving into the future. Here the question of religious affiliation and conversion surfaces again in an interesting way: at the end of his account of his father's life, Djakababa notes that after Yoseph Malo's death "he was given a Catholic burial and laid to rest in a room within the tomb of his (previously deceased) wives" (2002: 173). A year later, his youngest widow Dita Horo requested to

All photos reproduced from the Djakababa family album, with kind permission of Nelden Djakababa.

1956 photograph of Yoseph Malo taken on the occasion of a feast to celebrate his son's graduation from high school.

RAJA YOSEPH MALO
OF SUMBA

Cornelius Malo Djakababa
Introduction by DR. Janet A. Hoskins

Cover of Djakababa's book about his father (with an image adapted from a painting based on the 1956 photograph).

Painting of Yoseph Malo with his wife when they married in the presence of their grandchildren (also made on the basis of the 1956 photo)

A display of family regalia (and the painting) at Malo's reburial.

The Malo family gathering in Sumba.

The Djakababa
family gathering
at the reburial.

Calling Malo's
soul back with
oratory.

Beating the drums to summon Malo's soul.

Mass held at Yoseph Malo's reburial.

The tomb of Yoseph Malo in 2000.

be baptised as well, "to be on the same 'side' in faith with her husband and with her only son" (2002: 174). Djakababa then speaks in his own voice to express a certain ambivalence about conversions motivated more by a desire to have a close companion in the afterlife "rather than by conviction to the truth of the Catholic teachings". He adds: "In more recent years there have been more people in Puu Karudi who requested to be baptised Catholics, only hours before their deaths, just to be sure they will be in the same place with me in the other life. This certainly is quite a moral burden on my part personally as I prefer that each person should die in their life-long faith and worship, be it Marapu or Catholicism or others" (2002: 174). The book closes with this reluctance to embrace the idea of "conversion to modernity" in a community whose values were rooted in respect for the past.

Djakababa does not go on to tell his readers that he then arranged to rebury both his father and mother in separate, "modern" tombs decorated with crosses and inscriptions. When I visited Puu Karudi with him in 2000, we videotaped his visit to their graves, and I (along with my sister and daughters) paid our respects to the soul of this man we had never met, but learned so much about. Djakababa's goals in publishing his own version of his father's life are to present a text which will preserve his legacy for a different audience than simply those who may wander past his tomb: "It is to immortalise the memory of Yoseph Malo that for many years I had planned to write his biography" (2000: ii). The tomb was erected as the "most enduring and impressive symbol of family importance and renown for the Sumbanese" (Djakababa 1988: 53), but the book is intended to reach a wider, international audience, including scholars as well as family members.

Dialogic Methods and Hybrid Texts: How is a Life Story Told? And is This Different from the Way it is Written?

A number of recent writers have argued that life histories "are frequently offered as self-evident 'cultural documents' rather than as texts to be interrogated and interpreted" (Young 1983: 480). Gelya Frank has pointed out that the text is of course not identical to the person, but a version of the self constructed to present to the anthropologist. Autobiographical texts may appear "to offer a truer experience of the subject's life, a direct outpouring of consciousness, but here too certain conventions are invoked to structure the narrative" (Frank 1979: 83).

These conventions stem both from native traditions of storytelling and from the unique context of the conversation with an anthropologist. In order to read and write life histories in more imaginative and theoretically rich ways, we need to denaturalise the link between text and person. As Ruth Behar (1995: 152) has put it:

> Reading a life history text, and then writing it, calls for an interpretation of cultural themes as they are creatively constructed by the actor within a particular configuration of social forces and gender and class contexts; and, at the same time, a closer analysis of the making of the life history narrative as a narrative, using critical forms of textual analysis and self-reflexive (rather than self-ingratiating) meditation on the relationship between the storyteller and the anthropologist.

Yoseph Malo was not, of course, "the story teller" of his own life story in my case since I never had the chance to meet him during his lifetime. His style of self-narration was, however, imitated by Maru Daku, my first major source of his own life materials. And it was his presentation of oral materials which was remembered and recorded by H.R. Horo and, later, Cornelius Djakababa. The book published in January 2002 is a hybrid made up of the translated transcript of the narrative performance that I recorded from Maru Daku, texts prepared by myself, H.R. Horo and Djakababa, interviews with others who knew him, and library research by both myself and Mr. Djakababa. Readers' interpretations, too, will almost certainly vary, given the differing expectations that one might have of a scholarly article vs. a biography of a father written by his own son.

Since our initial contacts had been by mail, and our discussion at his home in Jakarta in 1986 was more of a friendly meeting than a formal interview, I had asked Mr. Djakababa in the summer of 2000 if he would be willing to allow me to videotape his telling the story of his father's life. I wanted to see what differences the oral format would produce, even after he had been working on a written version. With the assistance of my sister, Susan Hoskins, we taped a two-hour oral version of the same narrative — told in English, in the open "living room" of the Newa Sumba resort. In this narrative, Djakababa did insert certain details which are perhaps more likely to emerge in story telling than in written composition. The most striking of these was his description of his father's emotional reaction to taking a human head — feeling the hair slip from his hands because they were covered with blood, forcing himself to retrieve it and carry it back as a trophy. This level of subjectivity — and emotion — had been missing from the written accounts, which were matter-of-fact about the event. They did not betray the levels of subjectivity that a father might show in telling this story to his son, if perhaps not to a wider audience.

So the relation between the stylised oral narrative — the one that was in exactly the format of the "narratives with songs" (*ngara kedoko lodo*) — the still relatively formal interview, and the written text is interesting. Of course, since our respective written texts were exchanged over the mails and served to construct one another, they could also be said to be "in dialogue" in a certain way.

Maru Daku's text, recited to me and recorded in my home in 1980, was probably closest to the performance of his own life that Yoseph Malo was said to have done. It had the format of a traditional epic, was composed of narrated events alternating with songs, and does not include any of the trappings of written texts (footnotes, references, etc.). Mr Djakababa's book is a hybrid. It combines stories he presumably heard at his father's knee (and witnessed performed for others) with references to the texts I collected, quotes from published accounts (including my own and those of historians of the Catholic Mission), and personal asides and interpretations. Unlike Maru Daku's account, which stressed Yoseph Malo as a bard and traditional leader, his son treats him as an innovator and a good friend of the Catholic Church — even if a somewhat errant convert.

So my work is made up of a compendium of materials, some structured by the particular requirement of oral recitation (use of special speech forms and ritual verse) which are culturally valued and viewed as "unchanging" and "authoritative", others structured by the scholar's concerns to footnote, cite published references, and seek independent confirmation of facts.

Yoseph Malo now has one grandson (his namesake, Yoseph Djakababa) who is a doctoral student in History at the University of Wisconsin, Madison, and a granddaughter, Marion Broder, who is married to a finance executive in Whippany, New Jersey. In 2001, his first great-grandson, William Broder, was born into an American Jewish family but (on the insistence of his mother's family) baptised as a Catholic. His third grandchild, Nelden Djakababa, studied anthropology and psychology in Belgium, and completed a master's thesis in 2002 which analyses these issues from the perspective of her own generation. To do so, she interviewed her siblings by email, and quotes from both her brother and sister for the title: "My Grandfather was a Headhunter, and Wow, It is Cool!: The Present Telling and Reliving of a Sumbanese Family Narrative". For his grandchildren now living in the United States, the story of Yoseph Malo's life is valued because it is "different", it shows "perseverance", and evokes an exotic past that intrigues others. Marian speculates about what her own son might say about his family:

> I can see already that when William grows up and goes to school, he'll tell the story to his friends in "show and tell". He'll probably bring a *parang* [machete] to school ... maybe that's not a very good idea, he might get arrested. Anyway, it's going to be a great story to tell (Nelden Djakababa 2002: 52).

Nelden's thesis explores the intersubjectivity of the different stories in great detail, and also includes a personal experience which inspired her to continue this retelling:

> One night, I dreamed that Inna Horo came to me. She is my biological grandmother, the eighth wife of Yoseph Malo.... I saw my grandmother appearing in a manner similar with an old photograph of hers, a copy of which I have. But unlike the figure in the picture, she was smiling. She pressed her forehead with her right palm, and then she pressed the same hand onto my forehead. Many older relatives in Puukarudi have commented that my forehead is similar with that of my grandmother's. After doing that, she held my right hand in hers, and suddenly a pen appeared in my hand. She gently pushed my hand with the pen forward.... I have chosen a meaning to attach to that vivid dream. It is a simple realisation that I am part of a line of storytellers, in a universe of stories full of storytellers called humankind. In the dream, my grandmother urged my writing hand forward. I think it means that writing this thesis is my way of interrupting the ongoing story, to examine and negotiate it, before releasing it back into the flow of telling and re-telling (Nelden Djakababa 2002: 56).

Yoseph Malo's story is almost too rich for any single mode of interpretation and analysis. It is a narrative of enslavement, in the sense which Larson (2000) has developed in his treatment of similar stories from different parts of Africa. It is also the story of a colonial encounter, and the contrast between European missionaries and administrators and their local counterparts, in a sense similar to Vinson Sutlive's study of Tun Jugah (and especially his predecessor Temenggong Koh) of Sarawak (Sutlive 1992) — also someone who was both a headhunter and a colonial administrator of sorts. And it is an important story to the Catholic Mission in Indonesia, one beginning with the Jesuit Society and ending with the Societas Verbi Divini (whose headquarters are in Germany).

But it is also part of family memory and family tradition in a way that is different from the role that it can play in anthropological articles and books. When I sent the text of my 1989 article to Cornelius Malo Djakababa for his comments, he wrote to me that the facts were roughly consistent with what he knew from his father, but added: "It is strange to see my father's life used to prove or disprove anthropological theories" (personal communication, 1989). This is, as I see it, the crux of the dilemma: an audience of scholars, interested in cross-cultural comparison, will always have a different orientation from an audience of descendants, trying to cultivate their own legacy. This is true not only because descendants may have a tendency to exalt their forefathers (perhaps especially in societies which have a tradition of ancestor worship in some form or other), but also because their ties to a grandfather are subjective rather than objective, and full of affect rather than simply curiosity. The story of Yoseph Malo's sufferings and humiliations when he was captured as a slave is a personal story to them, one which I can experience only through a certain empathy and identification, but never in exactly the same sense that it is experienced by family members.

There is no easy solution that I can propose for this conundrum. I suggest, instead, that we simply remain aware of it, and be prepared to deal with it as anthropologists in the modern world are increasingly involved in the study of people who will be able to read and critique these studies themselves, and who want to speak on their own behalf, not through some scholar-ventriloquist. Many years ago, at about the same time that Yoseph Malo was taken captive, Karl Marx wrote with a European's casual arrogance, that "Some people cannot represent themselves. They can only be represented." This was the presumption of anthropology for many years: that it was our task to represent the illiterate, the marginalised, the "native" whose "point of view" could not be otherwise presented to a wider audience. That position is no longer tenable, and a new dialogue format has become essential to all our scholarship and historical research. This paper has tried to tell the story of one particular form that this dialogue could take, as a tacking back and forth between professional history and social memory, documented events and imagined subjectivities, and the many complex forms of responsibility which then come to entangle us within this dialogue.

Notes

1. Each lineage is associated with a named ancestral house. The House of Silver Heads was such a house, where human skulls were stored as valuables, including one said to be made out of (or perhaps decorated with) silver. The house still stands, though it no longer contains human heads today; they are said to have been hidden away in a secret place long ago. In the past, heads were sometimes buried under the house pillars. I photographed some examples in another village in 1980.

2. Maru Daku discovered that the two families were not simply related because Raja Horo was from Rangga Baki and Yoseph Malo married two women from the related village of Ratenngaro (one of them being Dita Horo, the mother of Cornelius Malo Djakababa), but also because each of them had his father killed by someone from the famous headhunting village of Ratenngaro. Raja Horo's father was killed in a feud which flared up when he was young boy, but his father was not beheaded because the two villages had many marriage ties and were part of the same language group and ritual domain (Kodi Bangedo). Yoseph Malo's father, Rato Malo Umbu Rangga, had his head removed and the skull was stored in the Uma Kakaku Amaho ("House of the Silver Heads") until the 1920s and 1930s, when he negotiated for its release as part of the counterpayment presented along with his Kodi brides. This family history indicates that "marrying into the family of one's father's murderers" was in fact not such an unusual practice in the Sumba of a little over one hundred years ago.

3. It would not have been necessary to marry two separate women from Ratenggaro in order to recover the head, since the skull was transferred as part of the counterpayment for the first wife. She, however, was said to have believed that Yoseph Malo never loved her, and married her only to recover his father's skull. The choice of her as a bride may also have been motivated by her own family's desire to marry her off quickly to someone from outside the area, since she was epileptic. Signs of mental instability were clear from an early age, and she eventually went mad and returned to her own natal village without bearing any children. Dita Horo, the eighth wife and Djakababa's mother, was also from Ratenggaro, and the marriage to her renewed the alliance on peaceful terms.

References

Versions of Yoseph Malo's Life

Maru Daku. 1980. "Ngara Kedokona a Toko Rara" ("The Epic of the Raja of Rara"). Tape recorded in Kodi in 1980.

Horo, Hermanus Rangga. 1981. "Kehidupan Raja Rara" ("The Life of the Raja of Rara"). Tape recorded in Indonesian in 1981. (There is also a misplaced written version of this story, which was consulted by Cornelius Djakababa at one point.)

Hoskins, Janet. 1984. "Spirit Worship and Feasting in Kodi, West Sumba: Paths to Riches and Renown". PhD Thesis, Harvard University.

———. 1989. "On Losing and Getting A Head: Warfare, Exchange and Alliance in a Changing Sumba 1888–1988", *American Ethnologist* 16(3): 419–40.

———. 1996a. "The Heritage of Headhunting: Ritual, Ideology and History on Sumba 1890–1990", in *Headhunting and the Social Imagination in Southeast Asia*, ed. J. Hoskins. Stanford: Stanford University Press, pp. 216–48.

———. 1996b. "Introduction: Headhunting as Practice and as Trope", in *Headhunting and the Social Imagination in Southeast Asia*, ed. J. Hoskins. Stanford: Stanford University Press, pp. 1–50.

———. 2002. "Predatory Voyeurs: Tourists and 'Tribal Violence' in Remote Indonesia", *American Ethnologist* 29/4: 797–828.

———. 2004. "Slaves, Brides and Other 'Gifts': Resistance, Marriage and Rank in Eastern Indonesia", *Slavery and Abolition* 25, no. 2 (August): 1–18.

Djakababa, Cornelius Malo. 1986. "The Life of Yoseph Malo by his Son". Typescript sent to the author.

———. 2000. *Life and Saga of Raja Yoseph Malo of Sumba*. Manuscript prepared for publication, and presented to the author when she visited the Djakabakas on Sumba.

———. 2002. *The Life of Raja Yoseph Malo of Sumba*. Jakarta: Atlanewa Publications (published in both English and Indonesian).

Djakababa, Nelden. 2002. "My Grandfather was a Headhunter, and Wow, It is Cool!: The Present Telling and Reliving of a Sumbanese Family Narrative". Masters Thesis presented to the Department of Social and Cultural Anthropology, Catholic University of Leuven.

Scholarly Bibliography

Abu-Lughod, Lila. 1991. "Writing Against Culture", in *Recapturing Anthropology*, ed. Richard Fox. Santa Fe, New Mexico: School of American Research Press.

———. 1993. *Writing Women's Worlds: Bedouin Stories*. Berkeley: University of California Press.

Behar, Ruth. 1993. *Translated Woman; Crossing the Border with Esperanza's Story*. Boston: Beacon Press.

————. 1995. "Rage and Redemption: Reading the Life Story of a Mexican Marketing Woman", in *The Dialogic Emergence of Culture*, ed. Bruce Mannheim and Dennis Tedlock. Urbana: University of Illinois Press.

Dubois, Cora. 1940. *The People of Alor*. Cambridge: Harvard University Press.

Frank, Gelya. 1979. "Finding the Common Denominator: A Phenomenological Critique of Life History Method", *Ethos* 7/1: 68–94.

————. 1985. "Becoming the Other: Empathy and Biographical Interpretation", *Biography* 8: 189–210.

————. 1995. "Anthropology and Individual Lives: The Story of the Life History and the History of the Life Story", *American Anthropologist* 97: 145–8.

————. 2000. *Venus on Wheels: Two Decades of Dialogue on Disability, Feminism and Cultural Biography*. Berkeley: University of California Press.

Gullestad, Marianne. 1995. "Why Study Autobiographies?" in *Everyday Life Philosophers: Modernity, Morality and Autobiography in Norway*. Oslo: Scandinavian University Press.

Haripranata, H.S.J. 1984. *Ceritera Sejarah Gereja Katolik Sumba dan Sumbawa*. Ende, Flores: Percetakan Offset Arnoldus.

Hoskins, Janet. 1985. "A Life History From Both Sides: The Changing Poetics of Personal Experience", *Journal of Anthropological Research* 41/2: 147–69.

————. 1986. "So My Name Shall Live: Stone Dragging and Grave-Building in Kodi, West Sumba", *Bijdragen tot de Taal-, Land-, en Volkenkunde*, 142: 31–51.

————. 1987. "The Headhunter as Hero: Local Traditions and Their Reinterpretation in National History", *American Ethnologist* 14/4: 605–22.

————. 1993. *The Play of Time: Kodi Perspectives on Calendars, Exchange and History*. Berkeley: University of California Press.

————. 1998a. "The Stony Faces of Death: Funerals and Politics in East and West Sumba", in *Messages in Stone: Statues and Sculptures from Tribal Indonesia*, ed. J.-P. Barbier. Geneva: Tribal Art Publications, Musée Barbier-Mueller and Skira Editore, Milan, pp. 167–99.

————. 1998b. *Biographical Objects: How Things Tell the Story of People's Lives*. New York: Routledge.

Keane, Webb. 1997. *Signs of Recognition: Powers and Hazards of Representation in an Indonesian Society*. Berkeley: University of California Press.

Kuipers, Joel. 1990. *Power in Performance: The Creation of Textual Authority in Weyewa Ritual Speech*. Philadelphia: University of Pennsylvania Press.

Langness, L.L. and Gelya Frank. 1981. *Lives: An Anthropological Approach to Biography*. Novato: Chandler and Sharpe.

Larson, Pier M. 2000. *History and memory in the age of enslavement: becoming Merina in highland Madagascar, 1770–1822.* Portsmouth, NH: Heinemann.

Linde, Charlotte. 1993. "What is a Life Story?" in her *Life Stories: The Creation of Coherence.* Oxford: Oxford University Press.

Lord, Alfred Bates. 1961. *The Singer of Tales: Homeric Epics as Oral Performances.* Cambridge: Harvard University Press.

Malinowski, Bronislaw. 1925. *Magic, Science and Religion and Other Essays.* New York: Doubleday.

Morin, Violette. 1969. "L'Objet biographique", *Communications* 13: 131–9. Ecole Pratique des Hautes Etudes, Centre d'Etudes des Communications de Masse.

Needham, Rodney. 1983. *Sumba and the Slave Trade.* Centre of Southeast Asian Studies, Monash University. Working Paper 31. Clayton, Victoria: Monash University.

Olney, James. 1972. "A Theory of Autobiography", in *Metaphors of the Self: The Meaning of Autobiography.* Princeton: Princeton University Press.

Postel-Coster, Els. 1977. "The Indonesian Novel as a Source of Anthropological Data", in *Text and Context: The Social Anthropology of Tradition*, ed. Ravindra Jain. Philadelphia: Institute for the Study of Human Issues.

Radin, Paul. 1926. *Crashing Thunder: The Autobiography of an American Indian.* New York: Appleton.

Reid, Anthony, ed. 1983. *Slavery, Bondage and Dependency in Southeast Asia.* St. Lucia: University of Queensland Press.

Rodgers, Susan. 1994. *Telling Lives, Telling History: Autobiography and Historical Imagination in Modern Indonesia.* Berkeley: University of California Press.

Rosaldo, Renato. 1976. "The Story of Tukbaw: 'They Listen as He Orates'", in *The Biographical Process: Studies in the History and Psychology of Religion*, ed. F. Reynolds and D. Capps. The Hague: Mouton.

Rosenwald, George and Ochberg, Richard. 1990. "Introduction: Life Stories, Cultural Politics and Self-Understanding", in *Their Storied Lives: The Cultural Politics of Self-Understanding.* New Haven: Yale University Press.

Sutlive, Vinson. 1992. *Tun Jugah of Sarawak: Colonialism and Iban Response.* Kuala Lumpur: Penerbit Fajar Bakti Sdn. Bhd.

Young, Michael W. 1983. "Our Name is Women: We Are Bought with Limesticks and Limepots: An Analysis of the Autobiographical Narrative of a Kalauna Woman", *Man* 18: 478–501.

4
A Toraja Pilgrimage:
The Life of Fritz Basiang

Roxana Waterson

Introduction: Forms of Autobiographical Narrative

As the "accelerated history" of the twentieth century has drawn to a close, we are in the special position of being able to look back on it and attempt to discern its patterns. Individuals who were born at the start of the century, and lived through all or most of it, have lived extraordinary lives which have been profoundly altered by unprecedented social transformations. My interest in presenting the following life history stems from this conviction: from the desire to record something of the life of a remarkable person; from a continuing fascination with the way his life embodied certain historical transformations; and not least as a debt which I have long owed to his family, who have their own concerns that his life should be remembered. The historian John Smail (1961), in an influential essay, proposed the need for an "autonomous domestic history" of Indonesia, one which would seek to avoid past errors of Eurocentrism, or of history written from the perspective of the winners only; his argument has of late received revived attention (Sears 1993). Life history research constitutes one potentially rich resource for contributing, in however small a way, to such a continuing project.

Jerome Bruner (1987: 31) has argued that "a life as led is inseparable from a life as told", and that the ability to tell it transcends cultural boundaries. "While the act of *writing* autobiography is new under the sun — like writing itself — the self-told life narrative is, by all accounts, ancient and universal. People anywhere can tell you some intelligible account of their lives. What varies is the cultural and linguistic perspective or narrative *form* in which it is formulated and expressed" (1987: 16). Any culture, he proposes, has its "tool kit" of narrative forms and heroes from which its members can build their own life stories. While this is doubtless true, his point about writing misses the fact that autobiography as a genre is by no means as old as writing itself, and in fact is more closely related to the history of publishing. Other ethnographers dispute the easy translatability of the genre: Birgitt Röttger-Rössler (1993) found difficulty in collecting autobiographical accounts from her Makassar informants in South Sulawesi, and concluded that notions of "public" and "private" identities in this society simply differed too greatly for informants to fulfil her original expectations (based on Western literary standards) that "an" autobiography would be primarily an account of an individual's inner life. On the other hand, she found that she had "accidentally" collected a wide range of biographical accounts instead, and that individuals did in fact recount a number of narratives about their own lives, which, although they defied her expectations, could be regarded as "a kind of autobiographical narrating" (1993: 372). These typically were event- or action-centred, and had to do with the public persona, as formulated in connection with ideas about *siri'* (honour, self-respect), and not with any confessional account of the individual's inner life or emotions. In fact informants were actively resistant to providing any narrative of the latter type, and clearly found her efforts to elicit them embarrassing. She suggests we should bear in mind that, outside of the Western context, autobiographical documents "constitute a narrative genre that has come into being only fairly recently through the collaboration of ethnographers and native informants" (1993: 367). Quite possibly, the fact that Fritz Basiang was so readily able to tell me his life story in linear fashion, and that he chose to describe it as a journey, already has much to do with his acculturation, his projection of himself into the wider world of the colonial Dutch East Indies and beyond. He was a modernist, embracing much that he saw as new and progressive, although he maintained an enduring if selective attachment to what he saw as valuable in his own culture.

Life histories are always the product of collaborations (Mischler 1986; Borland 1991; Behar 1992; Echevarria-Howe 1995). Caplan (1997: 22), presenting the personal narratives (both oral and written) which she gathered from her long acquaintance with "Mohammed", a Tanzanian, comments on the many possible ways in which the anthropologist may choose to execute the task of editing such texts — which is generally unavoidable in order to make them intelligible to a wider audience. She speaks of her eventual decision to write "a seamed narrative in which the ethnographer sews the seams and is seen to do so, but in which the people who are its sources — their voices and the occasions on which they speak — are made explicit". Life histories are also always in some sense unfinished products; Langness and Frank (1981) speak of the inescapable incompleteness of lives, as well as the impossibility of any final interpretation.

I started fieldwork in Tana Toraja, in the highlands of South Sulawesi, in 1978. During my time there, I came to know Fritz Basiang and his family more and more closely. In 1983, when he was 78 years old, I recorded several long conversations with him, in which he reminisced about his life, as well as providing an illuminating discourse on Toraja kinship principles and other cultural matters. I do not know whether he may have had his own reasons for deciding to talk to me about his life, beyond his courteous willingness to oblige me in my request. Given my inexperience, I inevitably found there were many more questions that I later wished I had asked him. He made his own selection too of what he wanted to include in his story. He chose to dwell on the historical events he had lived through, while remaining reticent about personal and family life. This might have been because of assumptions about what a life story should contain, or because he assumed that was what I preferred to hear about, or simply because he was more comfortable talking about those things; perhaps all of these. I was not to return to Tana Toraja for a number of years, and when I was finally able to do so, he had already passed away. I am keenly aware, therefore, that my account is in many ways inadequate and partial. As my interest in Fritz continued to deepen, however, his family helped to supply me with more information. In 1994, his son Daniel (Danny) spent considerable time with me going over the tapes (copies of which had by now become a valued memento for him also) and filling in details of explanation.[1] On a return visit in 1996, Danny for the first time produced the family photo album, which added a further dimension to the story and from which come the photos published here. On this and my next visit, in 1999, I sought out people who had known or worked with Fritz and gathered further recollections about him.

Shortly after this, Danny's elder brother Martin sent me a collection of hand-written notes which Fritz had made, mostly in the latter years of his life, which yielded still further details of reminiscence about the past. However imperfect, then, I hope that this account will convey something of a life which dramatically and adventurously crossed the boundaries between cultures, making a significant contribution to a newly emergent vision of what it might mean to be both Toraja, and Indonesian, in the twentieth century.

Life as Pilgrimage

Those who have reached old age in Tana Toraja now — or who were already old at the time I started my fieldwork, and have now passed away — belong to a special generation, the generation whose own lifetimes have encompassed all the remarkable and rapid changes that have taken place in Toraja society this century. They experienced all the transformations effected since the coming of the Dutch in 1905, the introduction of a colonial administration with its schools, its Christian Missions, its taxes and corvée labour, through the hardships of the Japanese Occupation, to the emergence of Indonesia as an independent nation, the troubles of the 1950s, up until the present, with the economic developments of the New Order, and the advent of tourism. Finally, before the century's end, 1998 brought still more dramatic transformations with the abrupt closure of the Suharto era and the manifold uncertainties about what was to follow on the road to Reform. In their own lifetimes, this generation have been witness to the corresponding transformation of world view that has accompanied the progressive shifts in perspective which these changes have brought about, as Toraja became aware of themselves as part of the greater entity of "Indonesia". This was the first generation to whom the possibility of a European education presented itself, and as a result of this, some were to embark on journeys that would take them far beyond the horizons of village communities that were the known world of their parents and grandparents.

Anderson has called these journeys "pilgrimages", particularly those that were part of an educational trajectory in the colonies. Only a few individuals had this opportunity, for educational channels were severely restricted in most colonies; the Netherlands East Indies were no exception in this regard. As Anderson points out, these institutions were organised in a tight hierarchy, whose geographical distribution led from village primary school, to local town middle schools, to tertiary institutions in a provincial city or, for a handful, to Batavia. A very few individuals might progress from here to the ultimate apices of the system, the metropolitan cities of Europe, before they found their path blocked to a permanent career either in Europe or in any other colonial territory. Then the loop of their journey would return them to their own colony. The experience of a newly "imagined reality" grew out of these journeys, and the lessons learned along the way, so that they played, Anderson (1983: 111) suggests, a crucial role in the emergence of nationalist identities and aspirations:

> From all over the vast colony, but from nowhere outside it, the tender pilgrims made their inward, upward way, meeting fellow-pilgrims from different, perhaps once hostile, villages in primary school; from different ethnolinguistic groups in middle-school; and from every part of the realm in the tertiary institutions of the capital. And they knew that from wherever they had come they still had read the same books and done the same sums. They also knew, even if they never got so far — and most did not — that Rome was Batavia, and that all these journeying derived their "sense" from the capital, in effect explaining why "we" are "here" "together". To put it another way, their common experience, and the amiably competitive comradeship of the classroom, gave the maps of the colony which they studied (always coloured differently from British Malaya or the American Philippines) a territorially-specific imagined reality which was every day confirmed by the accents and physiognomies of their classmates.

As the geographical extent of the colonial state, and its specialised functions, expanded, so too did the needs of the administration for trained, bilingual clerks and functionaries; educational provision enlarged accordingly in the early decades of the twentieth century (in Tana Toraja as elsewhere in the Netherlands Indies), so that "with every enlargement of the state, the swarm of its inner pilgrims swelled" (Anderson 1983: 106). In spite of the expansion of elementary education, however, the top of the educational pyramid remained so narrow that only a tiny fraction of students qualified for university education. High school standards were very high (comparable to the Netherlands) and costs were prohibitive for most Indonesians.[2] Even in the face of these restrictions, by the 1920s, Dutch-educated graduates were beginning to outnumber the positions available in government service or the "Western" sector of the economy, giving rise to the formation of an "intellectual proletariat"

(Veur 1969: 9). Van Neil (1960) provides a most illuminating analysis of educational developments in the period up to 1927; it was among this newly-educated minority that a nationalist consciousness was first to develop.

Fritz Basiang was a remarkable individual who exemplifies precisely the kind of educational pilgrim Anderson describes. Born in the very year the Dutch entered the Toraja highlands, the span of his long life (1905–93) encompasses the Toraja encounter with modernity. Being among the first Toraja to attend a Dutch school, he was also an early convert to Christianity. He was one of the first Toraja to travel to Europe, doubtless the first ever to visit Germany. Originally trained as a paramedic, he gained so much practical experience in medicine that he came effectively to work as a doctor, at a time when the number of doctors per head of population in Tana Toraja was tiny. In this role he performed outstanding service to his own people for many decades and was a well-loved and much respected figure in the community. Given the framework I have chosen for this account, the focus will be chiefly on the early decades of his life, though the later ones were by no means uneventful. In the first part of his story, we see him grasping every opportunity to change the course of his personal life; by contrast, the momentous historical events of his middle years, such as the Japanese Occupation and the subsequent struggle for Independence, acted upon him as upon others, leaving less room for manoeuvre as many people found themselves concerned chiefly to survive as best they could. When recalling his early life, he spoke in Toraja, slipping more and more into Indonesian once his account progressed to the point at which he had first left Toraja in pursuit of higher education.

Fritz's life in this sense may be compared with that of other Indonesians of his generation who have published memoirs of their lives or childhood. Indonesians have developed their own traditions of autobiography, and there are several well-known examples that deal with this period, not only by politicians or those who have had prominent public careers, but also by literary figures.[3] Two Sumatran examples, by Pospos (1950) and Radjab (1950), have recently been made accessible in English translation by Rodgers (1995); others include Nur Sutan Iskandar (1948) and Hamka (1951–52). It is perhaps significant that, with the exception of the latter, all of these are exclusively about childhood. Within them, the educational trajectory is a dominant theme, and they stop at the point where the author leaves his home region to pursue his education further afield. Rodgers notes how inextricably the personal is woven with historical events in these narratives. Published immediately before or after the achievement of Independence, the authors in effect look back as Indonesians, from the vantage-point of the newly-won Republic of Indonesia, to the world of a village childhood encapsulated within a local ethnic identity and culture. The newly-constructed modern self at the same time looks back, with a mixture of criticism and nostalgia, at a "traditional" world that has been irrevocably left behind with childhood. Ruslan Abdulgani's "My Childhood World", translated into English by Frederick (1974), presents a vivid picture of the more ethnically heterogeneous world of a Surabaya neighbourhood of the 1910s–30s, with many astute insights into the prevailing world view of its residents, including their ways of classifying the variety of non-Javanese (not yet perceived as fellow "Indonesians") with whom they had contact. He recalls his dawning awareness of the idea of "Indonesia" in the late 1920s, as nationalist movements began to gather momentum and the ideas of Dr Soetomo and Sukarno began to have an effect in the *kampung*. A few first signs of modernity could be seen in the children's enthusiasm for soccer, and the presence in his neighbourhood of a Sumatran doctor, who was "the sole representative of the world of Western science in the area" (Frederick 1974: 134). The neighbours were terrified of this doctor, and exchanged hair-raising stories about his supposed methods. He also remembers his mother supportively buying salt from poor coastal women, who made it illegally in defiance of the government salt monopoly. After hearing of Gandhi's historic march to the sea to make salt in breach of colonial monopoly in India, she tore his picture out of a magazine and pasted it on the wall, next to a picture of Sultan Abdulhamid of Turkey, who, she told him, had helped the Acehnese in their war against the Dutch. Dr Abdulgani's recollections may be regarded as of interest partly because he himself went on to have such a distinguished career, holding many important positions in the government of an independent Indonesia. But the narratives of those who are not famous can be of equal sociological and historical interest. A rare example is the unpublished life story of a young Javanese man, Soejtipto, written in 1928 and analysed by Kratz (1978). Starting from a difficult and unhappy childhood, the author tells of his efforts to develop his own philosophy of life, in a manner which in some respects is typically Javanese, in others distinctively modern in its confessional content, realism and directness of style, and colloquial use of language. In this instance, we know nothing at all about what happened to Soetjipto in later life; yet his account remains as an intriguing example of a newly emergent form of personal narrative.

Of particular interest in relation to Fritz Basiang's life story are the published memoirs of several contemporaries who were doctors. Earliest of these is the memoir of Dr Soetomo himself, who according to Anderson (1990: 245) was "the first prominent Indonesian to write something like an autobiography". This work, published in 1934, deals solely with the author's childhood. Oddly, it stops before giving any account of his years of political activity. Anderson points out the strange shape of this memoir, which radically departs from Western expectations of an "autobiography", arguing that it is nonetheless exemplary in its display of certain peculiarly Javanese concerns. He proposes that a major concern is the author's search for a new way to live without abandoning Javaneseness: "Being a good Javanese by becoming a good Indonesian" (Anderson 1990: 262). Already here, personal identity and social transformation predominate as themes. A second example is the autobiography of Dr Soemarno Sosroatmadjo (1981). Born in 1911, he grew up in East Java, where his father, like Dr Soetomo, was an administrative official. With this relatively privileged background, he was one of the few to receive Dutch-language education, which qualified him for entry to NIAS (*Nederlansch-Indische Artsenschool*, Netherlands Indies Medical School) in Surabaya, from which he graduated in 1938. Posted to a remote part of East Kalimantan, he delivered health care to the local Dayaks, journeying largely by canoe to upriver villages. He went on to achieve high rank in the Indonesian army, and served as Governor of Jakarta under Sukarno. Most recently, the autobiography of Dr A.A.M. Djelantik (1997), a son of the Balinese Raja of Karangasem (b.1919), vividly describes yet again that inexorable educational progression which carried the author, first, from the palace in which he grew up to the H.I.S. (*Hollandsch-Inlandsche School*, Dutch Indonesian Primary School) in Denpasar; next, to Java to attend the M.U.L.O. (*Meer Uitgebreid Lager Onderwijs*, "More Comprehensive Elementary Education", a lower secondary school) in Malang, and A.M.S. (*Algemeene Middelbare School*, a higher secondary school) in Yogyakarta, where students were lodged with Dutch families to encourage more thorough absorption of Dutch culture and manners; and eventually to study medicine in Holland. Here he survived the war years and the German Occupation partly in hiding, with the help of Dutch friends.

Djelantik was keen to serve in remote areas on his return to Indonesia, and together with his wife, a Dutch nurse, encountered a variety of dangers and adventures in Buru, Sumbawa, and North Sulawesi, before returning to work in Bali where he became Chief Medical Officer, later working overseas for some years as a malariologist for the World Health Organisation. These published works are obviously more substantial than the account I am presenting here. All of the above individuals came from more privileged backgrounds than Fritz Basiang, and have had more distinguished and high-profile careers. Their access to a more complete education in the Dutch language made it possible for them to qualify as doctors, an opportunity which was denied to Fritz. But in spite of these differences, their accounts provide many interesting parallels in experience. Like Fritz, they all lived through the Dutch colonial system and the passage toward a modern Indonesian identity. The training as a doctor in itself must have ensured a radical change in world view, providing a thorough indoctrination into scientific rationalism and a humanist philosophy. All chose to practise their medical skills where they were desperately needed, in areas where at that time the health service was in its infancy and conditions were often primitive. And for all of them this progression was also a political one, in which each came to share the vision of an independent Indonesia, and used their skills to contribute in the most practical way possible to improving life for ordinary people.[4]

A Village Childhood

Basiang (his original name), was born in 1905 at Maroson in Banga, in the westerly Toraja district of Saluputti. He was the second child of Ne' Pilo and his second wife, Lai' Kanan. He had three elder half-sisters from his father's first marriage, and had an elder brother Palino' and three sisters from his father's second marriage. Ne' Pilo was a local aristocrat with a considerable reputation for courage and fairness in dealing with the Bugis who at that time had settled in considerable numbers in Banga and other regions around the market centre of Rembon. In the late nineteenth century, the Bugis from Sidenreng, in the west, attempted to wrest control of the Toraja coffee trade away from Luwu', to the east, and when coffee prices fluctuated, found it profitable to trade in slaves as well. This trade was greatly intensified by the advent of modern firearms, which they offered in exchange. A

number of Toraja headmen, being eager to obtain the new rifles for
the pursuit of their own ambitions, colluded with Bugis mercenaries
in raiding remoter districts for slaves, causing severe depopulation in
the more vulnerable areas.[5] It was a time of chaos, and Saluputti was
one of the regions most severely affected.

Ne' Pilo's original Toraja name was Titting, the name by which his
family and fellow-villagers always called him, but later in life he liked
to keep company with the Bugis, who gave him the name La Pira or
La Piro, which local Toraja pronounced as Pilo. During the 1880s and
1890s, Pilo deftly cooperated with these Bugis infiltrators in order as best
he could to protect his community from their depredations, exercising
his influence to save many people (particularly, it is said, those of noble
families) from being sold into slavery. As a result of these interventions,
he could have greatly enriched himself by accepting land offered to him
by grateful people in return for his protection (as other local leaders,
greedier or less merciful, certainly did); he could have owned land all the
way from Banga to Ulusalu. Basiang recalled his father as being a man
of few words who, when he did open his mouth, always said something
worth hearing.

Basiang's earliest memories were of herding buffaloes with other
village boys, from about the age of six. The lyrical quality of these
recollections fits with a general Toraja pattern reported also by Hollan
and Wellenkamp (1996: 50–1) in the life histories they collected. Herding,
they note, "demands a great deal of initiative and independent action", and
consequent freedom, though it can be arduous to be out in all weathers
with the responsibility to keep temperamental buffaloes out of others'
rice fields and gardens; the herding period is one that "holds considerable
psychological and social significance" for many of their respondents, being
remembered as "a bittersweet time ... of relative freedom, satiation, and
rebellion". Basiang and his companions would take the buffaloes out on
the hillsides all day long, returning home in the evening. They would
whoop and call to each other, each with their own special call, to find
who else was out herding, and then they would gather for company
and work together to tend their charges. When they were hungry, they
would eat food brought from home in a woven reed bag (*kapipe*), or help
themselves to peanuts, corn or ripe bananas from a neighbour's garden
(this is considered acceptable Toraja practice, within limits — cf. Hollan
and Wellenkamp 1996: 52). Sometimes they would light a fire and steam
some food inside bamboos; sometimes they cooked buffalo milk inside a

pumpkin taken from someone's garden. They would coat the pumpkin in clay before baking it, a slow but delicious process; one had to be careful once it was cooked, in order not to break it and spill the milk. One herdboy might tend as many as ten buffaloes, some of his own family, others belonging to neighbours. In those days, he recalled, there were still "few people and plentiful resources". There was much more uncultivated land — open grassy areas rather than woodland — in this part of Toraja then than now, and it was his impression that people then had owned more buffaloes than they commonly do nowadays.[6]

He also remembered people performing corvée labour (D: *heerendienst*) for the Dutch, making roads and wooden bridges. The District Head would be in charge of organising this labour and ensuring that it was carried out until allotted tasks were completed. Under the Dutch administration, Banga formed a District and the District Head was a man called Tapparan. His first sight of a Dutchman was when his father once took him to Ma'kale (the small town founded as an administrative centre by the Dutch) on market day in order to sell some rice. He had to find a friend to tend his buffaloes that day, and felt obliged to hurry home after, for fear that the buffaloes, if unattended, might eat somebody's gardens — an early training, as he put it, in responsibility. They walked all the way there and back (about 15 km each way), attending the market which was held on a patch of open ground near the large pool built by the Dutch, which still forms the centre of the little town. There he caught sight of the Governor or *Controleur*, and was struck by the extreme whiteness of his skin. The *Controleur* had introduced orange trees (*lemo cina*) to Ma'kale, a number of which he had planted near the site of the present Catholic Church. By 1909 a school had opened in Ma'kale; it was staffed with teachers from Ambon, Timor, Manado and Sangir. The Toraja, Basiang observed, tended to act submissively toward these fellow-Indonesians employed by the Dutch, and obediently followed their orders.

"Family" for Basiang included a wide network of relatives, and like many Toraja children he spent time in more than one household while he was growing up. At one point he was fostered (*disarak*) by a friend of Ne' Pilo who lived in the same village. His job was to feed this person's dogs, but on one occasion he pulled a dog's tail while it was eating and it bit him in the face. After this, Ne' Pilo took him home again, and he went back to herding. Sometimes he also went to stay with his grandparents at Surakan for a few days, and from there, would go on to visit a first cousin of his grandparents at another village, Buttu, and go out with the buffalo herders there. Buffaloes in Toraja are very rarely used for ploughing, but hold supreme value in a prestige economy which focuses on their sacrifice in funeral rituals. Consequently, emotional attachment to a carefully-tended buffalo was liable to end painfully, though he laughed in recalling it so many years later:

> When this *nenek* ("grandparent") at Buttu died, I felt it very much, because a buffalo I had tended there was the first to be slaughtered in the *ma'palao* ritual (a stage of the funeral ceremony). My father tried to prevent me seeing it because I was so fond of that buffalo, and in those days the buffalo did not have its throat cut (*ditinggoro'*) quickly, but was hacked to pieces (*na ta'tak tau*). When I saw them doing that, I yelled at all the people and cursed them!

The wife of the deceased moved to Basiang's home village, Tapparan, from Buttu, because she was on her own and had no children, and for a time, Basiang went to live with her. Later, his father moved back to Maroson in Banga, where another elderly relative gave Basiang a puppy to raise. Basiang diligently applied himself to a training in Toraja economics: when the puppy was grown, he sold it to a man from Mamasa, and bought a pig, and when that was grown, he sold it and bought a small female buffalo calf. He raised this buffalo until it had a calf, his grandparent all the while keeping an eye on his progress.

Possibly a formative experience for the 13-year-old Basiang was the outbreak of the great influenza pandemic of 1918, which reportedly claimed the lives of ten per cent of the population in Toraja (Bigalke 1981: 254; Brown 1987).[7] The colonial government had not yet begun to introduce any modern medical services in the highlands, and had no help to offer the local population. Toraja still recall this as the time when people "were cut down like grass" (*ra'ba biang*):

> So many people were dying, you would bury someone in the morning, and there would be a new death by noon; you would bury someone at noon, and by the afternoon, there'd be another death. There was no medical service capable of reaching out to the population then; the armed forces had their doctors, but the people had no doctors yet — "natural selection" was good enough for them![8]

Later on, his medical work was to become Basiang's own contribution to his local community, as well as to the struggle for Independence.

Going to School

One day in 1921, Basiang's parents went to market in Ma'kale. Feeling the urge to follow them, he found someone willing to tend his buffalo for the day, and set out after them. Ne' Pilo had a regular arrangement to supply rice to the household of the Public Prosecutor (I: *Jaksa*), a Manadonese, in the town, and Basiang caught up with his parents there. Seeing him, the *Jaksa* inquired about him and suggested that it would be a good idea if he were to stay in Ma'kale and go to school. "I was silent, but in my heart I was very thrilled", Fritz recalled. His parents agreed, and so in that same year he started school.

Schooling at this date was open to only a tiny proportion of the population in Toraja. According to Basiang's own recollection, 12 village schools (D: *Volksschool*), with classes 1–3 only, had been opened by 1913, and 20–30 children were chosen from neighbouring aristocratic families to attend each of them.[9] But many noble parents were afraid to send their children; they thought the Dutch might carry them off to Holland, or send them from the highlands in military service, and some at first sent the children of their slaves as substitutes.[10] Perhaps for these reasons, Basiang had not attended either of the two village schools nearest to his home.[11] Ne' Pilo, however, knew the Prosecutor and trusted him, which was why he agreed to his proposal. Ironically, perhaps there was some intuitive truth in the parents' fear of school and its powers of acculturation; Ne' Pilo could hardly have imagined that he had just set his son on the first step of a journey that would really take him to Europe.

Basiang therefore moved to Ma'kale in 1921, where he first entered the regional elementary school (D: *Landschapschool*), graduating in 1926 to the intermediate-level *Schakelschool*.[12] Since the schools offered no accommodation for boarders, he lodged at the Prosecutor's house, where he helped out after school by looking after the household's ducks, geese and pigs, and fetching water from the well. He made himself a handy device to assist him in this daily task. It was a wooden wheel with a long handle, to which he attached a cross-bar on which he could hang an old tin can in which he carried the water. He felt proud when the Prosecutor saw him pushing it along, and admired his ingenuity. To keep the ducks and geese from straying, he built a fence around their pond. This earned him further praise, and he was entrusted with more jobs around the house. As for the school work, "Whatever I could do, I liked; I liked everything." School also included instruction in Christianity.

Basiang was given the job of ringing the bell for church on Sundays, and began to join in the services. In his written notes, he recalls:

> Headmaster Patti asked me to ring the bell on Sundays. I thought to myself that if I hit the bell with a big stone, it would be sure to make a bigger noise. I gave it two or three good blows, and on the third one, it broke. Needless to say, I got a big scolding from the Headmaster.

In this new milieu, and under the influence of his guardian, Basiang in 1923 converted to Christianity. The Prosecutor's Christian name was Fritz, and he bestowed the same name on Basiang, who began to call himself Fritz also. But he always kept his Toraja name too, which has now become the family name used by his children. In 1924, the Prosecutor's family moved away, and he then lodged in a house shared by three Manadonese schoolteachers, a foreman in charge of road-building, a clerk and a prison warder. Subsequently, they too moved, and he took up residence with the new Prosecutor, a single man from Ambon. His family would come and visit him on market days, when they brought rice and eggs to sell. Sometimes his father would give him a little spending money to purchase vegetables or onions. There was no school uniform in those days:

> You felt special already if you had a short-sleeved shirt with two buttons on it, and a pair of shorts. On Saturdays, the headmaster of the school would order those with cleaner-looking clothes to go to the office of the *Controleur* (Governor). The orange trees he had planted were already bearing fruit, and he would give us some, and praise us to encourage us in our studies.

In 1926, the Ambonese Prosecutor moved from Ma'kale to Rantepao, the other emergent town in Toraja, and so he moved with him and attended school there. This school had one class of 30 pupils from all over Toraja. There were very few possibilities for a student to further his education beyond the *Schakelschool* level, but Basiang had obviously impressed his teachers enough that they encouraged him to enter the examinations for the *Normaalschool*, a teacher training school in Makassar (the provincial capital of South Sulawesi), which at this date took only one or two pupils annually from Toraja.[13] It is 300 km from Rantepao to Makassar, and Basiang started out on the journey by walking two days through the forest to reach the coastal town of Palopo. The Prosecutor sent someone with him to carry his luggage. From Palopo they travelled by car to Makassar, through the Bugis districts of Bone and Sengkang, spending a night in each, and finally arriving shortly before midnight of the night before the exam. Tired from the journey, Basiang felt that he had performed poorly in the exam; if only he could have arrived earlier and had a few days to prepare himself, he could have stood a chance of success. A Sangirese teacher at the Rantepao school, however, encouraged him to try again the following year, so in 1927 he set out for Makassar again. By now, the friendly Ambonese Prosecutor had moved to a post in Enrekang, (the district bordering Tana Toraja to the south), so this time Basiang and one other hopeful pupil set out to walk there, and from there were driven to Makassar. This time they both passed the exams, but it was to do him no good:

> But now, because we were both from Rantepao, and I was already a year older than the other boy, they chose only the younger. So I decided my future did not lie in that direction. So I went to work. Things were not as they are now, when anyone who can pass can be accepted; the Dutch at that time kept only a tiny number of school places available. People were capable, but they weren't allowed to (I: *orang bisa, tetapi tidak boleh*).

Bitter as he understandably felt about this setback, Basiang made the best of it and applied himself in his new job, as an assistant in the *Controleur*'s office in Rantepao. He wrote letters, answered the telephone, and helped to count the silver money with which employees of the Dutch were paid. There was now a German doctor, Dr Simon, and his family, living in Rantepao. He had come out originally with the Mission, but did not get on with them and contracted to work for three years for the regional government (of *Landschap* Rantepao). He was the sole doctor in Tana Toraja at this time. And now, in a manner which was to prove so characteristic of him, Basiang saw a chance and seized upon it:

> I often went from my Office to the hospital to take Dr Simon his letters. One day when I went to the hospital, I saw many young men of my own age gathered there. I was already friendly with the Doctor, because I always brought him his letters, so I asked him: "A lot of young men are here, Doctor, the same age as me; what are they doing here?" He said, "I've chosen these young people from all the different districts, to come here so I can train them as health workers." I said, "How would it be, Doctor, if Basiang were to join you, would you

take me on too?" Ah! He was very happy! But he said, "What about
your other job? Perhaps the *Controleur* won't release you?" But there
was no problem. I told the *Controleur* that the Doctor would be glad
to take me, and that I wanted to go too.

Discovering a Medical Vocation

Fritz had now found something that truly engaged him, and he plunged
into the new work with enthusiasm:

> So I started there in 1928 ... I liked the work very much. Once
> I was registered I was allowed to help the Doctor as a travelling
> health worker (*tukang tornieur*). So I followed him whenever he went
> around Tana Toraja on horseback. Every month, he had to go on
> tour, all around the different districts.[14] If I'm not wrong, there were
> more than ten of us assistants, who all went with him. And in each
> district there was a government rest house (I: *pasanggrahan*) for us
> to stay in. He would send out word that there would be a clinic the
> next day, and everyone would come. And then he would examine
> all the patients, and give them medicine — worm medicine, and
> vaccinations against cholera, typhus and other major diseases.... There
> was already a vaccination programme against smallpox being carried
> out. In that year, of my own desire, I went continuously with the
> Doctor and worked in the hospital. But in the evenings, we'd listen
> to his stories, then when we saw him nodding off, we'd think, "Ah!
> Now it's time to sleep, we're tired." We travelled all over the place!
> For twenty days or more at a time. In one month, we'd be on tour
> more than we were in the hospital. You can imagine: we'd travel
> on horseback from here to Sangalla', the place called Batuallo. As
> far as Ulu Uai — near the mountain that's tallest over there. Then
> down to Mengkendek, to Palesan, then to Buakayu, and from there
> to Mappa', and from there to Simbuang. It takes two days if you
> travel fast, before you reach Simbuang. From there, there were still
> two more places to visit, each of which took a day to reach, then
> we'd go on to Balepe', come down towards Sasak, then Bittuang.
> We'd spend the night in Bittuang, at Alang, and go from there to
> Baruppu', then after treating people there, when the medicine was
> nearly finished, we'd send a letter ahead to Rantepao, telling them to
> send more medicine on ahead to Pangala'. So I really got to know
> the whole of Tana Toraja, and almost all the village heads (I: *kepala
> kampung*) of that era, I knew them all, and there are some who still
> remember me.

In his written notes, Fritz recalled that the most common diseases at that time included malaria, yaws, scabies, syphilis, gonorrhoea, trachoma, and intestinal worms. Dr Simon found practical opportunities to further his pupils' instruction. If a pig was killed to feed the party at one of their overnight stops, he would use the animal to teach anatomy, explaining the passage of food through the body, and showing them all the internal organs.

Fritz's schooling, incomplete as it was, had already given him a degree of advantage over the others in that he knew more Dutch. Palilu, a surviving member of the original group of trainees, who later went on to become a pastor, recalled that Dr Simon made Fritz his personal assistant for this reason.[15] As for Fritz, he was planning ahead, his ambition setting him apart from his fellows:

> So for months, almost the whole of that year, 1928, I was thinking, "This is one kind of work that is really socially useful"; and I was wondering how I could go further. The idea was for the other health workers, after they had received sufficient training, and learnt what was considered important, to go back to their village clinics and work there, but I was looking for a way to go further, beyond just training with Dr Simon. So he said, "I will give you a choice of three places: do you want to go to Weltevreden in Batavia, or to Semarang or Surabaya?" Those three places all had large hospitals, all equally good. So I said, "If it pleases you, I will go to Weltevreden." So he said, "Write a letter for yourself, saying that you would like to do this work, and I will give you a letter of introduction explaining that you are the only one from Toraja." So I was happy. The answer came back: "You may leave and start here on 1 January 1929." So I had to hurry. I went to tell my parents about it and ask their help. There was a buffalo I had tended, still there in the village. We slaughtered it and sold the meat in Ma'kale, and with the money I paid for my journey.... So when everything was ready I set off, and the Doctor took me all the way to Palopo in his car. By then there was a motor road opened all the way to Palopo and the journey took only a few hours. By chance, Dr Simon knew a Javanese man employed by the Public Works Department, so I stayed one night with his family in Palopo, then I boarded a ship from Palopo to Ujung Pandang. That took one day, and the ticket cost Rp.12½. It seems cheap now, but in those days it was a lot! There by chance there was a soldier going to Java on furlough, so I travelled together with him, as a deck passenger, on a ship to

Surabaya. In Surabaya, we disembarked, and I asked the soldier's
family to help me find a place to stay, then travelled on again. By
chance, at the hotel where I spent the night, I met a Manadonese
who worked for the Controleur here in Toraja, who had been bitten
by a mad dog. He had to go to Bandung ... because in those days
that was the only place you could get treatment for rabies. So we
travelled on again together on the train. He was allowed to travel
First Class and I was only allowed to go Third Class. But because
I was with him, I was allowed to travel First Class!

Fritz was now discovering at first hand the much larger world of
the Dutch colonial empire, making chance encounters with people from
many parts of the archipelago and enjoying many new experiences.
Those he met were also on the move because of their positions within
the colonial hierarchy, and many further lessons in inequality and
politics were to follow. Interestingly, a training in medicine seems to
have led on to radical political activity for several early nationalists
in Indonesia: Tjipto Mangunkusumo, Gunawan Mangunkusumo,
Adbul Muis, Suwardi Surjaningrat, and Dr Soetomo, had all studied
at medical schools such as the STOVIA (*School tot Opleiding van
Inlandsche Artsen*, School for Training Native Doctors), which Van
Niel (1960: 51) suggests became a leading source for members of a
new intellectual elite. It was in Batavia that Fritz first became aware
of Indonesian nationalist aspirations:

Surabaya of course was very busy, compared to anything I had yet
seen. And my mind was opened as a result. And it was the first time
I had ever been on a train — it was a steam locomotive. I parted
from the Manadonese man at the Rabies Hospital in Bandung...and
from there I went on to Weltevreden. I got off the train at the
central station (Batavia Centrum). Then I found a taxi and asked
to go to the hospital. But the taxi put me off at the wrong place,
at the Central Hospital. But the people there said never mind,
and got someone to show me the way. I was given a place in the
hostel. The next day I was shown where I was to work. There were
people from all over Indonesia there, and most of them hardly knew
where Sulawesi was, let alone Toraja. So I had to say, Makassar,
and then they would know: "Ah, Makassar, Sulawesi." When we
met, we spoke Indonesian to each other [not Dutch]. In those years
there were already signs of a desire for Independence. The *Soempah
Pemuda* had been declared, but the Dutch controlled the political

situation tightly and suppressed these organisations.[16] Really, those who became members of those organisations were followed the whole time. The people in charge of hospital organisation, all the nurses at the hospital, were all Dutch. We Indonesians had to obey them and do whatever they said, even if you were of the same rank as a Dutch nurse. Sometimes, it made us unhappy, but no matter what, you had to accept it.... It was in Java where I first became aware, "Oh, there are people who think like this, whose ideas are quite different" [i.e. Indonesian nationalists]. Among them was our own doctor. He was from Ujung Pandang, but his wife was Dutch. But he was politically active. Sometimes the atmosphere was tense … Dr Leimena[17] was at Bandung then, and there were several groups of activists in Surabaya, Bandung, and Batavia. But they were not too obvious about it; they had to work discreetly, promote their ideas from within, being careful because of their positions within the Dutch administration. But when they came home from work, then for sure, when young people came to visit them, then they would speak freely of their ideas.

Fritz's father, Ne' Pilo (standing, far left) and his father's elder brother Palino (far right), photographed some time in the 1920s. (Neither the occasion, nor the names of others in the photo, are known.)

A studio portrait of Fritz taken in Düsseldorf, 1932.

Fritz in Essen, Germany, with Dr Simon and his son, Harald (far left) and small daughter.

Marta Gora (right), pictured with a friend in Surabaya before her marriage, while she was studying midwifery at the hospital there, 1929.

Marta in European dress, Surabaya, 1929.

Fritz (fourth from left) in a group of fellow nursing students in Javanese dress, having just passed their exams, Malang, 1936.

Fritz and Marta with their first child, Ida, in Malang, 1936.

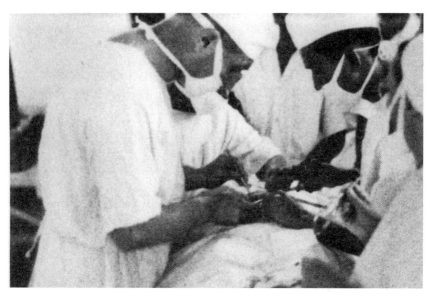

Fritz (right of centre) and Dr Goslinga (left) working in the operating theatre in Rantepao, late 1930s.

To Europe

For 18 months, Fritz worked at Weltevreden, before another turning-point presented itself to him:

> In July 1930, Dr Simon sent a letter saying: "Fritz, my contract is expiring. I must go back to Germany." I started thinking. I was still young, and hadn't yet completed my training as a nurse at the hospital; I still had a year and a half to go before I could qualify. I thought, "I am still young, I would like to go with him to Europe." So I wrote and asked him if he would agree to my accompanying his family to Europe. I said: "If you agree, please contact my parents, and if they have no objection to my going, send me some money so I can come home first for a few days. If I get the money, I'll know it means it is agreed." I received a reply that all was arranged. My heart was young and my ambition was to travel as far as I could. When the money arrived, it was only Rp.25, which was enough to take the boat from Tanjung Priok[18] to Makassar. Because in those days, to hire a car from Makassar to Rantepao cost only 1 ringgit,[19] so it was easy, even if I didn't have any money left when I got to Makassar, to pay for the ride once I got back to Rantepao. So I

went and told the director of the hospital that I wanted to go home. He was surprised. "You are the only one from Sulawesi, why are you leaving?" I told him: "I have to go home to see to some affairs, then I will come back." I didn't tell him I was going to Germany. I was afraid he wouldn't give me permission otherwise. So I left the hospital, came back to Rantepao for a few days, saw all my family, then we left right away for Europe.

For the first few months, Dr Simon remained on leave in his home town of Düsseldorf, living on his savings, for he had been highly valued by the Dutch Administration in Toraja and had been very well paid by them. Fritz was aware of this from his time of employment in the Governor's Office when he had had to count the money used for payment of salaries. It felt like a holiday to Fritz, though in the afternoons Dr Simon taught him skills, such as bandaging. The Doctor's original plan had been to work in Europe for six months before taking another contract to work in South Africa, or perhaps another African country. Fritz was prepared to follow him even there. Eventually, however, the Doctor accepted a position at Essen in a private hospital, Krankenhaus Krups. Here he also gave training to the local Red Cross, and Fritz would follow these lessons. At the same time he did his best to learn German:

> I had to learn it when I got there, because no-one else could speak my language. Only when I got back home, then I could speak to Dr Simon in Malay. But outside, I had to use German. And not only that, but all the time I was in Essen, I hardly ever saw another dark-skinned person. Only when the circus came to town, then there were all sorts of humans![20] You have to force yourself to learn because you are mixing with other people every day, and I studied hard by myself so I could talk to people. More than anything I had to learn the medical terminology, because all the books used were in German. All the surgical textbooks that I had were in German. In six or seven months I could get along; whatever someone asked, I could answer, and although I spoke haltingly they could understand me too, even if it wasn't perfect. So I was happy, doing what I was doing. But as to the future, I didn't know. Because up to that point, wherever the Doctor and his family went, there I had followed, and I always told myself, well, so long as I live, that is how it must be, and besides, I felt, I'm still young. So I said, however far this can lead me, that's how it must be.... I thought if I could get a Diploma in Nursing that was already sufficient to give me a passport to anywhere in the

world.... All I really wanted was to keep on travelling and do whatever I wanted, because it still didn't feel enough to help the people [in Toraja]. But to get into medical school would have been difficult, because for a start, you needed to have graduated from high school. Dr Simon said, "It's a pity you couldn't have finished high school." I said, "Yes, I regret it too." But still, I carried on trying to do and learn all I could, following whatever paths I could — if I could find a way, I did, and where I couldn't, I just told myself, "Well, it can't be helped".

Fritz had now reached the outer limit of his pilgrimage: his onward path was blocked by a number of obstacles. One of them was the inadequacy of the basic education he had been able to receive, even though this had already made him exceptional among colonised Indonesians. Lateral movement to a colony on another continent, following Dr Simon, presented itself as a possibility, though one which in the end was not to materialise. One senses in this account the possible conflict entailed in his relationship with Dr Simon, which had become both enabling and binding; attachment to his patron had brought him so far, yet now his fate rested upon the Doctor's own life decisions. For Fritz there was also the moral question, about how to use his knowledge to the benefit of his own people, which would predispose him ultimately to make the return journey to the point from which he had started. Retrospectively, this decision was presented to me in a somewhat simplified form, though at the time it must have entailed more confused emotions; according to his son, Fritz had formed a romantic attachment to a German nurse, and had considered the possibility of marrying her and settling in Germany, a course against which Dr Simon had expostulated since it would have defeated the aim which he also shared, that Fritz should return to where his medical knowledge could be put to the best possible use in helping his own people. Given the political situation, and the near impossibility for any foreigner to obtain German citizenship, such a course of action would have been highly problematic. For all of this was taking place in the years 1930–32, during Hitler's rise to power — years of economic collapse, mass unemployment, and mounting political violence. In 1932, the public endured an exhausting series of election campaigns, while Nazi murders of political opponents, and a wave of street battles, mostly between Communists and Nazis, claimed hundreds of lives and brought things to crisis pitch. It was this increasingly ominous

atmosphere which was in the end to prove the most conclusive factor
in deciding what to do next:

> Doctor Simon also thought the same way. And what he saw was that
> so much help was still required to meet the needs of the people. And
> that mattered to me too. So if he said, "You can stay for another year",
> I would, because I was still young and benefiting from his guidance.
> But the atmosphere in Germany was getting tense. There was going to
> be a General Election, and there were three main parties contesting it:
> the Nazis, the Communists, and the Centre.[21] This was 1932. Whoever
> won the election would become Chancellor. Things were already at
> crisis point. But the longer I stayed there, the more I said to myself:
> there may be war later on....The thing was, National Socialism was
> already strong, so sometimes, if the Communists gave their salute,
> with the clenched fist, the Nazis would start a fight. Those who were
> for or against were becoming polarised. If someone we knew gave
> the Nazi salute, we'd know they were Nazis. It was dangerous! If I
> met someone, and had to give the salute, they'd think I was a Nazi
> too! And there were many political meetings. We had to be careful
> about what might happen next. So at that time, I said to Dr Simon:
> "Really, I am not a citizen of Germany. I would follow your politics
> but..." — Dr Simon at that time was still a supporter of the centre
> party, but he was beginning to lean toward the National Socialists.
> That was already clear. But if I were to take German citizenship,
> that would mean that I must inevitably take sides too.[22] So I said:
> "If you don't mind, I will just go home. And what I have already
> learned here I feel is enough for me to be able to help my people as
> a nurse — if it were food, I have enough to give my fellow-Toraja
> something to eat."

There followed an emotional parting:

> He was ready to let me go. But there were tears in his eyes. He
> felt sorry that I must part from them. I had been there almost three
> years — 1930, '31, and '32. And Dr Simon's contract was almost
> over too. He was to change his job and become a doctor at a Police
> Hospital. He couldn't go to Africa any more, because the situation
> had changed. So there was nothing to do but come straight home.
> And by chance, Dr van der Veen ... was in Holland.[23] He was on
> leave there. He was already working on his dictionary then, and also
> writing school books in Toraja, for use in the village primary schools....
> Dr Simon sent him a letter asking him to help me find a place on
> any ship going to Indonesia, so that I could get home. So I felt a

bit relieved, of course. Dr van der Veen sent a letter saying, "Yes, there is one." So I prepared to leave for Holland, where I met van der Veen. I stayed three or four days there. I knew him quite well; for as long as I'd been working in Rantepao, I had known him. He got me a place on a ship leaving from Rotterdam. In those days the voyage took exactly a month. There was a Dutch colonel returning on the same ship. Van der Veen introduced me to him, and explained that I was returning home. So had I wanted to, I could have asked this colonel to get me a place in the [Dutch colonial] Army medical corps. Of course, I could have got in, but I said to myself: "Wah! never mind: we'll be at war with them one of these days!" — I already thought like that.

The Return Home

When I got home to Rantepao, in January 1933, the hospital was already finished — because when I left, in 1929, they were just beginning to build it — and the doctor who had taken over after Dr Simon was also Indo-German, but very old, from South Africa.[24] I went to the hospital and told him of my return, and he at once got hold of me and said: "Fritz, I give you no more permission to go anywhere; I need your help here!" I said: "I need to go somewhere first" [probably to visit his family in the village]. He said: "Oh, yes, I might say you can go for one or two days, but then you'll run off!" I said no. I told him straight, of my own accord: "I have come back here to help Toraja." And this old doctor was content with that. So I started to work with him as his assistant.

Thus Fritz's pilgrimage to Europe had brought him full circle, exactly in the pattern mapped out by Anderson. But this was by no means the end of the story, for momentous events were about to erupt into the quiet life of the Toraja highlands and alter them still more dramatically. In 1935 a new doctor, Dr J.J.J. Goslinga, was posted by the Mission to Rantepao, and Fritz worked with him for the next two years. Dr Goslinga's predecessor had achieved an agreement with the local government to build a leprosy treatment centre, and in 1935 Fritz was given the job of riding around all of the districts on horseback, to search out and register any people showing symptoms of the disease, collect medical histories, and register them so that plans could be finalised for the building of the centre. He registered more than a thousand people and helped to bring them to the centre. This work

involved considerable tact in overcoming the fear and stigma at that
time associated with the disease, to help sufferers accept treatment.
Fritz maintained his concern and interest in the leprosy centre for the
rest of his life, collecting donations of money or groceries from the
shops in town every Christmas, and continuing to visit the later much
reduced number of residents.

While he had been away, others had been travelling too: although
Dr Simon's original selection of trainee paramedics had been exclusively
male, the Mission had now recruited three or four young women too,
for training as hospital nurses. One of them was Marta Gora from
Tikala, who had just come back from a hospital in Surabaya, where
she had spent three years (1929–32) training as a midwife. Fritz found
himself working with her at the Elim Hospital in Rantepao. In 1935
they were married, and the following year their first child, Ida (Matilda),
was born. For many years, Marta remained the only trained midwife
in Toraja, and just like her husband is fondly remembered by many of
her former patients and those who knew her.

Dr Goslinga wanted Fritz to gain more experience as a theatre
assistant, and so the family moved to Malang (East Java) in 1936,
where Fritz worked with a specialist at the Mission Hospital, learning
at first hand about more complicated surgery. The broadening of
horizons continued in other ways too. While they were there, Fritz
learned Javanese; photos in the family album show him in a group of
medical students in Javanese dress, while pictures of Marta from her
earlier stay in Surabaya show her in both Javanese and European dress.[25]
One senses in these pictures how, with every outward movement, new
dimensions of identity can be tried on, and added to one's repertoire.
New relationships, too, must have shaped an ever-developing idea of
what it meant to be Indonesian, though unfortunately, Fritz did not
say much about the acquaintances he made in Java. The couple stayed
in Malang almost a year, and their second child, Katrina, was born
there. All the time Fritz was working harder and harder, gaining more
responsibility, and felt that he was making good progress. After their
return to Toraja, he continued to work as assistant to Dr Goslinga.
There was plenty to do, for his written notes record how the highlands
in these years were swept by a number of epidemics, including bacillary
dysentery and anthrax. The latter started among the buffalo population,
but could not be contained from spreading. Unaware of the danger,
people were slaughtering their sick buffaloes without realising that

contact with the blood of an infected animal could cause the disease to cross over to humans. Dr Goslinga and his assistants toured the districts regularly, maintaining a vaccination programme against typhus, cholera and dysentery. Together with other nurses at the hospital, Fritz also assisted Dr Goslinga in hundreds of operations for other conditions then common among the people, such as goitre, cleft palate, and stones in the urinary tract. Dr Goslinga in fact began to train him more actively to perform the operations himself:

> Dr Goslinga saw that it would most likely be a long time before there were enough doctors in Tana Toraja, but he said to me that he believed I would be capable of carrying out all the tasks that we had worked on together. He wrote a testimonial letter for me. And because he thought like this, he said to me, "Every time we do an operation, I am going to give you the scalpel, and I will explain to you what to do from beginning to end."

Fritz was now becoming a doctor, even though he could never officially qualify as one. It is worth pointing out here that, satisfying as this undoubtedly was for him, it also meant that he was still being paid at a very low rate that was hardly commensurate with the responsibilities he was taking on. He never mentioned this in our interviews (nor, according to his son Danny, did he ever complain of it within the family either), but there were big discrepancies between the salaries paid by the Mission to Dutch staff and to local Indonesians, including the medical orderlies. Plaisier (1993: 204n338), in his exhaustively detailed account of the history of the Mission in Tana Toraja, mentions a meeting held in 1935 at which "*mantri* [orderly] Bassiang" inquired about the right to free housing, to which all Mission staff except local medical assistants were entitled. One of the missionaries, H.C. Heusdens, was in favour of extending this right to Fritz, pointing out that the doctor's salary was 20 times higher than Fritz's, and even the Dutch nurses' salaries were much higher. He argued that "if we don't do this we will foster an inclination toward revolution". The argument that local people might turn to socialism if income inequalities remained so exaggerated was one that he repeated in later meetings, but he was defeated by others in the organisation, notably D.J. van Dijk, who remained set against any improvement in salaries and conditions for local workers. The impact on the Mission's budget was deemed too great; and the missionaries themselves were for the most part inclined to preserve existing status distinctions. Fritz was, however, the only one to benefit from this meeting, being granted a ten per cent pay rise, no doubt in recognition of the level of work he was now performing.

Dr Goslinga was so well known that doctors from Palopo, Duri, Enrekang and Makassar visited the hospital to see and work with him. In 1938, the hospital was visited by a Dutch eye specialist who performed dozens of cataract operations, as well as treating many trachoma patients. Fritz was detailed to assist him, and accompanied him further afield to Enrekang, Rappang, and Pare-Pare when he went on there to continue his work. From Pare-Pare, Fritz hurried home on receiving the news that his wife Marta had given birth to their third child (a son, Martin), but had haemorrhaged and was in danger. To his relief she made a good recovery, and after a month had regained her strength. After this he continued with the normal work at the hospital. But now the threat of war began to loom.

War, Independence Struggle and Rebellion — Two Troubled Decades

Things remained peaceful in Toraja until 1942, but with the Japanese invasion, which reached Makassar in February of that year, and into the highlands by March, all the Dutch had to leave their posts for internment camps. As uncertain as the situation now was, Fritz at least felt thankful not to be still in Germany:

> My predictions had proved themselves correct. I felt God had really looked after me. I felt it was a blessing I had left. And what I had guessed might happen, the way I had thought about it, turned out to be rather accurate, and not mistaken. Then the Japanese came, and I said, "The situation has spread to Indonesia too, in connection with the war in Europe...." After the Japanese invasion, all the Dutch were to be interned, including the doctor, and I was given responsibility for things at the hospital, insofar as I was capable. The Dutch doctor's place was taken by a Japanese army doctor — the Japanese took over everything, of course, including the hospital. They took over Rantepao without much trouble, because South Sulawesi had already fallen. Tens of thousands of troops arrived! There were air force, navy, and agricultural units, who immediately began to cultivate, make gardens, rear pigs and everything, to feed the forces. At the same time they also brought the Heiho [Auxiliary Forces]. The Heiho was an Indonesian force being trained to help the Japanese army. Or, to put it another way, they were labourers, who had to

do whatever the Japanese needed done — build roads, or whatever. They were brought from all over: people from Surabaya, Bataks, and all sorts, people from all over Indonesia, mixed together. Those who came here were already a mixture. So, at that time, we just had to do whatever work the Japanese wanted: we weren't in a position to resist or make trouble. In 1942–43, the schools were reopened, with teaching in Japanese, and the whole curriculum was altered.... It was difficult; the teachers were given some lessons in Japanese, and the few words they managed to learn, they carried with them to school, and taught them, then they'd go back and learn some more. So they still mixed it with Malay. They had to. The atmosphere then ... we didn't feel too badly oppressed. But in spite of that, the feeling was always confusing, unsafe. It was a time we can never forget.

In this atmosphere of uncertainty, Fritz now found himself placed more or less in charge of the hospital, under some supervision, and had to feel his way with his new Japanese bosses. In Sa'dan district, north of Rantepao, was the Sangkaropi' copper mine, which the Japanese took over. A specialist surgeon named Dr Suzuki was employed as doctor for the Japanese staff at the mine, and Fritz had to report to him:

He was of the same family as Minister Suzuki at that time. If anything came up I had to tell him. Because he said: "We want you to be the head of the Rantepao hospital." So if anyone was in labour or anything, they had to come and look for me ... and I would tell him, "Doctor, here is this patient...." Once there was a woman in labour. He said, "I am not a gynaecologist — I only do surgery. Surgery is my speciality." I said, "I can do the delivery, if you've no objection; do you want to watch while I do it?" He said, "Are you experienced?" I said, "Yes, I'm experienced." So I took charge of the delivery, and thank God, all went well. We went into the office. He took down one of the books there and said, "Whose are these?" I told him, "They belong to the Dutch doctor; he did a lot of work here, and I keep them so that I too can refer to them, and if I have to do something specific, I can look it up and be sure I don't make a mistake." He said, "How is this? Can you read German?" I said, "Yes, I can a little, I can understand it." He said, "Where did you learn it?" I said, "From a German doctor." He said, "Japan — Germany — friends!" clasping his hands together. He was pleased. And it felt like some protection for me. He was more inclined to trust me.

Fritz consequently took over more and more responsibility in the hospital, and established a reasonably effective communication with Dr Suzuki,

in a mixture of Indonesian and mutually understood medical terms. He
recalled one frightening assignment: the local Kempeitai (military police)
executioner and torturer, a man well known locally for his cruelty, came
with a toothache, and wanted to have the tooth pulled. Dr Suzuki was
warmly praising his assistant, but Fritz was alarmed that if anything
went wrong, the patient might turn nasty. He suggested, to no avail,
that the executioner might prefer the services of the Japanese dentist
who was staying south of the police station. Dr Suzuki replied that the
officer didn't care to go there; he wanted Fritz to do it.

> So I said, "I'll have a look first." I was thinking, "I'll feel it, and if
> it looks easy, then I can get it out without a problem, but if it's still
> firm and a bit difficult, and then it breaks, I'll have a job to get it
> out, because I haven't the right small instruments, only large tongs,
> nothing small enough to extract the root." But I felt it, and it was
> already loose, so I said: "If you, Sir, are willing, then I am brave
> enough to do it also." I was already thinking to myself, "I could pull
> this out even without any instruments, but I had better make a good
> show of it." So I said, "Very well, Sir, are you ready for me to pull
> it, so I can give instructions to prepare everything that's needed?" He
> said, "Yes, it's very painful, I can't sleep." I told my nurse to prepare
> the couch, and lay out the instruments and a glass of mouthwash,
> medicines, sterile cotton, and everything. I put it all ready so that I'd
> be able to work quickly. Then I invited him to lie down, and told
> one person to hold his head and others his arms, in case he tried
> to grab my arm and I might not pull hard enough. Everything was
> arranged as I wanted it. Then I asked him to open his mouth and I
> got ready. As a distraction I said, "After you open your mouth, Sir,
> would you give a strong cough, please." He opened his mouth and
> coughed; I already had hold of it, and yanked it; he said, "Aagh!",
> and I showed it to him: "Sir, it's out already!" Oh, he slapped me
> on the shoulder, and I thought, "I'll get a gold star for this!" I was
> so relieved that it had all gone well. Even though I could have got
> it out right away, my piece of theatre had served its purpose, and
> he was happy.

Fritz recalled the large numbers of Japanese stationed in the
highlands, including quite a number of doctors. There was a headquarters
at Barana' in Tikala, and military posts in Tallung Lipu' and elsewhere,
including almost an entire navy battalion at Sangalla'. Like others who
survived the Occupation, he remembered the severe shortages and
hardships which everyone suffered:

But all the while we were thinking, "How long can this go on?" We tried to get through each day, but we were always thinking, "What will happen tomorrow, or the next day?" That was always in our thoughts. And life was very hard. Everything was in short supply. You can imagine ... we would thresh our rice, and hide it inside big bamboos. Then we'd take a little and try to pound it without making too much noise, away in the gardens, and cook it there. Because the rice, all crops, were supposed to be handed over to the Japanese. Then you just had to do whatever you could to feed yourself.... If the Japanese had a surplus, they gave out some rations, if not, you just had to try and grow whatever you could to stay alive, and live from the produce of your own gardens. We gathered the edible plants from the rice fields, too. It was no use complaining. You had to work with determination and make do with whatever there was. Most of the townspeople went back to their own villages, so very few people — only those who had to — remained. We were subject to all sorts of oppression if we stayed in the towns. My wife and I didn't stay in town either; when we'd finished our day's work at the hospital, we went to Kalambe' and stayed at the school there.[26]

One of the only consolations in this situation was that he was still able to help people, with whatever medicines he still had; he would even request permission to go to the villages to give TB vaccinations, since he still had some supplies of vaccine left. Compared to other parts of Indonesia, it must be said that the Toraja experience was rather less terrible than some, because it was used chiefly as a supply centre and there was little fighting or resistance in the area. The end of the war did not bring an immediate end to uncertainty, however.

In August 1945, rumours at last began to reach Tana Toraja that the Japanese had lost the war. In Rantepao the people were summoned to the football field for the announcement that Japan had surrendered. They heard that Australian troops would be coming to take over — although it was to be mid-November before they actually arrived. In the ensuing power vacuum, the local political situation was distinctly uncertain:

At that time, there were not only Torajans, but people here from all over Indonesia, in the Heiho [Auxiliary Forces]. Among them, there were some who were already politicised. Right away, they took weapons from the Japanese when they surrendered.[27] Some were given up by the Japanese, some were just taken. They hadn't yet been surrendered officially, because it was a while before the Australians got here. The Dutch were still in the internment camp at Awan, near

Bittuang, and then, when the Australians came, they were freed. At
that time, the *pemuda Indonesia* were also emerging from underground
and becoming visible.[28] So once again we lived in fear from day to
day. You had to look out for yourselves, for you could say, whatever
happened next, the youth of Indonesia were certain to rise up; they
had their goals, and the Allies were coming with their own agenda
too. The situation was confusing, and no-one knew what was the best
way to face it. Then the NICA troops came, and the *pemuda* were
preparing to defend themselves, even with the very few weapons they
had; they planned to form a guerrilla force against them....[29] Some
Toraja were strongly pro-*pemuda*, some were pro-Dutch.... It was
difficult to predict how things would go.[30]

As one might expect, degrees of politicisation varied widely among
Torajans at this time, and awareness of what was happening on Java
was unevenly distributed. But Torajans were by no means completely
cut off from these events, even if news was difficult to come by. Those
who had a radio, Fritz recalled, could pick up broadcasts from Java,
but if NICA knew that anyone was listening to the radio, they would
confiscate it. NICA troops were now in Toraja in force, and they included
many seasoned soldiers formerly of the Dutch colonial army (KNIL).
They began to recruit as many Toraja youth as they could, using the
region as a training-ground.[31] At the same time, the youth movements
in Sulawesi were very vigorous, until in 1947 the special forces of the
notorious Captain "Turk" Westerling perpetrated a series of ruthless
massacres of independence activists in South Sulawesi, in which 40,000
people are said to have died. Fritz was a keen observer and talked at
some length about the unfolding of events in what was to be a period
of prolonged upheaval and uncertainty in Tana Toraja.

At that point, some of the youth were co-opted into the KNIL, but
a larger number had already taken to the hills as guerrillas. So for
people like me, ordinary *pegawai* (administrative employees) in the
town, it was a very troubled, difficult time. Finally, in 1949, when
there was a complete transfer of power from Holland to Indonesia,
then all the Toraja youth who had been in the KNIL were sent home
to their own people, and of course it was a big question what would
happen when they came up against those who had been fighting for
the Republican cause....[32] But in spite of all this, the way Torajans
were thinking — yes, although many of them had been pro-Dutch,
it was inevitable that the education we had received from the Dutch
would eventually be used against them!

These comments were doubtless informed by his own experiences. Just as Fritz had seized every opportunity to acquire training and then sought to exercise his skills independently, so the colonial education itself, with the exposure to ideas which it involved, was in the long run bound to add its own impetus to Indonesian desires for an independent nation. As for Fritz himself, he found himself now effectively doing two jobs. The Dutch Dr Goslinga had returned from internment, and so long as NICA forces remained in Toraja, there were also several Dutch army doctors helping out in the hospital. Fritz worked with them, but he also was left more and more to take care of the hospital administration, and in the continuing military confusion his position as a medic put him in a somewhat uncomfortable position of enforced neutrality toward the different parties in the struggle, since he had to treat the wounded of both sides. Danny told me that he had, all the same, done what he could for the independence fighters by passing medicines to them when he was able, and that he had regarded this as his contribution to the struggle.[33] At the same time, he felt the ambiguity of his status: although his incomplete basic education would forever disqualify him from becoming a doctor, he effectively now had so much practical experience that he operated as one anyway, and given the extreme shortage of medical staff in Tana Toraja, the other doctors were glad to let him:

> Dr Goslinga only did the medical work; the actual running of the hospital was left to me. He was always saying, "Fritz, you just take care of that." Anything that needed signing, the administration, I myself took responsibility for it. If there were an ambush or skirmishes between the troops anywhere, the wounded would be brought to the Elim hospital. Whatever happened, and no matter what I felt, I had to deal with it, together with them. The Dutch doctor, seeing my way of working at whatever I had to do there, handed over more and more of the work to me. Sometimes now and again, I would say to myself, "It's all very well that he trusts me, but the work is not easy!" I felt the situation was a difficult one to work in, but then my thoughts would return to the fact that this was my job. Winners may become losers, and friends may become enemies, but I must [tend to them all regardless]....
>
> All the doctors I worked with were very pleased because whatever we worked at together turned out well. A group came with the Health Minister from Java for a visit. I had just done a load of operations; some of the patients were already up and about, others were still in

bed recuperating. I did all this not to show up the other doctors, but because there were sick people who needed help. So I was helping. Really it was not my job — it should have been done by the doctors, there should have been specialists to do it. When the Minister's group was due to leave, I said to one of the doctors from Ujung Pandang who had come with him, "How is it, Doctor, that I haven't been scolded by the health team? Why has no-one told me, 'You can do this, but you shouldn't be doing that'?" He said, "Fritz, whatever you are able to do, you just do it, I will take personal responsibility for that...." At that time, I did a lot of operations myself — appendectomy, several kinds of eye operations, stomach operations, obstetrics — all sorts. And all these doctors gave me their assurance that I could do all this work. It's not possible really that a nurse can perform all the specialisations of doctors, but I had already gained experience as an assistant in all these fields ... and personally, I said, "I thank God that whatever I've undertaken has been blessed with success and has benefited the people. So long as the people are satisfied, that is enough for me!"

After Indonesian independence became a reality at the end of 1949, the military and political situation in South Sulawesi remained confused. Javanese troops from the Brawijaya and Diponegoro Divisions of the Indonesian National Army (TNI) were sent to secure South Sulawesi for the Republic. But there was conflict over the terms on which lowland guerrilla leaders were to be incorporated into the TNI. Notable among them was Kahar Muzakkar, who, denied his own battalion in 1950, gathered around him a group calling itself the South Sulawesi Guerrilla Union (KGSS). His lieutenant Andi Sose, who came from the region of Duri on Toraja's southern border, and had attended the *Schakelschool* in Ma'kale, was stationed in Tana Toraja. Sose's father was a Toraja noble from Mengkendek, who had married a woman from a high-ranking Duri family. Though Sose identified more with his mother's side of the family, he kept links in the southern Toraja districts, and counted some Toraja youths of aristocratic families among his followers. He was essentially a warlord running his own private army and financing it through his efforts to control local trade (Pasande 2002; Bigalke 2005: 242). In 1952 Kahar joined forces with the Darul Islam rebellion centred in West Java, and fought to create an Islamic state in South Sulawesi. Andi Sose at this point split from Kahar, and accepted a commission as captain in the TNI, his troops being incorporated as Battalion 720. They were now to co-operate with Diponegoro Battalion 422, which spent two years in the highlands from late 1951 or early 1952. But there was tension between Sose, with his aristocratic connections, and the markedly leftist Battalion 422, which was giving its support to claims for land redistribution in Toraja at this time. Within Andi Sose's forces was Company 2, made up of Torajans under the leadership of Frans Karangan. After induction into the TNI, Company 2 became alienated from Andi Sose as the latter's ill-disciplined troops began to commit outrages in Tana Toraja, and Andi Sose himself became more and more heavy-handed, demonstrating an openly pro-Muslim, anti-Christian stance. At the same time, tensions ran high as left-wing organisations supported an increasing number of peasant actions against large landowners in 1952–53. Andi Sose's oppression was made more disgraceful, in Fritz's opinion, not only because it appeared as a revival of age-old Bugis designs to dominate the highlands, but because his troops were by now supposed to be regular forces of the national army. He also recalled (as some others do) the capture of some of Andi Sose's troops, who, in spite of the trouble they had been causing, were not harmed but sent out of the highlands:

> We said we were living in a burnt-up world — villages were burned; at Rante, at Tondon, at Ma'kale, at Nonongan, houses were burned. Thank God there was still a group of people who said, "This is wrong, what these forces of the Indonesian Republic are doing".... Thank God, those people were not able to spread and deepen their hold over the whole of Toraja, and when they saw they couldn't succeed, they fled.

By 1953, Christian Toraja leaders were plotting an assault against Andi Sose and drew Frans Karangan and his troops with them into the action. Large numbers of villagers joined in the attack on Andi Sose's battalion, which after fierce fighting was driven out of Toraja.

> Then a number of them were captured, sent to Palopo, and put on a ship back to Ujung Pandang. In such a situation, supposing Torajans had been shortsighted, they could have killed all of them! But because people thought clearly, they sent all those troops back and put them "in storage". Because clearly it was they who had tried to make trouble in Toraja.

Andi Sose's troops were to be driven out a second time in 1958, when they were once again posted to Toraja to replace Javanese troops relocated to North Sulawesi to deal with the Permesta rebellion which began in 1957. Once again Fritz found himself treating the wounded on both sides of the conflict. And throughout most of this decade, Kahar's DI/TII (*Darul Islam/Tentara Islam Indonesia*) rebellion continued, taking its toll on Toraja villages whose men were sometimes co-opted into the guerrilla forces. Some communities then in turn suffered reprisals from Torajan regular forces of the national army for having supported the rebels. Peace and slow economic progress returned finally by the late 1960s, with the 1970s seeing an outflux of Torajans seeking higher education or employment beyond their homeland. Their remittances began to have a marked effect on the still overwhelmingly subsistence economy at home. There was also an influx of foreigners with the modest beginnings of a tourist trade which has grown considerably in recent decades. Fritz made little comment on the events of this period, which for him was a time of continuity and stability, as he worked at the hospital and raised his family. His travels were over, and his life and career had by now taken definitive shape; his narrative here ceased to focus on his personal experiences and reverted to more general subjects.

Unsettled though conditions were in the 1950s, this had not prevented some progress at the hospital. In 1935 it had been taken over by the Dutch Reformed Church Mission (*Gereformeerde Zendingsbond*), and when the Toraja Church (*Gereja Toraja*) became independent of the Mission in 1947, it continued its involvement in the running of the hospital. Fritz became the first chairman of the Church's Health Organisation (*Yayasan Kesehatan Gereja Toraja*), serving in this position until 1965. In 1952, he and his co-workers formed another committee to build a nurses' hostel. He succeeded in getting help from the Public Works Department so that this could be done at limited expense. In the following years he also ran a variety of health training courses.

Until his eventual retirement in 1971, Fritz remained at the hospital in Rantepao, working together with a succession of doctors. He joked how anyone with a problem would come looking for "Om [Uncle] Basiang". One of his nurses, Papa' Remas, who had worked with him as a theatre assistant for 15 years from 1957 to 1971, recalled his distinctive manner of working. He maintained strict hospital discipline, and demanded punctuality and efficiency from his staff. If a fly got into the operating theatre, whoever had prepared the theatre that day could expect to be given a banana as a "prize", as well as a stern lecture in front of the others. The hospital was still very short of supplies, so he would instruct the staff to bring their old sheets from home, to be washed and boiled over a wood fire to sterilise for use as dressings. In spite of these makeshift conditions, his strictness paid off in ensuring avoidance of post-operative infection. His boyhood ingenuity in fixing up useful appliances from available odds and ends still came in useful, too: in the absence of a proper lamp for the operating theatre, he made one himself out of an old car headlamp, powered by numerous batteries packed into a large bamboo tube. He went out of his way to help people in the community, and would receive patients even if they couldn't afford to pay. Sometimes, he would accept payment in cassava or vegetables. He did many operations to correct cleft palates; one patient, a young boy named Taruk, who had no money, paid for his operation in eels.[34]

Fritz had five children in all, most of whom grew up to travel adventurously, as he had, out of Tana Toraja. In 1957, when his wife Marta fell ill of cervical cancer, he himself operated on her. But the cancer was too far advanced, and he was unable to save her. After her death, he remarried. His second spouse was Damaris Palin, also a nurse in the Rantepao hospital, and a distant cousin of his first wife. For some years after his retirement, he still helped out at the hospital at times when he was needed, later concentrating on the cultivation of clove trees in his gardens. He was often to be seen on his bicycle, and children knew that he always had sweets in his pocket. He remained a beloved figure around town until his death in March 1993 at the age of 88. In keeping with his always sincerely held Christian beliefs, his children obeyed his wishes that his funeral be kept very modest, with the slaughter of only a single buffalo. This is still most uncharacteristic in Tana Toraja today, where if anything the renewed security and prosperity of the past few decades has led to an escalation of ritual expenditure. It also requires great skill on the part of those organising the funeral, to avoid giving offence to more traditionally-minded relatives.

There is a coda to this story. In 1973, Fritz went to Germany to visit his daughter Rina who was living there, and they set out to trace Dr Simon's family. Düsseldorf was almost unrecognisable after the heavy bombing it had sustained during the war, and subsequent rebuilding; but the street names were unchanged, and he even recognised the restaurant where they used to eat in Halberstrasse. A new house had been built on the site of Dr Simon's former residence, and the woman who lived there could tell them nothing at all, but they went into the restaurant and

Roxana Waterson

looked up all the Simons in the phone directory. The fourth call they
made connected them to Dr Simon's family, who with great excitement
immediately invited them over to their new house. They had to ask at
the Police Station for directions, which turned out to be not so simple:
having been told to cross the bridge over the Rhine and take the second
street they came to, they reached the river to find that there were now,
not one bridge as in the 1930s, but several. The second one they tried
turned out to be the right one. They found the house and rang the
bell; there followed an emotional meeting, especially with Dr Simon's
son Harald, who still remembered Fritz well. Dr Simon himself had
died in 1959. After Fritz's departure from Germany, he had taken the
job with the police; they saw his Nazi insignia still lying on his desk.
[This image sticks in my mind uncomfortably, though I know so little
about Dr Simon that I am certainly in no position to judge his motives,
nor those of his wife who presumably was continuing to dust them.]
Harald, still in his teens at the end of the war, had been blinded by
a stray bullet during the final German retreat. But he went to blind
school, learned to type, and studied law, and had subsequently become
a judge. His girlfriend stood by him and married him, and she and his
mother used to read to him and help him with his papers. Thus the
contact between the two families was renewed, 40 years later.

Conclusion

I began by setting the life of Fritz Basiang within the framework of the
colonial "pilgrimage" through education into modernity, as postulated
by Anderson. But this says more about the early part of his story than
the later parts. Other suggested frameworks for analysis may be helpful
in considering the life history as a whole. Mandelbaum (1973) and
Agar (1980) both suggest some categories of analysis which might be
applied to any life history, though they involve rather different methods.
Mandelbaum, taking the life of Gandhi as his example, draws attention
to the overlapping "dimensions" of a life — biological, cultural, social
and psychosocial (i.e. relating to an individual's subjective experience); the
"turnings", or moments when key decisions are taken concerning what
to do and be, and what not to be; and the "adaptations", or periods of
longer duration in which can be seen "ongoing development in various
spheres of behaviour", as the individual also must find the means to
cope with the changing conditions of life (Mandelbaum 1973: 181). Yet

underlying all these formulations, there remains what is individually unique and irreducible in any life history, the person's own creativity which cannot be fully accounted for. Marx's famous formula that people make history, but not in circumstances of their own choosing, finds an echo in Mandelbaum's insistence on the person as "both a bound actor and a free agent", caught up in historical events. No life can be reduced simply to categories of analysis; in studying the whole life of a real person, "the student tends to become especially aware of the person as an active doer and seeker, and not only as a passive recipient or a subject for scientific generalizations" (Mandelbaum 1973: 181). In the present case, the turning-points in Fritz's early life stand out clearly, as we see him seizing the opportunities to invent a new life for himself which would carry him far beyond the confines of the village life of his early childhood; one can see also the consistency with which he later pursued his chosen vocation, which he obviously found deeply satisfying, and the necessity to make the most of difficult conditions in periods of social upheaval.

Whereas Mandelbaum is in the exceptional position of being able to draw on a rich variety of first-hand and published sources, including Gandhi's own voluminous autobiography, Agar's approach differs in dealing more directly with fieldwork materials. A person's own recorded first-hand account can lend itself to more direct textual analysis. The coherence of any life story, Agar proposes, suggests the existence of "schemata" by which it is organised to form a narrative comprehensible to the listener. Agar does not deal in detail with the origins of such schemata. I have already presented evidence that the very idea of a "life history" has a degree of cultural specificity attached to it, but the ability to grasp a narrative structure, which Agar proposes is intuitive on the part of the listener, is something we may take as universal. Whether "intuitive" in this context is to be taken as meaning that it forms part of a person's "tacit" cultural knowledge (Polanyi 1975), or that it has something to do with the brain's circuitry (cf. Sperber 1985), or most likely both, is a question which there is no space to expand on here. The story also makes use of "background assumptions" (the cultural knowledge necessary to understand the content; these I have tried to fill in where necessary). Within the narrative, "episodes" stand out as separate stories embedded within the larger tale — such as, in Fritz's case, the story of how he got taken on by Dr Simon, or the episode of the tooth extraction. The various journeys, in particular, stand out in terms of the great amount of incidental detail recounted (more even than I have been able to reproduce here), while longer, more stable periods were condensed and passed over with little elaboration. This latter aspect of narration is typical of how memory works for all of us; yet still, the fact that so many of the detailed episodes are journeys remains a significant feature of the account as a whole.

Textual analysis, however, is never an end in itself for the ethnographer or historian, who is always using it as a route to some greater understanding of the cultural or historical world of the informant. "Themes" extracted from the narrator's own patterns of expression can for instance be drawn together to provide insights into significant "domains" of cognition (Agar 1980: 231–3); the way in which a story is told may provide surprising insights into the psychology of the narrator and even of the social group to which he belongs (Portelli 1990). It is to be expected, too, that any life account will be to some degree self-serving: this, I believe, is not simply because we wish to present ourselves in a good light, but becomes part of our efforts at coherence. There may be a psychological necessity to persuade oneself that key decisions, or even events which may have looked disastrous at the time, were all for the best in the end, and this becomes part of the stories we tell ourselves about ourselves. Peneff (1990: 36) suggests that the often pre-existing frameworks we select as a means to arrange our memories into comprehensible stories should be thought of as "mythical", in the sense that they provide the structure for narrative coherence. Especially pertinent to the present case is his observation that, while such mythical frameworks are common in all societies, they are "especially widespread in societies undergoing rapid development and change, where individuals tell their histories as a kind of progress or journey".

In Fritz Basiang's story, two themes that appear repeatedly are the sense of adventure, expressed in the desire to experience everything new and to travel as far as possible, and the desire to help his own people by doing something socially useful. While at first these themes run parallel to each other (it was necessary to travel and acquire knowledge first *in order to* be useful), at some point they might have come into conflict with each other (when it came to deciding whether to follow Dr Simon to South Africa, or to attempt to settle in Germany, rather than returning to Toraja). This tension is resolved, however, by his decision to return home, while the remainder of the narrative describes the transition to a more settled period, marked by the great consistency he showed in his adherence to the second theme, the ideal of service to others. Of course, another implicit theme, the experience of cultural transformation, is one that attracted my attention in the first place, so some comment is in order here about the dramatic shift in world view which his life encompassed. When I asked Fritz what was the greatest change he had witnessed in his life, he replied that it was the advent of education and all that came with it. Most specifically, he noted that this had greatly increased the geographical mobility of his children and their generation, for whom educational opportunities were hugely expanded. This fact is something that was also immediately observable from his family's genealogy. His initial break away from the traditional life has been followed by an explosion of diversity in the life paths chosen by his children. All but one have married people from other parts of Indonesia or overseas — his eldest daughter met and married a Batak while studying economics in Java; his second daughter Rina married a Dutch man, a nephew of Dr van der Veen, and lives in Germany; one son, Martin, who has had a prominent career as a judge (recently retiring as Deputy Attorney General), married first, a woman from Palembang (Sumatra), and subsequently after her death remarried a Manadonese; his younger brother Danny travelled in the merchant marine, and married a Betawi woman from Jakarta before eventually returning to live in Tana Toraja; only the youngest daughter is married to a Torajan, though they reside in Jakarta. All the children share an outlook which is distinctly modernist, and if anything even more fervently Christian than that of their father, who was not outspoken about his faith but who undoubtedly influenced many people by example.

Christianity was the second innovation that dramatically altered his world view. His conversion is hardly surprising, given the strong emphasis placed on the teaching of Christianity in the schools he attended. Religion was very much a part of hospital life, too. In his written notes Fritz remarks that morning prayers were held daily, and that the ministers and evangelists who served as hospital chaplains were diligent in visiting non-Christian patients and encouraging their conversion. When they were discharged, they would often be given a letter of introduction to their local pastor, in the hope that they would continue to seek instruction in the new faith. Toraja Christians were aware that their conversion connected them to a world-wide community. In the past, travel outside the Toraja highlands was often difficult and dangerous, and hostilities often prevailed even between neighbouring villages. The slave trade of the late nineteenth century, which caused so much social disruption, meant that most Toraja who travelled out of their homeland in this period did so as captives to be put on sale in lowland markets. Although there was some Toraja resistance to Dutch takeover, the fact that the colonial regime put an end to these chaotic conditions has much to do with the relative lack of animosity toward the Dutch in Toraja people's memories. Toraja Christians sometimes remarked to me that one of the great benefits of their faith, as they see it, is that being part of a larger world community of Christians makes travel safe for them in distant parts of the world such as Europe, Australia or America. Fritz too commented that once, in 1932, after he had been in Germany three years already, he had received a letter from his parents saying that they were concerned about him and were anxious to see him again. "I wrote to them in reply that they shouldn't worry about me, that I was with good people and that the reason I had been able to travel so far in safety was because those people were Christians." Encouraged by their son to consider conversion, they were among the first in the Banga district to accept the new religion. Although Fritz made no mention of this in our interviews, he had sponsored the building of churches in his home district, at Maroson, Buri and Surakan, as well as raising donations for the building of churches in other places. In more traditional vein, he also organised the rebuilding of a family origin-house (*tongkonan*), Tondok Tanga, at Surakan (which had originally been built by Fritz's grandmother), and contributed to the rebuilding of a *tongkonan* of his second wife's family, at Batulelleng outside Rantepao. He always spoke warmly of the strong bonds of mutual support between kin which he saw as characteristic of the Toraja kinship system, as an aspect of his own society which he truly admired. One may note here that the rebuilding of origin-houses remains in Toraja one of the most highly valued acts and the mark of a successful career; modern church-building is in many ways an extension of this traditional pattern by which successful individuals demonstrate allegiance to their places of origin. The summation of a more traditional Toraja career, though, is one's funeral, the size of which, and the number and quality of buffaloes slaughtered, will be remembered by descendants and discussed for long afterwards. Dutch Reformed Church missionaries were hopelessly unsuccessful in their efforts to end a ceremonial economy which they perceived as shockingly wasteful, and funerals today continue to be the most important social occasions in Toraja life. Fritz however had taken to heart the mission's attitudes toward this issue, and firmly eschewed any desire for an elaborate funeral, with its connotations of rank, and the economic burdens that it inevitably places on the deceased person's children. Given the value that he still attached to kinship relations, he had obviously had to give considerable thought to how to extricate himself from the prestige economy. He had cleared most of the ceremonial debts which he had inherited from his father, Ne' Pilo, in order that his children be free of them. He would still attend funerals, but without taking a pig, only other contributions such as palm wine. He would make a point of leaving early, before the meat division took place. In this way he avoided receiving meat, and thus reduced his participation in funeral exchanges without actually severing his links with kin. Since he served people so generously in other ways, they could not take too much offense at this minimalist approach to the traditional ceremonial obligations. In this respect his attitudes were distinctly modernist, and his career ended unconventionally.

Fritz Basiang's life stands out in several ways, besides his exemplary record of service to the community. Spanning almost the entire twentieth century, as he remarked himself, "I can honestly say that I have had to face all kinds of experiences in my life." Through his own energies and initiative, at the same time as he gradually discovered himself as an Indonesian, he also traced for himself a passage toward a radically new way of being Toraja. Along the way he left deep impressions on many of those who knew him.

Notes

This chapter is a revised version of an article that originally appeared in *Indonesia and the Malay World* 29:83 (2001): 5–50, a journal published by Taylor and Francis (<http://www.tandf.co.uk>), and is reprinted with permission.

1. I am especially grateful to Danny for all the help he gave me. I have also drawn some details from a brief memorial chronology of Fritz's life produced by Danny at the time of his funeral. There are one or two minor discrepancies between the dates given in this account and those given me by Fritz himself in the interviews. I have chosen to keep to the latter since it is the interview materials that I am chiefly dealing with here.

2. Detailed statistics of enrolment in the different types of schools in the Netherlands East Indies from 1900–40 can be found in Veur (1969).

3. See also Watson (1989) and Sweeney (1990) for discussion of a range of Indonesian and Malay autobiographical writings.

4. One other example which I have not been able to consult is mentioned by Watson (1989: 10). It is the privately published autobiography of a Minangkabau doctor, Dr Mohd. Ali Hanafiah Gelar Sutan Maharaja, who studied at the STOVIA from 1916–26 and, like the others mentioned here, gave medical service to his community under three regimes, the colonial, Japanese and Republican: periods which the author himself observed "have a meaning and special character all of themselves, influencing my life, and indeed the life of our whole nation" (Hanafiah 1977).

5. A full account of this period can be found in Bigalke (2005).

6. The perception that life was easier in the past, and pressure on resources less, is one repeated to me by many older people in Toraja.

7. This was one of the severest disease pandemics in human history, claiming perhaps 20 million lives worldwide, including at least 1.5 million in Indonesia (Brown 1987: 235). It appears to have been brought into the battlefields of western Europe by American troops in the last summer of World War I, and spread from there in three waves, partly as a result of the massive movements of people occasioned by the war (Crosby 1989). Distinct memories of the pandemic are retained in Toraja; some thought the "winds" of war had blown across the world unleashing pestilence — not an inaccurate description in fact.

8. He used the Indonesian, *seleksi alam.*

9. The three-year *Volksschool* was first instituted in 1907 (Veur 1969: 2). This was a breakthrough since for the first time, a Western-style elementary education thus became available to Indonesians in rural areas. Establishment of the schools, however, depended on the degree of local initiative. According to Bigalke (2005: 151), those in Toraja were set up by the Dutch Reformed Church Mission (*Gereformeerde Zendingsbond*), and received some government subsidy.

10. This at least is a common memory in Toraja, though how many children of dependents may have actually succeeded in escaping their low status through this "crack in the school house door", Bigalke (2005: 151) suggests is questionable; cf. Volkman (1985: 37).

11. There was a school in Banga and another at Parappo, not far from Rembon market.

12. The *Schakelschool* or "Link School" had a five-year Dutch-language curriculum which, from 1921, prepared indigenous pupils for entry to secondary schools. Prior to this date, Malay-language primary education was a dead-end, and pupils had been unable to go on to secondary schools, where Dutch was the medium of education (Veur 1969: 4; Bigalke 2005:

150–4). Even then, there were only three institutions of Dutch-language higher education in the Indies, started after 1913, and all of them were in Java (Bigalke 2005: 155).

13. Renamed Ujung Pandang in the late 1960s, the city reverted to its older and better known name of Makassar in October 1999.

14. Clinics had been built in the different districts at Sangalla', Mebali (Mengkendek), Buakayu (Bonggakaradeng), Parappo (Saluputti), Bittuang, Pangala', Sa'dan, Nanggala and Buntao'. Rantepao and Ma'kale each had a hospital for admissions.

15. Interview with Pendeta Palilu at Dende', November 1999.

16. The *Soempah Pemuda* or "Youth Pledge" was taken at the Youth Congress held in Batavia in 1928. It was a radical pledge of loyalty to three ideals: one homeland, Indonesia; one nation, Indonesia; one language, Bahasa Indonesia. 1929 was a year of intensified activity among nationalists, matched by mounting repression by the Dutch administration. Political meetings were often broken up by the police. A contemporary Dutch perspective on these events is provided by Blumenberger (1931), a retired government official. The membership of PNI in particular expanded dramatically, and throughout this year, Sukarno was making frequent and provocative speeches until his arrest, with that of other PNI leaders, in December (Ingleson 1979).

17. An Ambonese who later (in 1957) became one of three Deputy Prime Ministers under Sukarno.

18. The harbour at Batavia.

19. 1 ringgit = 2½ rupiah.

20. Fritz here referred to himself in Indonesian, as *berkulit hitam*, in a comment which served to emphasise to me how different he obviously must have felt as a single Asian in a largely homogeneous white community. He met no other Indonesians while he was there. He seemingly had no incidents of racial hostility to recount; this may have been partly because he was protected by his relationship with Dr Simon. But it was a dangerous time to be different in Germany. The comment about the circus is of some historical interest since in fact, a recent film has documented how black and mixed-race Germans did tour in the Hillerkus Afrikaschau circuses or acted in films and "ethnic" shows in an attempt to escape Nazi persecution in the 1930s. In 1932 Hitler gave a speech to crowds in Breslau, in which he ordered all Africans, Jews and others who were not Aryans to leave Germany or face the concentration camps. (Some Africans in Germany came from German colonies and had fought for Germany in World War I; others were from French colonies and had been deliberately deployed by France in the occupied Rhineland as an extra "humiliation" to Germany

[or so many Germans perceived it] after the Treaty of Versailles.) (See Michael Barnett and Delroy Constantine-Simms' film, *Black Survivors of the Holocaust* [Afro-Wisdom Films, 1997], and the review of it in *Anthropology Newsletter*, May 1998, p. 13.)

21. I am unsure whether Fritz was here referring to the Social Democratic Party (SPD), the largest moderate party of the time, or to the smaller, Roman Catholic, Centre Party.

22. This was probably not a viable option in any case. Criteria for citizenship in Germany have always been highly dependent upon German descent, and some Germans of colour had their citizenship revoked later, during the War.

23. H. van der Veen was a highly talented linguist who was employed by the Dutch Reformed Church Mission. He collected and published several long texts of Toraja ritual chants, translated the Bible into Toraja, and with the aid of his Toraja assistant, J. Tammu, compiled a Toraja dictionary. The house he lived and worked in Rantepao was built on land rented from Basiang's family and later became the Basiang family home.

24. According to Fritz's written notes, this would have been Dr Esser, who succeeded Dr Simon (1930–33). He was followed by a Dutch doctor, Dr Buitelaar (1933–35), before Dr Goslinga took over in 1935.

25. It was a rule at the STOVIA medical school that all Javanese and Sumatran non-Christian students wear native dress while in attendance at the school. This was deeply resented, since it was felt to be discriminatory and humiliating (Van Neil 1960: 54). Possibly a similar rule accounts for the predominance of Javanese dress among the medical students in the photo.

26. At his wife's village in Tikala. According to Fritz's written notes, the patients from the hospital were actually evacuated to emergency shelters at Pangrante. Even the doors and windows were removed from the hospital and taken there, in case the hospital might be bombed. Fritz and his wife were often called out to the villages to attend not only to local people but also to Chinese evacuees from Ujung Pandang, who had settled in various parts of the highlands. Sometimes people would come with a horse for Marta or Fritz to ride to accompany them to distant hill villages. In attending childbirths with complications, they often worked closely together; he records one night when they were called to Sareale, high on the slopes of Mount Sesean, to deliver a breech birth. The baby was presenting its hand; between them ("and by the grace of God", he adds) they succeeded in turning it and ensuring a safe delivery. At other times they might be called out to different locations, and not see each other for two or three days at a time.

27. Bigalke (2005: 207–8) describes these incidents in more detail.

28. Literally, "Indonesian youth". Bigalke well describes the somewhat confusing uses of this term at the time: while in Java, it signalled a "revolutionary activist", in the Toraja region it became a label for any "nationalist" or "activist", moderate as well as radical. In the aftermath of the Japanese defeat, various *pemuda* groups were forming, with some tensions emerging between those who were Christian and those more closely aligned with the Muslim-dominated *Pemuda Republik Indonesia*, which formed in October under the leadership of *pemuda* from Palopo (in the neighbouring Bugis region of Luwu') (Bigalke 2005: 202–10). Fritz is here also using the term in this broad sense.

29. NICA (Netherlands Indies Civil Administration) forces were responsible, under the terms of the agreement signed between the Netherlands government and the major Allied powers, for restoring Dutch judicial and administrative power in Indonesia.

30. As Bigalke describes, in Tana Toraja the desire for Indonesian independence was tempered by anxieties about being absorbed by lowland Bugis or Makassarese power centres in any emerging new order, involving loss of Toraja autonomy and perhaps enforced Islamisation. The Dutch regime had provided a buffer against such developments. At the same time, old rivalries between the leaders of the southern districts around Ma'kale, and those of the Rantepao area to the north, reasserted themselves in the new political landscape that was unfolding (Bigalke 2005: 210–6).

31. In the three years 1946–48, three classes of Toraja KNIL were recruited, totalling around 1250 people, and trained for 8 months before being sent on active duty in South Sulawesi or Java (Bigalke 2005: 211–2). Some of them deserted and joined South Sulawesi guerrillas.

32. In the event, some returning Torajans demobilised from KNIL were absorbed into the company of a local Toraja commander, Frans Karangan.

33. Danny added that later, when a national effort was under way to compile lists of local Independence Heroes (with the right to interment in the local Heroes' Cemetery), Fritz was proposed for inclusion in the Toraja lists, but he typically declined the honour.

34. Interview with Papa' Remas (Pak Musa Tambing), June 1996. Another friend who remembered both Fritz and his wife Marta was a retired minister, Pendeta Herman Rapa, whom I met in November 1999. He commented that he felt great respect and admiration for Fritz on account of the fact that with so little education, he had managed to go so far, and had really fulfilled the role of a doctor. He added that Marta had achieved a great deal with even less educational advantage, since she had had only three years of primary education.

References

Agar, M. 1980. "Stories, Background Knowledge and Themes: Problems in the Analysis of Life History Narrative", *American Ethnologist* 7/2: 223–39.

Anderson, B. 1983. *Imagined Communities: Reflections on the Origin and Spread of Nationalism.* London: Verso.

———. 1990 (1979). "A Time of Darkness and a Time of Light: Transposition in Early Indonesian Nationalist Thought", in *Language and Power: Exploring Political Cultures in Indonesia*, ed. B. Anderson. Ithaca: Cornell University Press, pp. 241–70.

Behar, R. 1992. "A Life Story to Take across the Border: Notes on an Exchange", in *Storied Lives: The Cultural Politics of Self-Understanding*, ed. G. Rosenwald and R. Ochberg. New Haven and London: Yale University Press, pp. 108–23.

Bigalke, T. 2005. *Tana Toraja: A Social History of an Indonesian People.* Singapore: Singapore University Press.

Blumberger, J.T.P. 1931. *De Nationalistische Beweging in Nederlandsch-Indië.* Haarlem: H. D. Tjeenk Willink & Zoon.

Borland, K. 1991. "That's Not What I Said: Interpretive Conflict in Oral Narrative Research", in *Women's Words: The Feminist Practice of Oral History*, ed. S. Gluck and D. Patai. New York and London: Routledge, pp. 63–75.

Brown, C. 1987. "The Influenza Pandemic of 1918 in Indonesia", in *Death and Disease in Southeast Asia: Explorations in Social, Medical and Demographic History*, ed. N. Owen. Singapore: Oxford University Press, pp. 235–56.

Bruner, J. 1987. "Life as Narrative", *Social Research* 54/1: 11–32.

Caplan, P. 1997. *African Voices, African Lives: Personal Narratives from a Swahili Village.* London: Routledge.

Crosby, A.W. 1989. *America's Forgotten Pandemic: The Influenza of 1918.* Cambridge, Mass.: Harvard University Press.

Djelantik, A.A.M. 1997. *The Birthmark: Memoirs of a Balinese Prince.* Hong Kong: Periplus.

Echevarria-Howe, L. 1995. "Reflections from the Participants: The Process and Product of Life History Work", *Oral History* 23/2: 40–6.

Frederick, W. 1974. "My Childhood World" (by Ruslan Abdulgani), *Indonesia* 17: 113–35.

Hamka. 1966. *Kenang-Kenangan Hidup.* Kuala Lumpur: Penerbitan Pustaka Antara.

Hanafiah, Mohd. Ali. 1977. *77 Tahun Riwayat Hidup*. Jakarta: privately published.

Hollan, D. and Wellenkamp, J. 1996. *The Thread of Life: Toraja Reflections on the Life Cycle*. Honolulu: University of Hawai'i Press.

Ingleson, J. 1979. *Road to Exile: The Indonesian Nationalist Movement 1927–1934*. Singapore: Heinemann.

Kratz, E.U. 1978. "Djalan Sempoerna: Eine Fruehe indonesische Autobiographie", in *Spectrum: Essays Presented to Sutan Takdir Alisjahbana on his Seventieth Birthday*, ed. S. Udin. Jakarta: Dian Rakyat, pp. 340–56.

Langness, L. and Frank, G. 1981. *Lives: An Anthropological Approach to Biography*. Novato, CA.: Chandler & Sharp.

Mandelbaum, D. 1973. "The Study of Life History: Gandhi", *Current Anthropology* 14/3: 177–206.

Mischler, E. 1986. *Research Interviewing: Context and Narrative*. Cambridge, Mass.: Harvard University Press.

Nur Sutan Iskandar. 1987 (1948). *Pengalaman Masa Kecil*. Jakarta: Balai Pustaka.

Pasande, D.S. 2002. "Menguak Tabir Menepis Prasangka: Analisis Sosiologis Mengenai Peristiwa 1953 dan 1958 di Tana Toraja". Master's Thesis, STT Intim Makassar.

Peneff, J. 1990. "Myths in Life Stories", in *The Myths We Live By*, ed. R. Samuel and P. Thompson. London: Routledge, pp. 36–48.

Plaisier, B. 1993. *Over Bruggen en Grenzen: De Communicatie van het Evangelie in het Torajagebied (1913–1942)*. Zoetermeer: Boekencentrum.

Polanyi, M. 1975. "Personal Knowledge", in *Meaning*, M. Polanyi and H. Prosch. Chicago: Chicago University Press.

Rodgers, S. 1995. *Telling Lives, Telling History: Autobiography and Historical Imagination in Modern Indonesia*. Berkeley: University of California Press.

Röttger-Rössler, B. 1993. "Autobiography in Question: On Self-Presentation and Life Description in an Indonesian Society", *Anthropos* 88: 365–73.

Sears, L. (ed.). 1993. *Autonomous Histories, Particular Truths: Essays in Honour of John R. W. Smail*. Madison: University of Wisconsin Center for Southeast Asian Studies.

Smail, J. 1993 (1961). "On the Possibility of an Autonomous History of Modern Southeast Asia", in *Autonomous Histories, Particular Truths: Essays in Honour of John R. W. Smail*, ed. L. Sears. Madison: University of Wisconsin Center for Southeast Asian Studies, pp. 39–70.

Soemarno Sosroatmodjo. 1981. *Dari Rimba Raya ke Jakarta Raya: Sebua Otobiografi*. Jakarta: Gunung Agung.

Sperber, D. 1985. "Anthropology and Psychology: Towards an Epidemiology of Representations", *Man* (N.S.)20: 73–89.

Sweeney, A. 1990. "Some Observations on the Nature of Malay Autobiography", *Indonesia Circle* 51: 21–36.

Van Neil, R. 1960. *The Emergence of the Modern Indonesian Elite.* The Hague/ Bandung: W. van Hoeve.

Veur, P. W. van der. 1969. *Education and Social Change in Colonial Indonesia (I).* Athens, Ohio: Ohio University Center for International Studies.

Volkman, T. 1985. *Feasts of Honour: Ritual and Change in the Toraja Highlands.* Urbana: University of Illinois Press.

Watson, C.W. 1989. "The Study of Indonesian and Malay Autobiography", *Indonesia Circle* 49: 3–18.

PART II

Voices and Fragments

5

Arifin in the Iron Cap: Confessions of a Young Man, Drowning

Robert Knox Dentan

[Acculturated Semai] no longer seem interested in traditional economic activities. But because of their low educational attainments, their choice of jobs is limited; you will find them employed as factory workers, security guards and cleaners among other things.

> Hasan Mat Noor, quoted by Faezah Ismail (1997)

The author of these confessions and the confessions themselves are, in a sense, fictional. Nevertheless, such persons as the composer of these confessions not only exist in "modernising" society, but indeed must exist, considering the circumstances under which that society has generally been formed. I have tried to present to the public in a more striking form than usual a representative figure from a generation still surviving.

> Paraphrase of Fyodor Dostoyevsky
> *Notes from Underground* (1864)
> [1972: 13; Ellis 1991: epigraph]

[T]he muslim priest fitted orphan boys with iron skullcaps to insure their adult idiocy and enhanced begging capacity.

> C. Blaise, review of V. Mehta, *New York Times Book Review* (21 Nov. 1979): 7

Robert Knox Dentan

Introduction

> Thirty-eight murders were committed in 1907 [in Perak].... In
> Pahang there were four cases of murder, one being the murder of
> five women and children by an elderly Sakai [Orang Asli] who was
> left in charge of them at a camp at Chenik, on the Pahang river
> (Taylor 1908: 20).

> ... Storytelling is a way of mourning the dead (Alexie 1996: 48).

This is a case study.[1] But really, it's just about what you can read in
the newspapers, in your hotel room, waiting for a plane to take you
somewhere else. The topic is how a man born among the Semai,
traditionally among the least violent peoples on record, turned violent.
The presentation follows the rules of empirical anthropology: raw
data, methodology and contextual narrative, interpretation, conclusion,
separated from each other into tidy boxes. Orderly.

Like empirical anthropologists, traditional Semai place a great value
on order. When you don't follow their complex rules for maintaining
cosmic order, they say, fierce thundersqualls sweep in from the forest,
the earth collapses, and great tectonic dragons rise writhing into the
dim light as the darkling waters that lie beneath the dissolving earth
burst forth, and everything safe and familiar drowns. Something like
that happened in this case, and it pushes against the tidiness of the
presentation.

You can get in touch with the powers of disorder, Semai say,
by going into trance with the help of a familiar spirit. Or sometimes
those powers just take you anyway. *Blnuul bhiip*, "blood intoxication",
is like that, for example. You see spilled human blood, your own
or someone else's, and your terror puts you through a series of
psychic experiences that are like the stages of trance. Sometimes
the process ends with the dizziness and nausea that affect people
who begin to dance into trance but stop before the familiars enter
them. Sometimes it continues, and you yourself become compulsively
violent.

As to the man himself: I don't even know how I should spell his
name. In the police reports it has one "f", the proper Arabic spelling,
but the newspapers give it two. His Semai name was Bah Pin, short
for Arifin, but that didn't show up on his identity card or in the
newspaper stories. I only met him twice, under difficult circumstances,

for a few minutes each time. But, for a little while in 1992, he was pretty famous in Malaysia.

A Note on Method (Such As It Is)

This sort of case study illuminates a reality not accessible to more abstract formal language. To paraphrase Benedict Anderson closely (1990: 155n), it is sad that it should be such records of judicial processes, where the stakes, at least for the accused, are so high, and where all parties, for their own reasons, are deeply concerned to question, justify, and accuse, that bring the alien anthropologist his keenest sense of the pain of people's ordinary lives. Worse than sad, maybe, making ethnographers and inquisitors allies.

Traditional descriptive ethnography has come under fire, because the authors used to be people like me: old white Anglophone men, based in universities, who added "master narratives" to the other indignities which, sometimes by virtue simply of the relative power of their native countries, they inflicted on "subaltern" peoples. The shift in praxis over the last half century to authors from other social categories has not, in the minds of the critics, outdated their critique. I tend to agree with them. With one caveat: talking about "postcolonial" studies bothers me. What's "post-" about colonialism? The policies of the educated ruling classes in Malaysia towards indigenous peoples like Semai are almost indistinguishable from European colonialist policies, e.g. by Euro-Americans towards Native Americans (Dentan *et al.* 1996, Endicott and Dentan 2004).

But the intellectual problem is that "culture", the topic anthropologists feign to address, doesn't really exist, except as an abstraction in their own minds. What exists, Buddhism tells us, is suffering and the lies people tell each other about it, the sort of events this narrative addresses. I set about collecting narratives like this (e.g. Dentan 1993, 1999b, 2001, as well as several manuscripts) to document changes in Semai society, planning to conflate them into a "master narrative". And you can do that, write wonderful ethnographic accounts, like Le Roy Ladurie (e.g. 1975) and his followers. But in "master narratives"

> ...we pass
> through each other
> like pure arrows
> or fade into rumor (Ondaatje 1997: 711).

If we want to understand how culture works, we need to understand it on the ground, where it happens, in individual lives. We need to try to recreate those lives as vividly as we can, so that people can imagine them, imagine *being there*, not just read *about* them. And it's not just personal for Arifin, but for me as a would-be moral being talking to and about him. Intellectually and imaginatively, that's why we need life histories.

The presentation is "narrative" ethnography (cf. Eber 1995, McClusky 2001, Niman 1996). That is, I try to present facts as I experienced them, in sequence and in the context of my own responses, so that readers can make their own evaluations of both the facts and the research:

> people are invited to enter into experiential relationships with events through which they themselves did not live. Through such spaces people may gain access to a range of processual, sensually immersed knowledges, knowledges which it would be difficult to acquire by purely cognitive means (Landsberg 1997: 66).

Why do any ethnography? Isn't it, at least in part, because we humans need to make connections with others in order to understand who we are? When we encounter horrors like the ones I'm talking about, we need not to recoil. Rural Semai don't. The murderer I met in the country in 1992 has a *muh nicneec*, bad name/reputation, among people who know what he did, although they don't usually talk about it to outsiders. But most Semai don't think of criminals as a qualitatively different breed from ordinary people, the way so many Westerners do. There's none of the post-punishment Americans inflict on people who have committed crimes, the public humiliation and ostracism, the denial of ordinary rights. So Semai find it easier to connect with murderers, for example, than Americans like myself do.

The essentialism that soaks American folk notions of violence was in my head too, when writing this up, making me think *once a murderer always a murderer*, as if murderers were different from the rest of us in some fundamental way, the way Lombroso thought a century ago (e.g. 1911); but I couldn't sustain that feeling, that Arifin was *only* a monster, because I did know his life history, a little. I think, finally, that all of us humans floundering here in life need to ask the question about our inquisitors Alain Resnais asks at the end of *Night and Fog*, his 1955 documentary on the Nazis, as the camera pans slowly around the wintry Auschwitz death camp:

> Are their faces different from ours? …There are those who sincerely look on these ruins today as if the monster were dead and buried beneath them; those who feign taking hope again as the image fades,

as if there were a cure for the sickness of these camps; those who pretend to believe that all this happened only once, at a certain time and in a certain place; those who refuse to see. Who are deaf to the endless cry. [RKD translation]

These are the Simple Facts of the Case

Expat's wife tells of guard's attack
By Anita Gabriel

KUALA LUMPUR, Mon. An American expatriate's wife told the magistrate's court here today that she thought the security guard in her house had killed her cocker-spaniel when she found bloodstains on the floor at the entrance to her house.... [S]he had just returned from dinner at a friend's place two or three minutes drive away when her toe hit a large stone as she was walking towards her garage.

"I called for my guard and he explained to me that he used the stone to get rid of stray dogs," she said.

As she entered the house, she discovered bloodstains on her cream-colored tiles and uttered, "Oh God, he did it ... he killed my dog."

At that moment, the guard approached her and threw a stone which hit her forehead.

"I started screaming for help and threw my amah's shoe at the guard. He threw another stone which also hit my forehead," she said.

["I realised I could not fight him and ran inside the house and latched the front door and picked up the phone to call for help but it was dead," she said.

"I went upstairs to my bedroom but the children and maid were missing and there were blood stains on the floor."]

"[M]y sons were not sleeping on my bed and [I] saw some bloodstains around it," she said.... She said she used the cellular phone in her room and called a friend who lived about 20 metres from her house, Mr. David Frediani....

["I called David ... with a hand phone and asked him to come over after telling him the guard was trying to kill me."]

David said as he was running towards Sunita's house after receiving her call, he saw someone running away from the compound.

"I shouted to the man to stop, but he continued to run," he said.

Asked ... to describe the man, David said he was wearing a light-colored shirt and a pair of dark trousers similar to a guard's uniform and seemed to be holding something.

Idealised Ethnic Dress.

Atop "good" Malay-style dress, Risau wears distinctively Semai appurtenances: bark cloth, crossband and headband with flowers. He carries a distinctively Semai blowpipe and quiver but does not wear the loincloth despised by Malays. Chaba' Jinter, 1962.

Semai Men in Malay-style Dress.

This is the dress of Pahang men when they are dressed up. In both Pahang and Perak it would be worn to go among Malays, and in Perak it would be the at-home dress of men who could afford it.

Mocking Aboriginal Dress. Semai are aware of Malay feelings about loincloths, and they themselves mock the loincloths of their ancestors (*mai manah antum*) which they say were too narrow and worn too high. Chaba' Jinter, Pahang, 1962.

Semai Man and His Son. The man on the right wears Kelantanese Malay dress, transmitted to the Semai via their northern neighbors, the Temiar. The son dresses like a poor Kampong Malay. They are feeding wild chicks. Chaba' Jinter, Pahang, 1962.

Earlier, Sunita's husband, Rakesh Talwar, 42, a business manager
with Colgate Palmolive..., said the maid, "Netty," had been with them for
four years.... [A]bout 9:45pm, he went upstairs and found his children
sleeping in his bedroom ... he described the behaviour of the security
guard in his house that day as "normal, chatty and friendly."

New Straits Times (21 July 1992)

[Long text in brackets is from Anonymous (1992), "Security guard tried
to kill woman, inquiry told", *The Star* (21 July).]

* * *

About the missing children. Kabir, the elder brother, was 11 years old.
Arjun, the younger, was seven. Kabir's grown-up teeth were growing in
crooked, and he had to wear orthodontic braces. That night it was so
hot and humid that the boys had taken off their shirts and, I suspect,
had dropped them on the floor in an untidy heap for Netty the maid to
pick up. Kabir wore shorts, striped black and white; Arjun wore baggy
red sweatpants. The little boys wiggled too much to sleep in the same
bed, though they liked the idea of sleeping together in their parents'
bed when their parents were away, boys are like that; and one or both
usually wound up sleeping on the floor, I imagine, as happened that
night. I hope they weren't afraid of the dark.

The boys couldn't have been very big. The top of an 11-year-old's
head comes about level with your shoulder. The nose of a seven-year-
old who's hugging you gets buried just below your sternum. The hugs
feel good, but even when their arms are plump they seem fragile.
You worry about how easy it is to break children, and you want to
encapsulate them against the buffeting they're going to get from life.
You know it's going to hurt.

* * *

Statement under Interrogation[2]

Report No.	1569/92	**Station**	Pantai
Name	Arifin bin Agas	**Nickname**	Pin
Identity Card #	A 1365320		
Ancestry	Orang Asli	**Language**	Malay

Date/Place of Birth	1967 Kuala Lipis, Pahang
Age	26
Occupation	Security Guard
Work Address	GWEN KENS SECURITY SERVICE
	No. 1, Petaling Garden, Petaling Jaya, Selangor
Home Address	No. 1, Jalan Othman, Petaling Jaya, Selangor
Other Addresses	Kampong Potdixon, Kuala Lipis, Pahang
Work Telephone No.	7929246
Home	—
Father's Name	AGAS BIN ?
Father's Address	Deceased
Recording Officer	Inspector Dollah Daud at C[awangan] S J[enayah]
P[erdagangan] office, Jalan Hang Tuah,	
Kuala Lumpur on 25.4.92 at 1100	
Translator	from to

Text: On 25.4.92 at 10:30 AM when I was at Office D5, IPK, Kuala Lumpur I was asked by PPP Poh to record a statement under authority of Sec[tion] 113 KAJ from a S[us]P[ect] DPC 69358 brought before me a SP wearing a black jacket, blue jeans and his name was determined which was given as ARIFIN BIN AGAS ID[entity]C[ard] A1365320(B). I examined the SP's body and no wounds or bruises of any kind were observed. The SP had already said that his education was to the Third Level at Clifford Middle School, Kuala Lipis, Pahang. After talking for approximately 20 minutes with SP it was determined that the SP could speak and understand the Malay Language well. I asked him after that whether he was feeling alright or not and [he] said he was alright and wanted to make a statement in the Malay language.

[signature illegible]

Before recording a summary statement from ARIFIN BIN AGAS IDC A13653220(B) I read the following warning in the Malay Language.

"IT HAS BECOME MY DUTY TO GIVE A WARNING TO YOU THAT YOU ARE NOT OBLIGED TO SAY ANYTHING OR TO ANSWER ANY ANYTHING, BUT ALSO THAT ANYTHING YOU SAY, WHETHER IN ANSWER TO A QUESTION OR NOT, MAY BE GIVEN IN EVIDENCE."

Q: In what language do you want to speak?
A: Malay.

Q: Do you understand the warning which has just been read and explained to you?
A: Yes.

Q: Is it the case that you want to ask any questions in connection with the warning [you have] just received?
A: No.

Q: Is it the case that you want to provide any information in connection with the warning (you have) just received bearing on this case?
A: Yes.

Q: Is it the case that you have received any inducements, threats or promises to give a statement to me?
A: No.

Q: Is it the case that I have been in the position of inducing, frightening or making any promise at all to you so that you will give a statement to me?
A: No.

[signature illegible]

S: Is it the case that you are giving this statement of your own free will?
A: Yes.

S: What do you know about this case?

I have worked at Gwen Kens *Security Service* since 3 March 1992 as a security watchman until the date I was arrested. On 23.4.1992 I was assigned to work as a watchman at Address NO. 20 20, Jalan Turi, *off* Jalan Ara, Bukit Bandaraya, Bangsar, Kuala Lumpur. I was assigned starting at 7:00 PM 23.4.92 until 7:00 AM 24.4.92. At approximately 8:40 PM the owners of the house left to go to a *'Party'* leaving the babysitter and the (2) children. Approximately at 11:00 PM the babysitter informed me that someone had rung the doorbell three times, and each time the bell rang she went out but there was no one there. After that I patrol the area to see if everything's okay and shine my light all over the area and there wasn't anything, all the surroundings were quiet and dark. After patroling and there isn't anything I take a container of rice from my bag but suddenly there appear (3) Chinese men all dressed in dark (black) clothes and one of those men points his pistol at my head and at that time also I determine that one man also is carrying a pistol and the other is carrying a knife. After that that man (who was holding the pistol) asks me what *lu*[3] do here. I answer I am working and in the middle of eating. Then I ask him in return How could you get in here sir, and he answered, don't sweat it you don't want to know that. I ask him in return, who do you want to see and he answers I want to give you a job, I try to be brave and answer I'm in the middle of a job right now, why would I want another job, that man says *Lu* don't babble on any more and at that time he threatens me with his pistol to my head, he says don't make any noise or [I'll] blow off *Lu* head and [you'll] die right here. A few seconds later the babysitter comes out because of the noise. Hearing the door open that man pulls me into a dark area behind a Casuarina tree. The babysitter comes right up to us because she doesn't see us. One of the men takes a concrete block and hits her in the area of the nape of her neck (2) times, afterwards that man orders me to drag the babysitter along with the concrete block to the grassy place where we're standing. After that one of the gangsters looks for some way to hide the babysitter. After I see the babysitter get hit I feel myself trembling, my thoughts are so mixed up and confused that I panic and can't think what to do. Finally one of the gangsters finds a way to hide the babysitter. He orders me to drag the babysitter to the septic tank of the house. After that while I'm dragging the babysitter to the grass one of the men throws stones in the direction of the babysitter the number was a lot, finally the man orders me to throw stones around the babysitter and drags the babysitter to the septic tank and I also drag the babysitter into the septic tank.

Afterwards the three Chinese men are going up to the parking area and one of them threatens [me] with his pistol to my head in a brutal way directs me to go into the house and he takes me somewhere in the house I don't know [where] and the (2) other men wait outside. When we arrive inside the house the man takes a piece of wood like a *'Pingpong racket'*[4] a long piece about a foot long. At that time I try to resist but to no avail because the weapon still menaced my head. Finally the man directs [me upstairs] to a story that I have never entered. When we got up there we run across two children asleep (it is believed in their room) one is sleeping on a bed and another beside the bed, I don't know whose boys they are. The man then gives me the *'Pingpong racket'* piece of wood and orders me to whack the heads of the boys several times, I do not recall what part [I] hit. So then I am forced to carry the boy outside on my shoulders (just one) but to no avail because [the little boy is too] heavy and the man forces me to drag the boy downstairs and outside to the septic tank. Afterwards the man forces me to go upstairs again and take the boy and drag him downstairs but he directs me to carry the boy outside by a different route but it is found that the door is locked and I drag him back upstairs again and then out again by the door [I used] before and forces me to carry him straight to the septic tank. While I was coming out [of the house] carrying the boys it was observed that the two men who were waiting outside were not to be seen. After I put the third boy into the septic tank the man forces me to put the lid back on the septic tank to close it. After that the man directs me to go to the parking area and when I have been in the parking area for a few minutes I hear a car coming into the house and at that time the gate in the fence isn't open yet, and at the same time the Chinese man drags me to the dark place behind the Casuarina tree. I see the owner of the house get out of the car (a woman it is believed of Indian ancestry) and finally asks me why there are many stones scattered around the parking area and I tell the owner of the house because there were people throwing left-over stones into our yard because around the gate in our fence there had been several dogs hanging around. I have been forced by the Chinese man who is still behind me to tell that, to the owner of the house. After that the woman goes into the parking area and through the parking area to the front steps and at the same time the Chinese man who is behind me hands me a big lump of stone and forces me to throw that stone at the woman and I throw it right away and I see the woman fend off the stone her hand hits my left arm and her fingernails scratch my left arm. While this is happening the Chinese man has already vanished. Finally I get my bag and my food and climb out over the fence to go to the Pantai Police station that's the local Police Station.

When I got to the traffic light by the *'Pantai Medical Centre'* I met my supervisor named Ramakrishnan and I told him what had happened. I urged him to go to the Pantai Police Station ahead of me to make a Police report but he said he wanted to meet with the gentleman who owns the company first to discuss the matter. When we got to the Jalan Gasing area, P/[etaling] Jaya, we met up with the car belonging to our boss and went up to his car and and told the story of what had happened and they still insisted on going to the house where it happened, but I still insisted on going to the Station to make a *report* but they were insistent about going to the spot where the incident happened. So we went to the place where it happened.

When we got to the place where it happened I observed a lot of people and Police officers everywhere in the area and a police officer took my arm after I turned myself in. Then the Police directed me to show the place where the babysitter and the children of the owner of the house were hidden and I showed it to the Police. At the same time the Police surrounded the house because they suspected there was something going on on the roof of the house. Finally I was taken to a patrol Car and [it] took me straight to the station and after that I don't know anything that happened later.

Q: Is it the case that you could recognize the three Chinese males [you] described if you met them again?

A: I could if I saw them inside a week [from now]. I won't be able to remember if it's been a long time.

Q: Could you give a sketch of the three Chinese males who were with you at the site of the incident?

A: (1) The man who put the pistol to my your head. He spoke broken Malay Language, Age 20–30ish, Height 5 feet 6 in. hair with a little gray in it, no moustache, no moustache, clothes dark black including hands.

(2) The man who held a pistol.
Spoke brokenly in the Malaysian Language,
Age approximately 20ish,
Height 5 feet 5 in, no moustache, clothes dark black including hands.

(3) The man who held a
Spoke brokenly in the Malaysian Language, Age approximately 20ish, Height 5 feet 5 in, no moustache, clothes dark black including hands.

[signature illegible]

(Dollah Daud) Insp.
Investigating Officer
Criminal Affairs Branch

* * *

What I remember first about him, the thing that haunts my memory of him almost as much as the teeth, is how *small* he looked in the enormous visitors' gallery in Pudu Prison where inmates in fetters mill around waiting for their visitors. It's not that I usually think of Semai as small people. Many are, I suppose, but I don't normally notice people's size once I've started talking with them. Besides, some of my Semai friends, Tony and Juli for example, are taller than I am. But in that Victorian prison gallery, among burly Chinese gangsters and elongated turbaned Sikh murderers, Arifin looked *tiny*. The clear plastic handcuffs he wore looked like children's toys, not serious manacles for a dangerous criminal.

* * *

Expert: Dislodged teeth belonged to dead boy
By Anita Gabriel

KUALA LUMPUR, Tues. — A dental specialist told a special inquiry here today that a great deal of force must have been inflicted on an 11-year old boy to have caused five of his teeth to be dislodged.... Dr Sharifah Fauziah replied that either a severe punch or a blow with a hard and heavy object could have inflicted such trauma on the deceased.

It was a direct blow which hit him on the face, she said, adding that the impact of the blow would have been the same if he was sleeping, sitting or standing....

[Arjun Talwar sustained a fatal haemorrhage on his brain as a result of blows on the head by a blunt object.... [T]he fatal wound ran along the ear to the eye and the brain tissue could be seen protruding from one of the wound[s]. There was depressed fracture bone on the left side of the head].

Korporal Majid Jaafar, 38, a zone supervisor at Pantai police station who was patrolling the area said he was stopped by a woman, Sunita Talwar, who told him her children and amah had been kidnapped.

He entered the house and found some bloodstains on the stair case.

Later, at 12.10am when Majid was outside the house, an Indian and a Malay man, (whom he identified as Ariffin) approached him.

The Indian man, named Ramachandran, had told Majid that the guard, Ariffin, was on duty in the house during that night.

When Majid asked the guard if he was involved in the incident, he said the guard replied: "Ya, Encik" ["Yes, sir"].

"I then handcuffed him and asked him to lead me to where he had hidden the children and the amah," said Majid.

Majid alleged that Ariffin told him the bodies were kept in a hole and voluntarily led Majid to a sewage tank behind the house.

When they reached the place. two other police officers who had accompanied them, shone a torchlight into the hole — about 15 feet deep — and saw three bodies, he said ... it was not possible for them to be alive because the hole was very deep and the lid of the tank was shut tightly....

Another witness, Jumri Ahmad, 41, an ambulance medical assistant, said.... "Their eyeballs were dilated and fixed and there was no movement. I checked and found that there was no pulse and they were not breathing."

There were traces of blood on the younger boy's (Arjun) left ear and Kabir had suffered injuries on the right side of his head....

He said he also moved the body of the younger boy whose head was under his elder brother's body. [Dr. Abdul Rahman Mohamad Yusof.... said he also found a few broken teeth consistent with a woman's on the floor and a broken chopping board near the blood smear beside the main staircase ... [and] blood splashes on the staircase consistent with blood dripping from injured persons in a standing position.... "A cloth was found inside Kabir's mouth and his right eye was swollen. Punch marks were also found on both jaws," he added.

He said Fernandes sustained several injuries on her face with missing teeth, broken jaws and her nose was covered with blood.]

New Straits Times (22 July 1992)

[The first long text in brackets is from Anonymous (1994), "Boy had fatal head wound, court told", *The Star* (29 January); the second is from Anonymous (1994), "Murdered brothers and maid possibly dragged down the staircase, court told", *The Sun* (28 January).]

* * *

"I had never touched the blood of a human being before," Arifin told me.[5] He "was scared", he said, and *bingung*, "unaware of his surroundings", "in a daze". He couldn't recall the details of hauling the corpses to the cesspit, just dragging them along by the heels, face down. He thought they were dead, he said. They didn't make any noise, or move. But he was too frightened to check.

The most visible distress Arifin showed during our conversation was when we were talking about the little boys, about how their parents felt. "They love their children," he said, frowning in pain and shaking his head. "I have children. I love my children. Who doesn't love his children?"[6]

* * *

> I wander thro' each charter'd street,
> Near where the charter'd Thames doth flow.
> And mark in every face I meet
> Marks of weakness, marks of woe.
>> From William Blake, *London* (1994 [1794]: 83)

That evening I wrote up my notes in a small slightly seedy room in the small slightly seedy Chinese hotel where I usually stay in Malaysia, on a banged-up Olivetti portable several keys of which no longer worked. My family had been back in the US for a couple of weeks. I was lonely. The story seemed disgusting and full of corruption. *What kind of work is this I do?* Vision of myself: pale, big-nose naked-headed alien scavenger, lurking in the shadows for some new morsel of carrion to gulp.

The crowd downstairs at the hotel seemed tipsy, noisy and stupid. Ill at ease and depressed, always uneasy in crowds, I went out to walk in the light evening rain that fell in slanting lines through the night. Earlier that evening, along the Klang River valley to the east, the rising heat and haze from the truck-choked roads and smoking factories had sucked in cooler breezes from above the Indian Ocean. The sea breezes carried dense banks of acrid smog inland, swallowing the sky and obscuring the dark hills to the east of the city. The bloated sun had bled itself out over the ocean, in layers of particulates that reflected its rays in gorgeous oranges and reds, the atmospheric tinge Semai call *nyamp*, and fear. Now it was dark and cooler.

Pale raindrops pockmarked the greasy sidewalks. An occasional dying gust of wind picked up scraps of plastic bags and blew them flapping down the streets like mangled *ruwaay* headsouls until they caught on some sharp projection or barrier and went limp. The gutters in Kuala Lumpur are mostly covered now, so you can't smell them, though the smell of damp was everywhere. You can't see the moon or stars, of course. The bright lights prevent that anyway. But, just up the street from my hotel, on the bridge across the confluence of rivers that gives the city its name, the dark takes over. You can't see the fragments of plastic and styrofoam, just see and hear and smell the rivers, swollen with rain and run-off, feather-flashes of white foam like frantic fish lashing with their tails, and gleaming darkness. Blues time for damp aging Americans.

This area used to belong to Temuan, another group of Malaysian indigenes, "Orang Asli" to use the official government term for West Malaysian indigenes in general. Chinese miners drove the Temuan out, and the British sided with the miners, and the Temuan got nothing. The people moved to a new place, away from the burgeoning city. For many years the government used this new settlement, conveniently close to the capital, as a sort of Potemkin village for their policies towards Orang Asli. They bussed visiting dignitaries there. See how much like a Malay peasant settlement this looks! Plank houses, TV antennas, fruit trees, Vespas. Then they decided to build a new airport and drove the Temuans out. It's all government land anyway.

There's something about rivers. You see one, you think of another. I thought about William Blake's "charter'd Thames", in his time newly penned between embankments, as these rivers were in crumbling concrete spillways.

> In every cry of every Man,
> In every Infant's cry of fear.
> In every voice, in every ban,
> The mind-forg'd manacles I hear.

> (Ibid., p.83)

But the Klang is different from the Thames. Now that the rainforests that used to absorb rainwater are gone, the Klang floods almost every year, obliterating roads and cars and buildings, burying them in featureless mud. Listening to the dark waters smash against their manmade banks, I recalled the enormous flood dragons I'd first heard of on the Teiw Tluup in Pahang, thirty years earlier, swimming in huge mindless menace through the cold abysses beneath the earth.

On the wet streets and sidewalks all around, misting the distant neon lights, the unseen rain was falling.

* * *

To: R.K. Dentan
From: C[olin] N[icholas], Center for Orang Asli Concerns
Date: 24 July 1992
Re: killing of maid and two children (US nationals) in April this year, see newspaper
cutting for details. The accused is a Semai man who is married to a Malay and
had 'masuk Gob'. For most Orang Asli [indigenous people, like Semai], he is as
good as a Gob.

* * *

Arifin was born *maay Tluup*, a Telom River person from northwest
Pahang state, in the settlement of Cba' Lanaw "Slimy Delta", near
Cba' Jnteer, where I worked in 1962. So I could understand his dialect,
although it had been 30 years since I had spoken it, and we kept
slipping into the Waar River dialect which was the Semai I had used
during most of my 1991–92 fieldwork.

During the mid-century Communist uprising the British "regrouped"
the Telom people around a "jungle fort", Fort Dixon, in order to
facilitate their control of the "aborigines". It was the first in a continuing
series of lessons in powerlessness. In 1979, when Arifin was about 12
years old, the Malay-dominated government "regrouped" about 1,300
Telom people, almost everyone, to a 2,860-acre Regroupment Scheme
near Betau, about 40 miles from Raub and 20 from Kuala Lipis, still
in Pahang state. They said it was so that they could deliver services
better, but most people knew that the greed of the Sultan of Pahang
for logging money was an important factor.

The Betau Regroupment Scheme is like any reservation. Loggers
have deforested it. There is not enough land for traditional Semai farming
or agroforestry to be self-sustaining, and the rivers have been fished
out. The clinic goes unstaffed, but Malay power is everywhere. Little
Bah Pin had to speak Malay in school, where the teachers were and
are Malay and the children are ashamed to speak their own language,
which they call *nroo' maay miskin*, a language for the pathetic poor.
Malays appear on television, glamorous, rich, self-assured, everything
a boy might want to be. Malay men molest Semai women at will,
and laugh about it. Malay politicians visit occasionally, hectoring and
lecturing the people, condemning their laziness and ingratitude. The
little boy must have paid attention, and learned. Three years later, he
converted to Islam and *moot Gɔp*, as Semai say, became a Malay.[7]

He always "minat" Islam, he said, had a liking for it, and, he said, (just as Malays say, wrongly) "Semai have no religion." No, he didn't convert just to get married, although, to marry a Malay like his wife, he would have had to. He and his wife's family had talked a lot about Islam. He loved his wife, he said. She had had a hard time giving birth to their first child. Before that she had had a job of her own, but afterward he told her that she had enough to do at home, and that they could live on his wages. It's a Malay attitude: Malay men should support their families, unlike Semai, for whom marriage is a partnership. Arifin had never returned to Betau, although he had kept in touch with his *tnee'*, an older kinsman of his generation, who worked at the Indigenous Peoples' Hospital in Gombak, near Kuala Lumpur.

* * *

"Just Following Orders, That's All"
Hand Printed Statement by Arifin

In fact on 28/4/92 I was employed at the Bangsar Indah condominuium in Maarof Lane. On 23/4/92 [I] left home and arrived at the office at 6:30 PM and was sent to the company van with my colleagues and supervisor, Mr. Ramachandran 6:45 PM [we were] on our way, my supervisor Mr. Ramachandran told me to work at No. [20] Turi Road and I was just following his orders, that's all. 7:15 PM [we] arrived at No. 20 Turi Road [I] got out and right away I rang the doorbell and the door was oipened by the babysitter.

At 8:00 o'clock PM the gentleman and the lady went out in their car and did not inform me to where. At 8:40 8:20 PM the gentleman came back by himself in the car and went inside the house. Minutes later a taxi arrived. The gentleman got in the taxi with a *bag* and I helped him take the *bag* and the taxi left.

I and the babysitter went into the courtyard and the babysitter closed the gate in the fence with a *remove control,* and the babysitter went into the house. And I sat down in a chair in the car *paking* [parking area].

At 11:00 PM I felt hungry and went to the water pipe in front to wash my hands. After washing my hands I went back to where I had been sitting and sat down and opened my *bag* to get the supper which had been packed by my wife.

Suddenly the babysitter came running out in a rush to the gate in the fence, not looking to the left and saying there'd been someone ringing the doorbell. And at the same time I was startled and surprised not because the babysitter was had come running out in a rush to the fence gate but because while I was getting up suddenly three Chinese men appeared beside the place where I had been sitting. These criminuls were all three in dark clothes, hands, shirts and pants and one of the criminuls had a scar on his face, and two had pistols and one was armed with a knife. One of the three criminuls chased the babysitter, picking up a stone from under a tree along the way and right away hit the babysitter. The babysitter fell down and the criminul dragged her onto the grass. Then I tried to resist but was unsuccessful, because the criminuls at that time hit me too. I fell down and [I tried to] get up one of the criminuls who had a big strong body and a scar on his face pressed me down and menaced me and threatened that if [I] resisted or did anything the criminuls would kill me. Also at that time 2 of the criminuls went into the house 10 minutes later the criminuls came out and threatened [me] and forced me to drag the corpse to the privy pit and after that they forced me to gather stones to be thrown [to cover up the body]. In the circumstances [I was] extremely scared and extremely panicked. I was just following orders, that's all.[8] After I was finished following the orders of the criminuls....

Suddenly the criminul yanked and pulled [me by the] arm and shoved me behind the wall by the entry door to the stairs blocked by a tree. A car drove up and entered the compound the mistress of the house got out of the car. And [the criminals? passage unclear] circled around from there. Mistress stepped away and entered, asking how the rocks got that way. As directed by the criminuls I said in a shaking voice there was someone throwing stones into here from outside, because dogs were hanging around in front of our fence gate. Mistress stepped up to the doorstep to enter the house. At that point the criminal threw a stone in that direction and at the same time the criminul also directed me to throw stones in that direction, pushing me in the direction the stones were thrown. I saw mistress lying there. I was staring and looking back, suddenly the criminuls had disappeared from my view.

At that moment mistress jumped me from behind. I tried to push her away but was scratched by her fingernails in the area of my left arm. My fear and panic increased. I grabbed my *bag* and ran away from there as fast as I could without looking to the right or left. I was thinking I wanted to get help and *report* to the police station. But suddenly on the way I heard someone calling my name. I was startled and stopped, looking back in the direction of the voice and I went closer it was my supervisor Mr. Ramachandran. I quickly informed my supervisor [what had happened]. I wanted to *report* to the police station, but my supervisor prevented me, saying there were many police already waiting for [me at the house] and the supervisor told me to get into his car. But it turned out he drove his car to the house of our *boss,* saying he wanted to have a discussion with the *boss*. The *boss* and *Mr*. Huang were already waiting in the yard of the house. Right away I told the *boss* and *Mr*. Huang that I wanted to *report* to the police station but the *boss* and *Mr*. Huang prevented me. The *boss* and *Mr*. Huang said I couldn't because there were a lot of police waiting for me where the incident happened. I fell silent and did [not] know what to say.[9] I was sent away from the *boss's* house and got into the car of my supervisor Mr. Ramachandran, and the *boss* and *Mr*. Huang each got into their cars. On the way Mr. Ramachandran picked up the knife with a piece of paper in his car and threw the knife away and I recall the place and we went straight to the place where the incident happened. I felt confident because there were many uniformed police and I met with the police and told them the truth about what happened. The police handcuffed me and beat me up and I fell down there and right away they took me to the police station. At the police station [I] was beaten and questioned and interrogated. And I told the truth about what happened. But the police didn't believe me and didn't admit that there were other people including the three Chinese men who committed the crime, and that my supervisor prevented me from making a report (*report*) to the police and that my supervisor threw the knife away. And after beating [me] up and interrogating [me, they] put me in the *lock-up*. The next day I was taken to the main hospital to be examined and back to the police station [where I was] beaten up and interrogated. After I told them [the story] that was not true and the police believed it, then the police put [me] into the *lock-up*. And on the second day early in the morning I was taken out and beaten up and interrogated again and they took the line that I threw the knife away and that the mistress had gone to a *party*. [I] told them the truth that the person who did it who threw the knife away was my supervisor Mr. Rama Chandran and in my report I said I never touched the knife who[ever] threw it away, And also whether mistress went out to a *party* I didn't know because the gentleman and the lady went out without informing me.

After I told them the truth the police still didn't believe me. And [when] I told them what wasn't true, then they believed me. Then the police took me to the place [I] mentioned where the knife was tossed by Mr. Ramachandran. I and some plainclothes policemen went looking for it together and one of the plainclothes policemen with white hair found the knife next to a ditch and the policemen ordered me to come over to the knife and point [at it]. One of the policemen took my picture. And the policemen ordered me to pick up the knife and give it to a policeman. And the policeman put it in a *plastic* bag. After they were finished, the

police took me back to the station. Back at the station I was beaten up
and interrogated and kept in the *lock-up*. During my time in the *lock-up* I
was given food and water but I couldn't manage to eat or drink because
all my body and my head were always hurting. I was locked up for two
weeks. I tried to eat because I was extremely hungry but I couldn't, not
even a spoonful, without vomiting and I asked for first aid but the police
promised, but only broke their promise. After that I was taken to court two
times. I tried to speak but was not allowed to by the police. On 6/5/92 I
was sentenced under sec[tion] 302 k.3rd. without an inquiry or evidence
and taken to Pudu Prison and given medical help in the prison hospital,
and my condition got better so I'm OK now.

* * *

My visa was to expire in a couple of weeks and I was preparing
to leave Malaysia when Colin Nicholas of the Center for Orang Asli
Affairs told me Arifin was Semai. I called Balaguru, the chief counsel,
to talk to him about "blood drunkenness", *blnuul bhiip*, which I thought
might be a defense. Balaguru checked me out with Anthony Ratos,
a former official of the Department of Orang Asli Affairs, who as a
Tamil-Malaysian was eased out when the Department decided that all
its senior officials must be Malays. Ratos has remained an active and
admirable supporter of Orang Asli causes.

Meanwhile, I checked Arifin out with Semai friends, who dismissed
him as "really a Malay" and regarded my involvement in the case as
quixotic and idiosyncratic, not necessary for me as an advocate of Semai
causes. Balaguru called back and suggested we meet. At the meeting,
he gave me the statements by Arifin I have reproduced in this essay,
and suggested I should talk with Arifin in person. I was unprepared
for the suggestion but decided on the spot to accept the invitation.

I was uneasy. Arifin was in a struggle for his life. If I hadn't thought
I might be able to help his case and that speaking Semai might be a
relief, I don't think I would have talked with him. As it was I didn't
prepare an interview, and we didn't talk long. And I don't think speaking
Semai was a relief for him; and, since Malaysian law does not recognise
"temporary insanity" or "irresistible impulse" as defenses, my attempt
to be useful to him failed.

* * *

Guard: I had no reason to kill the three
By Jocelyn Lee

Ariffin also alleged he was beaten by policemen after being arrested at the scene of the incident when he followed Ramachandran back to the house.

He said that he was stripped of his shirt and pants and threatened by a policeman called Maniam who, together with other policemen, hit and slapped him and dragged him around when he fell.

He suffered injuries on his head, legs, arms and body, including a split lip.

New Straits Times (18 March 1994)

* * *

When I spoke with Arifin's pro bono lawyers in July, 1992, just before I had to leave the country, they said they did not know what to make of his story. K. Balaguru, a large intelligent Tamil-Malaysian man with a beautiful basso profundo voice, said he was "reserving judgment" on whether Arifin was telling the truth. The other Tamil lawyer said that he had "spiritual" evidence that Arifin was telling the truth, but declined to elaborate. The Malay assistant counsel, a young woman, found Arifin's apparent sincerity convincing, as did one of the other assistants, a slight Tamil man.

The story was more convincing when Arifin told it, leaning forward, gesturing brokenly with his manacled hands, eyes moist with the intensity of his need to be believed, to be freed, to be allowed to live. In the official statements the "I" disappears sometimes, so I had to add it in brackets; the verbs of which Arifin is the object almost all deal with subordination and intimidation, like most modern Semai lives: *they ordered [me], they forced [me], they threatened [me]. I just did what I was told, only that.* In his account, Arifin does not make anything happen, only acts when acted upon, does what the vague threatening alien powerful people around him want him to do, becomes what they want him to be. He isn't an actor, he's scarcely a person. The story may not be true to fact but it seems true to Arifin's life.

But in prison he still looked the way he wanted to look, like a little Malay, the way Malay propagandists say Semai really are, little brothers of the kindly Malay elder siblings who will tell them what they must do to grow up to be full human beings, Malays. A good-looking, small man with a little pencil mustache that made him look slick, like a Malay lady's man. His lawyers said that his wife and in-laws described him as "a perfect husband, obliging and friendly, always willing to go out of his way to help". I can believe it: a good father, a perfect husband, a hard worker. An exemplary little Malay man, though that never got in the papers, and the Malay-language papers were as careful to point out that he was an aborigine as the other Orang Asli were to point out that he was a Malay. The English language papers got his name wrong. To his interrogators he was nothing.

* * *

Inquiry told of guard's request
By Anita Gabriel

KUALA LUMPUR, Wed. — A security firm supervisor told the magistrate's court here today that a guard from his firm had disposed of a knife in his presence and later asked to be taken to a police station.

Mr M. Ramachandran, 39, of Gwenkens Security Sdn Bhd, said he received a call from his superior earlier telling him that there was trouble in a house to which he had earlier assigned a guard. Ramachandran said that after the call, he was driving to the house in Taman Bukit Bandaraya when he saw the guard — Ariffin Agas — along Jalan Gasing at 12:10 am and asked him what had happened.

"I told him to get into my car. As we were approaching the Pantai police station he took out a knife from his silver-coloured bag and told me to throw it away...." [T]he guard, who was clad in uniform, told him "*Saya terpaksa buat.*" (I had to do it).[10]

Questioned by defense counsel Mr K. Balaguru whether the guard had said "*terpaksa*" or "*dipaksa*", Ramachandran said he was sure the guard had said "*terpaksa.*"

"He wanted me to take him to the Brickfields police station but I said we would go to the house where the incident had taken place first," he said. ["I took him to the house as I wanted to find out what had happened."]

When they reached the house, they were met by a police officer who later handcuffed the guard.... [T]he police officer had questioned the guard roughly.... [T]he guard, who had been working with the firm for two years, had never caused any problems.

On the day of the incident, the guard usually assigned to Talwar's house was on leave.... "Mr Talwar wanted an English-speaking guard and therefore I assigned Ariffin," said Ramachandran.

He had personally sent Ariffin — who seemed normal — to the house that night....

Insp. Sheridan Mohammad, 39, said he had found a lot of blood stains in the house. They were found in the stairway, in the television room leading to the master bedroom and in the hall. [He said that during a search he found part of a chopping board with blood stains.]

He found two teeth in the television, two on the carpeted floor and one more on the dressing table in the master bedroom....[T]he first body that was brought out was that of Arjun, who wore a pair of red track pants but was shirtless.

"Then they took out the body of another boy (Kabir) who wore a pair of black and white-striped shorts and then a woman clad in a green skirt and T-shirt," said Sheridan.

Later, from the postmortem report, he came to know that a handkerchief was found in Kabir's mouth.

Sheridan said later, when he returned to his office, Ariffin — who was kept in the lock-up — told him he had thrown the knife somewhere along Jalan Pantai Baru.

"He told me he would show me where he had thrown the knife," said Sheridan.

Together with a team of policemen and the guard, he went to the place and discovered the knife.

New Straits Times (23 July 1992)

[Text inside brackets is from Rajeswari Kandiah, "Guard had blood stains on uniform, inquiry told", *The Star* (23 July 1992).]

* * *

Arifin was framed, he told me. He didn't even get to read the confession he signed. The cops figured he was guilty, so they didn't bother looking for the Chinese ninjas, or for footprints, or for fingerprints, just beat him and beat him and beat him until he was willing to say anything they wanted him to say.

But Ramachandran was the one who set him up, he said. When Ramachandran threw the knife out of the car, he threw it over the roof, so that it landed on Arifin's side of the car, as if Arifin had tossed it out. Besides, no knife was used in the killings. The cops made

Arifin pick up the knife before they bagged it. That's why it had his fingerprints on it.

A supervisor ought to drive a company car, he went on, but Ramachandran was driving a different car when he picked Arifin up, as if he had been out on non-company business. Ramachandran was an alcoholic who used to be under Arifin's supervision. But he accused Arifin of bringing a woman into the office — "my wife," said Arifin — and got Arifin demoted, and took Arifin's job as supervisor.

* * *

Guard had blood stains on uniform, inquiry told
By Rajeswari Kandiah

KUALA LUMPUR: The uniform of a security guard was stained with the blood of an Indian maid who was found dead together with two American children in a septic tank.

A government chemist, Primulapathi Jaya, 39 … said Ariffin's uniform was not stained with the children's blood… [H]e did not detect any seminal stains in the skirt which Natalia @ Netty was wearing.

He said her skirt and panties were not torn and there was no indication in her brassiere that she had come into contact with a hard surface.

He detected human blood on two rocks found in the garden of the house.

[Counsel representing the little boys' parents] added that the mother, Sunita, was in a state of trauma as a result of her children's death and if this case was prolonged, she might not be able to recover.

"She is presently receiving psychiatric treatment," he added.

[The first paragraph and a half is from *The Star* (23 July 1992); the next section is from the already quoted report by Anita Gabriel on the same date in *The New Straits Times;* the last two paragraphs are from an anonymous account, "Guard to stand trial for triple murder", *New Straits Times* (26 July 1992).]

* * *

Pudu Prison, where Arifin was kept, was a relic of colonial days. It sat among the glitz and colourful plastic modernity of Kuala Lumpur like a toad in a toybox, gray, ugly, a reminder of the days when Anglo-American theorists focused a lot of intellectual effort on bondage and discipline, repression and punishment. Like Albion and Attica Prisons in New York, Pudu Prison was a nineteenth-century outpost in the closing days of the twentieth century, a solid grim scary penal colony from the past.

Under duress, prisoners had painted the outside of the exterior wall, under the razor wire, flat childish pictures of the lowland tropical rainforest which most prisoners had not seen and now would never see: a forest now to all intents and purposes extinct on the peninsula, stereotyped palm trees out of primary school spelling books: *Ini ialah hutan*, "This is a jungle." In west Perak, on the coast washed by the holy Ganges, they put up fences around the polluting trash the get-rich-quick developers leave, and paint Day-Glo green palm trees on the fences, not only so as not to offend tourists passing by but also as a half-hearted pretense that things are still all right.

See? Palm trees (filth). Everything's fine (don't look too hard).

It's the same principle both places, I think. At least they didn't call it a "correctional institution". In 1996, they turned it into a tourist site, though in 1998, when the prison was 103 years old, there was talk of re-opening it to hold refugees fleeing to Malaysia from the disastrous Indonesian economy, people seeking to "enjoy proper meals", the police said.

Normally, you could get your picture taken there, I guess, the way tourists have pictures taken of themselves in the ovens at Auschwitz.

The *South China Morning Post* covered the proposal to reopen the prison (Stewart and Grant 1998).

* * *

Guard guilty of killing two children, maid
By Jocelyn Lee

A security guard was found guilty of killing two children and their maid.... The five-man and two-woman jury returned a six to one majority verdict against Ariffin Agas on all three charges...Ariffin, 26, ...remained impassive when the verdict was delivered by the foreman... High Court Judge Datuk Syed Ahmad Idid...told them [the jury] not to concern themselves with the consequences of their verdict and "must disregard any attempt to touch your emotional feelings."

New Straits Times (27 March 1994)

* * *

REFLECTION: LETTERS FROM A PUDU PRISON OF THE MIND

Wear the mask of circumstance long enough and inside
the face deforms, curves to fit the shape that binds
it, becomes what it seems to be because *pain needs to happen*,
don't stand in its way.
                    Kathe Koja, *Kink* (1996:167) — her italics

He did it, didn't he?
Yes.
How do you know?
He told his *tnee'*, his older cousin, his *tnee'* told my friends,
my friends told me.
He's a piece of shit.
No one is a piece of shit.
Tell that to the kids' mother.

* * *

In 1907 the old man in the epigraph killed women and children too,
stupidly enough to get caught by the British. The Orang Asli involved
weren't Semai, but the circumstances are a little like those in Arifin's
case. As traditional Semai got older, they got closer to demonic *halaa'*
power, the power of shamans and tigers, a gift of the thundersquall
Lord God. Malays in Trengganu, who may be acculturated Orang Asli,
connect *halaa'* and violence:

> [M]y next-door neighbor was almost strangled to death one night
> by her mistakenly jealous husband... Her husband is a classic
> example of *Angin Hala*, the Wind of the Weretiger, which
> makes one quick to anger and heedless of its consequences
> (Laderman 1991: 71).

Something demonic in Semai terms is going on, something like *blnuul
bhiip*, blood intoxication, which begins in panic and turns to cold mindless
murderousness, wraps you in a moral Cloud of Unknowing.

Writing this paragraph, I was in fear that the mother of two little kids
I knew and loved was beating them. The boys were about the same age
as Arjun and Kabir. They loved her, and she loved them. She never did
hurt them too badly, even when her bipolar disorder and agoraphobia,
her terror and rage, just got out of hand. Back then, she was under stress,
and I knew what she did when that happens, had seen the carpet burns

and bruises. She's ok now, I think. We don't see the family much any more. But it was that sort of helpless horror I felt.

I wish I could learn from this experience of mine, and use it to make sense of what happened on Jalan Turi that night. But it simply makes me feel more inarticulate and tentative. I want to turn away from him, don't you? There's nothing heroic about him. What he did was horrific, disgusting, stupid, greedy. You want not to have heard his alibis, not to understand them. I was ashamed after talking with him, afraid that I might be like him, even a little bit. Your only protection is to turn away, to say, *Monster! MONSTER. Not-me.*

But my *job* is to understand, isn't it? There are words and concepts I could use here: "identification with the oppressor," "imitative dependence," "panic disorder," "obsessive-compulsive behavior syndrome." But what happened is worse than this distanced jargon can encompass. All I can try to do is to recreate it, to make an account that ties *everything* together: Arifin's love for his children, the scattered teeth, "identification with the oppressor", the Betau Regroupment Scheme, the elision of ethnic and personal identity, the fear, the dazedness, and the blood.[11]

* * *

WHAT MAY HAVE HAPPENED: A VISION

> Whoever undertakes to write a biography binds himself to lying, to concealment, to flummery... Truth is not accessible (Sigmund Freud, cited in O'Brien 1994: 291).

> ...I do not, in the conventional sense, know many of these things. I am not making them up, however. I am imagining them. Memory, intuition, interrogation and reflection have given me a vision, and it is this vision that I am telling here (Banks 1989: 47).

> In certain kinds of abusive betrayals of children... escape is not a viable option. Here, the ability to detect betrayal may need to be stifled for the greater goal of survival. A child who distrusts his or her parents risks alienating the parents further, and thus becomes subject to more abuse and less love or care. In situations like these, it may be more advantageous to be blind to the betrayal (Freyd 1996: 10).

I think of little Bah Pin at the Betau Regroupment Scheme, learning
every day how worthless he is, how wonderful Malays are, how easy
it would be for him to change, to become a complete person instead
of an impotent ignorant savage. When who-you-are is under assault
all the time so that being you is only suffering, one type of relief is to
become like the people assaulting you, to become as much like them
as you can so they won't hurt you any more. If you can stop being
who you were, and become who they are, then you can feel safe. It
may be an illusion, but it's a relief. That's what psychoanalysts mean, I
think, when they talk about "Stockholm syndrome" or "identification with
the oppressor" as an "ego defense mechanism." You hurt me, because
of who I am. If I become you, you stop. I think that must be what Bah
Pin did, when he was just 15 years old, and "became a Malay".

But it's a hard act. You can't be sure that the new you is you. Arifin
wasn't able just to be Malay in the easygoing way most Malay men are.
He had to be *convincing*. He wasn't just a good Malay husband and
father, he was a *wonderful* husband and father; not just a good Malay
man, but a *perfect* Malay man. He had to smash little Bah Pin entirely, to
hollow himself out. Going back to Betau was scary and painful for him, I
imagine; I know he never went.[12] Agas, his father's name, isn't a Malay
name: it means *gnat*, a tiny powerless annoying insect. Who wants to
claim that heritage when you can join the powerful? Maybe he was always
as intensely involved in being convincing as he was when I talked with him.
He convinced his younger lawyers of his innocence by sheer willpower.

* * *

> I was always conscious of many elements showing the directly
> opposite tendency. I felt them positively swarming inside me,
> these elements. I knew they had swarmed there all my life,
> asking to be let out, but I wouldn't let them out, I wouldn't, I
> wouldn't. They tormented me shamefully...
> Fyodor Dostoyevsky, *Notes from Underground* (1972:16)

I don't know why he was inside the house that April night. Maybe
— no one can ever know — someone really did put him up to it. Maybe
he was just curious about how rich Americans live. In the event, he stole
nothing. But I can see him, standing in the master bedroom in his clean
pressed Malay rent-a-cop uniform, feeling his authority, looking down
on the two sleeping children, powerful the way any waking person is
more powerful than one asleep, any adult than a child, looking down

on them with an adult's love for children, for oneself as a child, but also the way he used to imagine Malays looking down on little Bah Pin, with pity and contempt, despising their fragility and weakness, feeling his power, his allrightness.

Then, I imagine, little Kabir stirred. Perhaps his lips parted, as if he was about to call for help, to reveal that the guard was no guard at all, just little Bah Pin pretending to be what he was not. Revealed, about to be caught out, about to lose his job, not to be the good provider any more, the perfect husband and father, just what he was born as, just disgusting graceless little Bah Pin, Arifin shoves his handkerchief into the boy's mouth, forcing the soft lips against the sharp braces, and in the process of trying to keep the boy quiet he makes the mouth bleed. The blood spurts from the cuts the braces and teeth make; and all the ancient Semai horrors flood into the hollow in his mind, and swamp his brittle compulsive new self, and the new familiar safe Enci' Arifin drowns, and he *-buul bhiip*. Blindly he smashes the head too, trying to silence the accusatory mouth, love and revulsion bursting within him, and in mindless terror and rage lurches into his little massacre.

I don't know whether he brought the grinder up from the kitchen just in case he had to defend himself or whether the children had taken it to play some sort of little boy game. But I know that almost all the wounds he made were to the head and face, smashing identity, spraying fragments of teeth everywhere.

* * *

I think he did everything his betters told him he was supposed to do to be a complete person, and so became a monster.

Subject: Aripin Agas
Date: Fri, 19 Nov 1999 01:29:15 +0800
From: "Colin Nicholas" <coac@tm.net.my>
To: "Bob Dentan" <rkdentan@acsu.buffalo.edu>

Dear Bob,
This is just a short note to inform you that the N[ew]S[traits]T[imes] of 17 November reported that the Federal Court turned down Aripin's appeal and that the death sentence is upheld.

Colin

Appendix I: Semai At Betau Regroupment Scheme

Child Health

	Stunted	Underweight	Year of Study [N]
preschool	52%	60%	1988 (111 children)
ages 7–10	35%	27%	same study
ages 0–8			
girls	37%	32%	1992 [59 girls]
boys	40%	34%	1992 [70 boys]

Notes

1. The Harry Frank Guggenheim Foundation supported the research of which this article is an outgrowth. The Jabatan Hal Ehwal Orang Asli, the Malaysian equivalent of the Bureau of Indian Affairs, permitted me to conduct it. For background on Semai non-violence, see Dentan 1979, 1992; for "blood intoxication", Dentan 1995, Robarchek and Dentan 1987; for Semai thundersquall beliefs, Dentan 2002a, 2002b, Freeman 1968, Robarchek 1987; for Semai trancing, Dentan 1988.

2. Arifin's lawyers supplied me this document and Arifin's second "confession". My student, friend and colleague Irid Farida Agoes kindly made a rough translation from the Malay. I have amended her translation and am responsible for any errors. To preserve the sense of police documentation I have followed the punctuation of the original, including typos. To preserve the feeling I get from the document I have tried to be as literal and simple as possible in translation, e.g. translating Arifin's "penjenaiah" or "pengjenaiah" (for Malay penjenayah, criminal) as "criminul". I translate "anggota", *member* (in this case, of a gang), as *gangster*.

   It is important to remember, I think, that Arifin survived poverty, bad schooling and other forms of institutional racism on his path to no. 20 Turi Road. That he could speak English well enough to work for Americans is eloquent testimony to his ambition and hard work. Although English is the second language of Malaysia's business and ruling classes, government schools don't do a good job of teaching it to Semai kids (Dentan 1993). One result is that most Semai cannot read the environmental impact assessments that sketch the effects of development projects on their communities, even in the uncommon instances when EIAs address the issue (Nicholas 1997).

   The constant contempt took a toll too, I imagine.

   > Shame ... can be understood as a wound in the self. It is frequently instilled at a delicate age, as a result of the internalization of a

contemptuous voice … rebukes, warnings, teasing, ridicule, ostracism, and other forms of neglect or abuse can play a part (Robert Karen, cited in O'Brien 1994: 198).

3. Arifin is trying to mimic a Chinese accent in which he imagines "you" as the derogatory *lu*, "the form of 'you' used only to Chinese cooks" (Burgess 1986: 395). Arifin addresses the supposed Chinese with the more polite Malay "Encik", which I have translated as "you sir". Arifin refers to his boss with the very deferential honorific pronoun *beliau*.

4. This object shaped like a pingpong bat is probably a *sengkalan*, on which Semai and Malay cooks grind curry or hot peppers. The fact that Arifin apparently could not recall the name of this common household utensil suggests that he was disoriented either when it was being used to beat the children or when he told his story.

5. *Pe' prnah ng-caap bhiip sn'ooy* in Arifin's Semai.

6. *Ki-hoo' knoon ki'. Mong knoon egn am-hoo'. Boo' d' to' ki-hoo' knoon ki'?* in Arifin's Semai.

7. To *masuk* (Malay) or *moot* (Semai) *Gɔp* in Semai is to "enter Malay[ness]", that is, to become a Malay under Malaysian law, by speaking Malay at home, following Malay customs and becoming a Muslim. As far as I know, Arifin's original ethnicity never appeared in the English language press, although the Malay paper *Utusan Malaysia* (19 March 1994) was careful to identify him as a Orang Asli, an indigenous person. So, in the end, the conversion which was to have made him a Malay failed, as far as the people he wanted to join were concerned.

   Colin Nicholas' many useful publications on Orang Asli include *Pathway to Dependence* (1994) and *The Orang Asli and the Contest for Resources* (2000).

8. In Arifin's Malay, "saya cuma mengikut arahan saja".

9. "Saya diam saja [tak] tau kata apa-apa", two Malay phrases which for Semai signify defeat in an argument and thus subordination.

10. The Malay root "paksa" refers to compulsion. The form *terpaksa*, "was compelled", does not specify whether the compulsion is external or internal: the agents could be Chinese ninjas or some sort of obsessive-compulsive drive. The passive voice *dipaksa*, "was coerced", specifies external agency and thus, like the passive voice in American bureaucratese, evades responsibility.

11. Fort Dixon, where Arifin was born, was a relocation centre during the Emergency of the 1950s, a Communist uprising which prompted the British to begin the process of uprooting Semai from their ancestral lands to prevent their supporting the rebels. The Malaysian government, partly for security reasons, partly for administrative convenience and partly to

facilitate dispossession, has continued this "regroupment" (for details, see Dentan *et al.* 1997). Hence Arifin's removal to Betau when he was about 12, along with 243 other families, about 914 people; sanitation there is poor and the water supply inadequate (*Utusan Konsumer* 1997; Khor 1994: 129).

Most men are occasional labourers, with an average income extremely low by Malaysian standards, under RM250 (less than US$100). The best description of Betau, from which the description in the text comes, is by a courageous Malay anthropologist who at one time thought the project would benefit Semai but now recognises that it has failed (Hasan 1989; cf. Dentan *et al.* 1997: 95–6; Nicholas 1994; Khor 1994: 129). The area of the regroupment scheme is 1.5% of the area the people once occupied. See Appendix 1.

Although one rationale for this dispossession and displacement is to facilitate delivering government services, the delivery of those services is slapdash and erratic. Thus at Betau and similar "relocation centres", 80% of children between two and six years old are significantly mal-nourished, as are over a third of the adult women; more than three-fifths of the kids have protozoan infections, and half the adults have goiters due to iodine deficiency. Malnutrition is pretty much standard for Semai children in "Relocation Centres" (e.g. Khor 1994; Lim 1997, Wan Nazimoon *et al.* 1996). It's also not a bad "index" (as social scientists say) of the contempt in which the government holds the Semai people. After all, Malaysia is not a poor country. An inadequate diet as a child is also probably one of the main reasons Arifin was so small.

For Malay stress on Semai ingratitude and sloth, see Dentan *et al.* (1977: 91, 114–6, 136–8). Anderson, as usual, has a wonderful analysis of this rhetoric (1993):

> 'Look at all we have done for you! Where is your gratitude?' is what they hear day in day out.... [I]ngratitude was a typical accusation by Dutch colonial officials against 'native' nationalism: 'Look at all we have done for you, down there, in terms of security, education, economic development, civilization.' The language is that of the superior and civilized towards the inferior and barbarous. It is not very far from racism, and reveals a profound incapacity [on the part of the Indonesian upper class] to 'incorporate' East Timorese, an unacknowledged feeling that they are really, basically, foreign.

The difference between ethnocidal assimilation of the Malaysian sort and its genocidal Indonesian counterpart is as important as differences get. The Malaysian ruling classes eschew systematic physical violence. But there is a significant overlap, and the ineluctable double-bind message is the same: "You're hopelessly beneath us, but try to become us anyway."

12. Shunning home would not be unusual for a person in Arifin's position. Sherman Alexie, a Spokane/Coeur d'Alene novelist, writes of a character who is doing well in the white world:

> Through her intelligence and dedication, Marie had found a way to escape the reservation. Now she was so afraid the reservation would pull her back and drown her in its rivers that she only ventured home for surprise visits to her parents, usually arriving in the middle of the night. Even then, she felt like a stranger and would sometimes leave before her parents knew she was there. And she rarely spoke to any of her reservation friends (1996: 34).

References

Alexie, Sherman. 1996. *Indian Killer*. New York: Atlantic Monthly Press.

Anderson, Benedict R.O'G. 1990. *Language and Power: Exploring Political Cultures in Indonesia*. Ithaca: Cornell University Press.

———. 1993. "Imagining East Timor", *Arena Magazine* 4 (April/May) <http://eng.hss.cmu.edu./theory/Anderson.html>.

Anonymous. 1997. "Pahang Govt taking public for a (river) 'ride'?" *Utusan Konsumer* 27(13): 7.

Banks, Russell. 1989. *Affliction*. New York: Harper Perennial.

Burgess, Anthony. 1986. *Little Wilson and Big God: The First Part of the Confessions*. New York: Grove Weidenfeld.

Dentan, Robert Knox. 1979. *The Semai: A Nonviolent People of Malaysia*. New York: Harcourt Brace and World.

———. 1988a. "Ambiguity, Synecdoche and Affect in Semai Medicine", *Social Science and Medicine* 27: 857–77.

———. 1988b. "Lucidity, Sex, and Horror in Senoi Dreamwork", in *Conscious Mind, Sleeping Brain: Perspectives on Lucid Dreaming*, ed. Jayne Gackenbach and Stephen LaBerge. Boulder, CO: Lynne Reiner, pp. 69–108.

———. 1990. "The Rise, Maintenance, and Destruction of Peaceable Polity: A Preliminary Essay in Political Ecology", in *Aggression and Peacefulness in Humans and Other Primates*, ed. James Silverberg and J. Patrick Gray. New York: Oxford University Press, pp. 214–70.

———. 1993. "A Genial Sort of Ethnicide [sic]", *Daybreak* (Autumn): 13, 18–9.

———. 1995. "Bad Day at Bukit Pekan", *American Anthropologist* 97: 225–31.

———. 1999a. "Enduring Scars: Cautionary Tales among the Semai of West Malaysia", in *Traditional Storytelling Today: An International Sourcebook*, ed. Margaret Read MacDonald. Chicago: Fitzroy Dearborn and New York: Garland, pp. 130–3.

———. 1999b. "Untransfiguring Death: A Case Study of Rape, Drunkenness, Development and Homicide in an Apprehensive Void", *RIMA: Review of Indonesian and Malaysian Affairs* 33(1): 17–65.

———. 2001. "A Vision of Modernization: An Article on a Drawing by Bah Rmpent, Child of the Sengoi Semai, a Traditionally Nonviolent People of the Malaysian Peninsula", *Journal of Anthropology and Humanism* 26(1): 1–12.

———. 2002a. "Disreputable Magicians', the Dark Destroyer, and the Trickster Lord", *Asian Anthropology* 1: 153–94.

———. 2002b. "Against the Kingdom of the Beast: An Introduction to Semai Theology, Pre-Aryan Religion and the Dynamics of Abjection", in *Tribal Communities in the Malay World: Historical, Cultural and Social Perspectives*, ed. Geoffrey Benjamin and Cynthia Lau. Leiden: International Institute for Asian Studies and Singapore: Institute of Southeast Asian Studies, pp. 206–36.

Dentan, Robert Knox, Kirk Endicott, Alberto G. Gomes and M.B. Hooker. 1995. *Malaysia and the Original People: A Case Study of the Impact of Development on Indigenous Peoples*. Boston: Allyn and Bacon.

Dentan, Robert Knox and Ong Hean Chooi. 1995. "Stewards of the Green and Beautiful World: A Preliminary Report on Semai Arboriculture and Its Policy Implications", in *Dimensions of Tradition and Development in Malaysia*, ed. Rokiah Talib and Tan Chee-Beng. Kuala Lumpur: Pelanduk Publications, pp. 53–124.

Dostoyevsky, Fyodor. 1972. *Notes from Underground/The Double*. Jessie Coulson, tr. Harmondsworth: Penguin.

Eber, Christine. 1995. *Women and Alcohol in a Highland Maya Town: Water of Hope, Water of Sorrow*. Austin, TX: University of Texas Press.

Ellis, Bret Easton. 1990. *American Psycho*. New York: Vintage.

Endicott, Kirk M. and Robert Knox Dentan. 2004. "Into the Mainstream or into the Backwater? Malaysian Assimilation of Orang Asli", in *Civilizing the Margins: Southeast Asian Government Policies for the Development of Minorities*, ed. Christopher R. Duncan. Ithaca, NY: Cornell University Press, pp. 24–55.

Freeman, Derek. 1968. "Thunder, Blood, and the Nicknaming of God's Creatures", *Psychoanalytic Quarterly* 37: 353–99.

Freyd, Jennifer J. 1995. *Betrayal Trauma: The Logic of Forgetting Childhood Abuse*. Cambridge: Harvard University Press.

Hasan Mat Noor. 1989. "Pengumpulan Semula Orang Asli di Betau: Satu Penelitan Rengkas", *Akademika* 35: 97–112.

Kaplan, Bert. 1968. "The Method of the Study of Persons", in *The Study of Personality: An Interdisciplinary Appraisal*, ed. Edward Norbeck, Douglass Price-Williams and William M. McCord. New York: Holt, Rinehart and Winston, pp. 121–33.

Khor, Geok Lim. 1994. "Resettlement and Nutritional Implications: The Case of Orang Asli in Regroupment Schemes", *Pertanika Journal of Social Science* 2: 123–32.

Koja, Kathe. 1996. *Kink: A Novel*. New York: Holt.

Laderman, Carol. 1989. *Taming the Wind of Desire: Psychology, Medicine, and Aesthetics in Malay Shamanistic Practice*. Berkeley: University of California Press.

Landsberg, Alison. 1995. "America, the Holocaust, and the Mass Culture of Memory: Toward a Radical Politics of Empathy", *New German Critique* 71 (Spring–Summer): 63–86.

Le Roy Ladurie, Emmanuel. 1975. *Montaillou, Village Occitan de 1294 à 1324*. Paris: Editions Gallimard.

Lim, H.W. 1995. "Nutritional Status and Reproductive Health of Orang Asli Women". B.S. thesis, Faculty of Human Ecology, Universiti Pertanian Malaysia, Serdang.

Lombroso, Cesare. 1911. *Crime, Its Causes and Remedies*. Henry P. Horton tr., Boston: Little, Brown.

McClusky, Laura J. 2001. *"Here, Our Culture Is Hard": Stories of Domestic Violence from a Mayan Community in Belize*. Austin: University of Texas Press.

Nicholas, Colin. 1994. *Pathway to Dependence: Commodity Relations and the Dissolution of Semai Society*. Monash Papers on Southeast Asia no. 33. Monash, Victoria: Centre of Southeast Asian Studies, Monash University.

———. 1995. *Putting the "People" in EIAs: Assessing Environmental Impacts on Indigenous Peoples*. Paper presented at Malaysian Nature Society Environmental Impact Assessment Seminar (9 March).

———. 2000. *The Orang Asli and the Contest for Resources: Indigenous Politics, Development and Identity in Peninsular Malaysia*. Copenhagen: International Work Group for Indigenous Affairs.

Niman, Michael I. 1995. *People of the Rainbow: A Nomadic Utopia*. Knoxville, TN: University of Tennessee Press.

O'Brien, Tim. 1994 *In the Lake of the Woods*. New York: Penguin.

Ondaatje, Michael. 1997. *The Collected Works of Billy the Kid. Running in the Family. In the Skin of a Lion. The Cinnamon Peeler*. New York: Quality Paperback Book Club.

Robarchek, Clayton A. 1986. "Blood, Thunder, and the Mockery of Anthropology: Derek Freeman and the Semang Thunder-God", *Journal of Anthropological Research* 43: 273–300.

Robarchek, Clayton A. and Robert Knox Dentan. 1986. "'Blood Drunkenness' and the Bloodthirsty Semai: Unmaking Another Anthropological Myth", *American Anthropologist* 89: 356–65.

Stewart, Ian, and Jenny Grant. 1995. "Hungry Illegals Flood Malaysia for Free Jail Rice", *South China Morning Post* (6 March).

[Taylor, W.T.]. 1908. *Resident General's Annual Report. 1907.* Supplement to the Perak Government Gazette, 1908. Kuala Lumpur: Federated Malay States Government Printing Office.

Wan Nazimoon, W., *et al.* 1994. "Effects of Iodine Insufficiency on Insulin-Like Growth Factor-1, Insulin-Like Growth Factor Binding Protein-3 Levels and Height Attainment in Malnourished Children", *Clinical Endocrinology* 45: 79–83.

6

Marking Time: Narratives of the Life-world in Thailand

Annette Hamilton

This Man and Nature world view is very much influenced by the
Buddhist philosophy which views life as part of nature and the
universe; life in all forms, therefore, cannot escape the natural
laws which govern the universe. The concept of these natural
laws includes the three characteristics of life — the three "marks
of existence" — namely, the Impermanancy [sic] ("Anica"), the
Unsatisfactoriness ("Dukka"), and the No-self ("Anatta"). These are
facts of life. Thus, the central tenet of Buddhist philosophy rests
on the premise that the world and things in it are in a constant
state of flux. Nothing is permanent, for change is a natural law.
This is the nature of all things.

(Suntaree 1985: 175)

Modern environments and experiences cut across all boundaries of
geography and ethnicity, of class and nationality, of religion and
ideology: in this sense, modernity can be said to unite all mankind
... it pours us all into a maelstrom of perpetual disintegration and
renewal, of struggle and contradiction, of ambiguity and anguish. To
be modern is to be part of a universe in which, as Marx said, "all
that is solid melts into air".

(Berman 1983:15)

The experience of modernity has been theorised in many ways: as the loss of primal or communal sources of identity, as the reimagination of the world through technologically mediated collective representations, and as an unavoidable commitment to highly rationalised forms of production, consumption and exchange (e.g. Berger 1977; Berman 1983; Lyotard 1984).[1]

In considering the transformations of human life which have taken place over the past century, it has become a commonplace to contrast certain fundamental value systems and philosophies supposed to characterise "the non-West" with those central to "the West": on the one hand, a state of acceptance and recognition of nature and humanity's place in it, and on the other, the inherent nihilism of an expansive and technologically driven system. Whether it is Heidegger's melancholic grasp of the transformation of both humanity and nature to a form of "standing reserve" (Heidegger 1977) or the contemporary enthusiasm of development agencies promoting on-line learning as a means of producing "human resources" in the developing world (the latter of course providing a clear example of the domination of the former in the realm of values), a notion of the overcoming of one system of thought and meaning by another seems unavoidable.

Thus modernity is thought to result in a uniform transformation of value systems, practical applications, social life and political forms. Western thought seems to attribute an inherent, perhaps metaphysical, power to the material, technological level, thus resulting in the movement of all societies following a uniform direction associated ultimately with the United States as key exemplar of Western modernity.[2]

The processes of social transformation in the twentieth century have been vividly apparent in the non-Socialist nations of Southeast Asia.[3] However, the way in which these rapid social, economic, political and cultural changes have impacted on individuals and local communities in those societies has been unevenly charted. Analyses of the social impact of large-scale development projects have generally been confined to the consultant's report and the NGO advocates. Everyday changes to the life-world, and their long-term consequences, are much more difficult to grasp, in part because they can only be rendered significant in retrospect. This involves not only engagement with individuals, but also with national and local history. Higher level international events, for instance wars, provide a different point of common impact.[4]

One obvious method of approaching this problem is through the use of life-histories or individual narratives. The centrality of the life-history in anthropology has always seemed rather uncertain. As Waterson has pointed out elsewhere, a full exploration of its possibilities, as a genre of ethnographic writing, has been "patchy and inconsistent" (Waterson 2001: 5). The life-history or life-story inevitably overlaps with the idea of "oral history", which has raised many issues around veracity and accuracy, from the viewpoint of a positivist historical perspective. In anthropology, concerns with the accuracy or rigour not so much of the informant's memories but of the ethnographer's forms of elicitation and recording have also resulted in questioning of the validity of much life-history writing, or at least the recognition of its collaborative nature (Behar 1992; Linde 1993; Peacock and Holland 1993). The life-history in its purest form is understood as an individual's account of the shaping of his/her own life within his/her own time and cultural frame. The creation of a narrative about the "self" is sometimes thought to be both universal and necessary (cf. Bruner 1987; Rappaport 1990). The fact that even conceptualising "the individual" as an entity which can give an account in this way is already a deeply culturally-determined proposition has belatedly been recognised (Röttger-Rössler 1993). Caplan (1997) approaches universality in another way, suggesting that issues of common human concern such as events in the life-cycle (birth, marriage, family issues) and ideas about illness, death and the spirit-world can provide a common framework through which the life-history can contribute both depth and comparability to ethnography.

Many anthropologists have the experience of entering the life-world of particular informants who become exceptionally close — as friends, quasi-kinsmen, and in a real sense, co-authors. To assist in the creation of their life stories (and it must always be a creation, due at the very least to the need to render speech as text) often seems like an ethical imperative, giving them a dignity and recognition which would otherwise be impossible, since their "stories" could never normally enter circulation beyond their immediate local or, in exceptional circumstances, national context.

However, there are other reasons for recording the lived experience of the people anthropologists encounter. In the research on which this paper is based, my primary interest was to explore the responses to twentieth-century modernity in a small town and its hinterland in Thailand. My particular interest concerned the impacts of mass media, especially cinema, radio and television. It became clear that exploring the commonalities and differences in recollection requires an understanding of local as well as national history, and leads to the creation of a series of overlapping fragments rather than a monovocal text unified by the ethnographer's already established perspectives. This question was of particular interest in Thailand because of the extent to which the twentieth-century nationalist project had obscured or suppressed local particularities, histories and memories from the "national" consciousness and public culture.[5] Modern education, literacy and the mass media created spaces in which the idea of a homogeneous nation with a single history could emerge, yet the distinctiveness of a local shared experience, a phenomenology of place, may be sometimes informed by national narratives and sometimes posed against them. The encounter of individuals with the local and the national (and also the extra-national) and the way their personal experience has shaped them, opens up a more nuanced understanding of the way in which large-scale social forces impact on individuals, communities and regions.[6]

In the case of Thailand, the process of nationalist narrativisation began in the nineteenth century and by the 1980s successive administrations within the Kingdom had produced a consistent, homogeneous version of Thai culture and Thai history. Even remote hinterland villages were drawn into this world-view through mass public education using a common curriculum. The spread of electrification to more than 90 per cent of the country by the mid-1980s meant that television broadcasting (indirectly state-controlled) brought a particular view of citizenship and cultural identity into universal experience. The ideology of citizenship was ostensibly on the Western model supported by a parliamentary democracy, although a complex oligarchy punctuated at various times by *coups d'état* and military dictatorships might provide a better description. Many, especially among the educated elite in Thailand, argue that an authentic Western-style democracy remains unrealised.[7] The power and significance of the Monarchy has steadily increased since the 1960s and suggests a distinctly pre-modern context for ostensibly modern social institutions.

The history of the Chakri Dynasty, and the sequence of Rama Kings (I–IX) is central to the sense of Thai history and identity circulating within the Kingdom. However, Kings Rama IV, V and VI, in spite of their various *rapprochements* with modernity, were absolute monarchs. The overthrow of the absolute monarchy in 1932 is an aspect of the

Thai past which until recently has been largely ignored or glossed over in public culture. Presumably for many living in the Kingdom far from Bangkok, and for many minorities, these events may have had little relevance. But in the area of my research, the overthrow of King Rama VII by a group of dissatisfied upwardly-mobile members of an emerging middle class, many educated in Europe and imbued with modern ideals, provided a lynch-pin of historical consciousness. To a lesser extent so did the events of World War II, even though this too is an episode which has until recently received little or no public attention.[8] The "reading" of these events may have been specific to this region, but the arrival of technological changes which transformed whole districts and lives were experienced in common with rural and small-town people everywhere in Thailand. In Hua Hin these elements of twentieth-century modernity were absorbed readily and enthusiastically, and the changes they brought with them seem not to have created any sense of crisis or disruption and were, on the contrary, thought to have introduced a far better quality of life and greater satisfaction.[9]

Memories in Hua Hin

Hua Hin is a town on the western shore of the Gulf of Thailand. First settled in the 1830s, during the time of King Rama III, it remained a remote rural area until the building of the railway connecting Bangkok with Malaya in the 1920s. It can readily be reached by road, about 3–4 hours, and by rail, a similar journey. Best known today as a popular tourist resort, Hua Hin was the premier seaside town of the Bangkok elites from the 1920s to the present. My interest in local identity, narrative and history led me to seek out the older residents of the town, from a variety of backgrounds. However the immediate impacts of tourist development, apparent between my first visit in 1984 and subsequent fieldwork in 1987, also called for an engagement with this, the most recent manifestation of global modernity. In another paper I have sketched elements of Hua Hin's early history and its transformation in the late 1980s and 1990s into a site of intense national and international tourist development (Hamilton 1994). I was appalled by the destruction of what were obviously "heritage" environments as tourist development proceeded. The demolition of the wonderful teak houses in the old village, with its sea-front location and vibrant fishing community, and of the gracious early twentieth-century Western-style bungalows along the beachfront to the south, seemed a catastrophe. As high-rise condominiums and apartment buildings sprang up, creating a Miami-like atmosphere displacing the fishermen and small-scale farmers along the beachfront they had occupied since the 1830s, as Western tourists began to pack into the town and bars sprang up along the old laneways, as vendors providing hot food and drinks on the beachfront were banned and removed from the sight of the wealthier tourists now basking in front of international hotels (French, German, Spanish) it seemed that surely the older residents would have some views, some comments, some sentiments to express on this radical transformation.

But, in line with the commonsense Buddhist philosophy expressed at the beginning of this paper, in this respect I was disappointed. My interviewees, aged mostly between late 50s and early 80s, expressed no demurral with the events taking place around them. What struck me most was their expression of satisfaction and what one can only call contentment. "Everything changes", they said, "and we can do nothing about that, because it is the way things are." "Don't you feel upset about these changes?" I would ask, as Mor Chui sat in his carved teak chair in front of his wooden house, his vast collection of herbal medicines in careful arrangement in his apothecary's shop behind him, while a ceaseless thrum of motorbikes sped up and down the narrow laneway, ridden by fat white (or rather red) men with tiny Thai girls looking to be about 14 clinging to the back. "I am very happy", he said. "I am pleased now that I am old. I have few duties and can relax. My family is here with me. I don't need anything."

In a moment I will return to him, and introduce some of the other people I spoke to at that time, most of whom have now passed away. Today the old fishing village is given over to backpacker and other low-rent tourism, or to fancy high-class seafood restaurants on the beach front. The local fishing industry, the small hand-crafted fishing boats, the racks drying squid, are largely gone. Whole sectors on the outskirts of the town are given over to townhouse development, while up in the hills are golf courses, horse-riding farms, luxury mountain spas and resorts. Some members of the original families, the "Hua Hin natives", have prospered through these developments, now being proprietors of hotels, guest-houses and so on, but many family members have left, mostly working and living in Bangkok.[10]

Hua Hin thus is a microcosm of the rapid transformation which occurred throughout Thailand in the boom years of globalisation and capitalist expansion. The interviews with the elders which I undertook at what turned out to be an important expansion phase of this process stand as a memorial to a different kind of consciousness, and give some surprising insights into the relation between large-scale historical events and the way these interweave into the experience and interpretation of the individual.

Like most villages and towns in Thailand, Hua Hin has an origin story. This story is told in various local publications, most of which rely on published accounts of Hua Hin's history including those found in "funeral books" published in 1977 and 1984.[11] The Krasaesin accounts state that Hua Hin was first settled in 1834 by two families who previously lived in Petchaburi Province.[12] These two founding couples are remembered as Nai (Master) Tong who was married to Nang (Miss) Yuu Krasaesin and lived originally in Bang Charn, and Nai Wat and Nang Nongkaew of Bang Kaew. Nai Tong and Nang Yuu's children included Nang Fuuk Krasaesin, who married Nai Choo Choontrakul. From this alliance sprang four of the famous old "Hua Hin native" families: the Krasaesin, Choontrakul, Tiemtad and Satukarn.[13] Early settlers from Petchaburi Province found Cha-am and districts to the north of Hua Hin occupied, but once arrived in Hua Hin various family members settled along the beachfront as far as Khao Takiab, now the site of a very famous temple. Not long after this new settlers, many of Sino-Thai origin, arrived from the south, in particular from Phuket and Pattalung. These arrivals gave Hua Hin its distinctive "southern" character, commented on by many who know the south well, such as the singing bird competition and the southern Chinese-style cuisine.

In this paper I will briefly tell the stories of four of the Hua Hin elders: three men from locally prominent families, each with a different background and life-trajectory, and a woman who spent her entire life in the fishing village as a day-labourer. Each of them lived in Hua Hin within a similar historical period, and their recollections touch on some similar events and aspects, but differ in the emphasis placed on them. Nevertheless they (taken together with the other narratives from the same set) provide an otherwise unrecoverable insight into local life and experience against the greater background of twentieth-century history and the Thai encounter with modernity. For almost all of the elders, tremendous significance was placed on their personal encounters with the Royal Family, most especially King Rama VII. They expressed great appreciation for the improvements to everyday life brought by twentieth-century technologies, including especially transport (the railway and the road network) and above all, electricity. Finally, these elderly people mostly expressed happiness in their old age and satisfaction with the lives they had led — an unexpected finding, and one calling for reflection on the role of cultural expectations and ideologies in shaping the subjectivity of ageing.

Khun Chun Satukarn

In 1988 Khun Chun Satukarn was the oldest surviving member of the Satukarn family, the early Hua Hin lineage described above. He was born in 1900 (Western Era calendar) in the original family home on the same site, on the corner of Tanon Poonsuk in the centre of the old fishing village. The house had been rebuilt around 1925–30. Without doubt this was the most magnificent of the teak houses in the old village, three stories in height, decorated with exquisite wood carvings along the upper floor verandahs. The house was large and well laid out, but modestly furnished and equipped, except for a large number of electric fans of all shapes and sizes.

Khun Chun lies on a banana chair in the front room.[14] His wife and one daughter are sitting at the far end of the room, and several young boys are watching TV nearby. Khun Chun is physically in excellent condition. His hearing and eyesight are very good and he speaks with great intelligence, dignity and reserve. Both his mother's and father's family were traders and after marrying they continued in the same business, selling food, clothes, tools, rope, fishing equipment and building materials, from the lower level of the original house which, as was commonly the case, served as both business premises and family residence. As a young child he helped his parents, who brought goods to Hua Hin from the town of Petchaburi by ox-cart. The business was successful and his father was ambitious for the lively and intelligent boy. At the age of 12 he entered a monastery school in Petchaburi, and at 16 went to study at the prestigious Wat Benchamabophit in Bangkok.[15] He was ordained as a monk there but remained only a few years before returning to Hua Hin.

Khun Chun was an acknowledged expert on the early history of Hua Hin, and described the nature of the town during earlier times. Surrounded by dense forest still full of tigers, with only a simple cart-track connecting the settlements to the north and south, the town was focused largely on the sea, although a single rice-crop was grown and fruit-trees and vegetable plantations flourished. Khun Chun, in talking about his life, began first by describing the historical past of the town and region, giving a brief genealogy of the founding families and describing the previous locations of the shrines memorialising them, some of which remain today.

He then began a detailed description of the history of the various *wats* (Buddhist temples) in the town and nearby. There was no *wat* at Hua Hin for a long time, and his uncle became a leader in the building of the first one, the real name of which is Wat Amparam. Khun Chun described the sequence in which the *wats* were built, how they got their names, and their successive transformation over time to the present.

When he was ten years old he believes around 300 people lived in Hua Hin. Life at that time was very different. People hunted in the jungle behind the beach for game and "wild chickens" (*gai paa*, jungle fowl). After the railroad was built in the 1920s many more people arrived. He recalled vividly, at around 16, his first ride on a rail-car which went between Petchaburi and Hua Hin during the early construction phase of the railway. After he returned permanently from Bangkok at the age of 20, he rejoined his parents in trading, travelling back and forth. There were only two ways to travel, on foot or by boat. The normal range of travel for everyone at that time was limited to Petchaburi or Prachuab towns, but by boat they could go further. He traded by boat, going to Samut Songhkram, Samut Sakhon, Petchaburi and to Prachuab, selling local salted fish and bringing back foodstuffs from Bangkok and thatching palm leaves from Samut Songhkram. He did not marry until quite late, at 35, and his wife, from Nong Salaa near Cha-Am was 22. The marriage was arranged completely by the parents as was the custom at that time. After his marriage he settled down to trade in his family's shop.

He and his wife had six children, five girls and one boy. All were born in Hua Hin, but only two remain in Hua Hin, the others working in Bangkok. They all had good educations and work either in banking or as schoolteachers. Education was very important to the whole family and it was his own father who founded the Satukarn School in Hua Hin, a well-known private school still functioning in 1988.

Khun Chun described the way, as a young man, he saw and participated in the traditional dance/dramas of old Hua Hin. *Lakhon*

Manora (a famous southern-style dance drama) was commonly played at New Year or on other important occasions, featuring southern performers who travelled up the Gulf as far as Ratchaburi. The *Manora* troupes stopped coming to Hua Hin about 50 years ago. *Lakhon Chatri*, a public version of the court dance-drama, however, continued to be played (and was still played in 1988). It is particularly strong in Petchaburi, where the main troupes are located.[16]

> Everybody believed in the spirits in those times. I believed in the spirits, and we still believe today although I think the new generations are really forgetting them. These spirits are like Gods, such as the Gods in Hindu religion, spirits which live in heaven or paradise. You ask the spirits for something, something you need or want, and if the spirits grant you that special favour, you pay them in a way they will like, for example, by arranging for a Lakhon to be performed in the street near your house. You look for the best troupes you can afford, and ask them to perform the whole Lakhon if you can pay. It might take two, three or more days to complete. For example, if you are hoping for a good rice-crop, you speak to Mae Porsop, the Goddess of the ricefield. When I wanted a son, after so many girls, I spoke to the spirits and when my wife did give birth to a boy I repaid the spirits with a Lakhon Chatri.

Khun Chun was happy speaking about these recollections of his early life in Hua Hin. However we came to a point where the atmosphere changed alarmingly. He was describing the way the King would come to stay at his seaside palace, Klai Klangwol, just to the north of the town, and the excitement this caused. I asked whether he (i.e. Khun Chun) was in Hua Hin when the events of 1932 took place. He became extremely agitated. At first he said "Local people didn't feel anything about it, they knew about it but it made no difference." Then he turned away in silence. And a moment later he said: "No, I can't talk about this any more. Please turn off that tape recorder. Why are you asking all these questions?" He did not want to go on with his story if it involved the recounting of this event.

In 1932 King Rama VII (Prajadhipok, reigned 1925–34, younger brother of King Vajiravudh 1910–25 and grandson of King Chulalongkorn) was in residence at Klai Klangwol in Hua Hin when the first events resulting in the overthrow of the absolute monarchy by the People's Party on 14 May took place. A popular history by M.L. Manich Jumsai gives a bland version:

After having seized control of the capital the People's Party at once sent a representative to see the king at Hua-Hin and to invite him to come back and rule the country as a constitutional monarch. The king consented to cooperate with the People's Party (Manich Jumsai, n.d.: 571–2).

Other accounts differ markedly, including tales of the King fleeing from the Palace with nothing but a small carry-bag and being captured by the People's Party supporters and returned by force to Bangkok where he was required to approve a permanent constitution on 10 December 1932. I had hoped Khun Chun would be able to cast a local perspective on these confused stories, but instead he became worried and silent. I turned off the tape-recorder and reassured him that there was no need to speak of it if he didn't want to. We could talk about something else. "Very well", he said. Then, dropping his voice, with the tape recorder still off, he said "Everyone here was on the side of the King." He gazed for a time out the open door.

Only later, talking to his daughter, did I learn that he and many others had attempted to rescue the King from the palace. News of the events in Bangkok had arrived with the train the next morning, and local men had armed themselves with staves, knives and whatever else was to hand in the hope they could prevent the King from being harmed. They had arrived too late, however, as the King had been removed by boat. The Hua Hin loyalists felt ashamed and fearful, retreating to their homes thinking that the police or soldiers would arrest them.

In later conversations, Khun Chun returned repeatedly to the question of the King and the Royal Family, and his personal feelings about the subject. He spoke no more of his role in 1932, but subsequent to the first interview described an event which he had previously omitted. Prior to 1932, when he was still a young man but after his return from the monastery in Bangkok, he had the honour to personally serve the King. At that time the King came often to Hua Hin, and Khun Chun saw him from a distance on many occasions. But the high point of his life, he said, occurred when the King agreed to participate in a Buddhist religious ceremony at the new *wat* in Hua Hin, built by his uncle:

> The King came as usual to Hua Hin in May, in the heat of the summer. A ceremony for the opening of the new *wat* was being held and the King was required to speak the words of a long prayer. This prayer was in the religious language (Pali) and although His Majesty was very able to speak in this language, he did not know all of the words

of this prayer. And because I had studied Buddhism for four years in Bangkok the Abbott requested that I personally lead His Majesty in this ceremony. It was the greatest honour of my life. I spoke the words, and the King followed behind me. I was close to the King's person and I heard him as he repeated the words of the prayer after I said them. This is the occasion of my life I can never forget.

Although World War II and the presence of the Japanese was an important event for the nation, he said it had very little impact on his own life. He continued as a trader and the Japanese were very good customers:

There was no trouble with the Japanese soldiers as far as I was concerned. They came and bought things from me and spoke to me politely. But they did insist that we accept their paper money in payment. Nobody knew whether this money really had any value or how to understand it. But we became used to using both kinds of money and it was all right. The Japanese came and went and we did not hear very much about the war until we saw many aeroplanes and then we heard that Bangkok was being bombed. Many people who had houses on the beach came and stayed here, and this was also good for business.

After the war, things continued much as they had been, but he considered that life got better and better. Electricity, for example, was something he was very happy about, although he could not recall exactly when it occurred:

The electricity came to Hua Hin and immediately people's lives improved very much. At first I had just one electric light in the house, but as soon as I could I put electric lights in each room. When there is light the house feels more cheerful and safer. Before, we never knew if a robber or bandit might be walking around or was trying to get into the house. Sometimes my wife and children were afraid at night. And oil or kerosene lamps are dangerous, they can easily be knocked down and then there is fire. Many times there were fires in the village and sometimes I thought this house would also be burned. With light in the house, and in the street, people could feel confident, and could walk around outside without fear. Not only the light, but now we could have a fan. As soon as the electricity arrived, I bought a fan. There weren't many, they were very expensive and only imported, but I went straight to Bangkok on the train and bought one, I didn't care what it cost. This brought new comfort to my family, especially in the hot season. I bought many other fans. [He gestured to the collection in the lounge room].

Khun Chun's recollections were not personal, nor did they reflect conflicts or social difficulties. Although much has changed over the past 20 years, he seemed quite unconcerned, saying that really it had nothing to do with him.

> Today I am very happy. I have nothing to do. I can sit here and listen to the radio with the fan on. My daughter and grandchildren are here with me. [His wife died some years before but he did not dwell on this at all]. I finished with my business and no longer have to worry about money or any of those things. All my children have had a good education and are successful. Do you know what I like to do now? I go travelling and see the world! I see other places in Thailand. Only a short while ago I went for a holiday on Koh Samui. My life is so much better today than it was in the past.

Later I discovered that Khun Chun is a very wealthy man. Although living modestly in his family house, he owns parcels of land all over town, on which restaurants and other tourist facilities have been built. His life story is one of determination and success, in terms of the potential horizons available to someone of his time and place. His education and Buddhist studies, his stable family life and his financial acumen have combined to provide a way of relating to the transformations of the twentieth century which he has stitched seamlessly into his own highly localised life and experiences. The rupture, the most alarming event he recalls, is not related to the technological or social impacts of modernity but to its effects on the institutions of the traditional Thai monarchy, while his most significant experience was the moment when he came closest to it in the person of the King.

Mor Chui

Mor ("Doctor") Chui, aged 93 (in 1988), is said to be the oldest man in Hua Hin. He is very famous as a healer, using traditional methods only. His daughter Acharn Chennai is a local schoolteacher, and he lives with her and her family members in another of the old teak houses of the town, next door to the house where his wife was born and where his deceased wife's sister continues to live. He retired from active medical practice in 1987, feeling he was too old, but many still come by to ask his advice and purchase medicines from his shop. His shop and house are now faced by the bars of *Thanon Farang* (Foreigner's Street), with a ceaseless passing parade and endless cacophony of country and western music and demented drunken laughter from the tourists who wander from bar to bar and race past on their motor-cycles.[17] However he sits quietly on his chair in the laneway. Mor Chui was born in Petchaburi, but his mother was from Hua Hin, from one of the old "native" families. He had a female twin sister, three younger sisters and one elder brother, all of whom are dead apart from the brother who lived in Bangkok. His father was also a traditional healer, and his mother a housewife who also farmed rice. He became a monk at the age of 18 and studied medicine in Bangkok, where his uncle was also a monk and traditional doctor. He left the monastery and married at the age of 39; his wife was considerably younger and the marriage had been arranged by the parents. As is customary in Thailand, he joined his wife's family in Hua Hin, obtaining land and building a house next door to them. He travelled all over the region on foot, giving treatment, and this was the main aspect of his life. He had three sons and four daughters, all born at home in Hua Hin. For the birth of the first three, the attending nurse was a lady of King Rama V's Queen, a midwife practising half traditional and half modern medicine. He has ten grandchildren.

Mor Chui's story was frequently interrupted by his daughter, who began by explaining that we would have to wait a while as someone

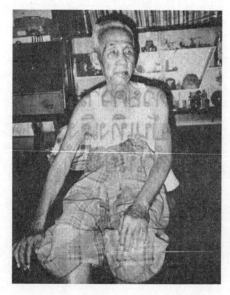

Mor ("Doctor") Chui, the famous traditional healer, who is said to be the oldest man in Hua Hin.

Source: From the Thai magazine *Sinlapa Wattanatam* (Art and Culture), 1990.

had just come into the shop looking for medicine for their baby.[18] Old people, she said, still had faith in traditional medicines. When small babies were ill and had fever Mor Chui treated them by putting traditional medicine on the baby's tongue, treating as many as 40 or 50 babies each day. The workload was very high. But today he has finished his practice as a healer, although he still sells medicine. People come with their own formulas which they have obtained from some other healer, although some still ask for his formula. Malaria was a problem in those days, but not in the town because people would recover due to the medicines. Hua Hin in those times was a centre of civilisation, everywhere else nearby was a jungle. Mor Chui said:

> A famous proverb goes: "if you are going to the jungle you should make
> sure you prepare a pot". This means, you are sure to die, and you will
> need the pot so your ashes can be taken home after cremation. There
> was one big epidemic, when many people died, long ago, before I came
> to Hua Hin. Nothing as bad as that ever happened again.[19]

Mor Chui spoke of the difficulties of travelling, on foot or by ox-cart, during his early years as a traditional healer:

> In those times my father and I had to find many kinds of medicine to
> treat the people. You could buy medicine in Petchaburi and in Kuiburi.
> Chinese traders travelled around and some of them sold herbs and
> medicine. People often suffered from accidents, wounds, and fever.
> Some were attacked by wild animals such as tigers. Some became ill
> because of spirit-attack. My father and I treated people with our own
> Thai medicines from the jungle. My father knew which medicines to
> use and how to prepare them. There were jungle medicines growing
> here in the mountains [gesturing to the west of the town towards the
> Tenasserim range region on the Thai-Burma border]. The Karuang
> [Karen, a hill-tribe group] gathered many different herbs from the
> high mountains and brought them here to this very house. Sometimes
> traders would go up there and exchange dried fish and rice for them.
> I went myself once with my father but I was afraid and ran away.
> My father understood. He did not request me to make that journey
> again, I remained close to the coast travelling on foot from place to
> place. There are many places, spirits and stories belonging to the land
> around here. I learnt these stories from old people but today they
> are written down and people can read them. You have to be careful
> because there are places where spirits live and in those days you did
> not know where they were if you did not ask local people. In the
> jungle there is nobody to ask.

Mor Chui's daughter interrupted him and began to recite the origin tale for Prachuab Khiri Khan province, the tale of Chao Rai:

> This story is a famous one and everybody knows it here; Chao Rai is one of our really important spirits belonging to all our local people, the people who are born in this province. Other provinces have their own stories. But today the Chao Rai story is known everywhere and people don't know it belongs to this province.[20]   ·

Mor Chui continued to reflect on the healing practices in earlier times. He made tablets as well as mixtures for drinking and putting on the tongue. He was one among a number of "doctors" in Hua Hin at that time — the others were Mor Ood, Mor Poowang, Mor Set, Mor Men; all are dead now. The medical training included diagnosis, which was done by considering the colour of the skin, the face, particularly the eyes, pulses, temperature and so on. Sometimes the sick person came in the morning and returned in the evening so Mor Chui could see what difference there was; this could help in the diagnosis.

Generally only men could become healers, but this was largely due to the methods of teaching and learning.

> Healing not only concerns the body. It is necessary also to understand the flow of energy (*raeng*) and this is not ordinary knowledge.[21] Some women became healers, but it was hard for them because they had to gain the knowledge from monks. Mostly they only learnt if their father had been a monk. The exact skills would depend on the teacher. One famous female massage doctor lived here, and she was also a Mor Duu (spirit-channeling diviner). Petchaburi town is the place for healers. It is the real centre of culture: Hua Hin has a history, but not of the cultural kind as in Petchaburi.

It was difficult to obtain a sense of continuous narrative in these conversations. Mor Chui was keen to reminisce about specific events, most particularly those associated with his training and professional practice as a healer. The broader world appeared to have made no strong impact on him until the arrival of radio and then television in the 1950s and 1960s. The major exception was the period of the Japanese residence during World War II:

> Japanese soldiers were all around here. They were camped on land belonging to the Railway Hotel and they often came to my shop. They asked often for clean water which I was happy to give them, and then they would buy food, always paying for it. They were very

polite and disciplined. If anyone did anything wrong the senior officers would punish them in public. Mostly they stopped in Hua Hin, on their way either north or south.

He paused here and looked around cautiously, lowering his voice.

I could not understand this problem with the Japanese, or why there was a war. The Japanese were strange but they did not seem to be fierce or hurtful. And yet for some reason there sprang up a strong group of Seri Thai [the Thai liberation underground] in Hua Hin. Why they did this I cannot say. Later on I heard about the enemies of the Japanese, and bombs falling on Bangkok not long after the Japanese arrived here. It was important to be quiet in those times. But there were no bombs here. If they had bombed here, I don't know where we could have run away to.[22]

Although there were many traditional healers, there were also many modern doctors in Hua Hin and people began to go to both kinds of doctors. Some of the modern doctors spoke against the traditional healers, but usually they helped each other.

The modern doctors moved to Hua Hin because it was the King's town. Many important people had their summer houses here. When the King came here, so did the important people, and their families. Even in the time of King Rama VI this began, because he had a palace at Cha-Am (about 50 km north of Hua Hin). When King Rama VI came to his palace in Cha-Am he got off the train here in Hua Hin and had a small car on the railway to go back to Cha-Am. King Rama VI supported modern medicine. The Kings liked to bring modern facilities to the people.

Life changed very quickly after electricity came:

Electric power really changed our lives. Before that, people had small oil lamps, using coconut oil, and if they had to walk about at night they used bright wooden torches. People were frightened of tigers, robbers, *phii* (malevolent spirits). I went straight away and bought light bulbs. As for other things, I bought a refrigerator. But I didn't worry about television, until about ten years ago [mid 1970s]. I like television. It allows people to hear the news quickly, and become more modernised.

Mor Chui doesn't think anything really important happened in his lifetime. He is satisfied with what he has done, but none of it was really important. The saddest thing was the death of his wife. But apart from that, life is much better now. He doesn't have to do anything, the children come back and help in his business. When transportation improved it was much better for him because when people became sick they would send a car to get him — much better than having to travel on foot or by cart.

Khun Tuck Dechapanya

Dechapanya is another of the traditional Hua Hin families. Khun Tuck Dechapanya is aged 59 but looks much younger. He represents the generation of men immediately below the senior elders. His life was much more broadly focused than theirs, he travelled widely, and had a number of occupations which reflected the considerable influence he was able to wield. In 1988 he was the manager of the Tananchai hotel. Formerly he was Lord Mayor of Hua Hin, and at one time worked for army TV (Channel 5), travelling in many parts of Thailand. He still has many friends in the Army. Because of his experiences and education he speaks good English. He had his own tape recorder and co-taped our conversations, speaking part of the time in English.

The first thing he stated concerned his name. He gave the English spelling "Tuck" and stated that King Rama VII presented the name to him. Moreover, King Rama VI presented the name Dechapanya to his family, hence he is doubly named by Kings. His father was the District Officer under Rama VI, and came from Ayutthaya, but his mother is a Petchaburi native. He is the youngest of four. The whole of his family is famous, he says. His eldest sister's son-in-law was Chief Prosecutor in Bangkok; the second sister was a teacher in the King's Palace School at Hua Hin, now retired. His brother was Deputy Governor of the main gaol in Bangkok, and his son is the movie star Annason Dechapanya, who was a big star in TV dramas, but now is not so young. Khun Tuck was the only one born in Hua Hin, the others were born in Bangkok. His father moved to Bangkok during the time between King Rama VI and Rama VII, which is why they were born in Bangkok.

His father, after retiring from the position of District Officer, became Lord Mayor for a year. Before that he opened a shop specialising in art, called Prasat Sin. His father's name was Khun Prasat. But when he was just a small child his father was a trader. He died when Khun Tuck was still young. Although his father had been an important man, after his death the family found he had left very little money, and Khun Tuck was obliged to work at all kinds of things to get income for the family: he worked in the rice-fields, cement-construction, and also in Thai medicine. His mother found plants and bought herbs from Bangkok. He was also a ball-boy on the local tennis court where Bangkok elite people played when they were visiting Hua Hin. After living in a number of other provinces, he returned to Hua Hin and opened a photography business.

He told the now-familiar story of early days in Hua Hin, stating that early settlers came from Baan Laad, Petchaburi, and have many remaining descendents in Hua Hin. He described in detail the sequence and problems of road construction in the area, over 60 years ago, stressing how much people liked the road and of course the new railway, since it brought a wider variety of goods, better trading conditions, and above all because they could now go by train to Bangkok. This opened up many new opportunities. Before this, people were frightened to travel: particularly frightened of meeting tigers on the laneways. They used ox-carts and sometimes horse-carts.

> In those times people lived only on the beachfront and there were no people living in the country behind Hua Hin. The people who live there now, growing pineapples and other things, mostly came from somewhere else, from Nakhon Chaisri, Nakhon Pathom, and from Ratchaburi. They are not the same as Hua Hin people, who know nothing about running plantations. The main thing they do know is trading, fishing, and how to make charcoal for fuel.

His wife was a Hua Hin native from a fishing family. He said he wanted to marry with "a native", since they would understand each other well. They grew up together, went to the same school, and were neighbours, but they were happy to wait to marry until they were both 23. They have four boys and four girls, all born at home in Hua Hin. Like the children of the other men discussed above, they have all done well: one works for Thai International in air-traffic control, two are traders, one runs a restaurant, one works in a savings bank, and one runs a sports shop. One is a magazine artist, and the youngest is studying at a university in Bangkok.

Speaking of early life in Hua Hin, Khun Tuck described attending many local events. There were occasional performances of *Lakhon Chatri*, *Lakhon Nora* and *Nang Talang* (the shadow plays from the south). More striking to him was the *Mae Sii*, or trance dancing, involving young girls, normally around 14–18, who meditate and are then possessed by spirits. In this state they can dance beautifully, even if they have never danced before. They can see in the dark, and walk around with their eyes closed. Many *Mae Sii* dancers lived in Hua Hin. He referred me to a woman called Pong, now a crab seller in the market. Others live in the fishing village. There was a similar trance dance for boys, called *Ling Lom*, the white monkey. Boys would pray, and then the monkey spirit would enter them. They would dance and shake so hard it would take six people to hold them. Khun Tuck himself has had extensive meditative experience, and has the ability to see inside a sick body. Once he had symptoms of appendicitis, and the doctor told him he needed an operation. But he meditated, and in this way he was able to see the wind which showed him a seed inside him. Then he meditated on water, and this washed the seed out. When the doctor next saw him he was healthy and well, to the doctor's surprise.

Another means of curing people is to see colours. There are many colours, but he himself knows only the yellow-gold colour, which can be directed inside the body to cure sickness. The colour is visualised by the healer, then sent inside the sick person, and thereafter there is no pain. The red light of the spectrum is the most powerful, but dangerous. He uses these techniques to cure his own mother, who is now 93 years old and healthy. He massages, meditates and cures her.

The "revolution" of 1932 marked a turning point for local people, he thought, saying that life was much better before, when the King was truly in charge. Even today, it would be better if the King was really in charge. Only under the King's direct guidance can the nation flourish, in his opinion. Ever since 1932 the King has been forced to accept the influence of others. He would say no more on this topic.

He recalled well the dramatic events of 8 December 1941 when the Japanese arrived at many places on the coast, including at Prachuap town, where the brave Thai soldiers lost their lives trying to repel them. Not until the next day did the Government tell them to allow the Japanese to pass, but by then most of the soldiers stationed at the Prachuap base had already died. Soon the Japanese set up camps in Hua Hin, and he often saw those who lived on the golf course, shooting with machine guns at the Americans flying overhead. Rich people who had houses here came from Bangkok to stay because they were frightened of the bombing. The Japanese printed their own banknotes, called Kong Tek banknotes. Everything was exactly the same, 50 satang and 1 baht, but a lot of people did not think it was real money. They printed them in Prachuab Khiri Khan and used them to buy fish and rice. If people wouldn't accept that money the Japanese became angry and hit them on the head.

During the war people only found out about things by seeing them, for example seeing a plane in flames which had been shot down, and seeing the *farangs* (foreign white people) going along packed into the railway cars (on their way to the Burma-Thailand railway camps). There were no newspapers. There was one radio station, Radio Thailand, and in Hua Hin there was only one radio set and it belonged to his father. They had to use very large batteries, and in the evening they put the speakers through the window so people could sit down outside to listen to the radio, to hear what had happened about the Japanese and the Americans. People were very nervous.

> Even today people think about the Japanese people. There were problems with the Japanese soldiers and young Thai girls, they raped them, they would bathe naked and grab the girls. The Japanese wanted to stay in the King's Palace [Klai Kangwol]. But people said, please, you have an Emperor, you respect the Emperor, you should respect our King in the same way. And finally they did do so, and didn't use the King's Palace, which pleased all the people here who were looking after it, the gardens and so on, not knowing when the King would come back again. The Seri Thai did a lot to help the Thai people, taking the kids and women to villages to protect them from the Japanese.

Electricity came about 40 years ago, immediately after the war finished, and it belonged to the State Railway. It was very cheap, people only used one or two light bulbs, there was no TV and nothing else. One 60-watt light bulb cost only five baht a month. Then people got radios, big ones which did not use batteries. People also got irons.

> Television came about 30 years ago and there was only one channel 4, then later the army presented channel 7 (now Channel 5). Everybody loved television. Television is good for people. It means you don't have to go out of the house, people have home entertainment and get some knowledge as well. But a lot of people are watching too much, staying up till midnight. Long before the war there was cinema. The name of the local cinema was Wik Ta Klong. Ta Klong is the name of the owner. He used a generator. I like movies. Right now I have cable TV, and I tape things on the video so I can watch when I have some free time.

Reflecting on things generally, Khun Tuck thought that the most important thing he saw in his life was the war and the Japanese soldiers when they lived in Hua Hin. It was both terrifying and exciting. He knew the First World War had been important too, but he was too young. But the Second World War was etched in his memory, since it made him think about life and try to understand things which otherwise he would not have thought about.

> I saw a Thai pilot who was shot down, the aeroplane went down in flames. We ran over to see the wreck, thinking he would certainly be dead. But he stood up and walked away from the plane even though it was burning fiercely. How was it possible that he did not die? He said he was wearing a magic shirt. Everybody now knows about the magic shirts the pilots wore, I think they still wear them today. Two famous monks made the cloth, a kind of red sweater. Soldiers wore them too, and then nobody could shoot them. So the enemy called them "ghost soldiers", even if you shot them nothing would happen, they thought they were spirits because they never got shot by the enemy.

Unlike many of the older people, Khun Tuck was more aware of the kinds of social changes which the twentieth century had brought to Hua Hin. As a result, he could not say that he was truly happier now than he had been in those former times.

> There was a more brotherly feeling in the old times. People lived together with a good neighbour policy, not like now. Today's society is very hypocritical. Before we didn't know about corruption. But right now every place takes money under the table. If you don't put money under the table you are not successful. Before our democratic time, in the time when the King had absolute power, it was better, there were not these problems. Also, the tax. OK, in those days, the officers would come to check the shop. "OK, can you pay? How about two baht, or four baht a year?" And then you could bargain: "How about three baht?" And the officer would say, "OK, OK, three baht". Another shop, it might be four or five baht. Today it's not like that. People have trouble. The old people, if you ask them all around here, like me, before, when the King controlled everything, it was much better, all the people were very happy, it is true. Everything today is about money and business. The income is much better, but people lose money because they have to spend a lot more, and to pay the social tax.[23]

Khun Chooey Santet-Witanon

Aged 74, Khun Chooey represents the other extreme of Hua Hin society. Her whole family, including her parents, was born, raised and remained in Hua Hin. She was born in the same street where she now lives, near the waterfront. Her house is a somewhat dilapidated timber structure beside which are metres and metres of squid-drying racks. This part of town is not for the sensitive of smell. Her family members have mostly been "employees", *rap chang*, labourers paid by the day, although they also did some trading on their own account. They all worked in the fishing business, one way or another. Apart from when she was a small child and lived down the road, she has always lived here in this same house and has never moved. She never went to school; she was too poor and had to take care of her brothers and sisters. She cannot read or write. In Hua Hin in the early days when there was hardly anyone living there, she used wood from anywhere around for cooking, and got fresh water from a pond nearby. She carried it in a jar every day to her house. Her husband was also born here. He was a fish trader, selling fish in Hua Hin but also taking it to Nakhon Pathom and Ratchaburi by train, mostly steamed mackerel and dried squid. The mackerel was caught in Hua Hin, cleaned and washed, then steamed on small plaited trays over salted water in which they placed a large basket. The water had to boil for half an hour, after which the mackerel would stay fresh for over two days. When they were very busy they sent out by train 400 trays at a time, with 800 fish in all.

She and her husband had been born in neighbouring houses and had known each other all the time as they grew up. They loved each other right from when they were children, so it was not an arranged marriage. She had seven children, all of whom still live in Hua Hin except for one in Bangkok. Other than this one, they too all work in the fishing industry, buying and selling fresh squid, dried squid and so on. They all live in the same area, and although they are married they continue to work together. Fifteen grandchildren have been born and are growing up nearby. Khun Chooey however has travelled quite widely. When she was 50 and the children were old enough she went to Penang, and twice to Chiangmai, and has visited many famous temples around Thailand. She travelled by train, car or bus.

She participated in *Mae Sii* as a young girl. It happened several times, always at Songkhran (Thai new year):

Someone tied cloth over my eyes, and I heard people singing. I felt sleepy. I didn't know what was happening. I don't know why they selected me. I was 11 or 12 the first time. I am a faint-hearted person, not strong, so that's how the spirit can enter me. When the spirit goes in it is the spirit of a woman dancer, who then makes the body dance. All I know is that *Mae Sii* is the name of that spirit, who goes into several girls at the same time. I don't know any story about her. It just happens to you. It still happens today.

Khun Chooey revered the King when he came to Hua Hin. She told of lining up near the railway station in the hot sun to see him arrive from Bangkok when he came in his special royal carriage. He always came in high summer, and there were not many shade-trees along the laneway in those days. Because she was an unimportant person she did not expect to get close to him, but once when she was still a girl he looked straight at her and she felt as though a spirit were entering her. She was very excited. She was about 18 when "wicked men" forced the King to give up his Kingdom, and she and her family and everyone they knew were very sad and felt as if they had lost their own father.

During the war she was very afraid and constantly ran away to hide. People thought the Japanese would do bad things, but nothing happened to her or her family. In the end she just accepted the Japanese soldiers, and sold them fish. "They bought a lot of fish but paid in bad money":

All my life the one most important thing is money. Lacking money is terrible, nothing is as bad as not having enough money. Working and making money is the most important thing, a person must be diligent and work hard and then they will have enough. Now life is much better, I don't have to work so hard. My family has enough money for our needs, we can eat rice easily every day. But still, I get into a bad mood sometimes and I shout at everyone.

Khun Chooey is very positive about the many changes which she has seen come to Hua Hin in her lifetime. She doesn't mind living here with all the cars and motorbikes and people walking around. The arrival of new people, increasingly over the past few years, has meant more and more money has come to the town and her dried squid sells very well.[24]

Conclusion

It is difficult to find an adequate way to write about what somebody has told you about his/her life and experiences. Life history, oral history, narrative, interview: whatever it is one seeks in these kinds of enquiries is elusive. Many parts of people's lives and experiences do not appear in an account like this. Most notably, the kind of personal narrations, with possible explanations for actions or events, such as might be elicited in a Western tradition, were never brought forward. People did not appear to construct their individual senses of self through sequential narrations. There seemed no sense of "who one is" as being something separate from "what one saw and did". My enquiries called forth certain kinds of memories and accounts, foreclosed others; and yet they revealed aspects of Hua Hin about which I could have had no idea otherwise, and commonalities in peoples' experiences which appear in no history book or formal account. They also highlighted the differences in experience and interpretation even among those who shared so much common time and space.

The experience of "modernity", as conventionally measured by technological change, was readily and enthusiastically embraced by everyone I spoke to. Nobody pined for the old days, although some mentioned the greater sense of intimacy in former times when the population was so much smaller and more stable. Yet the benefits seemed far to outweigh these costs. Ordinary expectations and behaviours were punctured occasionally by alarming externally-imposed events which were thrust upon them, but which they nonetheless managed to assimilate and "normalise". The closeness of the King, both physically and symbolically, seemed to bring comfort and a sense of special distinction to Hua Hin people, especially the "native" families. The extent of upward mobility across generations was also notable for these families, whose lineages began with simple farmers and traders in the early nineteenth century and who today include numerous descendants in upper middle class occupations with capital investments in the town. Although the transformations of modernity were indeed taking place — even the overthrow of the absolute monarchy can be attributed to the early globalisation forces which led to the rise of a Western-educated class calling for "democracy" — these meta-narratives had no purchase at the local level. Western power and hegemony, present though it was and increasingly visible during the tourist boom of the 1980s, seemed not to be a matter of concern or even recognition. There were *farangs,* but even though they were here in the same space, they were not really part of the same world, although their money was. For older people in Hua Hin, spiritual forces, which saturated the local environment, the presence of the King, and the practices of work and family, created their twentieth-century world. Notions of some transcendent Western metaphysical power seem from their perspectives to have been both unnecessary and unthinkable.

Acknowledgements

The research on which this paper is based was funded by Macquarie University Research Grants and by the Australian Research Council. The National Research Council of Thailand gave permission for the research to be carried out. My thanks are due particularly to Khun Thippawan Thampusama (now Abold) who assisted in the research with the Hua Hin elders. The generous participation of these people, and many other Hua Hin residents, is something for which I am deeply grateful. I hope to repay their cooperation by writing a book which will trace the many aspects of Hua Hin history and everyday life into the twenty-first century. I particularly want to thank Michael Niblett for his unfailing support and contributions during the period of field work in Hua Hin, and his insightful comments on many aspects of the research.

Methodology

Interviews and conversations were mostly held in people's homes or nearby. The original interviews were guided by a set of questions which were presented as the recollections prompted by previous questions were exhausted. However each respondent was free to go into whichever details or comments seemed appropriate at the time. Many conversations were interrupted and resumed at a later time. Some people asked me to come back because they had forgotten to mention something. Tape recordings and written notes were made where people agreed. Sometimes they requested that no notes were made, and these requests were always honoured. People sometimes spoke of matters they did not feel were appropriate for a public record, in particular local issues and events which were of concern, and might have repercussions. Any matters of this kind have been omitted.

Notes

1. These are among the most influential early works in English, published at the point where "post-modernism" was emerging as a social theory rather than an aesthetic movement. Since then the number of works devoted to issues around modernity has expanded far beyond the capacity to list them here.

2. The advocates of "modernisation" during the 1960s in Southeast Asia, in the context of "the threat of communism", seemed to operate on this neo-functionalist proposition, but little seems to have changed by the 1990s when, after the fall of the Soviet Union, neoclassical economics provided the underpinning of a moral crusade brought to Russia by countless technical advisers who believed economic liberalisation could occur overnight and would result in "democratisation". See Cohen (2000).

3. Today the latter are also experiencing similar processes, even while their ostensible political ideologies and discourses have not shifted significantly, a matter which calls for empirical investigation and theoretical discussion. The entry of nations such as Laos and Vietnam, and especially China, into a form of market-based para-capitalism while maintaining Socialism at the ideological level raises questions about the efficacies of State-promoted ideologies in changed material contexts.

4. The consequences of World War II across the Asia-Pacific, and its profound effects in reshaping the lived and imagined world of its inhabitants, has hardly begun to be recognised. Many studies of individual communities and groups have touched on the topic, but no systematic analysis has yet been completed.

5. Anderson (1983) opened up the question of the nationalist project and its relation to print media, through his concept of "imagined communities". My thinking is obviously indebted to his pioneering insights in this area. For the nationalist project in Thailand, and some of the ways in which it has emerged, see Reynolds (2002); this is a revised edition of the 1991 edition. Reynolds' new chapter "Thai identity in the age of globalisation" carries the analysis into the conditions of the late 1990s.

6. I explore the relation between local and national media in Hua Hin in Hamilton (2002), and consider broader themes in the relation between popular media and national narrative in Hamilton (1992, 1993a and 1993b).

7. And others suggest it may be unrealisable, due to the seemingly pervasive networks of power and influence which operate beyond the "mainstream" and yet are in one way or another supported by it; see Pasuk and Sungsidh (1995).

8. However, from around the mid-1990s, Thai cinema and television has turned to World War II for inspiration, with many *lakhon* (television melodramas) being set in that period. Thailand's position during World War II was that the Japanese could not be resisted, and should instead be tolerated and permitted to use Thailand for their own purposes without any formal submission. The melodramas dealing with this period generally focus on love affairs, in one notable case being concerned with the fate of a Japanese soldier left behind in Burma after the war — perhaps inspired by the Japanese film *The Harp of Burma*, without acknowledgment.

9. I carried out research in Hua Hin in 1987–88 for several periods, the longest of which was six months. Subsequently I returned to the town for two- or three-month visits until 1992, and again for several weeks in 1999. Acknowledgements appear at the end of this paper. For the aspect of the research discussed here, I interviewed around 30 older residents and their families with the assistance of an educated Bangkok woman who was working in the local council at the time. Interviews were taped and some notes were taken. I also collected a wide cross-section of documents including funeral books and local histories.

10. In addition to work in Hua Hin, extensive interviews were carried out with villagers living in the rural zones between the coast and the Tenasserim Range. A restudy of Hua Hin and its hinterland villages would provide valuable insights into the consequences of Thailand's "decade of globalisation" and the subsequent economic downturn. Many assumptions are made about the way these macro-level processes impact on individuals and families, but there is little in the way of concrete evidence of a "before and after" nature.

11. It is customary when an important person dies to mark their passing with a publication of some kind. This might be about the individual and his/her family history, or about some aspect of life which particularly interested the deceased. Especially valuable information on early Hua Hin was provided in two commemorative books, the first for Khun Somboon Krasaesin, entitled "Family Genealogy", which provides a comprehensive account of the many branches of the Krasaesin family (privately published in 1977), and the subsequent commemorative book for Mr Arun Krasaesin, "The History of Hua Hin", privately published on the occasion of his funeral in 1984. These books are not identified by author and are locally printed. Some collections of funeral books are found in the National Library in Bangkok, but otherwise are kept in family hands.

12. Petchaburi Province, to the north of Prachuab Khiri Khan, is one of the oldest and most important provinces in Thailand. Located 160 km to the southwest of Bangkok, it abuts the Burmese border and provided a front-line of defence during the Burmese wars against Ayutthaya. Originally

surrounded by a wall, Petchaburi town is full of crumbling ruins and old *wats*, famous cave temples full of Buddha images and on the mountain top (Khao Wang) is the recently renovated palace of King Rama IV. Hua Hin's early population came from this province, which continues to provide a steady stream of immigrants to both the town and its hinterland region.

13. Actually the Krasaesin family almost certainly came from Pattalung originally. "Krasaesin" is a very significant place-name in that province, although the Funeral Books do not make this connection.

14. It is always difficult to know which tense to use in recounting narratives of people's lives. I have chosen to use the present tense in describing the circumstances under which the person was living at the time I got to know him or her, and the past for the recounting of their previous experiences. This is admittedly awkward, but I am not sure of a better solution.

15. Wat Benchamabophit remains a temple under royal patronage and a major landmark in Bangkok. It was built of white Carrara marble at the turn of the century, under the patronage of King Chulalongkorn (Rama V). The fact that he was admitted to study in this *wat* suggests he had been picked out by his temple superiors in Petchaburi.

16. See Grow (1991) for an excellent account of *Lakhon Chatri* in Petchaburi.

17. This made talking to him, or any of his family members, extremely difficult. The original interview was drowned out by the cacophony and only fragments appear on the tape-recording. Inside the house was little better due to the ceaseless presence of the television, which was on during all broadcasting hours to drown out the noise outside. Finally it became apparent that around 6 a.m. was the best time for discussion, and further talks with him and his daughter took place at that time in the public laneway. This of course meant that many other early morning passers-by joined in the discussion. See note below.

18. The problem of obtaining life histories or narratives where nobody, least of all elders, is ever left alone raises many questions about the significance of "individual" narratives, and the contexts in which they can be told, which should be addressed as a methodological problem in this kind of work.

19. This was most likely the influenza epidemic of 1918. The impact of this, the first truly global epidemic, on populations in the Asian region, has received little attention, but see Brown (1987).

20. The story of Chao Rai is known now all over Thailand due to its popularisation in a television series and publication in cheap book form. These provincial origin myths account for the physical features

of the landscape — mountains, islands — as the result of the action of powerful figures in a mythic past, much as do Aboriginal mythologies in Australia.

21. *Raeng* refers to energy, power or force and can be used with reference to potency as of drugs or herbs, and the ability to transmit, as in electricity. Mor Chui commented elsewhere that *raeng* is a kind of electricity, but only after he had first seen what electricity could do did he fully understand what it meant as far as the body is concerned. However, it also has a spiritual meaning which is understood in Buddhism, and this is why healers can only really learn their knowledge from monks.

22. The Allies sent a wave of "Flying Fortresses" to bomb Bangkok on 4 January 1942. The Thai Government was incensed by this, because the Government had requested help from the Allies to prevent a Japanese occupation and had been ignored. As a result Thailand declared war on USA and Great Britain in January 1942, a declaration which was not reciprocated by the United States (Haseman n.d.: 29). The Seri Thai was formed by those who supported the Allies, carrying information, supplying Western soldiers in camps on the Burma-Thailand railway, and training guerrillas to fight the Japanese if the Allies should land. The Free Thai movement was supported by Thais in the USA and England, many of whom had been studying there when the Japanese invasion occurred. This account is provided in Jumsai (n.d.: 577). For a more detailed and thoroughly researched account see Haseman (n.d.).

23. People in Thailand complain endlessly about the "social tax". Whenever someone marries, leaves, has a death in the family or undergoes some other important event, all their co-workers and neighbours are expected to make a financial contribution. Moreover, police officers and others in official positions often send an invitation card to people who don't even know them, saying they need money, and people feel obliged to pay it.

24. Dried squid is considered a special delicacy and is sold in many forms, including packaged as a snack food. However, it is also sold by vendors from a wheeled cart on which the squid is hung. The squid is hammered out to soften it and sold with a spicy chili sauce. Squid vendors purchase the squid from dryers such as Khun Chooey and her family. The squid vendor's cart is also a common sight in Bangkok, especially in the suburbs.

References

Anderson, Benedict. 1983. *Imagined Communities*. London: Verso.

Behar, Ruth. 1992. "A Life Story to Take Across the Border: Notes on an Exchange", in *Storied Lives: The Cultural Politics of Self-Understanding*, ed.

G. Rosenwald and R. Ochberg. New Haven and London: Yale University Press, pp. 108–23.

Berger, Peter. 1977. *Facing up to Modernity*. New York: Basic Books.

Berman, Marshall. 1983. *All that is Solid Melts into Air*. London: Verso.

Brown, C. 1987. "The Influenza Pandemic of 1918 in Indonesia", in *Death and Disease in Southeast Asia: Explorations in Social, Medical and Demographic History*, ed. N. Owen. Singapore: Oxford University Press, pp. 235–56.

Bruner, J. 1987. "Life as Narrative", *Social Research* 54/1: 11–32.

Caplan, Patricia. 1997. *African Voices, African Lives: Personal Narratives from a Swahili Village*. London: Routledge.

Cohen, Stephen. 2000. *Failed Crusade: America and the Tragedy of Post-Communist Russia*. New York: Norton.

Grow, Mary Louise. 1991. "Laughter for Spirits, A Vow Fulfilled: The Comic Performance of Thailand's Lakhon Chatri Dance Drama", PhD thesis, University of Wisconsin-Madison.

Hamilton, Annette. 1992. "Family Dramas: Film and Modernity in Thailand", *Screen* 33: 259–73.

———. 1993a. "Cinema and Nation: Dilemmas of Representation in Thailand", *East-West Film Journal* 7: 81–105.

———. 1993b. "Video Crackdown, or, the Sacrificial Pirate", *Public Culture* 11: 515–32.

———.1994. "Dizzy Development in Hua Hin: The Effects of Tourism on a Thai Seaside Town", in *Culture, Identity and Urban Change in Southeast Asia*, ed. Marc Askew and William Logan. Geelong, Vic.: Deakin University Press, pp. 149–66.

———. 2002. "The National Picture: Thai Media and Cultural Identity", in *Media Worlds*, ed. Faye D. Ginsburg *et al*. Berkeley and Los Angeles: University of California Press, pp. 152–70.

Haseman, John B. n.d. *The Thai Resistance Movement during the Second World War*. Bangkok: Chalermnit Press.

Heidegger, Martin. 1977. *The Question Concerning Technology and Other Essays*. New York: Harper Torchbooks.

Linde, C. 1993. *Life Stories: The Creation of Coherence*. New York: Oxford University Press.

Lyotard, Jean Francois. 1984. *The Postmodern Condition: a Report of Knowledge*. Minneapolis: University of Minnesota Press.

Pasuk Phongpaichit and Sungsidh Piriyarangsan. 1994. *Corruption and Democracy in Thailand*. Bangkok: Chulalongkorn University, Political Economy Centre.

Peacock, James L. and Dorothy C. Holland. 1993. "The Narrated Self: Life Stories in Process", *Ethos* 21/4: 367–83.

Rappaport, H. 1990. *Marking Time*. New York: Simon and Schuster.

Röttger-Rössler, B. 1993. "Autobiography in Question: On Self-Presentation and Life Description in an Indonesian Society", *Anthropos* 88: 365–73.

Reynolds, Craig J. 2002. *National Identity and its Defenders*. Chiangmai: Silkworm Books (revised and expanded edition, first published 1991).

Suntaree Komin. 1985. "The World View Through Thai Value Systems", in *Traditional and Changing Thai World-View*. Chulalongkorn University Social Research Institute. CUSRI/SEASP Bangkok.

Waterson, Roxana. 2001. "A Toraja pilgrimage: the life of Fritz Basiang", *Indonesia and the Malay World* 29/83: 5–50.

7
Traversing Invisible Borders: Narratives of Women Between the Hills and the City

Yoko Hayami

In 1996, I was on my way up to the hills of Northern Thailand, a familiar ride I had often taken since beginning fieldwork in the hills in 1987. Waiting for the daily public transport, a pick-up-truck ride from a bus station in Chiang Mai, I came across a little farewell scene. A young teenage girl, who looked as though she might be Karen, arrived on the back of a motorcycle driven by a rather flamboyant young man. As she descended from the back seat, she stayed talking to the young driver. The pick-up truck departing from this station would take us up into the hills on a six- or seven-hour drive, the latter half of which was primarily through Karen country. When I began visiting the area in 1987, there was only one truck per day, but in the subsequent decades, with increasing mobility especially of youths between the hill villages and the city, they had increased it to two round-trips per day, and even then, the trucks were always full. Almost all of the people who sat around the station were Karen from the remote hills that were the pick-up truck's destination, and therefore, many of them were acquaintances, or at least, familiar faces. There was nothing much like a schedule, and the truck started when there were enough passengers and when the driver was ready. During the long wait, the passengers inquired of each other in Karen, asking each other from which village they came, for what purpose, and so on. The girl, however, continued talking to the bike driver in Thai. She twisted her body nervously, touching her hair and face, as if to express her discomfort at being positioned between the Karen villagers in town, and the flashy looking plains-dweller who assumed a taken-for-granted intimacy with her. After a while, the truck was ready to depart, and the girl mounted the pick-up truck, waving good-bye to the bike-driver. Nobody spoke to her for the first half of the six-hour trip. After lunch, the bus drove on into higher elevations, and as we began to see Karen villages along the winding highland road, the girl started talking to the Karen youths in a relaxed tone, so different from her tense and nervous manner which I had observed in the city bus terminal. Somewhere along the road, she had crossed an invisible boundary.

Experiences of Mobility and Women's Narratives

I take as a starting point that a local community or ethnic group cannot be a definable entity that corresponds to some culture, but is something that should be understood dynamically within the intricately interwoven webs of power, both far and near.[1] If so, in the face of the increasing mobility of Karen women from the hills who are spatially, politically, economically and socially positioned in the peripheries between the city and the hill Karen setting, what kinds of construction and negotiation of locality, ethnicity and gender can we find? Such mobility between periphery and centre is inevitably mobility between different fields of power. The moving subject is not a culture, nor an ethnic group, but a person. The person who traverses boundaries, or positions him/herself in the interstices, will objectify his/her own place of origin, and continue to question his/her own identity both ethnic and gender, in the processes and webs of power. Such personal experiences may be accessible through their daily actions, decisions, and narratives. By focusing on the latter, we may be able to find the effects and workings of power surrounding the person, and also, the construction of the narrating self through this very process. These two are inextricable.

In this paper, I examine the traversal experiences of Karen women through their own narratives.[2] Ong points out that female bodies are often symbolic of social boundaries and threats to such boundaries (Ong 1995: 6), so that in contexts of rapid social change, there is a tendency towards tightening control over women's morality and sexual activity. It has also been pointed out that those women who dare to be the first to travel away from home are often those who have for some reason lost productive means within the community, or lost their position in the community as a result of divorce, widowhood, or disablement (Moore 1988: 95). While men will boast their influences across regional and ethnic boundaries, women represent the local closed space, and femaleness is in turn represented by the social boundary itself (Tsing 1993: 250; Hayami 2003). It is true in hill Karen communities too, that norms regarding mobility and travel do differ between women and men, and travelling entails great risks for the women. The experience of travel sharply highlights both the condition of being Karen, and of being women.

However, the reason why I take up the subjectivity of women in this paper is not merely because women's travel and mobility as a phenomenon are different from those of men. To consider the agency of women as subjects, especially women in the peripheries, could lead us toward an important reconsideration of anthropological perspectives on persons as objects of study, and is furthermore a topic that includes many of the issues of feminist ethnography. If we adhere to a view of the subject as a modern or transcendent self that precedes discourse, (a view that is inextricable from the modernist cognitive duality between subject and object, male and female, which are themselves inherently hierarchical), then it would mean that agency will be possible only within the modernist subject thus defined, so that there is no scope for self-determination or agency for the self that is constructed in discourse and culture. Within this scheme where the constructing male subject is differentiated from the constructed female subject, agency becomes the monopoly of the former. This would then deny the possibility of women's agency, and would further lead to objectifying and essentialising women, thereby joining forces with the hegemonic discourse. However, if we take a contrary view and dissect the category "woman" itself, then feminism will lose the consolidated subject of its struggle. This is the dilemma.

Against such a perspective, Butler points out that for the subject who is thus "enmired" in culture, the construction precedes the subject's identity, and at once turns it into the object of negotiation. Agency is not to be found in the "I" before the encoding, but is mobilised within the very process of that encoding and constructive process. Rather than an alternative between a passive existence that is wholly at the mercy of the cultural mechanism on the one hand, or, a free decision-making subject on the other, agency is made possible in the very process of constructedness, or the construction is the precondition for agency (Butler 1990; Hekman 1995). The subject is constructed in multiple discourses in a particular cultural and historical space, within which it can seek to find a discursive space that enables its agency. To put it in Ortner's terms, "the importance of subjects (whether individual actors or social entities) lies not so much in who they are and how they are put together as in the projects that they construct and enact. For it is in the formulation and enactment of those projects that they both become and transform into who they are, and that they sustain or transform their social and cultural universe" (Ortner 1995: 187).

In this paper, I hope to look at the multiplicity and intricacies of power in the ambiguous territory of the travelling persons and their agency, through their narratives. Such a perspective will meet the phenomenon from the periphery, and while unquestionably being constrained by the powers that define the phenomenon from the centre, it will seek to examine the foundational process through which the subject and the phenomenon emerge.

The act of narration is founded on the relationship between the narrator and the audience. It is not as if we have here a communal effort within a power vacuum. Rather, the framework of narration in this paper is the event constrained in the form of the author's interview. The interview and the narration, as well as the representation of it through this writing, act to form another relationship of power. The possibility that researchers from first world countries may objectify and essentialise the voices of third world women, such that their work itself becomes a locus for an emergent power relationship, has been criticised sharply by Spivak (1988). Yet Ortner has redirected our attention back to committing ourselves to "thickness" of description, as our fundamental ethnographic endeavour (Ortner 1995: 173–4). If ethnography is the effort to understand the lives of others by using the "self" as the ultimate tool of knowledge, then the ultimate purpose of this thick description is to understand the subject that is constructing and acting out the project in the process of describing the multiple layers of power relationship (1995: 187). Moreover, she criticises Spivak's denial of the possibility of representing others, especially subaltern others, arguing that this in effect ends in dissolving the "subject" itself. Ortner, by contrast, holds fast to the claim that thick description in ethnography is the description of the other subject in the context of its "enmiredness" in webs of power.

In her introduction to the life history of Esperanza, a Mexican woman, Behar cites Benjamin's contrast between information and storytelling, and ponders, "it worries me that one does violence to the life history as a story by turning it into the disposable commodity of information.... One approach I took to this problem was to focus on the act of life story representation as reading rather than as informing,... I have tried to make clear that what I am reading is a story, or set of stories, that have been told to me, so that I, in turn, can tell them again, transforming myself from a listener into a storyteller" (1993: 13). This is the spirit I adopt in this paper.

The women I introduce here are neither typical Karen women, nor eccentric.[3] Because mobility and travel is more risky for women, women through their mobility recognise the multiplicity of webs of power, and through their individual experiences, respond to and make decisions in the face of it. In response to my requests, these women attempted in their own words to narrate their experiences.

Increasing Urban Migration from the Hills

I have been visiting a cluster of Karen villages in the northwestern corner of Chiang Mai Province in Northern Thailand since 1987. Ninety per cent of the population of the district are Karen speakers. Here, irregular labour mobility has been prevalent since the 1980s. The mobility of hill-dwellers from hills to the city itself is nothing new. There has always been seasonal labour mobility as well as irregular visits to the market, to medical services, etc., in the city. Yet travel for purposes of local petty trade and mobility for daily wage labour on the one hand, and the more recent migration of youths seeking opportunities for education and labour in the city on the other, differ not only in the age and sex distribution of the travellers but also in the perspective of the villagers who send them off (Hayami 1998).

It is impossible to quantify the changing mobility from the hills to Chiang Mai City not only for lack of statistics, but also because it would be meaningless to quantify such varied phenomena. According to one piece of research carried out in 1981, at the time there were seven hundred persons from the hills in Chiang Mai (not counting student dormitory occupants), of whom one hundred were said to be Karen (Vatikiotis 1984: 200). We may gather from this that urban migration among Karen was not as prevalent as among some other groups. In another piece of research five years later, we find indication of rapid increase, although 80 per cent of Karen migrants were male (Renard, Prasert and Roberts 1987: 34). From interviews and observations in the hills, I learned that it was in the 1980s that urban migration among male Karen youth became pronounced across the region, followed by a rapid growth in the numbers of young female migrants in the 1990s. Since the 1980s, economic growth in Thailand and the flourishing of the tourist industry brought an increase in demands for urban labour, and cheap hill labour was especially wanted. We began to come across hill Karen youths in gas stations, restaurants and hotels all over Chiang Mai city, and heard about increasing numbers of house maids and hospital orderlies. As a result of the Hill Tribe Policy since the 1960s, the hills had been targeted as the peripheries to be nationalised and territorialised in economic, social and cultural senses. In the hills, Thai language education was introduced, and the subsistence economy was threatened by severe competition and restriction of access to land resources. Urban migration in search of labour and educational opportunities began to increase. Christian organisations (especially Catholic and Baptist) responded to the increase, notably among young women, by expanding their dormitory facilities.[4]

The patterns of women's urban mobility from the hills are varied. Since the 1980s, in Chiang Mai City, there are places where we may observe women clad in "hill tribe costumes" entertaining tourists in restaurants, or selling handicrafts or other goods in the Night Bazaar (Toyota 1998). The fact that Akha women especially have appeared from such an early stage on the scene has been explained by the fact that those women, who have come across the national border from Myanmar, have preferred to make their own living in the city rather than to settle in villages in the hills where, disadvantaged as they are without land, they would have little choice other than to marry older men (Vatikiotis 1984). They sell handicrafts in Chiang Mai, and their colourfully costumed appearances have impressed upon the tourist scene in Chiang Mai the image of the "hill tribe women". However, until now, Karen women have been far less visible in the city. Not only were female urban migrants among Karen much less numerous until recently, but also those who did come to the city, both male and female, were less involved in commercial or tourist sectors, and mostly lived dispersed among the urban population rather than in ethnic clusters. There are few Karen in the recent squatter residences in the city which are occupied primarily by migrants from the hills. There are communities of Christian Karen in the city that have histories of far more than half a century, but aside from these, the visibility of the Karen population in the city has been low.[5]

From the perspective of the hills, travel and mobility to the city or to other places are differentiated according to purpose. One may go to study (*lae ma lo ta*), to visit somebody (*lae o ...*), go for labour (*lae ta*, or *lae ma ta*), go for trade (*lae cha ta bgae ta*), or go without any particular purpose (*lae ha*, which literally means "to go for a walk"). The latter three patterns apply mostly to men, while women today primarily go with the former two purposes and increasingly for the third. In many cases those who leave the village to study will continue to stay in the city after graduating and look for jobs, while others will go to work without seeking education in the city. If a woman goes to the city without any particular purpose, without any reliable company, she is criticised for "walking badly" (*ha na jo*). On the other hand, for a young man, aimless "walking" is not considered negatively. Rather, it will add to his experience and social network.

Among the hill-dwelling Karen,[6] kinship is organised bilaterally, and matrilocal residence is predominant. Women therefore most likely live close to their parents both before and after marriage, so that the parental house and village is their primary social arena. The youngest daughter, especially, remains with her parents, and is responsible for looking after them in old age. On the one hand, there are restrictive norms regarding their mobility, yet on the other, they are not hindered from such activities as petty trading or labour to gain income for their families.

Men, on the other hand, more likely leave their parental house and community after marriage. Even before marriage, they will travel to form wider social networks from among which they find their future brides. Thus, although even as an ideal, the gendered division of labour is not very pronounced, yet due to the restrictions on travel and mobility, male and female activities differ significantly. Men will travel beyond the surrounding forests to other regions, and through such travel experiences, they gain social and economic standing at home. They will form social networks through activities involving state agencies and markets. It is usually men who participate in projects brought in by the administration or by NGOs and other agencies. For Karen men, it is possible to experience and repeat sexual adventures with Northern Thai[7] (*Yau* or *Zau* in Karen) women, and then come back and marry a Karen woman.

Women, on the other hand, are said to have weaker souls[8] than men, so that if they wander out of the village into the forest alone, they are more easily caught by evil spirits in the forest. If they "walk badly" or aimlessly, they will be victims not only of evil spirits, but of the forest and the wild animals, or the *Yau* men roaming in the forests. The stereotypical image of *Yau* men held by the Karen is that they are morally unreliable, so that if a woman were to fall for a *Yau* man and marry him, the marriage is expected to be unstable. This is why both within and outside the village, it is safer for women to avoid contact. Should they dare to bring themselves in contact with *Yau* men, they will become the object of much gossip and condemnation. Once a Karen woman marries a *Yau* man, it is said to be difficult for her to find a Karen partner after separating with the *Yau* husband. Such women tend to remarry or continue relationships with non-Karen men. Especially in the city, once a Karen woman separates from a *Yau* man, she would be considered a "fallen woman" (*lau tae:* "fallen" in Karen, or *sia:* "broken", in the Thai idiom). Such stories were often heard in the hills. Stories of migrant women in the city are often recounted as stories of "fall", combined with the theme of the terror of AIDS.[9]

In order to avoid such "dangers" in the city, young women have had the choice of making use of Christian dormitories, staying with relatives or staying in respectable homes as live-in maids while studying or working outside. Women need to keep their urban experiences accountable. Up until secondary level, villagers perceive little difference in the relative usefulness of education for men and women. Young women have witnessed other women who have received an education and returned as teachers or clinic workers to the hills, earning respectable salaries. In the research area, up until junior high school level, there were more girls than boys who received education outside of the village.

Except for a very small minority, boys have tended to circulate between the city and the hills seeking daily or irregular labour opportunities. Women's average age of marriage is around 18. Girls in this age range are under strong pressure to get married in the village. Education away from the village has given them a pretext to delay marriage, as well as a respectable reason for urban migration, yet at the same time by putting off marriage, it has made it more difficult for them to find a suitable groom upon return after receiving a better education.

Narratives of Migrant Women in Chiang Mai

In 1997, I interviewed 30 young migrant Karen (aged 12 to 29) in the city, 25 of whom were women.[10] With a few exceptions, teenage girls gave me extremely similar responses: how they wanted to return to the hills after finishing their education, and find a salaried job in the hills, marry a Karen man, and look after their parents. When we consider the increase in hill Karen young women finding partners in the lowlands, mostly Thai, this is the normative and morally correct response for these young people, rather than a response that reflected the reality. In many cases the settings for the interviews were "hill tribe dormitories" in the city, or else I had sought out the interviewees and approached them, so the setting of the interview was such that I, a Japanese researcher, interviewed these young people knowing that they were Karen, and the interviewees also knew that I knew. It is possible that the interviewees may have made assumptions about what I expected to hear.

However, among women with longer experience in the city, now in their mid-20s, there were a few who responded quite differently. Weerawan, aged 23, was from northern Chiang Mai Province. In her village, she was brought up speaking Karen, but in the interview, she chose to speak in Thai. In fact, this was the only interview I conducted solely in Thai. In the coffee shop of the hotel where she worked, she explained to me that she no longer uses her Karen name, and introduced herself to me with her Thai name. She was the youngest of six siblings, and all of her older sisters and brothers married and stayed in or close to their parental village. After graduating from the local high school, she came to Chiang Mai, worked for two years to earn her tuition, then entered the night school of the Chiang Mai Teachers' College, working in the hotel coffee shop during the day. She lives in a room she rents with a *Yau* girl friend. Her shift is from six in the morning to three in the afternoon, after which from five in the evening to nine, she goes to college. She must work on weekends also, and in the afternoon she goes to the movies or shopping with her friends. Once, she had a Karen boyfriend who was at the Police academy. She

thought she would marry him, and he had mentioned it too. But he
went back to his village and married there. "He wanted a 'Karen bride'
from the village", she said. At present, she is not thinking of marriage,
and she does not go out with Karen men. She enjoys being with her
Yau friends. Her plan for the future is to earn her degree from the
teachers' training college, and seek a better-paying job. She goes back
to her village once in a couple of months, but she stays one night only.
Her only purpose is to see her parents, and as soon as she gets to her
village, she misses Chiang Mai.

Even though she has lived for a long time in the urban setting,
her life was affected by the norms and criteria of the hills. She was
made acutely aware of this when her boyfriend turned away from
her, which made her realise that she no longer fit the criteria of a
desirable "Karen bride" according to hill standards. As a result she
has learned to reconsider and measure her distance between the two
worlds. Thus, the future that she imagines for herself is a path that
is less binding in terms of restrictions of ethnic and gender identity,
yet it is one that will make it difficult for her eventually to return
to her natal village.

Malee, on the other hand, is a 28-year-old Catholic Karen from
western Chiang Mai Province. She is the fourth of five siblings, and
all of her siblings are married and have jobs either in the city or the
town near their home village. She stayed with her parents in the village
until she was ten years old, then came to Chiang Mai to study, staying
at the Catholic dormitory, and went to night school after junior high
school. Then, the Catholic sisters sent her to a nunnery in Nakhon
Pathom for two years. Now, she is living as a dormitory matron at
the Chiang Mai girls' dormitory, studying in the Teachers' college
weekend programme. She returns to her village during vacations to help
her parents in the fields. Unlike Weerawan, she would like to return
more frequently to her natal village, and whenever she does so, she
no longer feels like returning to Chiang Mai. Seventy per cent of the
youths in her village are away, mostly in Chiang Mai. It is therefore
quite normal to be away, but if she had a choice, she would like to
return and teach at the local school, and if possible, marry a Karen
man with equal educational background in the village. "But there is
nobody. My parents were pressuring me for a long time, but by now,
they seem to have given up. I think I don't need to get married. Once
I finish studying, I might become a sister (Catholic nun)." She has

never considered the option of marrying a non-Karen man, but would rather become a nun and continue to study. This would be a way to avoid both the pressure to marry, and the difficulties of being a single woman. Education and religion have provided a future path for her in which she does not have to forsake the identity that ties her to her natal village.

Both Weerawan and Malee are working part-time while paying for their own higher education. However, such independence and attainment render difficult the choice of returning to the village. The primary reason for women's urban migration is educational opportunity. However, having attained that educational goal, there are very few opportunities for jobs in the village, and neither are there many men who would be ready to marry an older woman with high educational qualifications from the city. A young woman who, far from *lau tae* (falling), or *ha na jau* (walking badly), is independent and achievement-oriented will, for the same reason, find her path to fulfilling certain norms and a particular lifestyle in the village closed. Because of this, in the narratives of these two women, we find that they are, as women from Karen villages, obliged to find a position for themselves somewhere between the hills and the city.

Of the interviews conducted in the city, the reason why I focused on these two women was that, right from the start of the interview, their narratives stood out from the normative responses of the others. But more importantly, both of these women persuasively led me away from all routine questions, since they had their own ideas about what they wanted to tell me. It seemed that for both Malee and Weerawan the telling of their own story was itself the act of connecting their past to the present and future in a meaningful way.

The Joy of Walking Around: Narratives of Travel as Adventure

In my own field village of S, urban migration by young people became pronounced in the 1990s. Most of them were young men going to look for wage work in the city. In villages in the area with better access to transportation, there was some observable mobility of young women who in most cases were taking advantage of kinship networks, acquaintances, or Christian organisations and their dormitory and other facilities in moving to the city. Women's migration begins in restricted form, and then gradually becomes popular in each community. In S village there were still only very few cases of young women's mobility.

Naw Khaepho is 24 years old, the eldest of the village pastor's nine children. At the time of this interview which I conducted in S, her natal village, she was already married with two children. Her husband is a Karen man from another village in the same district, although as a child he had been sent to school in Bangkok, and had subsequently continued to live there as a car mechanic. At the time of the interview the couple lived in S village with their children. Naw Khaepho herself had studied in a junior high school away from home in a school founded by the Karen Baptist Convention in the district, and had travelled farther than any other women in the village. It seemed she found in me a good listener to her tales of adventure, as often in our previous meetings she talked about life away from home. In the summer of 1998, I decided to interview her so she could talk to me more fully and freely about her travels. I took my tape recorder with me and asked her to tell me about her experiences away from the village. After graduating from primary school in the neighbouring village, Naw Khaepho went on to study in a junior high school in a Karen village in the sub-district centre. She stayed in her relatives' house, and came home on weekends.

> NK: When I was straight out of primary school I could speak only very little Thai, but in junior high school, we only used Thai at school. After three years there, I graduated and returned to this village, but I wanted to go to school again, so I went to a Bible school. The school was in Chonburi (southeast of Bangkok) and was founded by "Jesus Christ's Association for Thai People", a small private school run by an American/Thai missionary couple. But the students were mostly *chaw khaw* (hill tribe, in Thai). There were Khae Mussau (Lahu, in Karen), Khae Lissau (Lisu, in Karen), Khae Ikaw (Akha, in Karen) for example. There were Karen from all over the country. So we all used to laugh, saying "It's more like Jesus Christ's Association for *chaw khaw*."

After the two year study course, most graduates become evangelists. However, at the end of the first semester in her second year, the school moved to the northeast, and she decided to quit and returned home.

YH: Did you make many friends in Chonburi?

NK: Oh, so many. We went to many places together. The Chonburi beach, as well as Pattaya. Our teacher would drive the school truck for us so we all went together. It was really fun just going to many places. I didn't think I would get married for a while. If I did, I'd no longer be able to go anywhere. There was someone I was fond of, but I never thought of marrying him. He was a Thai from Bangkok. He was my teacher from junior high school. He later graduated from a Bible school in Bangkok, and is now a big pastor. He wrote me a letter recently and told me he is now a pastor with a church and said in the letter he earns ten thousand baht monthly. So, I told my husband, "you know, if I'd known I would have married him". But I didn't.

YH: Why not?

NK: I was having so much fun just walking around. I wasn't looking in his face. Besides, my mother said she didn't want me to marry Yau men. She said she wanted me to marry a Karen man. In those days I had never been to Bangkok. He came to our village, and he was waiting for me, but I just walked around. He came to teach Bible class in my second year in junior high school, and that was how we met.... I was fond of him a little bit, but there were others too. I wasn't of one mind. My father said he would be good, but my mother didn't. He was Thai, and he was from far away. I guess I didn't like him enough. Just a little bit. There were many others who wanted (*sa lo* in Karen) me. A soldier stationed in H village. The medical helper. Many others, in those days. They're all gone now. In those days, I always had plenty of sweets and candies beside my pillow that the men brought for me. Now there are none. Once you're married, that's the end of it. *A pho mu bgha* (married woman, in Karen) is of no use.

When I was in Chonburi, I had a Lisu boyfriend from Chiang Rai, and another from the south. It was fun to speak the Southern Thai dialect. We wrote letters for a while, but it didn't last. Once I'm back home, everything becomes so distant. I never thought of marriage at the time. Just friends. Fancying boys. If I go back to the village, I'll find some others, that's how I thought about it. I never thought about whom I would marry. I didn't even think I would marry my husband at first. My favourite was a Karen man from Mae Hongson.

We wrote each other for a long time. He was a teacher, but he wanted to study more at the teacher's college in Chiang Mai, and he said it would take one more year. He was tall, handsome, and nice. I even went to Mae Sariang to see him once. But he told me to wait one more year, since he was still a student. I think my parents were happy too. But I didn't wait for him, and got married. I met my husband at a district soccer festival. We met there, and he wanted me, and came to my village. I followed him to Bangkok, and we married when we came back. I didn't want to get married. Then, I went to Bangkok with him again. He was a mechanic, and had a job in Bangkok. First we were in Bangkok together, and after a while we had a child ... and came back. I had my son in a hospital in Bangkok. When he was four months, I came back to the village. The son's father[11] said it was better for our son, because the air is so bad in Bangkok. After one year, he also came back.

I was only 21 when I married. Too young. I still get letters from my friends from Chonburi and Bangkok days. But I don't read them much any more, because if I do, I'm disappointed. And feel lonely. Once my children are grown, I'd like to go to Bangkok and meet my old sweetheart. My husband knows about it too. Just recently, I got a letter from him. He (husband) asked if I could go alone. Of course I can. There was even a telephone number on the letter.

As she chatted on, listing her boyfriends and adventures, what Naw Khaepho seemed to want to tell me was less about her long list of boyfriends, which seemed only to be a device or prop for the story. What she wanted to tell me about was the joy and liberation of "walking around" outside and away from the village. As mentioned in the beginning, "walking around" for a woman may risk her reputation if not done properly. With all the joy and excitement of adventure in her narrative, yet Naw Khaepho narrates as if she was destined to return, and at all times, she is careful in her narration to emphasise that she did not cross the final threshold of her parents' wishes and the village norm. Even the Bible School, an unknown world to all villagers, was still "all *chaw khaw* (hill tribe)". The non-Karen world is one of adventure, full of possibilities and encounters that were unthinkable in the village, yet, now, she does not narrate them as a world she is realistically involved in. Her meetings with boyfriends in that world would remain symbolic of her relationship with the now distant world out there, allowing her to objectify her relationship with it and with her quotidian world of the village. The man she chose to marry was from a neighbouring village, and a man who could to some extent allow her to continue the mobility and adventure between this world and the other. She is passive about this issue in her narrative. Although she was currently the holder of the highest education of all the village women, and was capable of speaking Thai fluently, I had never heard her speak Thai in the village. It is as if she is careful not to bring her experiences of travel into her daily life and village relationships. She had in fact succeeded in realising the normative responses I had heard from young teenagers in Chiang Mai, but what she was trying to tell me in her narrative was her longing for a completely different world of adventure. Thus, while she follows the norms of the village community, yet by thus narrating her past experiences of the world outside, she is relativising her life in the village. After giving birth to two sons, Naw Khaepho began to take classes in the once-weekly adult education course in a neighbouring village that would give her a high-school degree. This way, she said, if there was any job available in the vicinity, she would be eligible. She is the pioneer among several young mothers who also take the once-weekly classes. It may also be said that her example, of having experienced travel and come back to the village to take up the full role of being a mother, has made it easier for the next generation of girls to travel far to get an education.

Narratives of Travel, Love and Morality

In the case of Naw Khaepho above, she travelled and moved about of her own free will. Now I introduce Naw Mupho, who was sent to Chiang Mai for medical treatment. Now 32 years old, at the time of her childhood there were no schools in the area, and Naw Mupho has not received any formal education. At 13, she had acute pains in one of her legs, and has been treated in hospitals on and off since then. Today, the leg is immobilised. When the pain started, she spent three months in a hospital in Chiang Mai, and then stayed on with a rehabilitation specialist. Altogether she was in the city for one whole year, at a time when it was extremely rare for a young woman from the village to be in Chiang Mai alone. Now, she is married to a man from the Northeast (Isaan) who is 30 years older than herself. They have two children, and live together in S village surrounded by her parents and siblings. It is the second marriage for her husband, who already has grandchildren in Isaan. At the time of their marriage, he was working in a pine oil factory in neighbouring H village, but is now retired, earning occasional cash from wage labour in the vicinity. Naw Mupho runs a daily store at home. With her husband's retirement money, they bought a rice milling machine. They collect fees from the villagers who bring their rice, and with the residue bran, she raises pigs for sale. When electricity arrived in the village, she was one of the first to connect a line to her house, and bought a TV and a refrigerator. On the terrace of her daily store she sells ice candy to villagers who come to watch TV, drawing the largest crowd of all the three daily stores in the village. With her own quick mind, and with the help of her husband and younger sisters who help her around the house, she is making her own living even though she cannot work in the fields.

Ever since the beginning of my field research in 1987 (at which time she was newly married), our conversation was mostly about Karen customs and legends. Her father is a medicine man well versed in the local lore. Like her father, she was always lively and talkative, and had a way of knowingly mixing Thai and Karen words and practices, giving interpretations of Karen legends and cosmology that differed from those of the elders. She often referred to her experiences in Chiang Mai during our daily conversations, and in the summer of 1998, I finally asked her, tape recorder in hand, to tell me about herself and her experiences.

> NM: At first (when I went for the first time to Chiang Mai), I couldn't speak a word of Thai. But I wouldn't understand anything unless I learned, so I had no choice. Eventually, I was good enough occasionally to translate for other Karen-speakers who came to the hospital.
>
> YH: So by then you had many friends in Chiang Mai?

This was one of my routine questions in the interviews I conducted with the urban migrant youths in Chiang Mai, which I used to inquire about their socialising network in the city. Her answer to this question decided the course of her subsequent narrative.

NM: I had many friends. I was in Chiang Mai from age 13 to 14. I
was still a child when I went, but was already a *muk'nau* (young
unmarried woman of marriageable age) when I returned. *Yau*
men wanted (in Karen, *sa lau*) me. Many of them.

YH: And you? Did you *sa lau* too?

NM: Yes I did. But I didn't really. I was still young. I only let my
favourite men treat me to meals. I did *sa lau*, but I didn't *ae
lau sa* (to love one another, or to marry).[12] There were two
Yau who did *sa lau* me. One was a soldier, and the other was
a musician. But I couldn't ever love (*ae lau sa*). I wanted to *ae
lau sa* with the soldier, but the other one said if I did he would
kill him. What was his name? I've forgotten now. It was 20
years ago.

She returned to the village at 14, but she still had to visit Chiang Mai
frequently to go to the hospital.

NM: And then, I met another one and this time we did *ae lau sa*. I
met him during one of my visits to Chiang Mai. He followed
me to the village, so we had no choice but to *thau bgha* (to
have a wedding and get married). But I didn't enjoy being
in Chiang Mai, and he didn't enjoy being in the hills, so we
kept going back and forth. He had a rice mill factory in Mae
Rim on the outskirts of Chiang Mai, and I visited his village
a couple of times. His parents were very good to me, but he
was always angry with me. In the beginning we did *ae lau sa*,
but soon he was tired of me. We actually had a proper Karen
wedding in the village. We had to. I was 18 at the time. He
followed me all the way to the village, and said he did *sa lau*
me, and then as soon as we got married, he was tired of me.
We parted within one year.

She explained that they were married out of necessity. According to
the hill Karen custom, if ever a man and woman who are not husband
and wife spend the night under one roof in a village, even if they are
complete outsiders to the village, they must be married before they
leave the village. If the woman is from the village, and if it is her first
marriage, then the wedding will have to be a three-day full traditional
wedding, as was the case with young Nau Mupho. Even if it is merely
formality, it is a must that the couple be married. For example, two

Thai school teachers who came to teach in the village for a short period, stayed in one house. Even though they were each married to someone else, they had to be formally wed before they departed, although the woman being a non-Karen woman with marital experience, it was only a simple half-hour ritual.

In Chiang Mai, being a young Karen woman from the hills with a physical handicap, Naw Mupho is doubly peripheralised; and is an easy target for lowland men. Back in the village, however, such experiences involving lowland men would become a source of stigma. Yet, she dared to bring her adventure right back into her village at the time, and furthermore, now she dared to talk about these experiences with me. Her actions, which she talks about below, would have been severely sanctioned had it been any other woman in the village than herself, but Naw Mupho was by then in some ways exempt from many of the norms that bound the activities of other marriageable young women in the village.

> NM: Then, I was with another *Yau* man. We met in Chiang Mai, he followed me here, we married, then we parted. Meeting someone, being attracted, then coming with me and *ae lau sa*, getting married, it was the same thing repeated one after another. And then I was still walking around (*ha*). Many others wanted to marry me, but I had had enough. A soldier who was stationed near here. A factory owner in P town, he came to ask for my hand, but I didn't want to marry any more. A health worker who was staying at the village headman's office also came. But I was fed up.... I worried that if I married, I would part again. *Yau* men will always be *Yau*. Right after I returned from Chiang Mai at 14, I wanted a husband all the time. Loving, and parting, loving and parting, some of the men, I cannot even remember their names. Isn't that awful? But then it was OK. Just being friends was enough. It wasn't *lo ti* (proper). I would talk love, but not *sa lau* (want) any more. This is how it is. Seeing them as friends is the best. Once we *ae lau sa*, then it meant as soon as we didn't want each other, we must part.

For Naw Mupho after her return to her village, her liaisons with the *Yau* men, seemingly outside the constraints of the Karen village norms, were in a sense a means of self-liberation in a life that had narrow options. Yet, at the same time, her experiences made her aware that in another way she was being exploited, and she had begun to develop a different relationship free of such worries. That was how she narrated her experiences to me.

> NM: They were all young. Until my son's father (referring to her present husband). Then, his father came and he wanted me. I didn't want to get married. If I had to, I would choose somebody younger. But my parents and my younger sisters all said I should marry him. They begged me to marry him. He's older, and he's reliable. There will be nothing to worry about, they said.
>
> NM's Sister: (She had been sitting with us during the interview.) If she didn't, then, she would *ha na jau* (walk badly, implying liaisons with men) some more. Young men are short-tempered. They would not be kind to my sister who cannot walk.

> YH: Did you like (*kwa gae*) your son's father?
>
> NM: Not in the least. He came to my parents and left a sum of money with them, and asked them to buy chickens and pigs to prepare for the wedding. I thought, "Oh dear, I must run away". I said I would go to P town (the district capital 50 kilometres from the village) to go shopping. I left the village, thinking I would visit my boyfriend in P town and would never return. At the time, my son's father was working in the pine oil factory in H village (the terminal for pick-up trucks going to P town). On my way to P town, I was in the noodle shop in front of the truck station. He came there by coincidence. We chatted for a while. I told him I was going shopping in P town. He just said "well then", and left some money in my bag. I didn't ask him to but he just left it there. After I got on the truck and departed, I thought about it. What should I do? If I didn't come back, would it be sinful of me? So, I just went and in P town I talked to my boyfriend. He said, "If you want to go home, I'll see you home." I thought and thought about it. My parents will be angry with me. Then, I returned home within the day. I returned, and I married.

For Naw Mu Pho, after her experiences of marriage and divorce with *Yau* men, her marriage to her present husband at the age of 21 came as an opportunity. She knew she had little better option if she wanted to stay in the village and make a living. She did not have to be told by others. Yet, by narrating the decision as she did, as an experience of escape, and her decision to come back, she has defined it as her own positive decision.

In her chapter on the travelling Meratus women and their experiences of love in Kalimantan, Tsing claims that these women talked about their "alien romances", experiences they gained through daring travel, not as a story of their own sacrifice, but as true love of the non-Meratus men towards them. Their courage in travelling away from their community implicitly throws local values and male privilege into question, and even though their romances with non-Meratus men are neither natural, easy, enjoyable, nor satisfactory, they refused to talk about these romances as experiences of tragic self-sacrifice (1993: 225–7). Love, in this case romantic love, in which personal relationship transcends logic, may exist outside of the framework of social norms and the apparatuses of power. Perhaps for that reason, it provides Meratus women, as it does Naw Mupho, a path to narrate their experience in the interstices of power.

Thinking back on my numerous interviews with hill Karen young men and women regarding their travel experiences, and the narrative forms chosen by those who seemed to want to tell me something about their experiences, I have observed that the young men primarily talked about their work and their fun life in the city, while for the women, the first and foremost topic they chose was relationships with men, love and marriage. Perhaps their choices were not unrelated to my own gender, age and personal characteristics as their interviewer. Women's mobility is talked about in terms of the terror of the "fall" (*lau tae*). Encounters with men are talked about in relation to this risk, and therefore cannot be free from normative constraints and difficulties. But it is precisely because of this that the narratives of women who have actually accomplished travel tend to focus on this issue. As subjects constructed in the process of such experiences of travel and male-female relationships, these young women choose to talk about themselves and find the locus for constructing their selves through their relationships with men in the experience of mobility.

Naw Mupho's experiences of love ultimately reflected the relationships of power surrounding her. In the hills, she depends on others physically and financially for her living, yet because of this she is to some extent free from the standard norms of the village, and is able to view her position at one step removed. For Naw Mupho, to talk about her love and her desire is a means to repel the overbearing powers that surround her. Yet love did not ultimately provide a path for narrating these webs of power from outside the web, and from her own experience of exploitation, she recognises this. In the city, she is doubly marked, and even as she talks about her experiences as experiences of love, she is in effect exploited. As she says, "*Yau* men will always be *Yau*", and in time she comes to reconsider her relationship with these men. At the same time, she talks about her marriage with her present husband, which would have been an inevitable choice in the eyes of anyone in the village, rather as her own moral decision. By narrating her experiences up to the time of her marriage in the language of love and morality, she finds an interstice that allows her agency.

Conclusion: Traversals and Narratives

In this paper, I have examined the narratives of young urban migrant Karen women. I have sought to uncover processes of subject formation in these narratives of spatial mobility and the traversal of cultural boundaries. What do we find through such an endeavour? Firstly, we considered the content of the narratives. In other words, what choices have these migrant women made, and what other choices might have been available to them? Secondly, what explanatory frameworks and narrative themes (for example, mobility and adventure, love, and morality) do the narrating women choose? From both of these perspectives, we analysed the ways in which the narratives are constructed, and in response how they themselves construct themselves as subjects in ethnic, gender and local terms, what paths they were able to take, and what were the possible paths which would have allowed them some exercise of agency. Thirdly, we considered the act of narration itself. As the audience for their narrative, I myself am an outsider/stranger who is not constrained by the norms and powerful forces that surround the narrators. I am a woman from another country, and as such, it is difficult for me to understand their experiences. At the same time, I was also a traveller, and to that extent the narrators may have felt they shared something with me. Both Nau Khaepho and Nau Mupho had even before the interview, often talked to me about their travelling experiences outside the village. This was striking in Naw Khaepho's case, since she rarely mentioned these experiences to other villagers. Thus, the things they chose to tell me were things that they would not normally talk about in a daily conversation with other members of their village, and the narration itself created a rather un-quotidian narrative space.

What then can be said of the act of writing this narrative, from a space once removed from the women's daily lives? As an outsider, I listened and I write, and I cannot avoid being a part of the forces that surround the narrating women. Yet in selectively textualising what I recorded in writing or on my tape-recorder, my project involved two purposes. Firstly, by using ethnographic description and narrative text in such a way that each throws light on the other, I hope to bring out in relief the webs of power surrounding the young women, and the ways in which their agency is activated. Secondly, I seek to illuminate the fact that their social positioning, their responses to it, and their narratives thereof, emerge within a specific conjunction of time and space. Yet paradoxically, I aim at the same time to draw their experiences nearer to ours, not to depict them as those of exotic others, but as something we can ourselves understand in relation to our own quotidian experiences.

Notes

1. The denial of approaches that view culture in segmented space have been critically reviewed from varied perspectives such as political economy, world systems theory, and the post 1980s ethnographic critique (Gupta and Ferguson 1997: 2). The questioning has also been instigated by conditions in the field. Mobility of people, commodities and information has increased both in scale and intensity. Centres and peripheries are even more multiply connected in varied balances of power, the process by which the periphery becomes increasingly peripheralised.

2. For the interviews in Chiang Mai, I did not use tape recorders. Notes were taken and I have textualised them based on my notes. In the interviews in the village, on the other hand, I gained permission from the women, and used tape recorders. The texts are transcribed versions of the recording, and I indicate where I have abbreviated. With the exception of Malee, who preferred to speak in Thai, all interviews were conducted in Karen.

3. Tsing took up with a few women among the Meratus people, who were socially peripheral and considered to be "eccentric subjects", revealing how their agency demonstrated the limits of the dominant discourse and categories. She shows how through their actions they challenge power and

at the same time reconfirm it (Tsing 1993). Historian Davis also attempts something similar for seventeenth-century Europe, approaching the cases of three peripheral women through documents written by themselves. While worlds apart, these two works both address women who are peripheralised by multiple emergent sources of power, in conditions of increasing urbanisation and state formation (Davis 1995).

4. There are a few Catholic student dormitories for youths from the hills. Here, many of the students work during the day as janitors and helpers in the Catholic school, then in the evening go to night school. In the five years prior to the time of the interview, the capacity of these dormitories increased 2.5 times, and 70 per cent of the occupants are Karen.

5. According to the Tribal Research Institute (1996), total "hill tribe" population numbered 740,000, of whom Karen constituted almost half.

6. Karen in the research area subsisted on rice grown primarily in irrigated rice fields. Besides this, they planted maize, pumpkins, taro, and other vegetables in their gardens. The rate of rice subsistence was low, and was augmented with wage labour, the gathering of forest products, and livestock rearing. Swidden cultivation of dry-rice had been undertaken to augment their production, until the early 1990s, but subsequently villagers quit due to stricter constraints by the government.

7. "Northern Thai" here designates a category of people recognised by the Karen as *Yau* or *Zau*. They are speakers of the Northern Thai (*khon muang* in Thai) dialect of the Thai language. Sgaw Karen in the hills primarily use this term to refer to the lowland Thai people. The term for Thai (*jau tae*) is used to refer to Thai people in official positions, or specifically to Thai people from "the south", which for the Karen in Northern Thailand include people from Bangkok, Isaan as well as Southern Thailand.

8. *K'la* in Karen, *khwan* in Thai. Karen consider there are 37 in a healthy body. If one meanders out of the body, it will be the cause of illness, and if the head *k'la* escapes from the body, it means death.

9. In fact of the three cases of HIV-positive women in the district, two had contracted the disease from their husbands.

10. In these city interviews, I did not use a recording machine. I started with a set of questions, and then let the interview go in any direction set by the interviewee.

11. This is one of the standard ways for a wife to address her husband in Sgaw Karen.

12. There are several expressions that are used in personal relationships, especially between women and men. *Kwa ghae* (literally meaning "to see

beautiful") is to like, *sa lau* (heart descends) is to desire, *ae lau sa* (to love each other) implies the existence of an intimate relationship, both physical and emotional, sometimes but not necessarily including a marital bond. The latter is differentiated from *thau bgha* (to marry) which refers to actually being wed.

References

Abu-Lughod, Lila. 1990. "The Romance of Resistance: Tracing Transformations of Power through Bedouin Women", *American Ethnologist* 16(1): 41–55.

Behar, Ruth. 1993. *Translated Woman: Crossing the Border with Esperanza's Story*. Boston: Beacon Press.

Butler, Judith. 1990. *Gender Trouble: Feminism and the Subversion of Identity*. New York and London: Routledge.

Davis, Natalie Zemon. 1995. *Women on the Margins: Three Seventeenth Century Lives*. Cambridge: Harvard University Press.

Gupta, Akhil and James Ferguson. 1997. "Culture, Power, Place: Ethnography at the End of the Era", in *Culture, Power, Place: Explorations in Critical Anthropology*, ed. Akhil Gupta and James Ferguson. Durham: Duke University Press.

Hayami, Yoko. 1998. "Mobility and Interethnic Relationships among Karen Women and Men in Northwest Thailand: Past and Present", in *Inter-Ethnic Relations in the Making of Mainland Southeast Asia*. Center for Southeast Asian Studies, Kyoto University.

Hekman, Susan. 1995. "Subjects and Agents: The Question for Feminism", in *Provoking Agents: Gender and Agency in Theory and Practice*, ed. Judith Kegan Gardiner. Urbana and Chicago: University of Illinois Press, pp. 194–207.

Moore, Henrietta. 1988. *Feminism and Anthropology*. Minneapolis: University of Minnesota Press.

Ong, Aihwa. 1995. "Introduction", in *Bewitching Women, Pious Men: Gender and Body Politics in Southeast Asia*, ed. Aihwa Ong and Michael G. Peletz. Berkeley: University of California Press.

Ortner, Sherry B. 1995. "Resistance and the Problem of Ethnographic Refusal", *Comparative Studies in Society and History* 37(1): 173–93.

———. 1996. *Making Gender: the Politics and Erotics of Culture*. Boston: Beacon Press.

Renard, Ronald D., Prasert Bhandhachat and G. Lamar Robert. 1987. *A Study of Karen Student Mobility to Northern Thai Cities: Directions, Problems,*

Suggested Courses of Action. Payap Research Centre, Payap University, Chiang Mai.

Spivak, Gayatri Chakravorty. 1988. "Can the Subaltern Speak?" in *Marxism and the Interpretation of Culture*, ed. Cary Nelson and Lawrence Grossberg. Urbana and Chicago: University of Illinois Press, pp. 271–313.

Toyota, Mika. 1998. "Urban Migration and Cross-Border Networks: A Deconstruction of the Akha Identity in Chiang Mai", *Southeast Asian Studies* 35, no. 4.

Tsing, Anna Lowenhaupt. 1993. *In the Realm of the Diamond Queen: Marginality in an Out-of-the-Way Place.* Princeton: Princeton University Press.

Vatikiotis, Michael R.J. 1984. "Ethnic Pluralism in the Northern Thai City of Chiangmai", PhD Thesis, University of Oxford.

8

Gendered Lives, Gendered Narratives: Stories from a Muslim Fishing Village in Southern Thailand

Saroja Dorairajoo

How does an anthropologist conduct fieldwork in a situation where the "field" has been visited numerous times by "hit-and-run" students of fieldwork? How can the anthropologist manage to collect data in a situation where informants, used to providing standard answers to pre-set questions, begin repeating these same answers to the anthropologist's spontaneous questions, or even in the absence of questions? How will the anthropologist obtain meaningful data in a situation where informants are suspicious of foreigners?

These were the dilemmas that confronted me when I went to do fieldwork for my doctoral dissertation in a small fishing village in southern Thailand, between November 1999 and August 2000. In this village of more than 1,600 inhabitants, 99.8 per cent were Malay-speaking Muslims; only four (members of one family) were Thai-Buddhists. This research site was not a "level playing field" where I could enter like Malinowski with pen and paper and record answers to questions I posed. For when I did try to follow the ways of the guru of anthropological fieldwork, brief answers were returned, some of which did not make good sense to me. In order to avoid frustration or having to quit and leave the field, I had to embark upon a different approach to securing information.

In this paper, I reflect on the strategies of data collection that I employed. Though they may appear to the reader to resemble conventional life stories, the methods used to elicit these stories were unconventional. These stories were transcribed without the use of pen, paper or tape recorders. Useful apparatus to "record" these stories included a "mental tape recorder", several brief hiatuses from the field to write up my mental notes, and numerous return trips to the field site in order to validate the veracity of my notes and observations. Although the methods I employed may be unconventional, warrant criticism or even perhaps be rejected as unscholarly, they did help in data-collection in a research site where it was impossible to do "pen-and-paper" fieldwork.

Methods and Methodology

In every graduate programme in social anthropology in the United States, a course on "Fieldwork Methods" is required reading for all students. There might be variations to this title, but the usual content roughly addresses the question of how to do fieldwork. Before taking off to the "field" or research site, one has to be inducted into the methods of doing fieldwork. Often, there will be basic mantras on "entering the field", and then more detailed advice on how to read facts or observations in the field. As many anthropologists lament, none of these courses, however, adequately prepares a student of anthropology to confront the field when he or she is actually in it. One anthropologist neatly explains why this is the case when he writes:

> The anthropologist who encounters people from other societies is not merely observing them or attempting to record their behavior; both he and the people he confronts, and the societal interests that each represents, are engaging each other creatively, producing the new phenomenon of Self and the Other becoming interdependent, of Self and the Other sometimes challenging, sometimes accommodating one another (Dwyer 1982: xviii).

The field, then, does not exist "out there", waiting for ethnographers to capture it with their pens, notebooks, cameras, video cameras and other modern gadgets that have become part of the anthropologist's toolkit these days. Rather, the field is created, in response to and in conjunction with its inhabitants, in reaction to and in association with the people the anthropologist encounters, in reply to and in negotiations with the multifarious situations incipient and emergent while they are there. Such interaction on a spatially and socially intimate, regular and, in many cases, eventually long-term basis often dictates the nature of the data the anthropologist obtains, the kind of data they have access to and even the kind of informants with whom they develop relationships. Such being the case, the p's and q's of fieldwork and the techniques of obtaining data are not often to be learned from textbooks but are constantly created, negotiated, effected and transformed in the field.

The nature of the field itself influences the technique of data collection. One important method of collecting data, in a situation where informants and researcher are acquainted on an intimate basis for an extended period of time, is the recording of life history or personal narratives of the informants. Caplan (1997: 14) points out that "personal narratives is a broad term and allows us to subsume within it a range of literature which not only encompasses the narrative or story of a life, but which is personal and focuses upon individuals". Paul Radin, one of the great early figures in American anthropology, argued that the only acceptable form of ethnology was life history (Caplan 1997: 9). While the reason for privileging this method of data elicitation is to understand the informant in his own words, Paul Rabinow (1977: 119) asserts that the data collected is "doubly mediated, first by [the ethnographer's] presence and then by the second order of reflection [the ethnographer] demand[s] from [their] informants". Crapanzano (1980: 8) further elaborates on this by writing that:

> The life history, like the autobiography, presents the subject from his own perspective. It differs from autobiography in that it is an immediate response to a demand imposed by an Other and carries within it expectations of that Other. It is, as it were, doubly edited: during the encounter itself and during the literary (re)encounter.

When I was approached to write this paper, I began to wonder whether the accounts or narratives that I had mentally recorded qualified as life history or personal narratives. I did not use a tape recorder to record any of the accounts that I present below. Almost all of them were mental records. And they were told to me in Thai Malay, but I present them here in English. The stories that I present were not just doubly edited, as Rabinow and Crapanzano seem to describe of life histories, but they were multiply mediated. I had mentally coded my informants' words and then later tried to transcribe them on paper in my own words as I could not always remember the exact words they had spoken. I am, therefore, re-presenting their words to you, the readers, as constructed from memory. I am creating complete sentences where perhaps there were none; I am perhaps putting unspoken words into their mouths. Furthermore I am translating from the Thai Malay language into English. Many steps of mediation have taken place. Are these accounts or narratives that I present here then valid? Were there ways by which I could have validated them? Can I call them "life stories"? Or perhaps they really were stories authored by me? Am I giving voice to my informants by presenting these stories here or have I robbed them of their voices?

While these questions may appear to make my narratives invalid, one needs to be reminded that "life stories" are not merely one-time records of an individual's life narrated to a researcher who records them on tape. As Linde (1993: 4) notes, a life story need not necessarily be a continuous record of a person's life history but could be "a discontinuous unit told in separate pieces over a long period of time". Life histories, as the objective account of history or ethnography (Kluckhorn 1945; Kroeber 1961, quoted in Linde 1993: 48) became the privileged texts for ethnographers to read their informants' external reality as well as their inner lives, psychological history or the psychological forces that define that cultural history. As such, these stories need not be continuous nor elicited texts but could be discontinuous, constantly edited, and unelicited texts despite the fact that life stories in anthropology have often been narrative accounts guided by questions from the anthropologist (Linde 1993: 47). Because of their ability to capture both the inner lives as well as external realities of an informant's lived and living experience, life stories become sites to learn about the complete social being of the informant. In my research village, the stories of the fishermen and women revealed three aspects of fishing life in southern Thailand in contemporary times. Firstly, a generic story of a fishing crisis in southern Thai Malay society served to create a meta-narrative that became a sort of legal document, which eventually led to legislation banning the use of push-net boats in Pattani, hence restoring the catch of the small-scale fishermen. Secondly, gendered narratives were created which served to reinstate the high status that the displaced fishermen used to enjoy prior to the reduction in catch caused by the push-net boats. Thirdly, moral narratives were created by women to redeem their status in the eyes of Thai Malay men who suspect the morality of these border crossers going to work in Malaysia.

How Can Life Stories Help Us to Understand Thai-Malay Fishing Society?

"Lor ning, takdo baghe dale laut" ("There's no catch in the seas these days"). When I first entered the village of Bang Tawar, in the southeastern coastal province of Pattani, almost every villager I met consistently greeted me with this phrase in the local Pattani Malay language. The villagers blamed the depletion of the coastal and marine resources on the push-net boats in Pattani (and trawler boats in Songkhla province) whose ecologically destructive methods of fishing reached deep down to the seabed and harvested all kinds of seafood including fry or minnow. Snigdha and Cook (2000: 11–2) give an account of how a push-net boat works:

> The boat propels a giant net that hangs from two large beams extending forward from the boat. The beams are made of wood or metal. Floats attached to the beam control the depth to which the beams are inserted. The beams have skis at the bottom to guide their motion along the ocean floor. The two beams, which form a "V", are connected at the bottom with a metal chain. The chain has two functions. One is to detect large boulders on the ocean floor. The second function is to disrupt the surface and drive all animal life in the area into the net....
>
> The push net destroys everything in its path — sea grass, coral reefs, and small animals. The ocean floor is normally wavy with mounds that serve as homes for small animals and baby shrimp. The push net smoothes out the ocean floor as it scrapes the bottom. There is no home for these animals after the push net makes its rounds in the ocean. Villagers often leave crab nets out at sea all night. When the push net passes through the area, it often rips the nets to pieces or swallows them completely.

The use of this method led to a drastic reduction in the catch, and thereby income, of small-scale fishermen. The negative impact of push-net and trawler boats on the lives of small-scale fishermen affected life along the entire coastline of Thailand, concentrated in the south (Ruohomaki 1999; Aksornloae 1986; Wattana 2000).[1] Many of the older fishermen, having been used to a life at sea since birth, felt totally unqualified to pursue alternative forms of employment. Yet the villagers told me that they were able to survive in such hard times without being afflicted by starvation. When I asked them how this was possible — that in the past when there was plenty of seafood to catch, people experienced starvation while in current times of dearth, starvation was kept at bay — the reply I got was, "These are the ways of God. Strange, isn't it? No one can explain why."

Despite my deep reverence for Islam and the divine, I felt that some other forces, besides divine intervention, were at work to keep the members of this fishing community from starving. However, not one informant ventured to meditate further on the issue, insisting on divine intervention in their lives. Further questioning hardly yielded further answers. But why? Were the informants not interested in saying anything more? Were they upset that I would dare question them further, thus in effect rejecting the powerful influence of the omnipotent being? Perhaps, but I soon discovered why the villagers were curt and compendious in their answers and unwilling to examine the issue at hand from various perspectives, as I would have liked them to. The village had received numerous researchers and research students, both local and foreign, who visited to ask about the fishing crisis. In addition, government officials, politicians, television producers and environmentalists came to learn about the small-scale fishermen's loss of livelihood. Almost all these visitors came on short-term visits, ranging from one day to two weeks, at the most. Their questions focused on the fishing crisis and the fishermen had ready answers for them, standard answers, brief and to the point. I was the first long-term researcher in the village but because I was a researcher, I was given these short answers too at the beginning of my stay in the village. Villagers believed I would be a hit-and-run researcher just like their earlier guests.

A more important reason for why the villagers were initially unwilling to allow me access into the deeper recesses of their lives was because they were suspicious of my identity. An unknown foreigner in a village could be a spy, fishing for incriminating evidence to charge them with some crime. But why this suspicion? I had gone to work in a Thai-Malay village in an area of the country where Malays were the majority. They had fought a separatist war against the Thai state from the early 1960s to 1990s.[2] When I entered the village, it had been a decade since this war had officially been declared over, but occasional acts of violence still persisted and the Thai-Malays were just recovering from the 1998 arrests of four high-ranking separatist rebels caught in Malaysia and deported to stand trial in Thailand (Sivaraman 1998).[3] Though the situation in Thailand was not highly tense at that time, I was entering Thai-Malay-Muslim country a year after the arrests had been made and there seemed to be some mistrust of foreigners. Though I was not a Malaysian and there was increasing resentment against Malaysians for betraying fellow Muslims (i.e. the separatist rebels) to the infidel Thai-Buddhist government,[4] I was a foreigner entering Malay-Muslim Thailand at a time when foreigners, particularly Malaysians, had compromised the trust of Thai-Malay-Muslims. When I first entered the village, many did not speak to me at all. I was a stranger, after all, and the question of how anyone could trust me became an important issue. I had discovered this when a fellow villager, thinking that I did not understand Malay, warned the people around me to be careful of what they told me as the data I wrote up as research findings might prove "damaging" to the village, an example being the drug problem, he stated.[5]

I, therefore, stopped asking questions; I avoided being nosy. I did not want to be subject to groundless suspicion. I therefore decided to do away with my incessant questioning. I would live with the villagers, let them speak, answer their questions and listen to what they had to say. These factors then dictated the nature of my fieldwork, a fieldwork which aimed to privilege the informants' voices and an ethnography which sought to construct itself primarily using uninstigated accounts by informants rather than using the answers to questions instigated by the researcher.

The stories or personal narratives[6] that I heard and recorded mentally were not offered in response to questions. As I mentioned above, I seldom imposed direct questions on my informants. Having sensed the caution that the villagers exercised in their interaction with me, I wanted to avoid being mistaken for a spy for a foreign government or the Thai state, and hence tried not to ask probing questions. At the same time, I spoke standard Malay but was not highly conversant in the local Pattani Malay dialect which was the linguistic medium in use in the village. My lack of fluency in the language was seen by the villagers as the reason why I hardly spoke much. Many a time, to break the monotony of the silence, men and women began telling me about aspects of their lives even if at first, I could not make complete sense of their words. By talking to me, villagers felt that they were at the same time teaching me the language. As for me, being forced into the position of listener had its advantages. I began to learn the language very quickly and by the end of three months, had attained a sufficient level of fluency to communicate effectively.

Such monologues were often initiated by my informants and were dictated by what they felt they wanted to tell me about. In a sense, they were responding to me as an Other, as Crapanzano states above. However, the subject of their stories was totally dictated by them, by their construction of an intention imposed on me, by their perception of what they thought I wanted to hear and by what they must have felt that I should have knowledge of.[7] That such dictation by the anthropologist's informants is salient in the presentation of any good ethnography is testified to by Plummer's (1983: 65) comment:

> At the very core of life documents is their subject matter: the continuous, lived flow of historically-situated phenomenal experience, with all the ambiguity, variability and malleability and even uniqueness that such experience usually implies. It is an account of the participant's experience, the way he experiences it, the way he chooses to verbalise that experience.

Listening to people talk about themselves, their lives, their emotions, their thoughts, their reflections, all of which are often classified under the genre of life history (Caplan 1997), then enabled me to understand how and why Pattani Muslim fishermen were able to survive the fishing crisis that currently confronted them. Focusing on people's stories or personal narratives enabled me to discover the survival strategies that the fisher folk of Pattani were adopting to cope with the fishing crisis. Focusing on the informants' stories enabled me to write a new story about the southern Thai fishing crisis. Focusing on the stories showed that, contrary to how they had been presented in previous studies, which had represented small-scale fishermen as helpless victims of the negative impacts of the fishing crisis, the traditional fisher folk were responding to the crisis in a positive way. Focusing on the villagers' stories revealed the transformations that had taken place in gender and inter-ethnic relations in this society. As a foreigner and outsider who was viewed as a potential spy and betrayer of village secrets, stories and narratives became the permitted site for my informants to allow me to enter their remembered spaces. Life histories, stories and narratives were the privileged texts for me to read their intents, emotions, desires, hopes, and fears and discover answers to certain ironies, answers that were not easily obtained through direct questioning. Since the question and answer technique did not work well for me in this case, I avoided using a pen and paper to record my informants' words. I was expected to put their words on paper only when they were responding to my questions. But when they were not responding to any questions and were merely speaking to or with me or telling stories, I was not supposed to record their words. I had to make mental notes. When I finally got the chance to write them down, such as when I returned to my apartment in the nearby university, I would try to remember their words and record them. Where my memory went blank, I used my own words to fill in the gaps.

However, this essay in stories told by the informants responding to non-questions should not be taken to mean that its course was entirely dictated by the informants themselves. What I have done here is to use the stories to "shape a particular preselected range of data into a meaningful totality" (Rosaldo 1979, quoted in Crapanzano 1980: 8). I have used the stories of my informants to answer the question that I posed at the beginning of the essay, "How is it that the fisher folk are able to survive despite the loss of their livelihoods?" Though the threads of the stories belonged to my informants, the weaving of these threads into a meaningful net was done by me. However, I was not merely the weaver of the net of stories that my informants seemed to have designed. As mentioned earlier, in some cases, I took charge of the designing as well because I was accessing my memory to transcribe my informants' words. The narratives that I present here were thus jointly authored by my informants and me.

Meta-narratives and Mini-narratives: Constructing the Fishing Crisis in Southern Thailand

Stories that people tell about themselves, their lives and their past are often selective, and are selections from a repertoire of not just happenings but also constructions. The way in which one tells a story often serves to bring about a particular desired outcome. In some instances, stories are concocted, events are created, effects are manipulated and outcomes are desired. In other instances, though, stories are told in very much the same fashion as they were experienced by the narrator. But the privileging of certain narratives and the prominence given to some events also serve to enact a desired end. Mini-narratives are sometimes strung together by informants and told in an inductive fashion to create a meta-truth. In other cases, different narratives are proffered according to the situation and target audience. Again, such narratives have a selective purpose, as in the kinds of stories women tell in the presence of men and those they offer when the men are not within hearing range. Yet other narratives are meant to create moral communities, in that the story-tellers use them to claim high moral ground, as seen in the case of the women working in Malaysia who oppose their moral, hardworking selves against their descriptions of the "loose, immoral" Malaysian women. In such cases, the ethnographer is actually not the intended recipient of the story but becomes the channel through which the story reaches its intended audience. In this case, the story needs the presence of the ethnographer in order to be told. The ethnographer becomes the channel that enables the story teller and her or his audience to unite as members of a moral community.

In the section below, I tell the story of the construction of mini-narratives by villagers with the intended consequence of creating a meta-narrative which could serve as oral testimony for legitimate ownership over certain natural resources. These narratives acted to create a historical scenario whereby those who utilised nature responsibly and conserved resources successfully were clearly interested in appropriating ownership over this history and hence over natural resources in the immediate vicinity of their dwellings. That I was seen as a possible agent in supporting the villagers' struggle for rightful and sole ownership over the coastal resources in the waters surrounding the village was one reason why the villagers were extremely interested in my having knowledge of this "truth".

The Thai-Muslim fisher folk of Pattani told stories of their "golden past", when there was mindful utilisation of natural resources by the local people, which ensured the survival and sustenance of the small-scale Muslim fishermen. Contrasting this meta-history of a golden era against the current situation, where illegal techniques of harnessing both marine and coastal resources by commercial fishers have not only destroyed the lives of the small-scale fishermen but also destroyed the natural resources of Thailand, gives birth to a kind of history that has the power to militate, to agitate, to activate Thais to protect not just the fishermen but the country's resources as a whole. Such active campaigning for upholding the usufruct rights of Thai villagers over the resources bordering their places of dwelling helped incorporate Thai-Malays into the Thai nation-state. This was an especially important development in that it helped spread the perception that Thai-Malays were no longer "enemies" of the state but active members pleading for protection of the country's natural resources. This view was also propagated through numerous country-wide seminars, as prominent Thai-Malay fishermen from my research village, as well as surrounding villages, spoke to varied crowds comprising government officials, politicians, academics and Thai-Buddhist villagers from various parts of the country. At these seminars, the fishermen once again narrated the story of the golden past and the present hell they experienced.

While the majority of the small-scale fishermen adversely impacted by the activities of the push-net and trawling boats were Muslims, the owners of the latter boats were predominantly Thai-Chinese and Thai-Buddhists, with a greater preponderance of the former. Several Thai politicians were also rumoured to be amongst the owners of such boats. Since this new fishing conflict came on top of the separatist revolt between the Thai state and its minority Muslim population, the stage seemed set for a re-kindling of the old ethnic tensions. However, an ethnic war did not erupt. Instead, the Muslim fishermen aligned with Thai-Buddhist Non-Governmental Organization (NGO) workers who entered the village with offers of help to solve the crisis and with money to create "development projects" designed to lift the Muslim fishermen out of poverty. This alignment went a long way towards incorporating the Malay-Muslims as legal citizens of the Thai nation-state and tried to remove images of them as potential threats to the Thai state, whose physical sovereignty had been threatened by these Muslims for more than three decades.

Dulu baghe mudoh, baghe muroh, lor ning baghe mahal, baghe payoh

This phrase, which roughly translates as "in the past, catch was easy [and abundant] but prices [offered for seafood] were low; these days catch is difficult [and much reduced] but prices [offered for the catch] are high", was parroted to me by every villager when I asked them about their lives. I used to be surprised at how each of them repeated the same phrase to me when I met them. Not a single word from the above sentence changed. I then realised what was happening.

In order for their voices to be heard at the level of the government agents, policy makers and funding agencies, the Muslim villagers began earnestly to highlight their plight to each and every outsider who was assumed to possess some measure of power, including research students and foreign journalists. This was done through a series of narratives that centered on the theme of life being better in the past but worse in contemporary times, following the drastic decline of coastal resources. These narratives had a common and central theme summed up in the phrase, *"dulu baghe mudoh, baghe muroh, lor ning baghe mahal, baghe payoh"*. The construction of this narrative was easily facilitated by the constant stream of research students, researchers (both local and foreign) and NGOs who visited the village. My host father in the village acted as guide and informant for all these visitors. Likewise, he became my unofficial guide and research assistant when I moved into the village.

Often Bae Soh took me to meet with the older people in the village. In fact, he nominated himself as my official teacher in the village and selected the people to whom I should speak. It was he who told me that I should be conducting interviews, since this was the job of a researcher. Whenever he brought me to a villager's house, he would tell the person that I was a researcher who wished to know about their lives, their problems, their hardship, after which the informants would start offering "standard" stories that were repeated by every villager to whose house Bae Soh took me. I later came to realise that such standard stories were offered to all research students,

Thai officials, Thai academics, and foreign researchers whom Bae Soh accompanied to interview the villagers. As a result of his seasoned role as the unofficial village guide and research assistant, Bae Soh had learnt that the visiting officials and researchers, both local and foreign, were often interested in finding out about the *panhaa oghe kampong* (*panhaa* being the Thai word for "problems" and *oghe kampong* the Pattani Malay word for "villagers"). In order to assess the negative impact of the push-net and trawler boats on the livelihoods of the small-scale village fishermen, these researchers needed information on life in the village in "the good old days" and they therefore sought out the older villagers for this information.[8] The knowledge of these villagers often confirmed that the current situation was bad enough to warrant being labeled a crisis. A typical story from an older villager went like this:

> In the past life was better, easier (*dulu sene*). It was easy to snare fish. Now it's harder to catch anything. But in the past, prices of seafood were cheap and although we managed to catch a lot we got little money. Now seafood prices have gone up but our catch has declined (*dulu baghe mudoh, baghe muroh, lor ning baghe payoh, baghe mahal*).... It was hard work but we caught a lot and there were so many types of fish in the sea. Now there isn't much fish around anymore.
>
> [Mr Deraman Samad, 70]

> In the past, life was better. My husband and I worked very hard. I went fishing with my husband at the age of 25 because he had no one to help him and was too poor to pay for an *awo* (crewman). Yes, there was starvation in the past. But that only happened to people who were lazy or unable to work. I never starved because my husband was hardworking. In the past, as I can remember, there were 20 species of fish here in Bang Tawar. Now, only nine of these are available. Of these, only four species, *ike plaleng*, *ike kembong*, *ike glamor* and *ike tambae* can we net a lot. The other five, we only catch occasionally and there are not too much of those. Of shrimp, there were ten kinds, now we net only four kinds. The same with *sotong* (squid).
>
> [Mdm Mok Ngoh Muji, 65]

This meta-narrative of the fishing crisis tended to dominate the mini-narratives of the older villagers, both men and women, "interviews" with whom were conducted in the presence of Bae Soh, and often by Bae Soh himself, since he asked the questions and I merely recorded the answers. "She has come to study the *panhaa oghe kampong*," was how people in the village of Bang Tawar referred to me. "She is an *anurak*." A Thai word meaning to love and respect, in this case, the environment, the term *anurak* was used in local parlance to refer to the Thai NGO workers who tried to alleviate the villagers' economic hardship by introducing development projects such as mussel rearing or making salted fish. Start-up capital for these projects came from these NGOs who in turn received money from the Thai government or from foreign NGO bodies such as the UNDP (United Nations Development Program) or DANCED[9] (Danish Cooperation for Environment and Development). These NGO workers also educated the villagers through a series of seminars and meetings where "experts", mostly academics or environmentalists, addressed villagers with information about the dangers of over-harvesting natural resources or harming the environment through the use of cyanide in fishing or the detriments of GM (genetically modified) foods, as an alternative to which they promoted the idea of "green foods" and "green markets". As I was conveniently assigned the label of *anurak*, the kinds of issues that dominated all my "interviews" with the villagers in the early months of my stay in the village were environmental, that is to say, fishing issues. Whenever I sat down next to a villager as he or she was bringing in the catch, de-netting the catch or just repairing a boat, the villager would immediately start telling me about the *panhaa oghe kampong* or villagers' problems even if I had not asked them any question at all. Since the NGO workers and the research students and researchers they brought along with them had typically asked questions about the fishing crisis, a meta-narrative about this crisis had been constructed. It had come to dominate the "life histories" of the older villagers. These were seen as the living testimonies to the beautiful life and bountiful sea harvest prior to the destruction of the coastal and marine resources by the illegal push-net and trawler fishers and over-fishing by commercial boats. The fact that all the older villagers I spoke to typically produced this meta-narrative revealed that this was a standard form that was narrated to the *anurak* or NGO workers or anyone who came to the village with the NGOs. Since I was first introduced to the villagers by the NGO workers who periodically came to visit me in the village, the villagers were convinced that I was a fellow NGO worker interested in hearing the *panhaa kampong* ("villagers' problems"). The meta-narrative about the seas teeming with life in the past compared to the decrease in catch at present became a highly saleable commodity, almost a legal document to be presented to the outsiders who could help the villagers solve the current fishing crisis that confronted them. That such an oral "document" could help in campaigning for new legislation to protect the marine resources and designate coastal resources as the sole property of coastal villagers, and to prosecute those who transgress these laws, was an important goal for the NGOs who worked with the villagers and for the villagers themselves. The Ministerial regulation of 1972, transacted under the 1947 Fisheries Act, bans trawler and push-net boats from operating within three kilometres of the coastline, and is meant to protect the small-scale fishers (Snigdha and Cook 2000: 8). The three-kilometre zone is considered their traditional fishing ground and they are granted sole access to fish in this zone (Ruohomaki 1999; Wattana 2000). However, the often relaxed attitude of the officials in enforcing this law has led to the encroachment on the traditional fishing grounds of the small-scale fishers and has cut into their catch. Despite succeeding in securing a decree completely banning the use of push nets in Pattani province in 1998, the villagers still find push net fishers operating in their traditional fishing grounds (Snigdha and Cook 2000: 9). The law has been bought with money, complain the fishermen, and they are gallantly fighting to get law enforcers to strictly enforce the ban. The small-scale fishermen, with the support of the NGOs, are producing oral narratives, akin to a legal document, to present to the higher authorities in order to force them to take action against the illegal push-net and trawler fishers.[10]

The fact that these stories were being generated and collected for presentation to the authorities was seen in the NGO promotion of sustainable development and conservation of the environment through the practice of local knowledge.[11] This latter body of knowledge was supposed to come from the local inhabitants themselves and was based on their social, cultural and spiritual manner of harnessing the environment. Narratives thus became almost legal documents for proof of ownership over resources utilised by a socially and ecologically responsible people who loved the environment. These standardised and oft-repeated narratives, which were created to help win legal ownership rights over the coastal and marine resources for villagers, met with success. In early February 2004, the Thai government declared illegal all forms of push-net boats in Pattani after testimonies collected from villagers were presented to the government. Push-net boats were immediately instructed to cease plying the waters of the Pattani Bay. This brought much happiness and relief to the small-scale fishermen who finally felt that their efforts had paid off. Their meta-narrative met with success as a legal document and to further prove that the fishing crisis was indeed triggered by the push-net boats, my villagers, as well as those in many of the villages surrounding Pattani Bay, reported to me in March 2004 that they were now netting about 500 to 1,000 baht worth of seafood a day when previously they could only catch seafood worth between 50 and 100 baht a day.

Male Narratives of Redemption

In contemporary fishing society in southern Thailand, Muslim fishermen have become not just national and ethnic, but economic, minorities as well. In a society where the man's role is to provide for his family by bringing in the catch, what recourse did Muslim men have to reclaim their status and their voices in a situation where they were no longer able to perform this role? A look at men's stories revealed the strategies that Muslim fishermen were adopting to reclaim their lost status as heads of the household.

During the nine months that I lived in his house, my host father, Bae Soh, spent his days sitting in the coffee shop, on the *sala* (sheltered platform) outside his wife's sister's house by the shore, or doing minor construction work around the house. His jaunts to the sea were few and far between and when they transpired, they lasted at most 30 minutes. His frustrated wife constantly scolded him saying, "How could you be so lazy? What will our (five-year-old) son eat?" Even the quiet and reserved Aning, Bae Soh's 15-year-old daughter, would occasionally blurt out in anger, "Why don't you go out and work?" The fishing crisis in southern Thailand has deprived traditional small-scale fishermen like Bae Soh of their livelihood and has led to their disempowerment within the traditional fishing society. Where in traditional Thai Malay society men earned their keep and fed their wives and children, the onset of the fishing crisis meant that men were no longer able to fulfill their traditional responsibilities. As a result, they were often disparaged by women and "working men" in the village.

Look at Dollah, sitting at home and chasing away the goats and chickens. He is able-bodied and yet he doesn't go out to earn money to feed his family. Shame on him, sitting at home while his wife supports the family.

[Pakcik Yakob, male, 68, diesel seller]

There's always something in the seas. All you have to do is to go out and catch it. Those men who sit around and avoid going to sea are plain lazy.

[Laila, female, 38, makes dried and salted fish]

I refuse to cook for him [her husband] or do his laundry. Let him do it himself. All he does is get on his motorcycle and hang out and he doesn't even look after the house when I am away selling fish.

[Mek Poh, female, 58, fish towkay]

Why should I cook for him [her husband] or wash his clothes? He doesn't go out to sea. It's been more than eight months since he last went out to the sea. I am old and not very fit and yet work while he goes playing kites with village children. Such childish behaviour!

[Mek Song, female, 60, makes and sells dried and salted fish]

In the sea of stories that had constructed the myth of the lazy fisherman, some men began to construct an anti-narrative against this myth. Now, the lazy fisherman image came about because many of the married men who did not go out to sea were able-bodied and still capable of doing hard work. Being used to a life at sea and having lived most of their lives in the village, these middle-aged men were reluctant to leave the village and their families to look for work elsewhere. In fact, they asserted that they were qualified to do no work other than fishing. As a result, the sight of able-bodied husbands and fathers sitting in the coffee shops smoking cigarettes, drinking coffee and engaging in talk with fellow fishermen made their wives angry. This anger led to insults hurled at the men and refusal to serve them. In order to reclaim their lost status and manhood, the displaced fishermen created an anti-narrative to counteract the female-created myth of the lazy fisherman.

When I chanced upon a group of disenfranchised fishermen sitting together I would sit down with them when there was an elderly woman in the group.[12] During such times, stories of men reminiscing about the "golden days" were heard.[13]

In those days, Bang Tawar was known as *telaga emas* (golden pond). There were lots of shrimp here and it was gold to us because shrimp fetched high prices. At times we would be able to net up to 1,000 kgs of shrimp a day. Yes, those were good times, until the push-net boats and trawlers came in.

[Dollah, 53, displaced fisherman]

Some of the fishermen expressed their frustration at the illegal push-net and trawler boats that devastated the coastal environment and wiped it clean of all marine life. The fact that these boats threatened their livelihood and, in effect, their manhood meant that this threat had to be countenanced in a manly manner.

I have often been frustrated by these boats and have, on a couple of occasions taken a gun and shot at these guys to chase them away. I do not know if I managed to kill anyone but I believe I hit someone because the boat left the area after I fired a volley of shots at it.

[Asae, 61, occasional fisherman]

The space for men to reclaim their manhood did not often exist merely in shooting at the illegal push-net and trawler boats. This was because the fishermen were well aware that the crew on these boats comprised illegal immigrants from Vietnam, Burma, Laos, or Cambodia. These foreign crewmen were poor just like the Muslim fishermen, and they came to Thailand to make a living and earn money. The real culprits were the boat-owners, often wealthy and influential Thai-Chinese from Pattani or other provinces as well as a small number of Thai-Buddhists.[14] While the shooting kept these boats away for some time, they often returned to continue their illegal but lucrative acts. Complaints to the marine police were as good as keeping silent, since the boat-owners paid off these officials so that little action was taken against the offenders, said the Muslim fishermen.

How then did these disenfranchised fishermen deal with the threat of the push-net and trawler fishers while regaining some semblance of respect for themselves? They did so in two ways. The first way did not bring forth any solution to the fishing crisis, but it helped these men reclaim their status within Muslim society, while the second approach helped confront the fishing crisis in a serious manner and also helped some of the displaced fishermen recoup their lost reputation.

In a society where Islam is revered, some of the fishermen have taken to joining the *dakwah* movement. They go around Bang

Tawar as well as other villages, urging the Muslim villagers to pray, entreating them to follow an Islamic way of life. Thirty-six-year-old Mahmat is an example.

> I used to go out to sea with my mother[15] and brother but I became sea-sick. I would vomit and fall sick and have to lie on the boat until we reached shore. That is why I don't go out to sea. Furthermore, there is very little to catch in the sea unless you have bigger boats with powerful engines and can go further out to sea. So, I stay home and look after the children while my wife goes out to the market to sell fish. It is humiliating to have your wife work and support the family but what keeps me going is Islam. I was a bad kid [used to do drugs] until I turned to Islam and joined the *dakwah*. Today, Islam gives me a sense of status and self. I have more respect for myself because of Islam. That is why I don't care what people say about me. I have surrendered everything to God and everything comes from Him.

For some displaced fishermen, then, it is their knowledge of Islam that elevates them in the eyes of their relatives and friends and gives them some status in the village society despite their inability to support their family.

Another such person is my host father, Bae Soh. As mentioned earlier, he does not go fishing often and does not make any money from fishing to feed the family. His wife nags him but yet has not divorced him for two reasons.[16] Firstly, there is his great knowledge of Islam. Bae Soh enthralls all around him with his knowledge of the Koran and Islamic principles. In fact, whenever I had any questions about beliefs pertaining to religion, Bae Soh's relatives would refer me to him. They always said that I should ask him as he knew the correct answer and they were afraid of giving me the wrong answer. Whenever someone tried to give an answer in Bae Soh's presence, they would always turn to Bae Soh for confirmation and if he said the answer was wrong, they would immediately defer to him and ask him for the right answer. Bae Soh would often recite some words from the Koran or Hadith and provide Malay translations for them. His knowledge of Islam, which comes from his year of studies at a *pondok* under the tutelage of a respected *tok guru*, was responsible for him being highly knowledgeable in Islam, said Bae Soh.

Another way in which Bae Soh and men like him earned respect from fellow villagers, relatives and family was through their relationship with the NGO workers. In the midst of the fishing crisis, the NGO workers came to play a very important role in the lives of certain villagers. Villagers' narratives addressed to NGO workers were often filled with the difficulties they encountered as a result of the fishing disaster. NGO workers exaggerated these narratives by bringing villagers to seminars, to protest rallies, to meet with senior ministers and politicians to voice their grievances. As mentioned earlier, these narratives became legal documents to push for villagers' rights to sole access to coastal resources in their immediate areas of dwelling. NGO workers also met with representatives from international aid agencies in order to obtain monetary aid to fund alternative development projects. The language villagers spoke in current times and the narratives they organised alluded to their real or assumed poverty and helplessness. These narratives won them sympathy, money and aid from external agencies. Villagers like Bae Soh, who helped NGO workers in their efforts, often received monetary hand-outs from these workers who compensated them for attending the seminars and rallies. This money was immediately handed over to the villagers' wives (since men are conventionally considered to be poor money managers). This kept the wives happy and helped the displaced fishermen recoup their lost reputation. At the same time, their association with the "powerful" outsider NGO workers (all of whom are Thai-Buddhists) elevated their importance in the village. In some cases, this association with the "powerful" Thai-Buddhists even helped them stay alive.

> The *kamnan* (village head) hates me. Once, she tried to "persuade" me to sign papers declaring unused village land as hers. As a village official, my signature would have carried weight in her illegal claim. I refused to sign knowing well that she wanted to build those environmentally destructive shrimp ponds on the land. Since then she dislikes me and I have heard her father issue threats against me. The reason why I am alive today is because I am friends with the NGO workers and if anything happens to me, the NGO workers would take action.
>
> [Bae Soh, 47]

Displaced fishermen like Bae Soh, who have suddenly become "lazy men" or may be nagged at by their wives or spoken of condescendingly by fellow male villagers, have been able to redeem their "lost manhood" and in Bae Soh's case, gain protection against physical harm, by aligning with the NGO workers. Joining the NGO workers meant that these Muslim villagers, many of whom had hardly travelled to other provinces in Thailand or to Malaysia or Singapore, were also taken on fully subsidised trips to other Thai provinces such as Chiengmai or Chiengrai to try and seek solutions to environmental problems or threats to livelihoods affecting the villagers. They were also taken to Malaysia and Singapore to observe successful farming and fishing projects that the Thais could emulate and implement in their own country. Besides helping in these various ways, NGOs also helped raise the status of these now well-travelled villagers in the eyes of fellow villagers. The following tale recounts this.

On a visit to a fellow villager's house, the villager commented on how Bae Soh did not go out to catch fish yet was able to sustain himself primarily from the money he received as a result of his association with the NGOs. The implication was that he was an opportunistic scavenger. Bae Soh immediately defended himself by recounting the following incident:

> Do you think it is easy and safe to do NGO people's work? Listen, I went to the UNCTAD meeting in Bangkok last week [January 2000] and there was this white NGO guy who took a cream cake and splashed it across the face of the chairman of the WTO. And we were all there when it happened. There was a scuffle with the police who arrested the guy immediately. See how dangerous this is, the work we NGO people do.

This story offered to the fellow villagers removed Bae Soh from the local scene of the village and placed him in the high world of international dignitaries and international conflicts and in the company of foreigners and the powerful Thai police. It gave him an identity removed from the village, an identity that raised his standing within the local community. The kind of stories men told served to elevate their status at a time when they were no longer able to perform the role of providing for the family from their traditional occupation of fishing.

Women's Narratives and Moral Communities

> Boys and girls are brought up to become men and women with different orientations, expectations and goals.... Women are oriented to domestic life by becoming wives and mothers; men are socialised towards communal affairs religiously and politically.
>
> (Chavivun 1982: 186)

> For Muslim women, trading is undertaken after marriage ... the undertaking of an occupation by women, particularly trading, is contingent upon marriage; the role of trader has developed in association with the role of being a wife.
>
> (Chavivun 1982: 178)

> Men fish but women sell the catch in the town.
>
> (Fraser 1960)

The stories that women told in the presence of my host father, Bae Soh, were very different from those they told when men were absent. When with Bae Soh, my host father, women almost always referred to the fishing crisis. They tended to parrot the men's narratives of the seas being devoid of food in contemporary times. That the "fishing crisis" narrative was essentially a gendered narrative constructed by men who had lost their prestige and status in society and was echoed by the women, in effect to boost the depressed statuses of these able-bodied fishermen who were unable to catch any fish or seafood, was telling of a society where men had failed in their role to support the family. While the women may actually be responsible for supporting the family, as was indeed the case as can be seen in the stories women told (see below), this issue was never even referred to by any male villager in the four years that I had known them. Perhaps this is not surprising since a defining feature of Malay-Indonesian societies is of men as breadwinners and women as home-makers (Brenner 1998; Swift 1965; Ruohomaki 1999; Fraser 1966; Firth 1943; Firth 1946; Carsten 1997). Women's stories, however, revealed that the economic backbone of Malay-Muslim fishermen society in Pattani was, in many cases, the woman.

While Bae Soh was away fishing or when I sat with a group of women among whom men had no place, women began to tell stories of their struggles and resilience. Moments like these gave insights into the lives women led. At the same time, they were also windows into the social structure of rural village society in Malay-Muslim Thailand (Watson 2000: 177).[17] A typical narrative was as follows:

> Look at me! I am sixty years old and I still buy some fish from fellow villagers, make dried/salted fish and sell it in the market for some money to eat. That man [her husband] has not gone out to the sea for the past eight months. He complains that there is nothing to catch in the sea. Instead he spends his time flying kites with the

village children. *Mace budok!* ("Like a child!") Not like a responsible
adult. I refuse to wash his clothes or cook his meal or give him
money for food. He is just being lazy. Look at me. My years of
hard work have left me with arthritis and my joints ache so much.
Here, darling, [to me] can you massage my legs. Because of my poor
constitution, I have to pay a villager to dry the fish, further cutting
into my small profits.

[Mek Song, 60]

In Malay society in rural Thailand, gendered division of labour
meant that men were invested with the responsibility of provisioning
the family and women charged with caring for the children and
managing the household. In the midst of the current fishing crisis,
such a gendered economic role saw some changes. Women were going
to work, mostly to sell fish in the market, to repair broken fishing
nets of the big commercial boats, to sell food in the village or in the
markets in town, or travel to Malaysia to work in the Thai-Muslim
seafood restaurants or as *au pairs* for the children of wealthy Malaysian
families. Women thus held money in their purses these days. However,
this is not a novel phenomenon. Women have always held on to the
purse strings in traditional Malay society. Despite their duty being to
bring in the money, men did not handle it. Women did. In Malay
fishing society of southern Thailand, men went out to the sea to fish
and brought the catch to their wives who then disposed of it to the
local buyer or peddled it at the nearby markets. Men were seen to be
frivolous with money. If they came into possession of it, they would
not only spend the money on food and clothing for themselves but
also squander it on un-Islamic indulgences such as alcohol, gambling
and mistresses, said the women of Bang Tawar (cf. Geertz 1961;
Brenner 1998).[18] It was therefore not surprising that almost every
woman in Bang Tawar held on to the purse strings. The only man
in the village who handled money solely by himself was Daud. But
then Daud was an anomaly. In the village where almost every fish
trader was female, Daud was one of the two males.

Look at Daud. He used to make lots of money in the past but he
squandered it on gambling and over-spending. That is why he is not
very rich. And he never gives the money to his wife. She is such a
pitiful creature, very quiet and stupid while her husband doesn't know
how to *simpe duit* ("save money") and loses it all.

[Bidoh, 44]

Daud was working at a job which was almost exclusively a female pursuit in Bang Tawar. Women were considered more prudent when it came to handling money and so they were charged with buying and selling fish in this fishing village. And why were they more prudent with money than men? As mothers, they were immediately concerned with the care and welfare of their children and, more than the fathers, the mothers were immediately charged with the physical sustenance of the children.

> If I had left it to my husband to provide for the family, the children would have starved. My husband is the *phuu yay baan* (village big man) and he often goes off to different places to attend meetings and seminars. He does not go out to the sea at all and his small salary of 1500 baht is not enough to pay for the family's expenses. Therefore, I had to set up this small café and make some money to feed my family.
>
> [Midah, 53]

Women's role as wives and mothers imbued them with prudence. Like Midah, they knew that they could not completely rely on their husbands to provide for the family. As a result, many married women's narratives were filled with stories about the hard lives they lived trying to raise their families.

The one story I recorded in full tells how Mek Yoh started life as a working child and still continued to work at the age of 53 while her husband had long given up his fishing. It was actually Mek Yoh's husband, Pakcik Dollah, who asked me to consult his wife when I once asked him what life was like in the past. Mek Yoh then sat me down with her, told me to take out my pen and notebook and record her story. It was interesting that she was the only informant who dictated that I put her story to pen and paper. Perhaps she felt it was high time someone recorded the "hard life" that she had undergone. Furthermore, this was the only time when a researcher had approached her for an account of her life since many of the researchers who came to the village were often speaking to the men about the fishing crisis. At the same time, her husband himself had advised me to ask her about life in the past. This was because he had failed in his role as a husband and provider.[19] Furthermore, Mek Yoh was an unusually strong and hardworking person. Also, as can be seen in her story below, her situation was unique. No young female child left the village to sell fish and very few women travelled to Malaysia by themselves for trading purposes. Mek Yoh was certainly a unique individual.

> My family was very poor. My father had died when I was a few years old and my mother remarried and went to live with her new husband in another village. I was raised by my maternal grandmother who sold food for a living. As a ten-year-old, I used to go out to the river mouth and collect water in an empty oil can and then carry it on my head to the village coffee shop for a small payment of 1 baht. In those days, we did not have water from pipes and we used the river water for all purposes. The coffee shop owner, Liping, used to pay me 1 baht for every can I carried. [Each can held approximately ten litres]. The cans were heavy and I was a small, frail girl at that time. I also did any and every kind of work that came my way. I used to help clean and prepare fish for salting. I used to buy fish from fellow villagers and then carry it on my head and walk to other villages to sell this fish. After I got divorced, I used to travel to Kelantan to buy clothes, houseware, canned foodstuffs, and other non-perishables to sell in Pattani. I used to travel alone on the train and buy these goods and return and sell them here. Yes, I would be scared but I had little choice. I was divorced and had to feed myself and my little son. Then I went into the food business. Since my grandmother was already selling cooked food, I learnt from her and eventually took over the business. I have been selling food for twenty-five years now and have managed to feed my family of five children and build this house. Yes, my current husband worked as a fisherman and did bring in money. But fishing was unpredictable and he did not catch much all the time. When catch began to decline drastically about five years ago, he stopped fishing altogether and sold his boat. Now he helps me grate coconuts for the curry and cares for our grandchild.
>
> [Mek Yoh, 53]

Though not all women in the village worked as hard or were as enterprising as Mek Yoh, almost everyone reported that life was hard and that they had to work to support the family. The concept of a gendered division of labour gave greater job opportunities for women compared to men, and so women could and would do any odd job that came their way, including maid services such as doing the laundry or washing dishes for a small fee or helping to clean and prepare fish for salting and drying, or preparing cooked crab meat for sale to seafood buyers. The latter job fetched a very high price but men hardly did this work. In fact, all they did was fishing, and when there was little catch they sat around smoking and drinking coffee or tea and reminiscing about old times when the seas were teeming with edible life. The narratives that women told about their hard lives revealed that without their financial contributions to the family, the current fishing crisis would have exploded to create an economic crisis in the community.

But why did women tell the stories of their hard lives only in the absence of the men, or in the presence of henpecked men like Pakcik Dollah? Could women only speak in the absence of men? Did the fact that Malay women were in charge of the household, while men were masters of the public and political front (Chavivun 1980: 186) mean that women's stories offered the chance for "women to back talk a world of male privilege and authority, to become subjects of their stories for a change", as may have been the case, says Mary Steedly, with the Indonesian Karo women she studied (Steedly 1993: 176)? Were their stories totally unacceptable in the presence of male "official" narratives?

I identified what I saw as two reasons for why women told their stories in the absence of men. Firstly, the stories that were told to a public audience of men and women, what I called legal or official narratives, had a purpose. They were meant to communicate the plight of the disenfranchised fishermen to those in power. Women's narratives, however, revealed that in these times where the men were not bringing in the catch, it was the women who were bringing in money through their work as fish traders, net repairers or as food sellers in Thailand and as restaurants cooks, waitresses or *au pairs* in Malaysia. The money they earned oftentimes helped keep starvation at bay. However, if these narratives were located in public space, they would contradict the legal and official narratives meant to seek redress for the suffering fishermen. Women's stories could only be told in private space, in the presence of other women. Another reason as to why women's stories were told in the absence of men was because these women's stories told of women providing for the family, in effect robbing men of their rightful cultural and religious roles as economic providers. In order to protect the man's public honour, stories that had the power to deprive men of their social roles were not told in the presence of men. And a man's honour and manhood rested on the honour and virtue of his womenfolk.

Women were therefore charged with the task of protecting men's honour by being good wives and daughters. Women thus served to protect their menfolks' honour by not publicly flaunting their status as economic providers. But did this mean that women never told stories in men's presence? No, they did. But the stories they told were meant to redeem their feminine status in men's eyes. The story below reveals one such case.

While many women found employment in Thailand, some travelled to Malaysia for work. Many young Muslims from Thailand, especially men, found jobs in Malaysia that would earn them enough money to pay for a bride in Thailand or give them enough money to build a house or set up a business in Thailand. Very few men stayed employed in Malaysia for a long time. This was because they missed their families in Thailand too much. "It's very difficult for a man to be alone, that is why there are very few male divorcees or widowers in the village," villagers used to say. On the other hand, it was quite normal for a female divorcee or widow to stay single, especially if she was 40 or above. An informal survey of women working in Malaysia revealed that the greater proportion were widowed or divorced and were solely responsible for providing for their children. They left these children in the care of their parents and went off to work in Malaysia, often as cooks or as waitresses in the *halal* Thai seafood restaurants, also known as *tom yam*[20] restaurants.

Women who travelled outside of home for work in the city or in Malaysia, away from the watchful eyes of their male relatives, were held in some contempt by some conservative Thai-Malay men. How did such women redeem their reputation in the eyes of these men? I recount the incident below which shows how women did this.

The protagonist is Mek Nah, younger sister of Kak Bido. Mek Nah is a *bujae* (divorcee) and she works as a cook in a *tom yam* restaurant in Kelantan. It is the eve of *Hari Raya Puasa* (*Aidil Fitr*)[21] and she has returned to Bang Tawar to partake in the festivities with her mother who lives there. Mek Nah is telling stories about Malaysian Malay women. Those present include her brother-in-law, Bae Soh, who is highly critical of women working in Malaysia. In a sense, her stories about Malaysian Malay women may be a way of upholding her moral self in the eyes of her brother-in-law. As Mary Steedly (1993: 1999) mentioned (see above), stories are always shaped for and by an audience. Mek Nah's story too was meant for her male audience, in this case her brother-in-law, who despised women in her position. In this case, however, as seen in all the stories women told above, women's voices could not be directly transmitted to the ears of the men. They were either hidden from their ears or if they needed to be told, as in Mek Nah's case, they could only reach the male audience through a conduit, a stationary vessel whose only function was to be the physical conductor of stories from the woman to the man. Mek Nah could not tell her story directly to Bae Soh. Prior to telling her story, Bae Soh had already painted a negative image of Thai-Muslim women working in Malaysia. For Mek Nah to challenge Bae Soh's assertion, she needed the presence of an assertive figure to "verify" her story by maintaining silence. Here Mek Nah did not need to speak as someone else (as Steedly shows powerfully in her ethnography, where Karo women often spoke out as mediums while in trance), but Mek Nah spoke "through" someone else. I became the person she spoke through in order to reach Bae Soh. I became the assertive figure through which this redemptive narrative was to reach the intended audience. My silence throughout Mek Nah's narrative only served to show that I believed in her by not challenging her. At the end of Mek Nah's story, Bae Soh's silence, like mine, revealed that Mek Nah had triumphed in her redemptive narrative.

> Malaysian Malay women are extremely lazy. They are so lazy that they even come to *sahur* (eating before the break of dawn during the fasting month of Ramadan. This meal usually comprises the leftovers from the previous night's dinner) at our restaurant. They bring newborn babies to the restaurant unlike Thai-Malays who never *sahur* in restaurants. And the father will be feeding a half-sleeping child. Many don't even *puasa* (meaning "fast", here referring the obligatory fast of Ramadan). They'll be working in their air-conditioned offices and when you ask them they'll say they have gastritis. Lazy! Although they have the religious police to catch such people even the policemen themselves don't fast. The girls come to our restaurant wearing long nails and nail polish and dye their hair red and wear short clothes. (Here, she uses her hands to point to her buttocks.) College students come during *puasa* and boys and girls will be holding hands and kissing during Ramadan. Then the girls fill Coke cans with beer and drink at the movies. Malaysian Malays are so lazy, un-Islamic and have low morals. And yet Malaysia is the land of Malay-Muslims

and look at their bad behavior, while Thailand is the land of Thai-Buddhists and yet the Malays here are better behaved. Malaysian Malay girls are worse than *anak daro siye* (teenage Thai-Buddhist girls).[22]

Thai-Malay women working in Malaysia, then, claimed a moral space for themselves within a male discourse that regarded their morality as suspect. These women drew upon the history of the Pattani kingdom of southern Thailand as the seat of Islamic civilisation (Nik Anuar 1994; Andaya and Andaya 1982). As Pattani Muslims, they saw themselves as high quality Muslims. They occupied a higher religio-moral category than the Malaysian Malay women, who were corrupted by a Western capitalistic system. As Thai-Malays who hailed from the high seat of Islamic morality in Pattani, these women had greater *akal* (reason) and greater control over their *nafsu* (carnal desires) than the immoral Malay women of Malaysia. Claiming a special position for themselves as highly moral Pattani Muslim women, they could redeem their unsullied status which might otherwise be called into question when working in a *tom yam* restaurant in a foreign country like Malaysia.

We can see how the stories told by women revealed their contribution to the household and their salient role in keeping starvation at bay. While divine reasons were earlier offered for why there was no starvation in the past, women's stories revealed their "God-given" ability to earn some money to put food on the table. However, this should not be seen as a situation of privileging men over women or engendering Muslim society in a negative way. The way in which women's stories were told actually served to uphold the status quo. It served to protect the reputation of the men, upholding their manhood, and it also served to confirm the high status of these Pattani Muslim women.

What Edwin Ardener (1989a, b) has called the "problem of women" — their simultaneous statistical presence and experiential absence in ethnographic accounts — is an effect of narrative misrecognition and erasure on both sides of the ethnographic divide, says Steedly (1993: 177) in her ethnography on Karo women. Karo women's stories became a measure of the misrecognition women face in Karo society and in ethnographic representation, she argues. In the case of these Pattani Muslim women, their stories offered in the absence of men, or expressed to men in the presence of an authoritative figure, cannot be read as erasure of women's voices or even narrative misrecognition. By examining the politics of the storytelling in these instances, we see how women's narratives are highly powerful. Their power resided in their ability to convene an audience (cf. Tsing 1990: 122), whether that audience was the intended target (as in the case of men's stories told to the ethnographer) or, whether that audience was the intermediary between the story teller and the intended male audience (as in the instance of Mek Nah's story). Convening an audience means telling the kind of story that counts for something to those for whom it is intended (Steedly 1993: 198). The powerful site where the audience and the story meet is where the narrative experience is constituted, where it takes shape, where it gains power. However, because these narratives are so powerful, they have the potential to be dangerous as well, to disrupt the social order and place women on top of men. In order for their stories to be heard but yet not disrupt the social order, women's stories had to be subsumed within male discourse. They had to occupy a status lower than men's in order to preserve the social structure. Women's stories are powerful enough to be offensive and destructive, just like the women themselves. Therefore, their stories, just like their selves, had to be contained and made to conform to the social order of things. Women's stories, like women, had to occupy a lower status in the scheme of narratives, in the scheme of the social world.

Conclusion

Life histories, stories and personal narratives are often the most important ingredients of good ethnographies. They provide the raw material out of which the ethnographer moulds her or his theoretical commentary on an aspect of human culture and society. In such texts, the authority or voice belongs to both the ethnographer and the owner of the life history or narrative. The mini- and meta-narratives created by the informants are codified, contextualised and constructed as a valid statement on a particular human culture, society or social institution.

Though life stories may be conjectured as mere fodder for the ethnographer's creation, I have tried to show in this paper that the ethnographer also becomes a tool in the field, effectively manipulated by her informants to create narratives that serve specific purposes. In the case of the Thai-Malay fisher folk among whom I conducted research, their constructed narratives became legal, gendered and moral scripts all intended to confer benefits on the owners of these narratives. The successful ways in which they achieved their aims then go to show that informants neither take a back seat in ethnographic presentations, nor are their individual voices superseded by the ethnographer's meta-voice. In fact, in the Thai-Malay case, narratives became the space where informants exercised power to win certain favours for themselves, favours which brought them the desired prestige, both socio-cultural and economic.

Because the power of scripting these narratives resided with the informants themselves, I did not collect stories or life histories in the classic way, recording every word of my informants with pen and paper. I heard people's voices of their own volition without their words being mere responses to my questions. I discovered what they thought and how they experienced the social world around them without asking them to account for their experience. In this, I had to ignore conventional recording methods. Memory became my tape recorder, and this essay has become the site for me to argue that I am trying to present my informants' voices, to represent their social experience using a string of words, a series of narratives over which both they and I share ownership. This dual ownership is in fact characteristic of any anthropological fact, because all anthropological data is elicited in the ethnographer's dialogic experience with her informants. There is no ethnographic data that emerges outside of the ethnographic encounter. As a result, despite the fact that the stories I have presented here do not follow conventional methods, I have tried to be true to my informants by using strategies that were in line with their dictates. Since my eyes, ears, and memory became the best recorders of their lives, I sought the aid of these human tools. But in writing, the only way to present these stories is in words, and so I have tried to recall as much of their words as I could. I did verify the contents of these words when I constantly returned to the field and would return to a discussion of some of the issues contained in the narratives that they had constructed during our earlier encounters. In such encounters, the "veracity" of the stories I recorded was confirmed, corrected or created anew. Contrary to the usual data-eliciting technique of asking questions and recording answers, I did not really ask questions. I just existed in the social and physical space of my informants and waited around for them to talk to me. This also gave me plenty of opportunity to observe how they talked to each other. Eventually their stories, and the contexts in which they were told, revealed how Thai-Malay society operated on a deeper level. To get at this level, I could not merely become a conventional recorder of life history with pen, paper and recorder. I had to serve as a conduit for my informants to talk to each other. Only then could I ultimately record their narratives here.

Notes

1. Ruohomaki (1999) gives an ethnographic account of the negative impact of trawler boats on the lives of the small-scale Muslim fishermen of Krabi. Wattana (2000: 27) writes that "[p]rocesses of fisheries modernisation and commercialisation, while quickly establishing Thailand as one of the world's top ten major fishing countries have, however, resulted in serious problems of overfishing and depletion of fish resources, which in turn meant loss of productivity and incomes for the majority of small-scale fishers".

2. Eighty per cent of the Muslims living in Thailand are concentrated in the south and speak Malay (an Austronesian language), espouse Islam, and share ethnic and kinship affiliations with Malaysian Malays. The majority ethnic Tai speak Thai (a language that belongs to the Austro-Tai family), and espouse Buddhism. Malays, therefore, differ in ethnic, linguistic, and religious terms from Thais. Further, Thai national identity is strongly predicated on an espousal of Buddhism, which removes the Malays from the sphere of "Thai-ness". With the rise of nationalism in Thailand, the Thai government's attempts to incorporate Muslims into the Thai nation-state by imposing the Thai language on them and sometimes forcing them to convert to Buddhism led to the outbreak of inter-ethnic violence and separatist wars.

3. Although Malaysian politicians as well as Malaysian Malays had covertly expressed sympathy for Thai-Malay separatists in the beginning, the then Malaysian Prime Minister, Mahathir Mohammad, became increasingly hostile toward them. Mahathir began to steer his foreign policy more in accordance to the ASEAN policy of non-intervention in the affairs of its neighbours.

4. One of the important principles on which Thai-ness is predicated is Buddhism and in this respect, the Thai state and its agents are seen as representatives of the Buddhist faith (Arong 1989; Thongchai 1994).

5. When I had unwittingly asked the villagers about drugs when I first entered the village, they immediately responded, "There are no drugs in our village." Then one day, when I was visiting Kak Laila's house, her

young nephew Nasir, who had returned for a short visit from Malaysia where he was working in a restaurant, came to say hello. He had a band aid plastered across his arm and when he removed it, there were scars from needles. Kak Laila immediately charged him with using narcotics, to which he remained silent. Then one day, about eight months into my stay in the village, my host father Bae Soh, blurted out, much to the chagrin of his wife, "Oh, Saroja, all the drug addicts in this village have left for Malaysia." On my first return to the village after I had left following fieldwork, my villagers greeted me with the news that eight young men in the village had been arrested for drug abuse. I was surprised that they volunteered this information freely and realised that my status in the village had somehow changed, from researcher to friend-cum-researcher.

6. I use the term "story" interchangeably with "personal narratives" because the stories that I portray are often selected pieces of information offered by my informants. They do not have a beginning or an end but are in fact encompassed by the narrative that I tell of the effects of the fishing crisis in southern Thailand.

7. One of the clearest examples of this intent came from my host father, Bae Soh. Once he told me, "When I meet Saroja's friend who is doing a political ethnography of Islam in southern Thailand, I talk politics, to Ajarn Nukul (academic-NGO member), I talk about the environment and village *panhaa* ('problems'). When I meet Ajarn Abdullah from *wor-or-sor* (College of Islamic Studies, Prince of Songkhla University, Pattani), I talk Islam."

8. Stories centering on "the good old days" are common among most fishermen living in southern Thailand. In the book *Empty Seas Empty Nets* (Snigdha and Cook 2000), fisherman Yuesoh Samae Ae tells stories about how life used to be better in the days before the entry of the push-nets into the villagers' traditional fishing grounds.

9. Established in 1994 as part of Denmark's environmental assistance to developing countries, DANCED funds projects that promote sustainable use of natural resources and the conservation of nature. DANCED's office in Thailand is at the Royal Danish Embassy in Bangkok <http://www.wisard.org/wisard/shared/asp/generalinfoserver/intermediate.asp?InstitutionID=8870>.

10. Thai NGOs often promote the concept of "local knowledge" referring to villagers' wisdom in harnessing their environment on a sustainable basis.

11. One of the most well-known fisherman of Pattani, Sukree Manasing, who works with NGOs to fight against the push-net boat owners reports he came to learn that the way to fight the push-net owners was to "collect data

so that we could tell the outsiders and make them aware of our problem" (Snigdha and Cook 2000: 52). He reports another incident when he went to a district official for funding for artificial reefs which he claims had increased the catch for the coastal fishermen. The official asked for evidence. Sukree reports, "… if you want to make the outsider understand you, you must have evidence to substantiate your claim — tangible evidence. We spent a year collecting data about what we could catch every day, how much it cost us, our income and the variety of sea animals. We presented the data to the director of the center. He told us we had clear evidence to support our work. He granted us the funds for the project" (Snigdha and Cook 2000: 61).

12. It would have been highly impolite and ill-mannered for an unmarried woman like me to be found alone in the company of young or middle-aged men.

13. Note that the men's stories during such times could be a reflection of the "normal pattern" of men wanting to present their glorious past in the presence of the anthropologist-researcher. In this case, however, this "glorious past" narrative also served the purpose of an anti-narrative to the "lazy fisherman" narrative.

14. While there are Muslim fishermen practising push-net and trawler fishing, the equipment used by these Muslim fishermen compare nowhere in size and magnitude to those of the commercial Thai-Chinese and Thai-Buddhist push-net and trawler fishers.

15. Mahmat's mother, Moksu, is one of the richest and most respected women in the village.

16. Failure to provide for the family is important grounds for divorce in this Muslim society.

17. Writing about the construction of a Javanese woman's autobiography, Bill Watson argues how the different chapters or stories told in the autobiography actually serve as introduction into the social structure of the community.

18. Brenner's Javanese informants explained this kind of gendered division by arguing that women have greater ability to control their desires and hence manage money well, rather than men who have a greater tendency to succumb to and financially satisfy their desires (Brenner 1998: 149–57).

19. Pakcik Dollah was younger than Mek Yoh by several years. She was his first wife while she had already been married twice before she met him. He was a young 19 year old at the time when he proposed marriage to her while she was twice divorced, 23 years old and had a 3-year-old son. Mek Yoh told me how Pakcik Dollah had been an irresponsible man during the early years of their marriage. He was always running off to

join travelling mendicants and was popular with women. Mek Yoh said the last straw was when a woman came to their house to look for him. "That was all I could bear. I went and consulted a *bomoh* (traditional magician) who taught me a spell with which I could make my husband become totally subservient to me. You can see what a homebody he is. He even washes the pots and pans, helps with the cooking and minds the children, things a man would never do. See the power of that spell." Mek Yoh's relatives often commented on what a hen-pecked husband Pakcik Dollah was and how he deferred to the powerful Mek Yoh for everything. His telling me to approach Mek Yoh for her life story may have had to do with his deference to her.

20. *Tom yam* refers to the spicy tangy Thai soup made of tomatoes, lime, chili, lemongrass and galangal, often containing seafood such as shrimp, squid or fish. *Tom yam* has become the hallmark dish of Thai food in Malaysia and *halal* Thai restaurants are known as *tom yam* restaurants.

21. This refers to the celebrations that mark the end of the fasting month of Ramadan, the ninth month of the lunar calendar. It is celebrated on the first day of the month of Shawal, which is the tenth lunar month.

22. Teenage Thai-Buddhist girls are often condemned by Malay-Muslim men and women for their moral lassitude.

References

Andaya, Leonard and Barbara Watson Andaya. 1982. *A History of Malaysia*. New York: St. Martin's Press.

Ardener, Edwin. 1989a. "Belief and the Problem of Women", in *The Voice of Prophecy and Other Essays*, E. Ardener. London: Basil Blackwood, pp. 72–85.

———. 1989b. "The 'Problem' Revisited", in *The Voice of Prophecy*, E. Ardener. London: Basil Blackwood, pp. 127–33.

Arong Suthasasna. 1989. "Thai Society and the Muslim Minority", in *The Muslims of Southern Thailand*, ed. A. Forbes. Bihar: Centre for Southeast Asian Studies, pp. 91–112.

Brenner, Suzanne. 1998. *The Domestication of Desire: Women, Wealth and Modernity in Java*. Princeton: Princeton University Press.

Caplan, Pat. 1997. *African Voices, African Lives: Personal Narratives from a Swahili Village*. London: Routledge.

Carsten, Janet. 1997. *The Heat of the Hearth: The Process of Kinship in a Malay Fishing Village*. Oxford: Clarendon Press.

Chavivun, Prachuabmoh. 1980. "The Role of Women in Maintaining Ethnic Identity and Boundaries: Thai-Muslims (The Malay-Speaking Group) in southern Thailand", PhD Thesis, University of Hawaii.

Crapanzano, Vincent. 1980. *Tuhami: Portrait of a Moroccan.* Chicago: University of Chicago Press.

Dwyer, Kevin. 1982. *Moroccan Dialogues: Anthropology in Question.* Prospect Heights: Waveland Press.

Firth, Raymond. 1946. *Malay Fishermen: Their Peasant Economy.* London: Paul, Trench, Trubner & Co.

Firth, Rosemary. 1943. *Housekeeping Among Malay Peasants.* London: Lund Humphries.

Fraser, Thomas. 1960. *Rusembilan: A Malay Fishing Village in southern Thailand.* Ithaca, NY: Cornell University Press.

———. 1966. *Fishermen of South Thailand: The Malay Villagers.* New York: Holt, Rinehart and Winston.

Geertz, Clifford. 1961. *The Javanese Family: A Study of Kinship and Socialization.* New York: Free Press.

Linde, Charlotte. 1993. *Life Stories: The Creation of Coherence.* New York: Oxford University Press.

Nik Anuar Nik Mahmud. 1994. *The Malay Unrest in Southern Thailand: An Issue in Malay-Thai Border Relations.* Bangi: UKM.

Rabinow, Paul. 1977. *Reflections on Fieldwork in Morocco.* Berkeley: University of California Press.

Radin, Paul. 1963. *The Autobiography of a Winnebago Indian.* New York: Dover Publications.

Ruohomaki, Olli-Pekka. 1999. *Fishermen No More? Livelihood and Environment in southern Thai Maritime Villages.* Bangkok: White Lotus Press.

Sanit Aksornloae *et al.* 1986. "Mangrove Resources and the Socio-Economics of Dwellers in Mangrove Forests in Thailand", in *Man in the Mangroves: The Socio-economic Situation of Human Settlements in Mangrove Forests.* Tokyo: The United Nations University, pp. 11–43.

Sivaraman, Satya. 1998. "Development-Thailand: Muslim Unrest Flares Up in the South". World News, Inter Press Service <http://www.oneworld.org/ips2/jan98/thailand2. html>.

Snigdha Vallabhaneni and Kathryn Cook. 2000. *Empty Seas, Empty Nets.* Bangkok: Wildlife Fund Thailand.

Steedly, Mary. 1993. *Hanging Without a Rope: Narrative Experience in Colonial And Post-Colonial Karoland.* Princeton: Princeton University Press.

Swift, Michael. 1965. *Malay Peasant Society in Jelebu.* London: Athlone Press.

Thongchai Winichakul. 1994. *Siam Mapped: A History of the Geo-body of a Nation*. Honolulu: University of Hawai'i Press.

Tsing, Anna. 1990. "Gender and Performance in Meratus Dispute Settlement", in *Power and Difference: Gender in Island Southeast Asia*, ed. J. Atkinson and S. Errington. Stanford: Stanford University Press.

Watson, C.W. 2000. *Of Self and Nation: Autobiography and the Representation of Modern Indonesia*. Honolulu: University of Hawai'i Press.

Wattana Sugannasil. 2000. "Fishing Communities in Southern Thailand: Changes and Local Responses", *Songklanakarin Journal of Social Sciences and Humanities* 6/1: 26–37.

Index

Abu-Lughod, Lila, 14–7, 26, 29–30, 90
Agar, M., 166–8
Anderson, Ben, 21, 128–30, 153, 166, 183
Anecdote, 17
Arifin bin Agas, 181–217
Ashplant, Timothy, 2, 3, 17
Autobiography, 3, 12–3, 17, 31n3, 31n4, 32n6, 116, 125–6
"Autonomous history", 6, 125

Bakhtin, Mikhael, 17
Bali, 22, 41–87
Basiang, Fritz, 20–1, 125–75
Bedouin, 14–7, 26
Behar, Ruth, 14, 18–9, 89, 117, 223, 257
Benjamin, Walter, 257
Berman, Marshall, 10, 221–2
Bertaux, Daniel, 24
Berteaux-Wiame, Isabelle, 24
Biography, 13, 90, 95, 108, 116
"biography in the shadow", 18, 89, 108
Borneman, John, 24–6
Brenner, Suzanne, 10, 11, 299, 300
Bruner, Jerome, 8, 31n2, 223

Butler, Judith, 255–6

Caplan, Pat, 19, 280, 285
China, 8–10
Christianity, 137–8, 169–70, 258–60
and Catholic mission on Sumba, 89, 99, 104–7
Crapanzano, Vincent, 280–1
"Crisis of Representation" in anthropology, 89
Cruikshank, Julie, 8, 10

Dialogical relationships, 17–9, 23, 31, 89, 116, 120, 223, 273–4, 281, 307–9
Djakababa, Cornelius, 23, 89–120

El Saadawi, Nawal, 13
Ethnography, 184, 223, 280, 284, 307

Frank, Geyla, 14, 18, 108, 116

Gamelan music, 56–8, 60–4, 66, 68–70
Generations, 11, 128, 130
Guha, Ranajit, 5

Headhunting, 89, 94, 103, 121n1–3
Healey, Lucy, 5
Heidegger, Martin, 222
Historical consciousness, 10, 25–6
Hua Hin (Thailand), 225–46

Identity, 25, 27
Indigenous peoples, 12, 199
Indonesia, 6, 21, 128, 131
  colonial period, 53, 94, 103,
    128–33, 135, 142
  Darul Islam rebellion, 162
  Independence struggle, 42, 128,
    159–62, 173n16, 175n28
  Japanese Occupation of, 20, 22,
    42, 74, 84n41, 128, 156–9
  massacres (1965–6), 42, 74,
    81n23, 84n42, 84n45
  New Order, 42, 84n40
Islam, 201, 283, 295–6, 305–6

Java, 10, 21, 131, 154, 169

Karen (north Thailand), 29, 253–74
Keesing, Roger, 13
Khun Chooey Santet-Witanon,
  243–4
Khun Chun Satukarn, 228–33
Khun Tuk Dechapanya, 238–42

Larson, Pier, 90, 108–9, 119
Life histories, 3, 26, 90, 117, 166,
  223, 245, 280, 291, 307
  analysing in sets, 24
  as unfinished, 127
  audiences for, 17, 19, 23–4, 26,
    116, 120
  of women, 5, 13–4, 306–7
  problems in analysis of, 4, 91
  representativeness, 6, 14
  turning points in, 166–7
  uniqueness of, 4, 14

Life stories, 3, 14, 223, 257, 281, *see
  also* life histories
Linde, Charlotte, 3, 223, 281
Lord, Alfred, 100
Lucaks, John, 30

Madé Lebah, 22, 41–85
Magic, 70–2, 83n39
Malaysia, 181–217, 300, 303–6
Malays, 187–9, 205–6, 212–3
  of Pattani, 278–309
Malo, Yoseph, 22, 88–121
Mandelbaum, David, 166–7
McPhee, Colin, 41, 52, 68–70
Modernity, 8–11, 221–4, 245
  and identity, 25, 222
Mor Chui, 233–8

Narratives, genres of, 17, 23, 31,
  91–2, 117, 126, 272
  about objects, 26
  audiences for, 19, 283–7, 292,
    303–7
  coherence, 3, 168
  contexts of, 26, 287, 303–7
  enforced, 28
  "episodes", 167
  ethnographic, 184
  gendered, 253–74, 278, 282, 293–307
  men's, 259, 293–8
  "meta-narratives", 287–8, 291–3
  moral purposes of, 282, 287–8,
    304–6
  and problems of translation, 44,
    281
  themes of, 42–4, 168–9, 273,
    286–7, 289
  therapeutic, 32n5
  transformative power of, 7, 102
  women's, 253–74, 298–307
Nepal, 7
Nora, Pierre, 1

Orang Asli, 199–200, 205, *see also* Semai

Oral history, 2, 15, 223, 245

Ortner, Sherry, 256

Parati, Graziella, 13

Passerini, Luisa, 17, 24

Pattani, 282–312

Performance, 23, 91, 100–3, 117–8

Personal narratives, 2, 4, 14, 31, 245, 284, 307, 310n6, *see also* narratives

Portelli, Allesandro, 2, 8, 14–5, 24, 168

Radin, Paul, 4, 44, 280

Rose, Nikolas, 8

Rosengarten, Theodore, 12

Röttger-Rössler, Birgitt, 126, 223

Self, construction of, 6, 223, 307
  as autobiographical, 7
  and modernity, 8

Semai, 27, 181–217
  at Betau Regroupment Scheme, 211–2, 214, 215–6n11
  bnuul bhiip, "blood intoxication" among, 28, 182, 213

Slavery, 89–91, 94–6, 102, 104–8

Smail, John, 6, 125

Social memory, 5, 9, 108–9, 120
  Politics, of, 103

Spivak, Gayatri, 5, 256

Spradley, James, 10

Steedly, Mary, 306–7

Steedman, Carolyn, 28

Storytelling, 17–8, 23, 91, 96, 117, 257, 284–6, 303–7

Subjectivity, 6, 15, 26, 31, 118, 120, 228
  of women, 255

Sumba, 22, 87–120

Tan Kah Kee, 8

Tana Toraja, 125–75

Temple, Bogusia, 7

Thailand, 28–9, 221–312
  and modernisation, 223–5
  monarchy of, 224–5, 230–1, 233, 234, 237–8, 240–6
  and nationalism, 224
  and "revolution" of 1932, 240
  Japanese troops in, 232, 236–7, 240–2, 244, 248n8
  hill tribes, 257–61
  Thai-Malays in, 284

Thompson, E.P., 5

Thompson, Paul, 2

Tonkin, Elizabeth, 18

Tsing, Anna, 255, 272, 274n3, 307

Watson, C.W., 12, 299

Women's narratives, *see* Narrative

World War I, 17, 242

World War II, 7, 14, 66, 156, 225, 232, 236–7, 241–2, 248n8

Young, Michael, 13, 116